A GOLDEN HAZE OF MEMORY

A Golden Haze of Memory

THE MAKING OF HISTORIC CHARLESTON

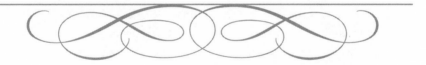

STEPHANIE E. YUHL

THE UNIVERSITY OF NORTH CAROLINA PRESS | CHAPEL HILL AND LONDON

Manufactured in the United States of America
Designed by April Leidig-Higgins
Set in MT Garamond by Copperline Book Services, Inc.

The paper in this book meets the guidelines for permanence and dura-
bility of the Committee on Production Guidelines for Book
Longevity of the Council on Library Resources.

Library of Congress Cataloging-in-Publication Data
Yuhl, Stephanie E.
A golden haze of memory: the making of historic Charleston /
Stephanie E. Yuhl.
p. cm.   "Organizational Memberships and Select
Authorship of Major White Cultural Leaders in Charleston,
1920–1940": p.   Includes bibliographical references and index.
ISBN 0-8078-2936-6 (cloth: alk. paper)
ISBN 0-8078-5599-5 (pbk.: alk. paper)
1. Historic preservation — Social aspects — South Carolina —
Charleston — History — 20th century.   2. Historic preservation
— Political aspects — South Carolina — Charleston — History —
20th century.   3. Charleston (S.C.) — Cultural policy.   4. Charleston
(S.C.) — Intellectual life.   5. Historic sites — South Carolina —
Charleston.   6. Memory — Social aspects — South Carolina —
Charleston.   7. Whites — South Carolina — Charleston — Politics
and government — 20th century.   8. Charleston (S.C.) — Race rela-
tions.   9. Group identity — South Carolina — Charleston.   I. Title.
F279.C447Y84 2005   975.7'915'043 — dc22   2004025292

cloth   09 08 07 06 05   5 4 3 2 1
paper   09 08 07 06 05   5 4 3 2 1

Portions of Chapters 1 and 2 have been reprinted from Fitzhugh
Brundage, ed., *Where These Memories Grow.* Copyright © 2000 by the
University of North Carolina Press. Used by permission of the pub-
lisher. Portions of Chapter 2 have also been reprinted from James M.
Hutchisson and Harlan Greene, eds. *Renaissance in Charleston: Art and
Life in the Carolina Low Country, 1900–1940.* Copyright © 2003 by the
University of Georgia Press. Used by permission of the publisher.

For Anthony,
without whom this
(and so much else)
would not be

CONTENTS

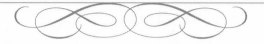

ILLUSTRATIONS

ACKNOWLEDGMENTS

I HAVE INCURRED many debts in writing this book. I want to begin by recognizing the wonderful scholars and professionals who have invested themselves in the success of this project. First, I thank my graduate mentors, Nancy Hewitt, Peter Wood, Syd Nathans, Bill Chafe, Rick Powell, Cynthia Herrup, and Bill Leuchtenburg, for their support and insights. Most especially, I owe a great deal to Fitz Brundage, whose sharp critiques, good humor, and unwavering friendship have left a powerful imprint on this work. Numerous colleagues and friends, from Duke and Valparaiso Universities and the College of the Holy Cross, as well as from Charleston, also deserve special mention: Alan Bloom, Martha Jane Brazy, Colleen Seguin, Alex Byrd, Mel Piehl, Mark Schwehn, Karen Turner, Theresa McBride, Ed O'Donnell, Mary Conley, Jim Hutchisson, Maurie McInnis, Keith Knight, and Lily Lee. Likewise, I am indebted to the various chairs, commentators, and audience members who attended to aspects of this work in conference presentations over the years. Numerous hardworking professionals at many libraries and archives contributed greatly to this book, including the staffs at the Charleston County Library, especially the generous and wise Harlan Greene; the Preservation Society of Charleston; the Gibbes Museum of Art in Charleston; the Charleston Museum, especially Julia Logan; the Avery Research Center and the Robert Scott Small Library at the College of Charleston; the Southern Historical Collection at the University of North Carolina at Chapel Hill; the Rare Book, Manuscript, and Special Collections Library at Duke University; the Historic Charleston Foundation; the South Caroliniana Library at the University of South Carolina; the National Geographic Society; and the Library of Congress. In addition, I would be amiss if I did not highlight the incredible goodwill and support proffered by the past and present staff of the South Carolina Historical Society during my many months conducting research in their midst, particularly Eric Emerson, Nic Butler, Mike Coker, Pat Hash, and the insightful and good-humored Steve Hoffius. I also thank Pamela

Gabriel, who graciously shared a wonderful old tourist map of Charleston. Of course, I am grateful to David Perry at the University of North Carolina Press for his support of this project, to the anonymous readers whose illuminating comments improved this work immensely, and to Mary Caviness for her good humor and skillful copyediting and for shepherding this manuscript to publication. Any errors or lapses in this book are singularly mine.

I also wish to thank the organizations that provided financial support for this project. The Women's Studies Program and the Center for Philanthropy and Voluntarism at Duke University and the Mellon Foundation funded a portion of my early research and writing. During a Lilly Foundation postdoctoral fellowship at Valparaiso University, I was able to carve out invaluable time and space to reconsider historical memory in Charleston. My home institution, the College of the Holy Cross, provided me with a Batchelor-Ford grant and a generous research leave that facilitated the writing of this book.

Finally, I am grateful to my dear friends Julie Manning Magid, Cindy Estes, and Jerry Kokolis, and to my family: to my parents, Kathleen and Eric, for instilling in me love of language and stories; to my siblings, for their constancy, friendship, and wit; to my in-laws, Jackie and Bub, for loving my children almost as much as I do; and, of course, to my children, Julia, Emmett, and Phineas, for being little beams of light and perspective in my sometimes narrow academic world. Finally, but really first, I owe so much to my husband, Anthony Cashman, to whom this book is dedicated with enduring love, appreciation, and respect. His true partnership makes it all possible.

A GOLDEN HAZE OF MEMORY

Introduction

hen expatriate author Henry James visited Charleston, South Carolina, in 1904, he was struck by the disparity between the city's robust past and its jaundiced present. Instead of the once bustling commercial, cultural, and political seat of the American South, James encountered an exhausted city still reeling from the effects of the Civil War—a city that was undeniably "thin," "vacant," "soft," "unrepaired, irreparable"—indeed, nearly monastic in its relation to the larger, contemporary American scene. "Whereas the ancient order was masculine, fierce and moustachioed," James observed, "the present is at most a sort of sick lioness who has so visibly parted with her teeth and claws that we may patronizingly walk all round her."[1] Years later, in 1922, Ludwig Lewisohn, a contributing editor of the *Nation*, who grew up in Charleston, echoed these sentiments. The state's economic and political power base had long since shifted to the up-country, usurping the historical prominence of the tidewater city and leaving in its stead a cultural vacuum. "A tiny tongue of land extending from Broad Street in Charleston to the beautiful bay formed by the confluence of the Ashley and Cooper rivers is all of South Carolina that has counted in the past," Lewisohn noted. "The memories that cling to the little peninsula are all that count today."[2] This is the story of how a group of elite white Charlestonians transformed these historical memories of loss and disintegration into a revitalized civic identity that rebuked the chaos of modern America and reasserted Charleston's relevance in national dialogues about race, politics, economics, and the social order.

For the first 200 years of its existence, Charleston enjoyed a prominent place in the American narrative. Founded in 1670 as "Charles Town," in honor of England's King Charles II, who granted the New World land mass called "Carolina" to eight lord proprietors, the colony flourished over the decades. Its population expanded rapidly with English, French, and Barbadian settlers, as did its physical layout. Religious tolerance characterized the colony despite the establishment of Anglicanism as its official church. The colony's economy thrived, based on the forced importation of African slave labor and a vigorous trade in commodities such as rice, indigo, and human capital. The emerging planter and merchant elite built wharves, public buildings, formidable plantations, urban residences in the distinctive single-house style, and an array of cultural institutions that reflected their consolidation of power.[3] By the mid-eighteenth century, Charleston was a booming crossroads of culture and trade for the British Empire enjoying its so-called golden age even as war with England loomed. When those troubles mounted, South Carolina sent five delegates, all of whom were Charlestonians, to Philadelphia for the First Continental Congress. The city later boasted several signers of the Declaration of Independence. And although the state's capital moved from Charleston inland to Columbia in 1789, the port town remained for several decades the vital pulse of the region.[4]

Of course, from its earliest years, the Charleston area also experienced its share of bloodshed and violence in the form of pirate raids, expansionist wars against local Indian tribes, and African slaves' resistance to white brutality and exploitation. In the 1739 Stono Rebellion, for example, approximately 100 slaves demanded their liberty from their masters' tyranny through armed force in clashes about twenty miles from Charleston. Approximately twenty-five whites and thirty blacks died in the battles, and white colonists clamped down harder on the peculiar institution. Nearly a century later, in 1822, local white authorities thwarted another potentially bloody slave rebellion allegedly planned by a free and literate black artisan named Denmark Vesey. Although Vesey and three other convicted coconspirators were publicly executed and their bodies left hanging for hours as a warning to all black Charlestonians, the very harsh response to the plot, which included the passage of laws further restricting enslaved and free black movement, revealed the precarious nature of the city's slaveocracy.[5]

Around the same time, Charleston's fortunes began to fade. Its port declined steadily as cotton and slavery expanded away from coastal regions and into southwestern outlets such as Mobile and New Orleans.[6] Antebellum Charleston was slowly becoming a "leisure capital" for its planter-professional elite, who reacted to this upstart competition by adopting an increasingly conservative approach to industrial stimulation.[7] In 1833, for example, officials would not allow new railroad tracks into town to connect its failing wharves with trade routes along the Savannah River. Instead, the tracks had to stop at the city limits and inefficient wagons had to haul cargo to the docks. In the words of historian George C. Rogers Jr., "The advantage of bypassing Savannah was thus lost on Charleston herself. And so Charleston held up her hand to the smoking engines and said, 'Do not enter.'"[8] Politically, troubling divisions emerged in the white social fabric as debates over nullification, constitutionalism, and states' rights raged. And while some determined writers, such as novelist William Gilmore Simms, tried valiantly to ply their craft in this environment in the antebellum years, other artists, such as painter Washington Allston, left the city, realizing the limits of Charleston's concern for high cultural endeavors.[9] By the time the first shot was fired on Fort Sumter in Charleston Harbor, signaling the beginning of four years of civil war, the "golden age" for elite whites had drawn to a close.[10]

Charleston's economic decline accelerated during and after the war. A major fire cut a swathe of destruction through town in 1861, and an eighteen-month bombardment by Union forces reduced more of the city to rubble in 1865. These events, coupled with the Confederate defeat and the eradication of slavery, left Charleston's white inhabitants demoralized and without the resources to rebuild. Northern reporter Sidney Andrews, who traveled to the South immediately following the Confederacy's surrender, found in Charleston "a city of ruins, of desolation, of vacant houses, of widowed women, of rotting wharves, of deserted warehouses, of weedwild gardens, of miles of grass-grown streets, of acres of pitiful barrenness — that is the Charleston, wherein Rebellion loftily reared its head five years ago."[11] Natural disasters, such as a major earthquake in 1886 and several hurricanes in the following decades wreaked further havoc on the city's infrastructure, as well as its area rice crop; a boll weevil infestation from 1917 to 1919 delivered a death blow to the region's cotton industry. And although some local promoters of the postwar era, such as newspaper editor Francis Dawson, dreamed of Charleston becoming "The Liverpool of America," the dominant attitude in the city was one of indifference.[12] Finally, with the rise of New South cotton mills in cities such as Spartanburg, as well as discriminatory freight rates that favored the state's inland regions, most white Charlestonians sat by and watched their port flounder, their markets fall away, and their young male entrepreneurs and professionals flee in search of opportunities elsewhere.[13]

Shifting political winds accompanied these economic changes and signaled a new era for white Charlestonians as well. Of course, the call for secession, and ultimately war, had come from Charleston. As Reconstruction waned, the elite white tidewater power structure continued to assert itself boldly in state politics. In 1876, for example, Charleston-born planter and former Confederate general Wade Hampton was elected governor with the help of organized bands of armed vigilantes, known as "Hampton's red shirts," who used violence and intimidation to prevent blacks from voting Republican.[14] With Hampton's "redemption" of South Carolina from Northern Reconstruction rule, white Charlestonians would once again exert major political influence for a time. However, the election of up-countryman "Pitchfork" Ben Tillman, an agrarian populist who publicly abhorred Charleston elitism, to the governor's mansion in 1890 profoundly undercut elite white Charlestonians' traditional power; they would not have one of their own serve as chief executive of the Palmetto State until the 1930s. As John Radford has argued, "What was left of Charleston's moral authority in 1865, had been eroded by 1880. Where in 1860 Charleston had been the symbol of an ideal and a center of national attention, in 1880 it was a minor seaport of little more than local economic and social significance."[15]

Aside from enjoying a brief boom in phosphate production in the late nineteenth century and the short-lived optimism surrounding the South Carolina Inter-State and West Indian Exposition hosted by the city in 1901–2, post–Civil War Charleston generally failed to embrace New South innovation.[16] And the expansion of Charleston's navy yard and war-related industries with the onset of the First World War did not alter significantly the city's dormant economy and its ambivalence toward modernization.[17] Even the second-term election in 1919 to the mayor's office of the charismatic progressive New South Democrat John P. Grace could not rouse Charleston from its complacent sleep. His promises of city services, paved streets, electric street lighting, and increased commercial enterprises did not radically uproot the city's entrenched social and economic conservatism. Grace did not garner cross-class support, in part because his vision of Charleston's future was an all-or-nothing proposition that required a complete break with the city's past, a concept too threatening to generations of elite whites raised to revere tradition.[18]

At the same time, more political harbingers of change were on the horizon, now from African American South Carolinians. W. E. B. DuBois's 1913 visit to Charleston inspired some in the black community to consider organizing politically. In February 1917, a group of twenty-nine elite blacks led by artist and mortician Edwin Harleston founded a local branch of the National Association for the Advancement of Colored People (NAACP).[19] Still, the First World War, which was to "make the world safe for democracy," failed to alter the experiences of black veterans who returned home to find Jim Crow and oppression alive and well. In response, black community leaders from across South Carolina held a statewide convention in January 1919 protesting segregation, lack of voting rights, and substandard schools.[20] In May of that year, violence erupted in downtown Charleston between white sailors and a black man. A bloody riot resulted that left three blacks dead and many whites and blacks severely injured. And although the city determined that the white sailors had been at fault and reimbursed damages to at least one black business owner, racial tensions seethed.[21] In the riot's aftermath, the NAACP galvanized support and successfully petitioned the city to hire black female teachers for black city schools.[22] A new day appeared to be dawning.

Most of Charleston's white civic and cultural leaders responded rather fearfully to these local and statewide economic and political challenges of the early twentieth century. Their solution: raise the drawbridge against the marauders of progress and seek solace in the city's past "glory." As historian Don Doyle describes it, "Old Charleston, besieged and subverted, retreated to the safe territory South of Broad, with its old mansions and its old ways. As the new century progressed, the old city became a museum, a sanctuary of artifacts and values that no longer ruled the South."[23] This is where our story begins.

IN A 11 JANUARY 1926 LETTER to the editor of the *Charleston Evening Post*, James Hagerty, a tourist from Chicago, celebrated the physical beauty and the "wealth of colonial relics" he encountered in the city. Convinced of the potential for a lucrative tourist industry, Hagerty blamed Charleston's essential snobbery, recalcitrant antimodernism, and undeveloped commercial sense for its failure to profit from the contemporary Charleston dance craze. "How your town is neglected from an advertising point," he declared. "If the people of uncultured CHICAGO, and the great Northwest, just had an idea of what you have to offer, you could take care of them. Talk about putting your light under a Bushel! . . . For Heaven's sake appropriate $100,000 this year for advertising, hitch your wagon to the 'CHARLESTON' and tell the world, yes it originated in your town, NEVER MIND YOUR DIGNITY. Your city is crying for improvement, your merchants want the business strangers will bring. Your working people will be as busy as the proverbial bee, if you will forget some of the non-essential past and live in 1926."[24] After just four days of exposure to Charleston, Hagerty was able to discern the dominant and connected attitudes of the city's ruling white elite: an exaggerated attachment to the past and a deep resistance to change. What he did not comprehend, however, was that his call to toss "dignity" aside and embrace for financial gain the Charleston (a "Negro" dance made popular by the runaway Broadway hit "Runnin' Wild") would have been considered heretical to many of the self-appointed custodians of the city's heritage. In 1926, the average member of Charleston's ruling white elite, while applauding Hagerty's appreciation of the city's historic artifacts, would have disagreed forcefully with the Chicagoan on at least two counts: first, that the city's past could ever be considered "non-essential" and second, that it should be forgotten. On the contrary, they would have argued that the past was vital to the city's identity and thus should be actively remembered and promoted.

As the James Hagertys of America lauded the rebellion and innovation captured by shortened hemlines, wagging hips, and cries of "Won't you Charleston with me," the town after which this Jazz Age anthem was named presented a very different face to the nation. In the years following the First World War, a coterie of elite whites, motivated by a perceived threat to their traditional way of life and a fierce civic pride, organized a network of cultural organizations dedicated to celebrating select aspects of the city's historic character. Together these individuals sought to preserve and enshrine Charleston as a place where remnants of a glorious past lived on, unmarred by the uglier sides of modernity. Through their efforts in fine arts, literature, music, and historic preservation, elite white cultural producers gave material expression to a version of Charleston that emphasized continuity of tradition, social hierarchy, and racial deference.

The elites' reinvented, indeed sanitized, interpretation of Charleston's past and present ignored the city's ethnic and racial diversity, omitted its entrepreneurial and commercial history, and erased the more violent realities of its slave-owning past and Jim Crow present. Instead, Charleston's white cultural producers imagined their city as the last enclave of genteel white aristocrats and subservient African American folk in an otherwise tumultuous nation. In doing so, elite whites cultivated a "usable past" that enabled them to assert their cultural significance in the present, to negotiate and accommodate the real and perceived changes modernity posed, to posit a critique of contemporary American economic and political culture, and to reinforce their claims to social authority. By the early 1930s, their efforts had helped produce

"Historic Charleston," a burgeoning tourist entity that lured thousands of history-hungry visitors to the city annually. Charleston's current multimillion dollar tourist industry testifies to the enduring impact and profitability of elite white cultural productions from the interwar period. James Hagerty would be proud.

The term "elite" can be difficult to define in many contexts, but in Charleston's white society of the 1920s and 1930s, the task is more transparent. Unlike in many other urban centers during this era, when business was the measure of the nation's greatness, one's claim to elite status in white Charleston had little to do with economic assets, corporate title, or capital liquidity. Certainly, some of the individuals central to the city's refashioning were serious professionals who at times profited handsomely from their cultural ventures, particularly before the Great Depression set in. The majority, however, were neither professional nor wealthy, particularly when they are considered in relation to the economic elites of other American cities in the 1920s and 1930s. In fact, many struggled to survive financially in their chronically depressed city. As artist Elizabeth O'Neill Verner, herself not a member of this caste, explained of her hometown in the 1930s, "The social lines are clearly marked but they are lines of blood and breeding and have nothing to do with bank accounts."[25]

Instead of meeting a contemporary economic standard, then, these cultural producers were "elite" by white Charleston's long-standing definition of the term — that is, they were the descendants of old-line families, many of whom were a part of the region's history from its earliest colonial days. Echoing perhaps the desires of the founders of the colony of Carolina who sought to establish a local "hereditary Nobility" to rule the region, a kind of "rural-urban squirearchy" emerged early in Charleston's history.[26] And yet, as George C. Rogers Jr. has argued, in its early phases this group was "quite willing to absorb new talent," which included merchants.[27] After the late eighteenth century, however, membership in this class solidified to include central clans that consolidated their standing through the accumulation of wealth in the form of land and slaves and related commerce; exercised their power in local and national politics; and self-consciously cultivated kinship ties, emotional bonds, and loyalties to each other to promote their shared interests. Of course, the reliance on family in "the creation of an elite culture" occurred in other early American cities as well, such as Philadelphia and Boston, but, as South Carolina family historian Lorri Glover argues, in eighteenth-century Charleston, the consequences were more formidable and enduring: "Class identity and commitment to protecting class interests ran deeper and [elite] control over their city was stronger largely because they enjoyed more extensive and intensive kin connections and greater cultural cohesion."[28] Frederick Cople Jaher's comparison of American urban elites in the nineteenth and twentieth centuries affirms and extends chronologically Glover's characterization of Charleston, especially in terms of the cultural prominence of the tidewater city's upper strata in the modern age: "If the Brahmins had an edge in intellectual, commercial, and financial vitality and in charity activities, the Charlestonians have better perpetuated their role in setting the tone for the fashions and rituals of the *beau monde* in their city."[29]

As their prominence persisted into the early decades of the twentieth century, Charleston's white elites continued to follow the social patterns set by their ancestors—what Jaher calls the "intergenerational bequests of rank and role"[30]—from three o'clock dinners to St. Cecelia Society balls. Their lives were deeply intertwined with each other: they resided in the same neighborhoods, joined the same clubs, were educated at the same schools, worshiped in the same churches, enacted the same holiday rituals, summered at the same beach and mountain getaways, intermarried, and, eventually, were buried in the same churchyards. Elites also assumed they would exert significant influence over their city's policies and inhabitants, as had their elders. Maintaining these kinship ties, social patterns, and life expectations not only provided significant "meaning and context for their lives"[31] but also fueled much of Charleston's formal cultural activity between the world wars, as it had the city's politics, culture, and economics from the colonial era through the nineteenth century.

Because the same names appear over and over again on the rolls of Charleston's cultural organizations in the 1920s and 1930s, one need only select a single name to begin to untangle the extensive and impressive web of blood and family. Take, for example, Susan Pringle Frost, the founder and first president of the Society for the Preservation of Old Dwellings (SPOD). Her cofounder, and savior of the endangered Manigault House, Nell (Mrs. Ernest) Pringle was a cousin by marriage. Susan Pringle Frost's great-grandfather, John Julius Pringle (born 1753), and Ernest Pringle's great-great-grandfather, Robert Pringle (born 1755), were brothers. Thomas Porcher Stoney (mayor 1923–31) and Burnet Rhett Maybank (mayor 1931–38), the mayors who vigorously embraced historic preservation as official civic policy, can also be linked to the Pringle/Frost lines. In turn, these two influential politicians were cousins by marriage to Albert Simons, an omnipresent force in the interwar years. A trustee of both the Carolina Art Association and the Charleston Museum, and a member of the Society for the Preservation of Negro Spirituals and the Etchers' Club (both founded in the 1920s), Simons was best known as the city's leading architect who shaped the public landscape as the main voice of the Board of Architectural Review. Through the marriage of Nell Pringle's daughter Margaretta to St. Julien Ravenel Childs, the Pringles became cousins to Albert Simons. Simons also served as a vital link between these families and the Stoney/Maybank clan, whose members included Sam Stoney, author, Gullah raconteur, and preservationist architect. Through marriage, Simons was also related to John Bennett, author and mentor to the city's inspiring literati.[32] And these individuals represent only a small tug on a single genealogical thread. The familial and institutional connections are everywhere in this story. Clearly, Charleston's cultural leadership drew upon these extensive and overlapping kinship networks — and their associative historical memories — for support and reassurance. Through them, elite whites were able to occupy positions of public prominence from which they exercised influence disproportionate to their numbers.

The elite white cultural refashioning of Charleston between the world wars involved the complicated interplay of modernization, social memory, and the uses of history in the construction and commodification of regional identity. It illuminates specifically the following questions: Who controls the identity and representation of a community? How is the power to articulate meaning claimed? Through what process is cultural meaning defined and redefined? How is it transmitted to individuals both inside and outside of the given community? And, finally, how are certain interests served and disfranchised in the process? At the center of this analysis are the linked concepts of historical memory and historical amnesia.

The role of history and memory (understood as both recalling and forgetting) in public discourse is a complex one that scholars are increasingly trying to elucidate. At its most basic, an articulated public historical memory might be best understood as, in John Bodnar's words, "a body of beliefs and ideas about the past that helps a public or society understand both its past, present, and by implication, its future."[33] But, of course, remembering the past is not merely an act of retrieving "pure" information; rather, it is a process of interpretation, of reconstituting the past in a meaningful and often therapeutic form. It is literally an act of re-membering. And while "history" should belong, as Pierre Nora argues, "to everyone and to no one, whence its claim to universal authority," historical memory is by definition subjective, constructed, and even, as in the case of Charleston, autobiographical.[34] Despite this definition, social groups often claim that their collective remembering carries the weight of "history" — of objectivity, authenticity, and timelessness — and is thus legitimate and seamless. Self-interested constituencies thus deploy historical memory for a variety of ends: to organize society; to regulate access to or exclusion from political, social, and economic power; to create and resist consensus identities; to invent tradition; and to control or challenge public discourse.[35] In many cases, the stakes are quite high.

As a tool for recovering an accurate account of the past, memory is undoubtedly imperfect and partial, and yet it is also ubiquitous and powerful. Scholars across the disciplines have found that the desire to reshape the past to meet contemporary needs and then call that entity "history" is a decidedly human impulse that transcends chronological, geographical, racial, and class boundaries.[36] In many cultures, it serves as a weapon of the strong, as a force of domination.[37] In others, as postcolonial scholars and social historians have underscored, historical memory can be a source of resistance to hegemonic narratives and oppressive power structures.[38]

Elite white Charlestonians availed themselves of both of these aspects of historical memory. On the one hand, they constructed what John Bodnar would call an "official public culture" based on memory claims in which alternate and dissenting interpretations were unwelcome, thus reinscribing "in ideal rather than complex or ambiguous terms" the traditional hierarchies that guaranteed their power.[39] At the same time, many of these individuals considered their historical commemorations a form of resistance to a more generalized modern American culture that had abandoned its agrarian values and racial organization, and had turned its back on Southern political philosophy. At first glance, it might seem absurd to compare elite white Charlestonians living in the Jim Crow South to postcolonial peoples elsewhere. And yet, vis-à-vis the exuberant national scene, the post-Reconstruction generation that comprised the core of the city's cultural activists often thought of themselves in just that light. They were the children of the conquered generation whose dreams of independence and the maintenance of the slave society that guaranteed their status died at Appomattox; they were grandchildren and great-grandchildren of the city's colonial and early-republican "golden age," when the city bustled with commerce and culture and national political influence. Indeed, for this early-twentieth-century generation, much had been lost through violence and degradation and a shift in national values. What was lost now required reclaiming — re-membering — for themselves and for their progeny before it was too late.

In order to transpose their personal and familial memories into an official public culture for the city, elite white cultural activists engaged in a sustained and energetic social process. As had their ancestors in earlier moments of "crisis," elites turned to each other — to their kinship and institutional networks—for affirmation and support. In these interactions, elites articulated, reshaped, and validated their individual recollections and made them concrete through monuments to their beloved city. In the process, historical memories were transformed from personal to group, private to public, ephemeral to material, local to national. The idea of a "legacy of memory" permeated this process. First, elites drew inspiration from inherited conceptions of place as their source of inspiration: they internalized the memories passed down to them from their elders and located their privilege to speak for Charleston in bloodlines and an inherited sense of place. Next, elites deployed a variety of strategies and forms—novels, concerts, historic house tours, and paintings—to create a tangible legacy for their memories that both fed and fed off of a growing consumer market. In particular, this 1920s and 1930s legacy influenced the way outsiders, especially visitors, would remember the city. Thus it was in the "contexts of community" with like-minded individuals that elite whites constructed the political entity "Historic Charleston."[40]

Examining how "Historic Charleston" came into being holds significance for our understanding both of the city in question and of the larger questions of how American public culture is shaped and what role the potentially elusive force of historical memory plays in this process. For Charleston, it is important to unpack and analyze critically the genesis of this public identity because of its persistence into the present. What might appear on the surface to be the rather dilettante workings of a small group of artists and preservationists has in fact become the central content of the city's most lucrative industry. Even with the current availability of African American historical walking tours and two recent city initiatives to develop both a local and a national museum of slavery, the essential elements of the Charleston mystique as shaped in the 1920s and 1930s remain in place today, despite the very different environment in which they now operate. Until a more inclusive representation of the past becomes the core of its identity, Charleston's fuller history and its public discourse about issues such as racism and poverty will continue to be obscured through the haze of a selective history, as will our national discourse about the past and its relationship to citizenship and power. From slavery at Colonial Williamsburg, to the Enola Gay exhibit at the National Air and Space Museum, to interpretations of the meaning of the Alamo, debates about public representations of the past run deep in contemporary American culture and often leave painful scars.[41] As part of these larger debates—in particular as a way to understand the various mechanisms and personalized influences behind the making of a "collective" memory—Charleston's specific story is illuminating.

Charleston's interwar story also offers the cultural historian a window to a fuller understanding of American regionalism—its manifestations, its successes, and, ultimately, its limitations. Charleston's reinvention of tradition and identity was part of a broader regionalist phenomenon of the 1920s and 1930s concerned with the impact of modernity on the American character. In Charleston, as in the larger regionalist circles, the philosophy and activities of cultural producers spoke to the complexities of an emerging, homogeneous American consumer culture, a growing interest in material culture, and an ennui with modernism that permeated American intellectual circles of the day.[42] When considered alongside contemporary regionalist and preservationist endeavors, such as the paintings of Thomas Hart Benton and Grant Wood, the literature of Mari Sandoz and Donald Davidson, and the development of Henry Ford's "Greenfield Village" and John D. Rockefeller Jr.'s "Colonial Williamsburg," Charleston's cultural activists become less an example of parochial Southern eccentricity and more an integral part of a widespread restorationist movement. Charleston's story also enlarges the specifically Southern regionalist canon beyond Faulkner and the Fugitive poets to include representatives from one of the South's historically prominent urban centers.[43]

As with their fellow regionalists, Charleston's cultural producers cannot be characterized as mere reactionary, backward-looking escapists; their general antimodernism was more complex.[44] While undoubtedly nostalgic about the past and highly critical of an unchecked gospel of progress, Charleston's cultural guardians were also very much preoccupied with the form the city's future would take. Therefore, they self-consciously turned to the past as a means of responding to the present. Their perspectives on modernity and innovation were as diverse as the individual personalities involved in the movement, and their professed opinions and actions were often rife with contradiction. Certain individuals decried the invention of the automobile, while others embraced aspects of the "modern" by sponsoring avante-garde events in the city, such as a lecture by Gertrude Stein before the Poetry Society and an exhibition of Solomon Guggenheim's nonobjective paintings at the local Gibbes Gallery of Art.

Without question, Charleston's cultural producers participated in the modernizing world. Their artistic and preservation efforts created a lucrative commodity, "Historic Charleston," for the emerging culture of consumption. The city became a magnet for those seeking a "romantic," "historic," "quaint," and "old-worldly" atmosphere. Its inhabitants, particularly its "primitive," "picturesque" African American working class and its "refined" and "noble" white "gentry," were the actors on this constructed stage. Through the commodification of the city's past, elite whites transformed Charleston from an overlooked and dilapidated backwater at the turn of the century into a major midcentury tourist spot, a transformation accompanied by decidedly modern changes in the landscape, such as paved roads, electric street lighting, two multistory modern hotels, a municipal airport, and even a towering steel bridge spanning the Cooper River, the city's eastern boundary. These nostalgic innovators employed modern technologies, such as radio and film, to promote themselves and their work. Finally, all were a part of the modern capitalist culture, seeking personal profits or organizational funds to continue their work.

Charleston's elite whites thus became a part of the very modern world that at first glance they seemed to deplore. They adapted to it and used it to their advantage to shape the city's cultural identity in a way that would ensure the endurance of the core of their values and traditions, even though those values and traditions might seem to be undermined by such developments. In the end, Charleston's elite whites operated in an environment similar to what Ian McKay, in his study of folklorists and antimodernism in twentieth-century Nova Scotia, calls "commercial antimodernism, structured by the very modern capitalism from which it seemed to provide momentary and partial escape, and reliant upon its fast-developing technologies."[45]

Studying Charleston's self-fashioning also challenges many academic conceptions of "Southern identity." Scholars of this school tend to discuss identity in a way that precludes sources of identification for American Southerners other than the region. The example of Charleston, however, complicates this narrow definition of identity by elucidating how an individual or group claims to be simultaneously "Southern" and "American." If achieving this balance is possible, or even desirable, as it was for many elite white Charlestonians between the world wars, then the notion of Southern distinctiveness must be more complicated. The Charleston example suggests that in at least some places in the twentieth-century American South, identity was not considered an either Southern or something altogether different proposition.[46]

The historic identity that elite white Charlestonians articulated and promoted in the decades between the world wars was undeniably "Southern" in content. It invoked traditional emblems associated with the region—Spanish moss, ionic columns, "genteel" white planters, "primitive" African Americans —that white American audiences understood as part of a symbolic vocabulary of "Southernness." At the same time, the spokesmen and spokeswomen for this movement diverged from more virulent forms of sectionalism, such as those promoted by the Vanderbilt Agrarians or the various Confederate veterans organizations, by emphasizing the *national* value of their city's character. These Charlestonians neither vilified all things industrial and alien to the region nor exhibited much interest in remembering, much less re-fighting, the Civil War. Instead, they highlighted Charleston's colonial, Revolutionary, and antebellum history, and the enduring cultural fragments of those periods present in the city in order to assert the national relevance of their values and to promote interregional tourism. Charleston's cultural producers downplayed regional divisions even while they exalted local continuities. In 1924, for example, bolstered by the town's increased publicity due in part to the successes of its writers, its artists, and its historic preservation movement, Mayor Thomas Stoney declared Charleston "America's Most Historic City"—not "the South's."[47] By conceiving of the city as the ultimate repository of nationalist history, then, elite white Charlestonians were able to reconcile the otherwise potentially competing identities of "Southerner" and "American."

Part of this reconciliation process relied on a national commitment to maintaining white supremacy, and understanding Charleston's cultural productions helps expand scholarly definitions of what constitutes the political culture of Jim Crow. Drawing on the work of Robin Kelley, who has reconsidered the possible meanings of seemingly passive or silent African American behavior during segregation, I found in Charleston a range of events and artifacts that contributed to the maintenance of racial segregation and oppression. By looking beyond the traditional "Whites Only" signs, Charleston's story reveals how museum exhibits, concerts, restored buildings, theatrical productions, and even walking tours reinforced white power and racial segregation within the city. The mechanisms of the Jim Crow South were multiple, pervasive, and often embodied in artistic guise.[48]

African American Charlestonians figured prominently in the cultural productions of elite whites, not as independent actors, but as constructed types. Elite whites appropriated black spirituals, folktales, voices, and images to weave an identity for Charleston in which African American primitivism served as a foil to white gentility. They blatantly ignored the presence of a thriving and long-standing black middle class made up of dentists, preachers, teachers, small-business owners, and even other artists. Instead, elite white cultural producers of the 1920s and 1930s allowed only a selective typology of African American figures into their historical drama—the domestic servant, the field hand, the street huckster, and the "old time" ex-slave. Thus objectified, African American "types" served to reinforce the city's racial boundaries by uniting whites in an understanding of themselves as superior to and paternalistically responsible for blacks and for the preservation of certain elements of black culture.

My original hope in examining Charleston's process of cultural construction was to discover a landscape rife with contestation. I imagined a city loud with dissenting voices, in particular African American voices, that challenged the elite white narrative of the past. Some evidence of black resistance to white cultural authority exists for the turn of the century. In one instance, for example, blacks complained so bitterly about a derogatory sculpture at the 1901 – 2 South Carolina Inter-State and West Indian Exposition that white authorities removed it from the Negro Building. Likewise, in response to the persistent defacing of a statue of John C. Calhoun on Citadel Green, city fathers were forced to place the father of nullification on a large column, away from possible vandals.[49] Unfortunately, no such episodes of opposition can be found in the public record for the interwar years. A severe paucity of black-authored sources means little or no evidence of resistance from the black community to this one-sided objectification. At least one black-owned newspaper, the *Messenger*, existed in Charleston during this period, but no complete copies of it survive in circulation. Nor do the extensive Works Progress Administration interviews with older black Charlestonians or the records of the local branch of the NAACP, founded in 1917 and relatively dormant in the 1920s and 1930s, shed much light on African American perspectives on white elite cultural endeavors. Oral histories I conducted with several elderly African American Charlestonians merely confirmed my suspicions that between the world wars, blacks and whites lived in very different worlds, despite the city's many integrated neighborhoods and a population ratio between the races that hovered consistently around 50/50. Not surprisingly, most black Charlestonians living under Jim Crow were poor, disfranchised, and preoccupied with basic survival issues. Their middle-class counterparts, meanwhile, directed their energies toward general "racial uplift," such as gaining economic and educational opportunities and improving medical resources for the community as a whole. Neither group left an account of resistance to the seemingly dilettante, but eventually far-reaching, artistic and cultural activities of the city's elite whites. As a result of these documentary obstacles, I have limited my discussion of Charleston's identity construction to the workings of elite whites — a discussion that is nonetheless deeply engaged with racial issues.

Referred to today as the "Charleston Renaissance," the city's cultural flowering occurred around the same period as the Southern Literary Renaissance and the Harlem Renaissance. Though it shared with these two movements a fascination with history's relation to the present and a vivid assertion of cultural identity, its similarities to them stop there.[50] Charleston's more serious writers, particularly DuBose Heyward and Josephine Pinckney, enjoyed professional relationships at various times with several prominent Southern Literary Renaissance figures, but by the time that movement came into full bloom around 1930, its Charleston literary equivalent was in decline.

Though Charleston's writers were self-conscious about their role in reclaiming the city's antebellum stature as a center of literary production, they tended not to use the term "renaissance" to describe their endeavors. Neither did Charleston's white artists, spirituals singers, or historic preservationists describe their activities as part of a specific renaissance. Instead, the term "Charleston Renaissance" itself is best understood as a form of contemporary memory-shaping. It is largely the recent creation of individuals seeking an attractive yet concise way to characterize the cultural stirring in the years between the world wars.[51]

Other "Renaissance" writers, such as contemporary African American and Southern writers like Jean Toomer, William Faulkner, and Howard Odum, scrutinized the burden of the past and struggled with questions of identity. In contrast, Charleston's writers and artists did not consider the past a negative burden. Nor did they feel compelled to ask, "Who are we?" Instead, they merely asserted what was to them a known quantity. Theirs was a largely uncritical approach to a received tradition of place that had been forged by the post–Civil War generation and that operated on an almost subconscious level. It was neither an intellectual journey nor a psychological challenge for them to articulate that they were Charlestonians. The city meant something fixed and worthy of preservation, an accumulation of history, family, land, and racial prerogative—little was problematic, alienating, or painful. It meant that they were the stewards of the home of America's last aristocracy. This was their operative identity myth—and this was the Charleston to which they gave life through their cultural activities.

In 1935, the Agrarian poet Allen Tate claimed that "with the war of 1914–1918, the South reentered the world—but gave a backward glance as it stepped over the border: that backward glance gave us the Southern renascence, a literature conscious of the past in the present."[52] Charleston's historical consciousness, however, did not spring full-blown out of the First World War. As they did the family silver, elite white Charlestonians inherited their basic conception of the city and themselves as historical, authentic, and important. They learned of the past at the knees of their mothers, fathers, uncles, aunts, and cousins and through volumes written by relatives, such as

Mrs. St. Julien Ravenel's *Charleston, the Place and the People* and Daniel Elliott Huger Smith's *Dwelling Houses of Charleston*.[53] They absorbed history through their physical surroundings, be it once-grand planter homes or "sacred" relics, such as Revolutionary War swords and colonial-era portraits hanging over the fireplace. Many elite whites internalized the importance of preservation by watching the efforts of female family and friends, such as members of the Colonial Dames, who fought to save the city's Colonial Powder Magazine from destruction at the turn of the century. These Charlestonians came to value black folklore and music through contact with family servants and the local-color literature of their childhoods.

When Charleston's elite whites began formally institutionalizing their cultural activities after the First World War, the main movers and shakers were relatively young people—all were born after Reconstruction. Although most were members of former slave-owning families, these individuals never experienced antebellum plantation life firsthand. Instead, they came of age in a decaying urban landscape surrounded by individuals who had witnessed the passing of that world, and thus the artists and writers identified with the previous generations' sense of loss. Received images of the colonial, early national, and antebellum periods and the people who colored them figured prominently in their conception of Charleston. Their understanding of the past, filtered through the recollections of their elders, was often several times removed. And yet elite cultural producers did not significantly alter the basic content of the previous generation's notion of place. Rather, they enlarged it and gave it imaginative representation to suit their psychological needs for continuity and control in a changing world. Their creative and preservationist impulses did not occur in a vacuum but rather in an environment where ancestors tread heavily and the call to remember imposed itself on the listener.

At the outset, Charleston's white cultural elites were concerned most with passing down to their children and to Charleston's future generations the sense of pride, reverence, and obligation toward the city that was their inheritance. They did not, however, adopt a fortress mentality and isolate themselves from external influences. From the very beginnings of the movement, they welcomed the leadership and participation of non-Charlestonians, such as John Bennett of Ohio, Hervey Allen of Pittsburgh, Alfred Hutty of Michigan, and Laura Bragg of New Hampshire, who were dedicated to the city's heritage but did not share in it directly. By the late 1920s, as their movement expanded, cultural producers also solicited advice from outside organizations, such as the American Institute of Architects (AIA), as well as the financial and moral support of increasing numbers of the new Northern property owners who resided in the city and the surrounding countryside during the winter season. Partially as a result of these alliances, Charleston's white artistic elites gave a patriotic cultural spin to their city's past and present and welcomed visitors and consumers from other parts of the nation. They encouraged outsiders to embrace their city and to propagate the traditions for which it stood. They encouraged all comers to share in their version of the Charleston experience.

By no means, however, did Charleston's artists and preservationists lead a democratic movement or create a populist identity for their city. On the contrary, they spoke primarily to themselves—comforting and reassuring each other that their world would endure and that their city would once again speak out in a proud voice to the nation. As their movement expanded in the late 1920s and early 1930s, so, too, did their audience. Writers cultivated relationships with New York publishers, artists with galleries across the nation, preservationists with prominent architects, spirituals singers with concert sponsors up and down the East Coast. Even with these increased contacts, however, Charleston's cultural producers mostly enlarged their already elite audience. They did not reach out to individuals or groups below what they perceived to be their elevated social class, and certainly not to other races. Although by the 1930s increased numbers of Americans from different echelons of society came into contact with their ideas through publicity, magazine articles, and tourism, they were not the original intended audience. Instead, Charleston's white elite cultural movement was designed as an exclusive dialogue, first, among descendants and ancestors and, second, between elite whites from different parts of the nation who were sympathetic to the expressed ideals.

In many ways, the history of Charleston's elite re-membering of the 1920s and 1930s resembles the self-conscious steps involved in staging a theatrical production. I have arranged the following study with this analogy in mind, dividing it into six sections, each of which provides an essential aspect of the production and performance of a play. In Chapter 1, which examines the role of historic preservation in shaping the urban landscape, the Society for the Preservation of Old Dwellings and the Board of Architectural Review create the physical scenery. After the historic backdrop is set, voiceless characters stride onto stage with the help of the artist's brush and the etcher's knife in Chapter 2. The poets and authors of Chapter 3 write the script to be enacted, and the Society for the Preservation of Spirituals provides the voices and sound in Chapter 4. Once all elements are in place, the production is mounted and marketed by the tourism industry of Chapter 5. In the afterword, the hard-fought efforts of the players climax with the production of an actual play celebrating the 1937 opening of the Dock Street Theatre, a restored landmark. This event, which brought federal funding and national political leaders to Charleston, signified the maturation of elite white historical re-membering and their cultural re-fashioning of civic identity between the wars. By clinging to their memories and little else, Charleston's white elites successfully situated their politicized notions of the past, present, and future at the center of city life.

CHAPTER ONE

A Golden Haze of Memory and Association

THE CREATION OF A HISTORIC CHARLESTON LANDSCAPE

Charleston is not the Island of Manhattan.
—Society for the Preservation of Old Dwellings, 1920

A white woman, dressed in flowing robes and armed with a large spear, sits guarding the harbor and buildings of a bustling, eighteenth-century port city. A ribbon declaring in Latin the motto "She guards her buildings, custom and laws" scrolls over the figure's defiant head. This, the official seal of Charleston, South Carolina, since its incorporation in 1783, illustrates the value Charlestonians have invested in their architectural treasures, placing them on the same level as their "customs and laws."[1]

In 1920, a group of elite white Charleston women wrapped themselves in the mantle of this allegorical spirit and asserted their role as guardians of the city's endangered historical landscape. Through the founding of the Society for the Preservation of Old Dwellings (SPOD), they launched a preservation movement shaped by a highly selective historical memory that is best described as personal, romantic, and heroic. Unlike their contemporaries at Greenfield Village, Michigan, or Williamsburg, Virginia, Charleston preservationists did not invent a historic landscape from scratch or from a small handful of buildings; rather, they worked with the city's existing structural resources.[2] The significance of a building depended on the extent to which it functioned for preservationists as a concrete reminder of traditional cultural customs and

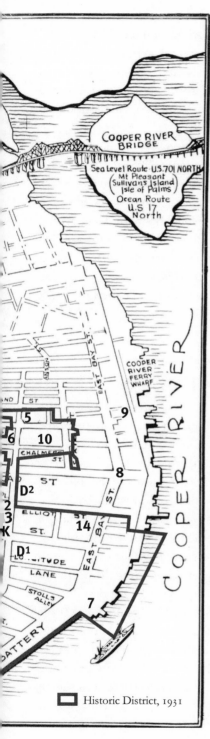

Sites

1 St. Michael's Episcopal Church
2 Post Office
3 Gibbes Art Gallery
4 Powder Magazine
5 St. Philip's Episcopal
6 Dock Street Theatre
7 Carolina Yacht Club
8 Exchange Building
9 Clyde Line Pier
10 Old Slave Market
11 Miles Brewton/Pringle House
12 Heyward-Washington House
13 Cabbage Row
14 Rainbow Row
15 Fort Sumter Hotel
16 Francis Marion Hotel
17 Manigault House
18 Charleston Museum
19 Robert Mills Manor Housing Project
20 Cooper River View Housing Project

Private Residences/
Studios of Key Cultural Figures

A John Bennett
11 Susan Pringle Frost (Miles Brewton House)
B Laura Bragg
C Edwin Harleston
D¹ DuBose Heyward
D² DuBose Heyward
E Alfred Huger
F Josephine Pinckney
G Nell Pringle
H Burnet Rhett Maybank
I Albert Simons
J Alice Ravenel Huger Smith
K Elizabeth O'Neill Verner
L Artists' Studios (Atlantic Street)

Select cultural sites and private residences/ studios in Charleston, 1920–1940, adapted from a tourist map from the same period (from Collection of Pamela Gabriel) values that were synonymous, in their hearts and minds, with Charleston. SPOD activists bestowed "sacred relic" status on the grand eighteenth- and early-nineteenth-century residences of the former planter class and ignored or advocated the "clean up" of more modest, usually black-occupied structures. In these preservation choices, SPOD members projected their interpretation of the past, and their claim to contemporary racial and class authority, onto the three-dimensional fabric of the city.[3]

As the 1920s progressed and historic preservation became more fashionable and potentially profitable, Charleston's movement altered accordingly.[4] Professional male architects and city officials assumed the movement's reigns from its early female volunteer founders. Whereas SPOD had been the engine of advocacy in the 1920s, the all-male, mayor-appointed Board of Architectural Review (BAR) arbitrated most preservation decisions by the early 1930s. Likewise, preservationists expanded their vision from saving individual homes to zoning an entire historic district in 1931. And yet, while the power to regulate Charleston's cityscape shifted hands, the elite spirit that defined the city's historic spaces and public memory remained constant.[5]

"Largely a Women's Organization": The Society for the Preservation of Old Dwellings

On Wednesday afternoon, 21 April 1920, a group of thirty-two white Charleston residents gathered in the front parlors of 20 South Battery, the home of Nell and Ernest H. Pringle Jr. They congregated at the request of Miss Susan Pringle Frost, a local realtor and a friend, and in some cases, relative, of those gathered. Between sips of tea and mouthfuls of mocha cake, the group listened enraptured to Frost's impassioned pleas that they organize themselves into a group to safeguard the city's architectural jewels. Although approaching fifty years of age, the stout and stern Frost presented a formidable figure that April afternoon. The suffragist and seasoned businesswoman knew how to motivate a crowd. Drawing upon concerns regarding the proposed commercial development of neighboring Citadel Square, Frost described in vivid detail the imminent destruction of the Joseph Manigault House at the corner of Meeting Street and Ashmeade Place for the construction of automobile garages on the site. Designed by Charleston banker and architect Gabriel Manigault for his rice planter brother Joseph, and built in 1802–3, the mansion featured elaborate ornamentation and a sweeping staircase; it was an outstanding local example of Adam-style architecture.[6] The potential loss of this Charleston monument—especially at the hands of a car garage—was

Preservation pioneer Susan Pringle Frost, shown here in the Manigault House, saw the architecture of her native city "partly through a golden haze of memory and association." Courtesy of the Charleston Museum, Charleston, South Carolina.

too much for the assembly to imagine. Frost further appealed to her listeners' racial and class anxieties by underscoring the "imminent danger of further deterioration on account of the class of tenants now occupying it."[7] To prevent such a tragedy, they created an association that became known as the Society for the Preservation of Old Dwellings.[8]

As SPOD's leader, Susan Frost became the most public face and voice of preservation in 1920s Charleston. Frost was a complex women who embodied both the traditional and the innovative, and her relationship to modernity is not easily categorized. She was a female business pioneer who broke the gender barrier for stenographers in the U.S. Federal District Court in Charleston, where she worked for sixteen years, supporting herself and her unmarried sisters. In 1909, she became a professional real estate agent.[9] Frost was very active in local women's club work; for example, she was the founder and president of the Charleston Equal Suffrage League, which advocated the National Women's Party's radical stance for an equal rights amendment.[10] At the same time, Susan Frost boasted an impeccably patrician Low Country lineage and identified strongly with the mores and manners of the past, regarding unwarranted change with a wary eye. As a result, she often sought compromise, which occasionally resulted in supporting contradictory stances. Take, for example, Frost's attitude toward cars. On the one hand, she consistently lamented the changes that the automobile wrought to Charleston's landscape, such as widened streets, demolished old homes, and unsightly filling stations. On the other hand, Frost was one of the first white women in Charleston to drive a car, which she used for showing properties to potential clients. While in some instances a threat, automobiles could also be a preservation ally, Frost pointed out, as they "now make all sections in close proximity, so that the old distinctions of up town and down town should have no part when it comes to the preservation of the best in architecture."[11]

Frost echoed the sentiment expressed by fellow Charlestonians Alice Ravenel Huger Smith and Daniel Elliott Huger Smith in their germinal 1917 publication, *The Dwelling Houses of Charleston*. "New and strange ideas, which, however suitable to places that have developed them, would be in Charleston merely imitation, and would perhaps destroy those very things that make the place so interesting," the Smiths wrote. "It is not what is new, however, but what is incongruous that should be avoided."[12] A practical visionary, the savvy Frost did not want to alienate potential allies among business and government interests in the city. Indeed, SPOD's second official meeting was held at the Charleston Chamber of Commerce. Thus, Frost articulated an ideal of preservation that embraced commercial, generational, and aesthetic concerns: preservation became "of vital and far-reaching importance to Charleston, possibly not in a commercial sense as some count 'commercial,' but certainly in a very broad sense 'commercial.'"[13] From the beginning, then, SPOD characterized its safeguarding of the past as a complement to rather than an adversary of commercial progress.

With Frost at the helm, SPOD members hoped that their organization would become a kind of consulting firm for the business community, able to "influence commercial interests to select for their business places localities in which old charm is not sacrificed."[14] SPOD envisioned preservation as a way to resuscitate the local economy by transforming dilapidated structures into "income-producing" properties, such as hotels, apartments, and even retail spaces.[15] On a smaller scale, from early on SPOD advocated charging tourists admission to gain access to Charleston's historic properties in order to offset preservation costs.[16] Frost also pointed to her own real estate career and the modest living she had earned from restored properties as an illustration of preservation's economic potential.[17]

SPOD was neither the first nor the only group of individuals who organized to rehabilitate the physical remnants of a remembered past. Its membership drew on a long tradition of organizing both in and outside of the South, such as the Mount Vernon Ladies Society, the Ladies Hermitage Association (Tennessee), the Association for the Preservation of Virginia Antiquities (APVA), and the Society for the Preservation of New England Antiquities (SPNEA). SPOD, however, differed from its organizational ancestors. Unlike the more reactionary APVA, for example, Charleston preservationists did not act as a last defense against change. They did not promote a wholesale return to the culture of the Old South.[18] Instead, they worked within a modern mentality, attempting to organize certain areas of the city as historic and representative of a revered past while allowing other spaces to develop along commercial lines. Charleston's preservationists balanced fears of unregulated development on the peninsula with reverence for tradition and a pragmatic approach to the modern age.

As with the automobile, preservationists sought to control the types of commercial endeavor allowed in their city, not to thwart them altogether or to return blindfolded to a past "golden age." Despite occasional rhetoric to the contrary, preservationists' behavior revealed that they were not waging a romantic war with modernity. Rather, they accepted and participated in the modernizing environment even as they struggled to ensure a prominent place for traditional values within it. Frost presented SPOD's position to the public in a 1928 letter to the editor of a local newspaper: "I want to bring out the fact that members of our Society are not opposed to progress, that we would like to see industries, smoke stacks, and everything that would advance Charleston commercially, come once more to Charleston; but we want them properly located, and not at the expense of the beauty and charm of Charleston's distinctiveness, which annually brings so many visitors to its doors."[19] Engaged in a delicate balancing act between past and present, preservationists tried to turn old buildings into bridges that spanned the generations and helped the Old South adapt to the New.[20]

Moreover, Frost considered historic preservation an effective vehicle for educating future generations of Charlestonians about their aesthetic inheritance by alerting them to their duty to stop the "desecration" of the city's historical landscape. "Let us keep to the things that have stood the test of centuries," she argued, "[the] beauty and dignity that [have] been handed down by those gone before."[21] Frost spoke of these properties and the imperative to protect them — and the cultural ideals they represented — in nearly sacred terms. To Frost, these buildings were more than mere brick and mortar. They were the visible remnants of an inherited set of values — of continuity, gentility, and order — that she and others like her perceived to be threatened in post–World War I Charleston. In what was also a critique of the ephemeral and homogenizing nature of contemporary culture, Frost contended that jeopardized buildings and neighborhoods, as well as the city's larger historic atmosphere — its cobblestoned roads, live oaks, and streets named after "early and respected citizens"[22] — lent "a certain stability and nobility of character and taste, which a modern age can ill afford to dispense with." Thus, afraid that the destruction of old residences would lead to the alienation of white Charlestonians from their heritage, as well as the "cheapening in the taste of the next generation in home building," Frost used SPOD to inculcate "in the mind of the public . . . a veneration"[23] of the city's finer buildings. Frost tirelessly propagandized SPOD's position: "Charleston is not the Island of Manhattan, straining at its natural limitations . . . — with us destruction is a cheap affectation — an impatient brushing away of an old order of culture, to ape the new wealth and up-to-dateness of newly grown cities." For Susan Pringle Frost, her people's historical memory was at stake. Without it, she scolded, "We are not worthy of these treasure houses that have been handed down to us, and treasures which will be required of us by her children and her children's children."[24]

Of the thirty-two individuals who responded to Frost's plea and endorsed her agenda on that April afternoon in 1920, twenty-nine were women. Although two men, including artist Alfred Hutty, delivered speeches at the first meeting, the six individuals who donated money for the immediate assumption of the Manigault House deed were women.[25] These white women followed a long tradition of female public voluntary activism in Charleston and the nation. For generations, American women had stepped across the prescriptive boundaries of separate sexual spheres and entered the public domain armed with a conception of domesticity that justified their activism. In order to ensure the integrity of their families and the society in which their children grew to adulthood, the argument went, women's domestic role obliged them to reform what they saw as society's ills. Thus, these predominantly middle- and upper-class white women mobilized for causes ranging from antiprostitution and poverty to temperance, better working conditions for women and children, and female suffrage. As they petitioned, marched, educated, delivered speeches, and wrote constitutions, women gained critical political skills while also remaining true, theoretically at least, to the submissive role required of domestic ideology. In the end, their activism changed the definition of women's public role in American society.[26]

From the Ladies Benevolent Society of the antebellum period to the Progressive Era's Equal Suffrage League of the 1910s, Charleston's elite white women were present in the public sphere. Some of this activist spirit extended to historic preservation. Indeed, some scholars argue that the historic preservation movement in America was born in Charleston in 1853 when Ann Pamela Cunningham issued her call to save George Washington's home in a local city newspaper, resulting in the founding of the Mount Vernon Ladies Society.[27] Female preservation work extended into the twentieth century with the local Colonial Dames' 1901 purchase and restoration of the city's eighteenth-century Old Powder Magazine.[28] Those gathered at Nell Pringle's home in April 1920 continued this tradition of women as the custodians of society's artifacts, identity, and welfare.

In Charleston, the centrality of women's participation in early preservation efforts influenced the kinds of spaces and structures that SPOD preserved, and that, in turn, helped shape the city's public character. In their two main efforts, the Manigault House and the Heyward-Washington House, Pringle and Frost and their colleagues selected the kind of site that was best known to them as women, the home. In fact, Frost chose the word "dwellings" for her organization's name specifically because it communicated her reverent conception of homes as permanent reliquaries of generations of Charleston's finest families.[29] By choosing spaces associated with private domestic activities over commercial, legal, industrial, or financial structures more often associated with men, the women of SPOD asserted the importance of historical continuity through the very personal lens of family and femininity.

In an attempt to breathe life back into the Manigault and Heyward-Washington houses, Charleston women went beyond financial support and placed themselves literally into the historic spaces. They held organizational meetings on the two properties and decorated them with their own furnishings, as well as period pieces borrowed from female relatives and friends.[30] Women SPOD members led tours of the homes, directing visitors through the historic spaces as guides to the past. This expression of female historical understanding reached its height in 1931–32, when Nell Pringle contemplated moving into the Manigault House to relieve some of the massive financial burden its ownership had placed upon her family. According to her husband, Ernest, Nell hoped to assemble there "the best pieces of her own furniture, and those of my sister . . . and the house will become a shrine for those interested in Colonial architecture and Colonial furniture." It was hoped that the lure of Nell as "permanent hostess" would make the place more attractive, more real, more alive to visitors, whose money would ensure the survival of the continually endangered home.[31]

The material culture of the Manigault and Heyward-Washington houses, then, may be described as an expression of an elite white female culture. Through these women's efforts and personal objects, the sites became more than palaces built by famous, wealthy white men. They became three-dimensional theaters where the everyday drama of domestic life, comprehensible to most visitors, many of whom were women, unfolded.[32]

A strong sense of ancestral worship and an evocative historical memory influenced Frost's public and private cultural activism, often clouding her practical business sense. She became involved in numerous money-losing projects for the sake of their historical associations. Of her financial struggles, Frost reflected in 1941: "I have never commercialized my restoration work, or my love of the old and beautiful things of Charleston. A friend told me once that I had too much sentiment to make money, and I think that is partly true."[33] Alston Deas, Frost's successor as SPOD president, best explained Frost's subjective, historically intuitive approach to preservation: "She saw it [Charleston] partly through a golden haze of memory and association, not only for its buildings, and streets, and vistas, but also for those men and women she had known, or of whom she had been told, who dwelt there, and created, through a period of many generations, the town. . . . She never lost sight of this personal feeling for the spirit of Charleston."[34]

Frost's desire to restore the eastern portion of Tradd Street, which had fallen into blighted conditions by the 1910s, including the presence of black-run brothels, stemmed from this "golden haze of memory and association."[35] She purchased the Georgian mansion at 61 Tradd, built and once-occupied by Frost's distinguished colonial ancestor Jacob Motte, a prominent banker, public treasurer, and legislator.[36] In doing so, Frost acted on an inherited conception of Tradd Street's former glory as one of the city's oldest residential and commercial centers. She sought to put it "back to where it was for so many years *before my knowledge*." To Frost, the *real* Tradd Street was a place she had never experienced firsthand but understood through the stories told by her elder kinfolk. It was the place where only "the best people" of Charleston—as opposed to its majority of contemporary African American residents—had resided.[37] To bring this reimagined past into the present, a demographic shift was required—the houses had to be restored and white occupants had to move in. Ironically, Frost relied upon the skills of Thomas Mayhem Pinckney, a local African American artisan, whom she hired to "reclaim" several Tradd Street properties from their status as black slums. By the early 1930s, numerous white residents, including artist and fellow preservationist Elizabeth O'Neill Verner, had moved into the area, increasingly pushing blacks out.[38] Frost's biographer, Sidney Bland, contends that the realtor's preservation choices were "in no small sense . . . responsible for creating the all-white Charleston south of Broad Street by World War II."[39]

Furthermore, historical memory powerfully influenced Frost in her daily struggle to preserve and maintain her own family home, an eighteenth-century mansion at 27 King Street. Built around 1769, the stately Miles Brewton/Pringle House figured prominently, if problematically, in Charleston history, serving as headquarters for both the invading British (1780) and the Union (1865) armies and as the home for five generations of Frost's family. For decades, Frost and her unmarried sisters followed the example of their unmarried aunt Susan Pringle and poured their hearts, souls, and meager finances into preserving this family mausoleum. "We shall not change a stone or plant, you may be sure," Frost wrote her cousin in 1919, "only restore it with tender hands to what it was as we remember it as chil[dren] there."[40] The "Misses Frost" were convinced of the national historic importance of their home and felt duty-bound to nurture its architectural legacy. To fund their work and pass on their conception of the past, the sisters opened their home to paying visitors for tours and even overnight stays.[41] The Frosts were, as Nell Pringle's daughter recalled, "very proud, they were emotionally bound up with it. . . . They were very noblesse oblige. They had a strong and probably very pathetic, probably ridiculous sense of honor and they loved that house."[42] SPOD, then, was the logical, institutionalized extension of Frost's personal devotion to visible reminders of Charleston's past.

To Nell Pringle, Frost's cousin by marriage and SPOD's first vice president, a home was also a kind of family reliquary—a theater of domestic performance that recalled the daily drama of love affairs, parenting, engagements, and child's play. The Bennettsville, South Carolina, native married into an old, prominent Charleston family long concerned with the preservation of, as her husband, Ernest, described it, "furniture, landmarks, tradition."[43] She felt a very strong connection with the Pringle women and was similarly preoccupied with preserving the past, committing herself, and, eventually, her health and her family's financial well-being, to saving the Manigault House. After an initial investment of $5,000 ($4,000 of which was to be returned by the subscriptions of others to a house fund that never materialized), the Pringles assumed the property's debts of over $40,000 and became the official owners in March 1922.[44] According to Nell Pringle's daughter, Margaretta, the timing could not have been worse. Shortly after, her father, Ernest, lost his job as president of the Bank of Charleston and went to work as a salesman for his younger brother's fertilizer plant. Eventually, he established his own investment business to support his wife, six children, *and* the Manigault House. That the Pringles undertook such a massive responsibility in the midst of a citywide depression can be explained by Nell Pringle's romantic attachment to Charleston and her commitment to keeping the legacy of its historical memory alive.[45] As her husband later explained, "So, in 1920, fresh from worthwhile accomplishments in war work, when my wife came to me, and gently said that she wanted to risk something—and give something, but not as much give as risk, for Charleston, and its preservation, but would hold her hand if I objected, what could I say, who loved both her, & Charleston?"[46]

Nell Pringle saw more in the sweeping piazza and fine mantlepieces of the Manigault House than a gem of Adam-style architecture. A reader of Victor Hugo and Sir Walter Scott, a devotee of the Stuarts and Bonnie Prince Charlie, Pringle indulged in fanciful imaginings about this domestic monument to the city's slaveholding, rice planter elite.[47] She became absorbed in the legends of the house, going so far as to paint "blood red" its secret staircase and to commission a wax work "to add to the eerie atmosphere."[48] For Pringle, this public space became the embodiment of all that was correct and worthy of protection in Charleston's premodern past. As hostess, she shared her interpretation of this past with her paying visitors. Tourist Sophie Collman from Cincinnati confirmed the efficacy of Pringle's presentation when she declared enthusiastically that a tour of the Manigault House provided "a glimpse into the past that will always be a charming remembrance."[49]

An undated short story, written by Nell Pringle probably sometime in the early 1930s, best reveals her historic understanding, her antimodern sentiments, and her intensely personal, emotional investment in the city's fine old residence. Set in "a chaste old city being allowed to crumble into memory as its old fashions, its old houses and its old honor are changed into a motory,

As the rallying point for the 1920 founding of the Society for the Preservation of Old Dwellings, the Joseph Manigault House (1803), pictured here, provided paying tourists with "a glimpse into the past that will always be a charming remembrance." Courtesy of the Charleston Museum, Charleston, South Carolina.

modern place of grease and cheapness," it is the story of one woman's struggle to stave off the "passing of the old order of things." The protagonist, Susan Snow, a barely disguised representation of Susan Frost, fights unsuccessfully to save the "Gault" house from destruction by "a city that was lulled into contentment by money in her hands, by moving pictures, jazz and motors." As part of a larger national cultural battle between the traditional and the modern, Snow considers the Gault mansion a bulwark against "the needless trample of commercialism" taking place in Charleston.[50]

In her short story, Pringle feminizes the Gault house. She characterizes it as a woman, a nurturing mother of children and lovers, a witness to "a past happiness we of this generation seek for in what we call 'success' but somehow are eluded." Likewise, she bestows upon each room and architectural feature a feminized, domestic referent, as she rhapsodizes:

Standing in the Gault doorway, there came visions of children having Christmas glee around a tree in the broad old hall—of the Ball held up in the drawing room for the daughters, and the wedding, where the cake and wine [that] stood for the feast were spread below in the circular dining room — a room architects have struggled in vain to copy, as well as the flying staircase, down which, with a laugh, the bride ran to join her husband, and then together they went out of the great doorway, across the piazza, down the twisted stone steps, running quickly over the flagged walks, through a quaint lodge, out far into a life of happiness.

Viewed through Nell Pringle's eyes, the Manigault House was first and foremost the repository of generations of elite white women's historical memory, the protective shelter of daughters and brides. "Destroying it," she concludes, "seemed like murdering an aged gentlewoman."[51]

Although Nell was an incurable romantic, her literary representation of the Manigault House's preservation tale should not be dismissed as mere post-Victorian melodrama. Instead, it stems from the very real hardship — the self-described years of "mental anguish" — she experienced in her desperate twelve-year battle to save the mansion.[52] Indeed, its preservation was, as one visitor described it in a 1928 guest book entry, "a fearful responsibility," shouldered entirely by the Pringle family.[53] Even the Pringle children joined their mother in the day-to-day struggle to keep the Manigault House from further deterioration by cleaning and painting the property and helping with fund-raising teas. Mary, the eldest daughter, actually left Charleston to accept a governess position in Baltimore to help pay for new plumbing.[54] Faced with city taxes and an urgent need for repairs to the long-neglected mansion, Ernest and Nell continually dug deeper into their pockets, eventually liquidating their bank stock. As the burden grew, Nell Pringle's physical and financial health declined. Her spirit broken, the mother of six children lamented, "I felt like a coward. The presence of my children were [sic] a daily reproach to me. I was a cheat. I had gambled away their education! I suffered only as a silly woman can."[55] In what must have felt like the ultimate surrender to the "motory" pressures of "grease and cheapness," Nell sold a corner of the Manigault garden to the Standard Oil Company. Standard quickly erected what architect and AIA president Robert Kohn called "a brand new and shining gasoline station in the best modernistic red, white and blue gasoline style."[56] The only ironic consolation was that instead of tearing down the mansion's elegant gatehouse, Standard put it to use as an Esso restroom.[57]

In 1933, Nell Pringle's association with the Manigault House ended when an anonymous patron stepped in to save the bankrupt property from the auction block, donating it to the Charleston Museum. The donor, Henrietta Pollitzer

Hartford Pignatelli, a native of Bluffton, South Carolina, was the descendant of a prominent South Carolina family that included a colonial governor. More important, however, she was the widow of Edward Hartford, the heir of the great Hartford A&P fortune and inventor of the Hartford shock absorber, who died in 1922. Armed with his fortune, Pignatelli followed the fashionable trend among America's rich and purchased a Low Country plantation near Charleston, Wando Plantation, in Berkeley County, South Carolina, to add to her long list of luxurious properties, including residences in Newport and on New York's Fifth Avenue. Ironically, some of the wealth that eventually saved the Manigault House, which was initially threatened by the construction of a car garage, came from a fortune based in part on the booming automotive industry.[58] This uncomfortable connection between preservation and the automobile was not unique to Charleston but can be seen in two major cultural endeavors of the period: industrialist and Model T inventor Henry Ford's building of his utopian "historical" outdoor museum, Greenfield Village, in Dearborn, Michigan, and John T. Rockefeller's restoration/reconstruction of Williamsburg, Virginia, from his Standard Oil millions.[59] With Pignatelli's donation, SPOD's first preservation effort concluded, only after the Pringles had spent over $50,000 to stave off real estate developers and antique hunters.[60] As a final and rather empty act, SPOD recognized Nell Pringle's singular sacrifice in a formal announcement of gratitude to the woman who had "at heart the interest of the future in the art of the past."[61]

Despite Nell Pringle's personal misfortune with the Manigault House, other preservation efforts gathered steam in Charleston in the late 1920s and early 1930s. A number of factors contributed to the increased popularity of such activities. Beginning with Alice Ravenel Huger Smith and Daniel Elliot Huger Smith's *Dwelling Houses of Charleston*, which depicted the city as a singularly romantic site of national historic import, where generation after generation maintained age-old traditions of gracious living, several books and countless articles in newspapers throughout the country served to propagandize the city's historic landscape and picturesque atmosphere. Nonfictional works by local elites, such as Albert Simons and Samuel Lapham Jr.'s *Early Architecture of Charleston*; Samuel Stoney's two collaborative volumes, *Charleston: Azaleas and Old Bricks* and *Plantations of the Carolina Low Country*; and Beatrice St. Julien Ravenel's *Architects of Charleston*, self-consciously showcased the architectural heritage of the city and its surrounding Low Country.[62] The relationship between these texts and the preservation movement was reciprocal—they benefited from each other's existence even as they encouraged their further growth.

The work of Sam Stoney, an architect, amateur folklorist, and "ambulatory encyclopedia for South Caroliniana" who traced his family back to Charleston's earliest seventeenth-century Huguenot settlers and eighteenth-century plantation owners, embodies the sentiment expressed in these near-hagiographic publications.[63] Much like his friends Susan Frost and Nell Pringle, Stoney conveyed an intensely personal and emotional connection to the city's buildings that went beyond mere aesthetic appreciation—they were part of the "legacy of memory" that elite locals were duty-bound to protect and pass on. In *Charleston*, he reasoned, "How is a man to describe with any sort of accuracy those things and those ways of living and thinking that after a fashion are more intimately parts of him than his feet and hands, his tastes or his abilities? The difficulty that comes from being a Charlestonian is that the things and thoughts, the memories and manners that make up the Charleston that count are too completely parts of one's heart and one's soul to be realizable. . . . Charleston is largely a matter of feeling."[64]

Just as publications like Stoney's helped to fuel an emergent Charleston-philia among wealthy white Americans, so, too, did the outbreak of the First World War. Prevented from traveling abroad, this cohort began wintering in the various warmer climes in the American South. With new highways and propagandistic literature to encourage it, Charleston's popularity as a destination city increased throughout the 1920s and 1930s. Many elite visitors "from off," as the locals described them, were enthralled by the local landscape and its historic associations and caught Stoney's loyal "feeling" for the place. They brought with them not only their much-needed money but also one of their fads, what Stoney's brother-in-law Albert Simons described as "the utterly unbalanced lust for Americana."[65] Correspondence among preservationists, as well as newspaper articles, throughout the period recorded anxiously the constant barrage of requests from antique dealers, Northern museums, and private collectors for antiques and architectural elements from Charleston houses.[66] With each passing year, silver, furniture, china, iron balconies and gates, woodwork, and even, at times, entire paneled rooms disappeared from the city.

Charlestonian Albert Simons, University of Pennsylvania trained and a vocal member of the Architectural Institute of America's Committee on Preservation of Historic Monuments and Natural Resources, was especially strident in protesting this practice of "selling everything of any artistic and historic value to somebody just because they have the money to buy and carry it off."[67] Simons, who was also a World War I veteran, lamented this phenomenon to an AIA colleague in New York City as the "one great danger

threatening our historic monuments that is much more ruthless in its spoila-
tion than any of the ravages of the wars, fires and storms that this city has
withstood."[68]

And yet it is not surprising that many economically strapped Charlestonians
took advantage of the market created by these wealthy winter visitors. Still,
"local public opinion," Simons contended in 1931, "is rather strongly against
this trade so that the antique dealers make their sales of interiors rather quickly
and silently."[69] The destruction of some of the city's finest residences, such as
the dismantling of the pre-Revolutionary Mansion House on Broad Street for
a New York buyer in 1928, further fueled the flames of resistance.[70] In 1932,
the *News & Courier* protested the continuation of this cultural vandalism,
decrying "the sale of Charleston antiquities to persons of other sections."
The article continued, "There is but one way to keep Charleston Charleston
and that is to keep Charleston Charleston, to save for Charleston the things
that are Charleston's."[71] This kind of fierce local pride and possessiveness
put many in the city on the defensive and roused them to support organized
preservation efforts.

Although many Northern visitors may have taken from Charleston, they
also gave in the form of tourist dollars and capital for preservation efforts.
This financial influx in Depression-era Charleston inspired support from local
leaders and merchants, who began to realize the economic potential of a tourist industry based on the city's architectural and atmospheric beauty. Simons
mused in 1939, "During the Depression, Charleston has been kept going by
the throng of tourists who have come here during the winter months. At the
present time presidents of banks and of the Chamber of Commerce and of
Rotary and of whatnots are all fanatical for preservation. Like all converts,
they are more Royal than the King, more Catholic than the Pope, and want
to preserve everything that is owned by somebody else, whether good, bad or
indifferent. Should the tourist trade lapse, their interest would evaporate."[72]
As the Carolina Low Country became increasingly fashionable for domestic
vacations among wealthy Americans, individuals such as E. F. Hutton and
Solomon Guggenheim purchased and restored elegant city mansions and area
plantations. Simons occupied a strange position in relation to this annual
"swarm of Yankees."[73] On the one hand an outspoken advocate of protecting
Charleston's historical resources *for* Charlestonians, Simons was also a working architect in an economically strapped town where few locals needed his
services. Despite his complaints of "Wall Street Planters"[74] and "working so
damn hard especially for a hoard of outlanders . . . I am getting quite fed up
on millionaires," Simons admitted in 1929 that "outside of the winter colonists

there is little local work. . . . While we have more just now than we can handle completely yet these incursions from without are extremely disquieting."[75] On a selected list of twenty-six city and country residences on which Simons and his partner Samuel Lapham Jr. worked during 1920s, twenty-two were owned by Northerners from places such as New York, Pennsylvania, Connecticut, and Massachusetts.[76] An impoverished SPOD also took advantage of these wealthy new arrivals. In a 1933 membership drive, the group targeted new plantation owners for funds to continue SPOD's preservation advocacy work.[77]

Without Northern capital, many of Charleston's historic properties might have deteriorated to the point of no return. Loutrel Briggs, a landscape architect from New York, for example, restored Cabbage Row, an African American tenement on Church Street, next door to the Heyward-Washington House, that provided the inspiration for "Catfish Row" in DuBose Heyward's popular 1925 novel *Porgy* was.[78] In some cases, wealthy non-Charlestonian property owners became so involved in preservation circles that they became something akin to honorary Charlestonians. The New York architect John Mead Howells, who purchased the Stuart House, and Victor and Marjorie Morawetz, owners of the Pirate House and Fenwick Hall plantation, for example, were all considered for membership in the St. Cecilia Society, the hallmark of "belonging" in elite white Charleston society.[79]

The arrival of Frances Emerson of Cambridge, Massachusetts, onto the Charleston preservation scene in 1928 provides a striking example of the integral role outside money and connections played in preserving Charleston architecture between the world wars. Simons escorted Emerson and her husband, William, the head of the Department of Architecture at the Massachusetts Institute of Technology, on a personal tour of the city. Enamored with the place and the man, the Emersons quickly became Simons's financial patrons for a volume he and Stoney were contemplating writing on Low Country plantations.[80]

In April 1928, deeply moved by the precarious position of many of Charleston's architectural monuments, Frances Emerson wrote to Simons, "It was sad . . . to see the Manigault House swarming with negroes, falling to pieces, and its lovely plaster ceiling at the top of the staircase wall already showing a large hole. I wanted somehow to protect that ceiling." She offered $500 for the establishment of a fund "to buy up, from time to time and place in the Charleston Museum such objects as fine wrought iron, old fan lights, paneled walls, or even a ceiling like the Manigault one."[81] Simons accepted the check on behalf of Laura Bragg, director of the Charleston Museum, and invested

Architect Albert Simons, whose decisions as the chief voice of the
Board of Architectural Review shaped much of Charleston's
historic landscape between the world wars. From the
Collections of the South Carolina Historical Society.

it, along with a matching gift by William Emerson, not in the Manigault
House, but in the community's second organized preservation target, the
Heyward-Washington House. One can imagine the depths of Nell Pringle's
disappointment. In 1930, Mrs. Emerson also donated $5,000 toward estab-
lishing the American Institute of Architects Committee for the Safeguarding
of Charleston Architecture (CSCA), a group comprised of national and local
experts to call attention to Charleston's preservation emergency.[82]

"A Movement Is Creeping, or a Creeping Is Moving":
Professionalizing Preservation

The efforts to preserve the Heyward-Washington House signaled the beginnings of a new era in historic preservation in Charleston, marked by male leadership, professional urban planning, and local and federal government involvement, as well as a more nationalist emphasis on the city's historical memory. In 1928, Susan Frost's loosely organized volunteer group became formally incorporated under a new president, Captain Alston Deas.[83] Deas's romantic attachment to honoring the "patriots" of Charleston's past and to preserving "Charleston as a historic shrine for the nation" was as pronounced as that of his female predecessor.[84] Although born in San Francisco in 1893, Deas descended from a much respected, old-line Charleston family. He had grown up in Charleston, taught at the Citadel, and considered himself a native. Others of his elite circle agreed, as his membership in such exclusive organizations as the St. Cecilia Society and the Carolina Yacht Club attest.[85] Deas's greatest achievement, however, was overseeing SPOD's cooperation with the Charleston Museum, the city's other main institution interested in preservation. Encouraged by Emerson's patronage, these groups together raised $13,000, $3,000 more than was needed, to make a down payment in the museum's name on the Heyward-Washington House in 1929.[86]

Built circa 1749, the endangered property at 87 Church Street quickly took center stage. In the decades following the Civil War, the colonial three-story brick mansion, once the elegant city home of the slave-owning Heyward family, from which author and preservation advocate DuBose Heyward descended, had fallen into disrepair and neglect. Over the years, the deteriorated building was used, among other things, as a boardinghouse, a bakery, and an African American tenement.[87] In addition to the opportunity to reclaim the family seat of one of their own, preservationists embraced the Heyward-Washington House for its larger historic importance and patriotic appeal. It was the home of Thomas Heyward, a signer of the Declaration of Independence, and could honestly boast that ultimate claim to preservation worthiness: "George Washington slept here." In May 1791, the house served as headquarters for Washington during his Southern tour as president.[88] With such an established pedigree, the house presented an ideal opportunity to declare to the nation Charleston's very real colonial and Revolutionary heritage intact and alive.

Furthermore, the Heyward-Washington House enjoyed a highly desirable location in the very heart of the future historic district below Broad Street. Unlike the Manigault House, located north of downtown in what had become

The Heyward-Washington House on Church Street, shown here in its derelict condition before the Preservation Society and the Charleston Museum spearheaded its restoration, became the city's first historic house museum. The arched entrance of Cabbage Row, the inspiration for DuBose Heyward's "Catfish Row" in the novel *Porgy*, can be seen adjacent on the left. From the Collections of the South Carolina Historical Society.

by the late 1910s a predominantly African American–occupied slum, the Heyward-Washington House was situated in the same neighborhood where many preservationists lived and where tourists, staying at the Villa Margherita or the Fort Sumter Hotel, passed their leisure time. The preservation and restoration of the site over the next several years, supervised by none other than the ubiquitous and talented Albert Simons, was a major success.

And yet not everyone in Charleston supported Frost, Simons, and their colleagues. Relatively speaking, the number of active preservation advocates was small, and many regular citizens either ignored or disapproved of their ardent efforts. Many of these critics failed to appreciate what they considered the vain and nostalgic enterprises of a bunch of has-been aristocrats. In a 1928 letter to the editor of the *News & Courier*, one city resident criticized as unprogressive and impractical the overly sentimental attitude surrounding preservationists' efforts at the Heyward-Washington House: "The old place on Church Street carrying a brass sign that George Washington was entertained there seems to have been vacant for years. Somebody is losing money on taxes, insurance, etc., but if anyone started wrecking the building to make way for something modern, that would pay its own way, the preservers would doubtless yell 'Bloody Murder!'"[89]

A major voice of opposition came from the law offices of prodevelopment former mayor John Patrick Grace, who criticized preservation as the "mania for mummies" and advised a more dynamic approach to the city's economic problems. "We must live with the living," he declared, "not with the dead." A second-generation Irish American who rode to office on the ballots of the city's immigrant and ethnic working-class wards—a historic part of the city that elite memory refused to acknowledge—Grace represented a more complex version of the city's past, insisting it was something other than the preservationists' leisure-filled, elite, romp. He emphasized instead the entrepreneurial commercial spirit that had made Charleston an international trading center in the eighteenth and early nineteenth centuries:

> Far be it from me to freeze the genial current of the timid souls who now seem satisfied only with memories. . . . If it suits them to mummify Charleston and to make of our city only a museum, let them revel in it. But there should be room enough also for others. . . . Why not awaken with this mercenary reverence for old things also the enterprise which made these old things? Instead of selling the ruins of what they built, why not build something ourselves? . . . I love the past, but I am living in the present and feel that it is the future to which we must look—even, thank Heaven, as our fathers did.[90]

In the end, much like the preservationists he criticized, Grace found in Charleston's past a history that suited his personal contemporary agenda, illustrating the plasticity and contestability of historical memory claims.

And yet at the very time that Grace wrote his tirade against a preserved landscape, it was becoming a dollar-attracting tourist and investment commodity. As long as preservation had remained a voluntary and largely female activity, it was tolerated socially and women were allowed to remain in leadership positions. With the shifting economic tide of the late 1920s, however, men assumed the helm of the movement. These individuals, such as Simons, Deas, his SPOD successor, E. Milby Burton, who became director of the Charleston Museum in the 1930s, and Robert N. S. Whitelaw, director of the Carolina Art Association and the Gibbes Art Gallery, understood well the importance of politics to preservation. As the women before them drew on female networks of support, these individuals called upon their powerful male relations and colleagues for help. Thus they enlisted the aid of the American Institute of Architects, of Mayors Thomas Stoney and Burnet Maybank (making both men honorary members of the newly renamed "Preservation Society"), of the South Carolina legislature for tax exemptions for the Manigault and Heyward-Washington houses, and of federal funding agencies to accomplish their preservation and urban planning goals.[91] Charleston's historic preservation movement experienced a gendered shift as it moved solidly beyond its initial local focus and amateur methods to a more nationalized, professional approach to the cultivation of a concrete historical memory.

The first manifestation of this new strategy occurred on 23 April 1929, when Mayor Stoney and the city council enacted the temporary City Planning and Zoning Commission to regulate and approve the construction of new manufacturing plants, schools, and gas stations in the older section of the city.[92] The council established a committee of influential volunteer citizens, including insiders Simons, Deas, and Maybank, to create a zoning ordinance for the city. Together, they functioned as architects and geographers of the city's public memory. Deas, for example, "undertook the definition of what buildings and, more importantly, what areas should be saved and drew up a list with descriptions."[93]

Realizing the scale of their charge, the committee recommended that the city hire a professional urban planning/engineering firm to conduct a comprehensive survey and to outline a zoning ordinance based on Deas's suggestions. As a result of his choices, the Pittsburgh firm Morris Knowles surveyed only pre-Revolutionary structures in the oldest quarter of the city, home to the bulk of Charleston's white elites, including Simons, Maybank, Stoney, and Deas themselves. On 13 October 1931, the Charleston City Council ratified the result, the nation's first government-supported planning and zoning ordinance. The ordinance created the twenty-three-block "Old and Historic District," protecting approximately 400 buildings from destruction. Six days later, Mayor Stoney signed the landmark legislation into law.[94]

The zoning ordinance established the Board of Architectural Review as its main operating arm to approve any exterior changes on structures within the historic district. The work of BAR fell to its chairman, Thomas Waring, editor of the *Charleston Evening Post*, and Albert Simons, who determined whether applied-for alterations could take place. As resident expert, the forty-one-year-old Simons exerted tremendous influence in determining the aesthetic and historical face Charleston would present to the world. Columns, fire escapes, balustrades, signs, fences, woodwork, and even exterior paint colors were all approved or disapproved by BAR in decisions that were based largely on Simons's training and personal tastes, or what he vaguely described as "a law controlling esthetics."[95] Historian Charles Hosmer, in his survey of Charleston's preservation movement, concluded, "It might not be an exaggeration to say that the whole historic district of Charleston emerged as a grand design from the drawing board of Albert Simons."[96]

Simons envisioned BAR as a kind of "free Architectural Clinic" through which he could educate citizens of Charleston and America in matters of "good taste."[97] A typical example of a BAR decision serves to illustrate his set views on beauty and the importance of indigenous styles for Charleston, down to the smallest detail. In 1932, he rejected the proposed building of a gate at the Church Street home of his friend Daniel Huger Jr., saying, "I do not particularly like their cribbing of a Long Island fence from 'House & Garden.' There is no excuse for this when there are so many good fences here in Charleston. 'House & Garden' and other publications of the same sort have done more to reduce American taste to a monotonous standard with rank New England flavor than anything else I know of."[98]

Through BAR, Simons sought to return the city's appearance to an imagined golden age, pre-1860, thus negating all historical developments that took place during or after the Civil War and presenting a unified and patriotic face to the nation. In particular, Simons chose to celebrate structures from Charleston's late-colonial and early-nineteenth-century past. "In this city more than any other city with a colonial past," Simons and his architectural partner wrote in 1924, "there exists today a continuous record of the architectural history of our country from the days of the first colonial settlements until the Civil War and the decline of architectural taste in the '70s."[99]

A proposal for a Hall of Charleston Architecture for the Charleston Museum, of which Simons was a trustee, further reveals the chronological bias of the city's cultural arbiters. The project outline claimed Charleston "as an illustration of one of the most highly developed of historic American cultures[;] the city is a public heritage and a public trust." The exhibit strictly defined the temporal parameters of this "public heritage" by showcasing examples of Charleston architecture "from the colony's beginning to 1860."[100] Simons himself made clear his admiration for the British stylistic associations of the earlier periods while denigrating "the Nineteenth century, that Tower of Babel, where the language of tradition was lost and architecture was confounded."[101] Marjorie Morawetz, one of Simons's wealthy Northern clients, shared this sentiment. Morawetz believed it was to Charleston's advantage to erase visible traces of its Victorian past by "bringing out its eighteenth[-] century beauty (much of which is hidden) [and] scraping off gingerbread ornaments etc."[102]

The privileging of the colonial, Revolutionary, and early-republican styles over later ones was based almost entirely on the personal aesthetics of the select group that directed the city's preservation program. These individuals declared a reverence for Charleston's history while at the same time ignoring significant parts of the historical record. For example, preservationists downplayed or ignored altogether those properties in large sections of the city that displayed the dreaded late-Victorian "gingerbread" style after their original architecture was destroyed by the "Great Fire" of 1861, which burned a 540-acre swath through the lower peninsula.[103] This could be explained by the fact that to preservationists like Albert Simons, who was born in 1891, the late-Victorian structures were more contemporary to his parents and himself than to the "great" Charlestonians of the distant past and therefore were easily categorized as unimportant "historically." However, a visitor looking at the protected landscape in 1940 might comfortably have understood that Charleston's *real* history ended in 1860. Because tourist literature and the city's cultural stewards all spoke of the pre–Civil War past as a heroic time when Old World gentility, a successful plantation system, and revolutionary patriotism reigned supreme—long before the ugly scars of sectionalism, defeat, and poverty came into being—a highly selective element of historical amnesia accompanied the preserved landscape.

As with earlier efforts, Simons soon learned that not everyone supported or appreciated the historic preservation impulse, the historic district, BAR's aesthetic control, or the movement's edited vision of the city's past. Simons encountered both the apathy and the hostility that SPOD had endured earlier with the Manigault and Heyward-Washington House projects. "I attempted to treat each case brought before us [BAR] as a doctor in the free public clinic would treat a free patient," Simons recalled, "I soon discovered the ironical truth that architectural advice given without charge was valued at what it cost the recipient: in short, valued not at all, and as often as not resented as an intrusion on the rights of the rugged individualist."[104]

Nonetheless, Simons's ability to mold Charleston's public historical landscape was not limited to his BAR work; it extended to choices resulting in the relocation of African American residents from downtown neighborhoods into New Deal–funded public housing projects on the outskirts of the city. During this period, Simons, who was considered a political liberal in Charleston, admitted that even he struggled with "instinctive racial prejudices hard to overcome even with the best intent . . . no matter how liberal we may wish to be."[105] This reality might have shaped his actions in regard to Charleston's black neighborhoods.

The migration of African Americans from the surrounding countryside into Charleston in search of work during and after World War I had placed tremendous pressure on the city's ability to house adequately its residents; the crisis level only worsened with the strains of the Great Depression. As Mamie Garvin Fields, a middle-class African American who grew up in Charleston, recalled in her autobiography, *Lemon Swamp*, "The tumble-down parts of Charleston got more tumble-down."[106] African Americans, whose death rates in the city were twice that of whites, especially suffered.[107] Photographs from the period, as well as a 1926 report on African American housing in the city, reveal the extent of the problem—many poor and working-class black, and for that matter poor white, Charlestonians lived in "unwholesome, unsanitary and even diseased conditions."[108]

In Charleston, historic preservation meant the structural renovation of old houses in areas where elite whites and poor working-class blacks had lived side by side for generations—in the great mansions and alley shacks and out-buildings, respectively.[109] Mamie Garvin Fields described the residential ar-rangements this way: "Days gone by, black and white people lived uptown and they lived downtown, the black families among the white families and vice versa."[110] By the 1920s, many buildings in these racially integrated neighbor-hoods had fallen into slumlike conditions. Preservationists' work resulted not only in restoring these structures but also in displacing African American oc-cupants and substituting in their stead white tenants or, better still, white buy-ers with capital to maintain the properties. Thus, urban "reclamation" along racial lines became part of the preservation strategy, ironically beginning the erasure of Charleston's historically integrated streets and neighborhoods.[111] After the Second World War, this pattern continued. Today, the "South of Broad" and Battery neighborhoods—the original "Historic Charleston" zone of 1931—are almost exclusively white.

In 1933 and 1934, Albert Simons represented Charleston in meetings in Washington, D.C., with various New Deal agencies to secure government funds for slum clearance near the historic district and the construction of white and black housing projects in Charleston. The goal was to improve the plight of the poor by eradicating African American slums in the downtown area and to provide "for more adequate negro housing in some other part of the city."[112] In 1935, with a $1.15 million loan from the Public Works Admin-istration, Charleston began building an African American public housing

A HISTORIC CHARLESTON LANDSCAPE

project midway up the peninsula, in the shadow of the Cooper River Bridge and away from the "Old and Historic District." The white housing project that was to coincide with this construction was delayed so further studies could be conducted. Many in the white community saw this as evidence of the New Deal's problack policies. To deflect such outrage, in a speech before the chamber of commerce, Mayor Maybank, a Franklin Roosevelt ally, cataloged the benefits of quality black housing for the white community, namely that healthy domestic workers meant less possibility of disease spreading in white families. This line of reasoning was not enough to assuage critics, and Maybank eventually added whites-only units to the project, the construction of which was completed in June 1937. In addition to racial motivations, then, it is clear that class concerns, namely the desire to push poor and working-class whites out of the historic district and far away from the eyes of tourists and elite white Charlestonians, influenced the location choices of early public housing in Charleston. Finally, in keeping with the Jim Crow laws, the city divided the housing project by race, naming the 75-unit white section Meeting Street Manor and the 137-unit black portion Cooper River View.[113]

The 1938–39 destruction of an African American neighborhood that bordered the historic district and the proposed construction of whites-only public housing on the site illustrate further the relationship between historic preservation and a racist housing policy. Near to at least three important historic buildings—St. John's Lutheran Church, the Unitarian Church, and the Marine Hospital—this collection of dilapidated houses just above Broad Street was also surrounded by several white-inhabited streets. According to the city housing authority, "Its crowded, poorly-lighted, evil-smelling tenements depreciated the entire section of the city."[114] White residents complained to local civic leaders, including Albert Simons, about the "disgusting fights, shrieks, pistol shots and vile language" emanating from the decayed shantytown.[115] One white resident described in detail a local knife fight to Mayor Maybank, playing the ever-powerful taxpayer/economic interest card: "As a native-born Charlestonian I feel ashamed to be a tax payer on this block as existing conditions are. . . . Visitors from another southern state were here (5 Pitt St) having just arrived—about to make their residence in Charleston! They were in utter dismay, annoyed and disgusted at such violence and at the confusion and noise caused by this negro fight—within view of the residents—happening in this section of our historic city where they expect to live!"[116]

African American residents also complained about the attacks on their neighborhood, but from a very different perspective. Many families resisted forced removal, declaring they would defy the orders to vacate. Hattie Jones,

Charleston's Housing Authority report of 1939 celebrated the construction of an all-white housing project, the Robert Mills Manor (top). Supported by federal funds and designed by Albert Simons, the project required the destruction of the largely African American Cromwell Alley neighborhood (bottom) and the relocation of its residents. *City of Charleston, S.C., Year Book of 1939.*

who lived with her husband and three-year-old twin boys at 22 Magazine Street, lamented, "It's a shame. It just ain't right to take our house away from us. No telling where we will have to go." Her neighbor Hanna Moore concurred, "They just can't come in here and tear down the building from under us. So they will just have to wait until we get some place to move until they start this work."[117] Despite their protests, the housing authority relocated the residents and commenced plans for the construction of another all-black housing project, the Anson Borough Homes, again far removed from to the downtown historic district.[118]

Matching the call for demolition of this neighborhood was the call for preservation. In July 1938, the Preservation Society circulated a petition to protect any historic buildings endangered by the proposed housing project. These included the county jail and the Marine Hospital, a building designed in 1833 by Robert Mills, the same Charleston architect who designed the Washington Monument, and that now housed the all-black Jenkins Orphanage.[119] Two months later, in September 1938, the worst natural disaster to strike the city since the earthquake of 1886 arrived in the form of a major hurricane, which left thirty-two people dead and caused over $2 million in damages. City officials successfully appealed to the federal government for aid, a portion of which saved the Marine Hospital from the wrecking ball.[120] Meanwhile, officials relocated the Jenkins Orphanage to a rural spot over ten miles out of town. The city continued the destruction of the black-occupied area and the construction of the Albert Simons–designed Robert Mills Manor, a 140-unit modern housing project for whites only, located downtown. A 1939 Housing Authority report boasted that the project "has entirely wiped out a section of the city which was a festering eyesore, a source of disease and crime, and a deterrent to the improvement of a great portion of Charleston."[121]

The completion of the Robert Mills Manor did not halt the process of racial relocation. Encouraged by the successful forced removal of black Charlestonians from the area by the local government, the Preservation Society launched a campaign in 1940 to continue the practice under private auspices. In keeping with its founder's belief that the replacement of black tenants with whites improved a neighborhood, the Society asked white residents of Archdale Street, which bordered the Mills Manor, to organize a "cleanup" campaign. At a SPOD meeting in January, preservationists lamented as "very undesirable" one local property owner's proposal to turn 23 Archdale into a "negro tenement." They voted to speak to the owner and press him to let his building to "white tenants" instead in a continuing effort to reclaim "this once elite neighborhood." At the same meeting, the president of William and Mary College, Dr. John Stewart Bryan, applauded Society members for serving as "valiant vanguards against vandalism."[122] Working together with a common yet ahistorical vision of a sanitized and predominantly white "Old and Historic Charleston," the Preservation Society and the city government succeeded in displacing large numbers of blacks from the city center that had served as their historic home for centuries. Historical amnesia had triumphed in the form of gentrification.

After two decades of preservation activity, by 1939–40, advocates considered the parameters of "Old and Historic Charleston" too limited. Due to the vision and energy of Robert N. S. Whitelaw, the city received a grant from the Carnegie Foundation to conduct a survey of historical structures in sections of the town not covered by the 1931 Morris Knowles survey and to plan for the city's growth accordingly. "We have become a tourist city and in all likelihood will become more so," Whitelaw explained, "but unless we protect ourselves with a plan for the future this source of revenue and individuals who are interested in us will work to destroy the very things that make us attractive."[123] Despite its scientific-sounding name, the Regional Planning Committee (RPC), which supervised the project, drew its members from established preservation circles. The committee included Whitelaw, Albert Simons, Samuel Stoney, E. Milby Burton, John Mead Howells, and watercolor artist Alice Ravenel Huger Smith. The same individuals, interests, and historical perspectives that put their marks on Charleston's early preservation efforts were in place to guide this more ambitious project.

As with earlier preservation work in Charleston, a large degree of subjectivity entered the process. In 1941, Charlestonian Helen McCormack, a former employee of the Charleston Museum and current director of Richmond's Valentine Museum, began the actual survey work, photographing and describing hundreds of the city's buildings. Despite the RPC's professed desire to concern "itself more with the actual qualities of the buildings it handled than with their historical or sentimental values," personal associations played a large role in its proceedings.[124] McCormack recalled that while working to identify "worthy" structures, "Miss Alice Ravenel Huger Smith took me on drives. She took her car and her chauffeur and we drove around and she pointed out things that she remembered that she thought were important." Smith's recollection of a site's past—her inherited memory about the place and its inhabitants—influenced her determination of a building's architectural historical significance, and thus influenced McCormack's.[125]

Subjectivity persisted as McCormack delivered her survey cards to the four members of the committee—Simons, Stoney, Smith, and Howells—

empowered with the final process of description and selection. In some cases, undeniable personal investments entered the discussion of a structure's merit. In weighing the value of a Legare Street house, for example, Stoney comically deemed it "Valuable (I was born there)," to which his brother-in-law Simons retorted, "Valuable to City (in spite of nativity of sGS [Samuel Gaillard Stoney]). Has lovely drawing room 2nd floor and an authentic ghost."[126] As Simons later explained, "No Charlestonian can be expected to speak or write about his city objectively for it is so much a part of the background of his mind and emotions that detachment is never possible."[127]

The final product, *This Is Charleston: A Survey of the Architectural Heritage of a Unique American City*, was published in 1944 by the Carolina Art Association with funds donated by city merchants to the RPC, renamed the Civic Services Committee since the onset of World War II. Sam Stoney composed the text that supported the volume's many photographs and maps. In addition to several well-placed insults directed at Charleston's toughest historic site competitor, Colonial Williamsburg, Stoney set forth the publication's pedagogical purpose: to educate Charleston residents, especially newcomers who had arrived during the war, about the city's heritage, embodied in its historic architecture. "The town is full of new blood, of people who do not know Charleston," Stoney explained, "and however they may appreciate the city's future, they can hardly recognize or respect what she has kept from her past unless they are given some knowledge of that past and the virtue of the landmarks it has left."[128] As keeper of the flame, Stoney focused his narrative, of course, on the city's colonial and early-republican heyday, thus encouraging his readers to internalize as their own the elite white view of the past.

The distance traveled by preservationists between the founding of SPOD in 1920 and the publication of *This Is Charleston* in 1944 was significant. Responding to changing economic potential, they transformed themselves from a small band of female amateurs into a larger group of male-led, government-backed professional policy makers, thus institutionalizing their personal and collective memories and ensuring their transmission to other Charlestonians and visitors alike. Although a superficial shift in leadership had occurred, Charleston's preservation movement never lost its "exclusive" mystique in the interwar years. By means more of disposition and willingness than deliberate conspiracy, the same few individuals—representing the city's most elite families—continually stood at the forefront. While their power to construct and define Charleston's official material culture expanded over time, the sentiment informing their conception of Charleston's past remained constant. From Nell Pringle to Albert Simons, local preservationists shared a romantic and heroic vision of the city's past, based on their very personal, often inherited, associations between Charleston's past and its surviving architecture. As Simons explained, "I think every Charlestonian has a certain amount of personal vanity invested in his city, and when they see something that they love and cherish destroyed, it hurts their vanity. They feel that their treasures have been diminished and they take it very personally."[129]

CHAPTER TWO

The Legend Is Truer than the Fact

ARTISTIC REPRESENTATION OF RACE, TIME, AND PLACE

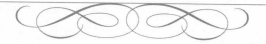

> I did not love the country because it was something to paint,
> but painted the country because it was something to love.
> —Alice Ravenel Huger Smith

On a crisp New England day in October 1937, watercolorist Alice Ravenel Huger Smith occupied a place of honor on the proscenium at Mount Holyoke College in South Hadley, Massachusetts. A public appearance outside of her native Charleston, much less hundreds of miles to the north, was a rare occasion for the graying sixty-one-year-old woman with large, soulful eyes and a rather frail though graceful demeanor. But even the homebody Smith could not resist the occasion; in celebration of its one hundredth anniversary, the esteemed women's college bestowed on her an honorary doctorate in literature. Unlike many of her artistic colleagues who received training abroad or in American art centers such as New York and Philadelphia, Smith spent her entire life in Charleston and received only a cursory "young ladies" education. Still, she was well regarded in her field and had exhibited in major galleries and museums all over the country and abroad. The previous year, she had published a series of watercolors depicting rice cultivation in nineteenth-century South Carolina, for which she enjoyed widespread public recognition of the sort conferred by Mount Holyoke.[1]

In her acceptance speech, the usually soft-spoken Smith offered a passionate portrait of Charleston as a refuge from the aches of modern America. As a representative of her people and her place on New England soil, she asserted, "We are living today in a nervous age. Everyone has a chip on his shoulder; every nation has a chip on its shoulder. The artists in the big cities fight against the hurly-burly, the tense struggle of modern life. I live in a backwater, where there is perhaps some sense of a certain disintegration, where there is also the memory, the tradition of a great civilization, a country in which there is a greater acceptance of life as a thing to be lived with the elements, with the skies and waters and the things that grow."[2]

Charleston's leading visual artists of the 1920s and 1930s embraced and promoted Alice Ravenel Huger Smith's notion of the Low Country as a site where memory and tradition endured in the tangible ruins of the region's past. Through their etchings, drawings, watercolors, and pastels, Smith and her colleagues exercised free use of artistic license and the privilege of selectivity in shaping a visual idiom of historic Charleston. Art historian Estill Pennington has argued that "to 'see' Southern art, one must pursue the old Southern dichotomy of fantasy and fact. . . . Reality, in the guise of objective historical accounting of goods and people, collides with the extensively evolved, and very sentimental lens through which the South has viewed itself."[3] In keeping with this tendency, Charleston artists constructed a world populated by genteel whites, picturesque working-class African Americans, and a time-haunted landscape of dilapidated houses and silent swamps. These images proved effective in communicating the artists' visions of place to tourists who visited art studios in Charleston and exhibits in galleries across the country. Many of these art-buying Americans returned to their homes armed with an "authentic" physical souvenir of a reinvented, historic, and romantic Charleston they could share with others.

Of all the artists who were active in the city during the 1920s and 1930s, none were more effective propagandists than natives Smith and Elizabeth O'Neill Verner. While the quiet and formal Smith dedicated her watercolor brush to memorializing the natural wonders of the Low Country, the gregarious and more assertive Verner etched the buildings, people, and scenery of her native city. Together, their personal lives, public careers, and artwork provide a remarkable record of the power of historical memory, historical amnesia, and the politics of representation in shaping Charleston's public identity.

From its colonial days through the late nineteenth century, several significant local artists, including Henrietta Johnson, Jeremiah Theus, Charles Fraser, and William Aiken Walker, worked in Charleston, but the city did not attain the status of "a Mecca"[4] for the arts—"a veritable mine of inspiration for etchers and painters"—until the late 1920s.[5] In 1928, the *Chicago Evening Post* described it as a center of American art, declaring, "Everywhere one turns there appears the inexhaustible picturesqueness of Charleston, and on every side an artist has set up his easel in devotion."[6] The city's art-friendly atmosphere, nurtured by shows by the Carolina Art Association at the Gibbes Art Gallery, as well as a healthy tourist market for Charleston images, encouraged the artistic expression of many locals, such as Antoinette Rhett, Minnie Mikell, Leila Waring, Edward von Siebold Dingle, Eola Willis, and Anna Heyward Taylor. As the city's cultural reputation grew during the 1920s, increasing numbers of Charlestonians, particularly elite white women, identified themselves as professional artists in the city's directories. In 1923, for example, only five persons listed themselves as such, whereas five years later that population had tripled to fifteen, reflecting the growing momentum of the local arts scene.[7] Likewise, in 1927, several Charlestonians formed the Associated Artists of Charleston, also known as the Sketch Club. This predominantly female group was affiliated with the Gibbes, where they shared studio space and collaborated on exhibits, art sales, and publicity.[8] The promise of warm weather and historic scenery lured artists from the North to Charleston as well. Two nationally renowned painters, American Impressionist Childe Hassam and American Scene painter Edward Hopper, led the list of notables, which includes Works Progress Administration artists George Biddle, Prentiss Taylor, and Palmer Schoppe, a student of Thomas Hart Benton. Of this artistic flurry, local author and sometimes etcher John Bennett observed rather hyperbolically in 1939, "There is, perhaps, no other city in America . . . not even lovely old New Orleans, not even raucus [*sic*], stupefying, arrogant New York, has been the mecca of so many transient draftsmen, adopted artists, and the source and birthplace of so many gifted, capable draughtsmen of exceptional skill and quality."[9]

Some acclaimed professionals, such as Alfred Hutty, went so far as to make Charleston their part-time home. The Michigan-born etcher visited the city briefly in 1919. He was so moved by its beauty that he wired his wife, "Come quickly, have found heaven."[10] He became a dominant member in Charleston's art circles, sharing his technical expertise through classes at the Carolina Art Association, exhibiting with local artists, and working with heritage-minded cultural organizations such as the Society for the Preservation of Old Dwellings and the Poetry Society of South Carolina.[11] Hutty's Low Country corpus comprised predominantly rural and urban landscapes, including his signature image, the gnarled, moss-hung live oaks. As art collector Duncan Phillips asserted only ten years after Hutty's arrival in the city, "[He] captures the essence of Charleston as it exists in the mind of the artist. He salvages what he can of the picturesque which is passing away, and gives permanency to that mood which the Northern visitor feels so poignantly in the Southern City."[12] Though Hutty's skill outpaced that of Verner, the subject matter and basic themes of his etchings do not vary significantly from those of his native-born counterpart. Hutty so wholly internalized the elite vision of Charleston that he became the city's foremost non-native visual interpreter, as well as a vivid example of the appeal of Charleston's image beyond its regional borders.[13]

While figurative artists such as Smith, Verner, and Hutty thrived in Charleston, the city was not a very welcoming mecca for artists experimenting with abstract forms. As contemporaries such as Georgia O'Keeffe and Paul Klee crafted their increasingly modernist "art for art's sake" images on canvases in New York, Charleston artists embraced a figurative yet always romanticized aesthetic. Charleston-born Robert N. S. Whitelaw, the young, innovative director of the Carolina Art Association throughout the 1930s and into the post–World War II period, actively encouraged the regionalist work of local artists through widely advertised exhibits at the Gibbes Art Gallery. However supportive of indigenous efforts, Whitelaw also possessed a broader imagination and greater toleration for the modern than most of the city's cultural producers. In 1936 and again in 1938, through Whitelaw's initiative, the Gibbes sponsored the first showing in America of abstract works from the private collection of Solomon Guggenheim, one of the city's prominent "winter residents." Although the exhibit attracted great numbers of visitors from the city, the collection found its final resting place, significantly, not in Charleston but at Guggenheim's modern art museum in New York.[14]

Historian C. Vann Woodward once declared that the South was not given to abstraction, and in Charleston art circles of the 1920s and 1930s, that was unquestionably true.[15] As American Scene painters, Charleston artists did not look abroad or to the abstract for inspiration but rather sought to depict the essence of their locale. They were part of the "Paint America" movement popular among artists in the interwar years whose approach to native subject matter was most often categorized as "social realist" or "regionalist." While social realists such as Ben Shahn employed art as a mode of exposing the nation's social, cultural, and political problems, which were exacerbated during the Great Depression, their regionalist counterparts celebrated the customs, folklife, and peculiarities of small towns and villages in a more patriotic, narrative style. Regionalists wanted to provide an alternative vision of American culture that was an antidote to the increasingly homogeneous, mechanized, and commercialized culture of modern America.[16]

Native Charlestonians Smith and Verner echoed this essentially conservative message, viewing their art as a manner of recording what they considered the endangered, morally superior, and indigenously "American" civilization of the South Carolina Low Country. Yet they differed from their famous Midwestern counterparts in a subtle and important way. In their elevation of the common man as the hero and hope of American society, Midwestern regionalists such as Grant Wood, Thomas Hart Benton, and John Stuart Curry created a democratic, populist art form that spoke to the concerns and aspirations of the average Depression-era American. The majority of their images — white farmers breaking rich soil or muscular pioneers moving westward across the prairie — attested to the supposedly universal American traits of moral fortitude, perseverance, and opportunity in a land of democracy.[17] The "common man" Smith and Verner depicted in their art, on the other hand, was the African American laboring in the fields or selling flowers on the city's streets. Instead of functioning as independent, patriotic, and heroic subjects, these African American types served as dependent, primitivist objects. They functioned as foils to the alleged civility and racial paternalism of the ruling white elites.

Thus, Smith and Verner fashioned an artistic illusion of Charleston as a world where all the whites were aristocrats and all the blacks were servants. Their white figures are largely shown as members of the city's elite or in historical terms as representatives of the region's slave-owner class. Their works provide no sense of the thousands of Charlestonians — from the Italian grocer and Irish streetcar conductor to the working-class Anglo-American with no ancestral claim on the plantation past — who comprised much of the city's white population. Likewise, Smith and Verner reinscribed what Henry Louis Gates Jr. calls a centuries-old "white fiction of blackness"; they constructed a strictly delineated typology of African American characters, most often representing their subjects as street hucksters, domestic servants, and agricultural laborers.[18]

In their racially integrated neighborhood south of Broad Street, Smith, Verner, and other artists came into frequent contact with African Americans who fit these types — and yet these artists must also have encountered members of Charleston's African American working class, the stevedores, ironworkers, and mechanics of their port city, as well its well-established black middle-class leaders and their formidable institutions, such as the Avery Institute, which educated the city's black elites, and the all-black Centenary Methodist Church.[19] During shopping excursions up the main business thoroughfare of King Street to Condon's, the city's largest department store, for example, Smith and Verner would have seen many African American–owned shops and dining establishments that bordered Citadel Square; they might even have bought a newspaper, as so many of their white neighbors did, from the popular black-owned Dewees News Stand.[20] Certainly, the artists were well aware that Charleston's African American community was not a monolith of uneducated, subservient types. Shortly before turning from etchings to pastels in the early 1930s, for example, Elizabeth Verner executed zinc print portraits of the Reverend Daniel Jenkins, a major black civic leader and founder of the city's African American orphanage, and his daughter, a trained opera singer named Mildred. Unlike Verner's much-reproduced flower women images, these prints were not re-created for the tourist market, perhaps because they were not commercially viable. Their existence, however, underscores the fact that Verner knew that a more varied and complex black Charleston existed yet deliberately chose to edit it out of her larger artistic repetoire.

Charleston's African American community boasted several accomplished artists who were active during the 1920s and 1930s and who captured on film and canvas images of a competing reality of Charleston—portraits of the "New Negro" middle class. For example, the work of two independent black photographers, Elise Harleston and Michael Blake, present a city peopled with elegant and educated black professionals who possessed the icons of middle-class American life—telephones, fur coats, fancy scroll-back chairs, and shining automobiles.[21] With such a limited clientele, however, artistic survival was difficult for black artists, as the example of Edwin Harleston illustrates. A member of one of the city's most elite black families, Harleston was educated at Atlanta University and the Boston Museum of Fine Arts and hoped to pursue his passion for painting professionally upon returning home. In Jim Crow Charleston, however, he found little welcome. So he took over his family's established funeral home, cofounded the local branch of the NAACP, and painted on the side. Harleston's view of Charleston's black population resulted in a much broader range of images than that of his white contemporaries. In his oil paintings, such as *The Honey Man*, *The Old Servant*, *Portrait of a Woman*, and *The Nurse*, Harleston resists dominant cultural stereotypes. His scope and realistic handling of subjects not as objects contrasts sharply with the narrow, picturesque styles of Verner, Hutty, and Smith. In recognition, in 1931, the Harmon Foundation of New York awarded him the prestigious Alain Locke portrait prize for his canvas *The Old Servant*. Meanwhile, at home he remained best known as a mortician.[22] The failed attempt of Laura Bragg, a Massachusetts native and the director of the Charleston Museum, to mount an exhibition of Harleston's paintings in 1926 testifies to the depth of the city's

Local black painter Edwin Harleston's *The Nurse* highlighted the agency and individuality of African Americans, a dramatic departure from the objectifying images produced by his white contemporaries.
Gibbes Museum of Art/Carolina Art Association.

entrenched racism. There was little room in the imagination of white-ruled Charleston for a professional African American artist of Harleston's high caliber, so it exerted its power to ensure that his competing vision of the city remained hidden from public view.[23]

The allowable public face of Charleston's art scene in the 1920s and 1930s was an exclusively white one that clustered its studios along Atlantic Street, a narrow lane paved with crushed white oyster shells in the heart of the old historic district.[24] On Sundays in March and April, the height of the tourist season, Smith and Verner and their colleagues held a joint "At Home," during which tourists could move from studio to studio for tea and a glimpse of the artists' portfolios.[25] They shared not only clients, materials, and exhibition space in local high-end tourist hotels but also a conception of Charleston's heritage to which they gave definition in their art. None was more effective in expressing their "collective" historical memory than Alice Ravenel Huger Smith and Elizabeth O'Neill Verner.

"This Rich and Tender Remembering": Alice Ravenel Huger Smith's Vision of the South Carolina Low Country

Around the corner from the Atlantic Street artists' studios and a few houses down from the Heyward-Washington House sits 69 Church Street, the home of Alice Ravenel Huger Smith. Born into an old-line Charleston family in 1876, Smith could scarcely escape the presence of the past as she grew to adulthood within the protective walls of this stately eighteenth-century mansion. Because of their strained finances, the extended Smith clan lived under one roof for much of Alice's life. Surrounded by her aunts and uncles, her amateur historian father, Daniel Elliott Huger Smith, and her grandmother, Alice absorbed the values and beliefs of a generation raised before the onset of the Civil War and loyal to its own selective memory of antebellum culture. It was in this household, wedded to the maintenance of elite traditions, that Alice Smith internalized as truth her elders' vision of the past, a vision that she, in turn, reified and passed on through her artwork.

Smith's childhood was characterized by a deep sense of the enduring legacy of deprivation and decline wrought by the Civil War, including the eventual loss of the family plantations. This once-wealthy patrician clan perpetuated in its children the idea of the gloriousness of the slave-based Southern plantation society that had preceded the bloody conflict, as well as the evils of a Reconstruction era marked by the oppression of Southern whites, and elites in particular, at the hands of an unscrupulous and undemocratic alliance among

Artist Alice Ravenel Huger Smith. Courtesy of the Charleston Museum, Charleston, South Carolina.

immoral Northern "carpetbaggers," Southern "scalawags," and ignorant, incapable African American freedmen that ruled the region. This historical interpretation held increasing national credence among white Americans, North and South, after *Plessy v. Ferguson* (1896) and the concretization of Jim Crow laws by the turn of the century. It was further popularized for generations to come by a group of historians working under Professor William Dunning at Columbia University, by D. W. Griffith's 1915 blockbuster film, *The Birth of a Nation*, as well as by Claude Bowers's 1929 best seller, *The Tragic Era: The Revolution after Lincoln.* Alice Smith fully embraced this historical interpretation, as evidenced in her memoirs by her description of her birth year, the moment of white "Redemption" in South Carolina, and her glossing over its more violent realities, such as the 1876 massacre of blacks in the Edgefield County city of Hamburg:[26]

> It was the year that saw the determined uprising of the people of South Carolina against the terrible Reconstruction government that for ten years followed the subjugation of the State by four years of war. The riots of 1876 that marked the overthrow of that orgy of misrule and oppression were my birthright, and poverty was the inheritance of the land in which I dwelt.

> But it was poverty so nobly met by our elders. . . . I have always been grateful that it was given to me to grow up even in the shadow of the shade of the great civilization that had produced the generation of the past.[27]

With all available funds reserved for sending her brothers to school, Alice Smith learned her history primarily in this "shadow of the shade" — tales of the past that "wove in and out of our childhood."[28] Smith accompanied her father, a Confederate veteran and accomplished antiquarian, on weekend walking tours of the city and its neighboring plantations and churchyards, searching for the homes and graves of heroes from Charleston's illustrious past.[29] Among the most memorable ramble was a fifteen-mile walk one Sunday afternoon to Middleton Place, an elaborate former rice plantation on the Ashley River. This landmark home of Arthur Middleton, signer of the Declaration of Independence, fueled Smith's historical imagination and her wistful associations with the land. "We strolled through its paths under the great oaks looking out across the fields and river," she recounted in her 1950 "Reminiscences." "We had no lack of history there. The settlement of the Colony and the growth of its laws and government brought one noted figure after another to walk those paths with us, and the Revolution brought another group for me to imagine. . . . I had walked a long, long way to take part in these especial gatherings in the footsteps of great men under these especial oaks."[30] History became an intensely personal endeavor for the young girl under her father's tutelage; she learned to take pride in having the blood of English and Huguenot colonial settlers in her veins. Of a cemetery walk one afternoon, Smith recalled, "We would visit hero after hero, we would meet famous soldiers and sailors, lawyers, judges, captains of industry and delightful old ladies, and many young ones too, for he had so many stories to tell us that history became real. It was not in a book, it was here and now."[31]

Smith, who was only twelve when her invalid mother died, was also deeply influenced by her paternal grandmother, Eliza Caroline Middleton Huger Smith. "Erect in her black dress and widow's cap, smiling but firm,"[32] Grandmother Smith loomed large in Alice's upbringing, sharing recollections of antebellum politics and life on the plantations of her youth, replete with parties, waltzes, courtships, and weddings. Her recollections, Alice Smith contended, encompassed not only her own living memory but also memories handed down from earlier generations. Infused with what Smith described as "the feeling and facts of her parents' days," Grandmother Smith bestowed on her granddaughter a legacy of oral narratives and visual portraits that swept from the Revolutionary War through the era of "Redemption."[33]

These vivid, memory-laden history lessons, with their emphasis on prominent people and impressive and genteel places, influenced the subject matter Alice Smith depicted in her artwork. Believing Charleston to be the embodiment of a praiseworthy past, she naturally turned to the streets of her native city that "carry you back to old times, with scarcely an effort on your part." To Smith, they provided "not an occasional glimpse of the past but the thread of the town's history from the beginning." With her father's early encouragement, Smith drew and etched the homes of Charleston's oldest families. All the while, she allowed her imagination to run free and ruminate on "those who lived within their thick walls . . . in the midst of very stirring and romantic events."[34] One contemporary critic called the result "an art of mood and symbol."[35]

Alice Smith came to this style in a rather roundabout way. Aside from a few art classes at the local Carolina Art Association school, which befit her status as the daughter of a patrician family, Smith was essentially self-taught. She sought out and found a mentor in Birge Harrison, a Tonalist painter from Woodstock, New York, who wintered in Charleston in the early part of the century and befriended the Smith family. While he refused to provide formal instruction to Smith, Harrison nonetheless exposed her to the blurred, poetic, and atmospheric approach of Tonalism. In addition, Smith spent a good deal of time studying and cataloging the large collection of Japanese wood-block prints owned by her close friend, former Harvard professor Motte Alston Read. From these Smith experimented with the Japanese wood-block techniques and aesthetics that influenced the fluid effect and composition of her later Low Country watercolors.[36]

After an early phase producing portraits, dance cards, ladies fans, and other ephemera, Smith dedicated herself to the creation of images, and in some cases text, for volumes and articles dealing with her passion, the history and architecture of the Low Country. To Smith, these early works were more than a means to financial gain. They were her main vehicle for explaining her understanding of Charleston to a curious outside world—and for promoting the preservation of the region's old ways. "The South to-day," she once wrote, "is so little understood and is so much misunderstood, that many things have escaped notice."[37] To help remedy this situation, in 1914 she presented a visual study of the ancestral home of her Pringle cousins, the structure Susan Pringle Frost struggled so long to restore, in *Twenty Drawings of the Pringle House on King Street, Charleston, S.C.*[38] Three years later, in collaboration with her father, Smith published an illustrated, book-length tribute to the city's architectural and historical glory, titled *The Dwelling Houses of Charleston*, which served as an inspirational text for the city's historic preservation movement. In 1922, Smith's illustrations of her cousin Elizabeth Allston Pringle's once rich rice plantations on the Pee Dee River accompanied the publication of Pringle's journals in *A Woman Rice Planter*. Pringle's text concerned her struggle to maintain the centuries-old but nearly extinct method of Low Country rice cultivation, and Smith's images depicted the distinctive geography and the scores of African American laborers at the heart of the production system since its inception over 200 years before.[39] Other projects sounded similar kinship and preservationist echoes, including a book on nineteenth-century Charleston miniaturist Charles Fraser and landscape illustrations for the writings of yet another Charleston cousin, Herbert Ravenel Sass.[40] By the mid-1920s, however, Smith largely abandoned the precision-oriented media of drawing and etching in favor of the more impressionistic practice of watercolor; her focus, however, remained the commemoration of Low Country history and culture. She increasingly turned her sentimental gaze to the natural beauty of the region surrounding Charleston, rendering its silent swamps, grassy fields, and heron-graced marshes in the translucent medium that, she argued, best suited her particular conception of those places.[41]

Through her publications, her art exhibits in cities across the country, her membership in regional arts institutions, and her contact with visitors in her Charleston studio, Smith transmitted her conception of the region beyond its boundaries. While her compositions traveled the country and even globe—forty-two exhibitions were held outside of Charleston during the period 1921–30 alone—Smith rarely strayed far from what she called her "country."[42] Artistically, she devoted her every image to the distinctive representation of Charleston and its lowlands. Critics heralded her as a visionary who used her brush to capture glimpses of the natural and historical world that she considered her birthright and inheritance. For example, a *Christian Science Monitor* travel reporter, who was a "paying guest" at Susan Pringle Frost's home during the winter of 1923, purchased a characteristic Smith painting, "a cerulean marsh with golden grasses and leafless trees moss-veiled in ash-grey." "In especial it was Alice Ravenel Huger Smith," she told her readers, "who helped to fix and intensify for me impressions that might have been pale and fugitive."[43] A *Chicago Post* review of a 1928 Smith watercolor exhibit in that city echoed this praise of the artist's ability to convey her region's atmosphere, which, he noted, "always wears a veil of mystery. . . . The poetic realism is convincing."[44] Closer to home, critic Henry Bellamann in the Columbia, South Carolina, newspaper *State*, acknowledged Smith's powerful and unchallenged position as interpreter of the Low Country. Describing her paintings as a material form of "rich and tender remembering," Bellamann asserted, "Her work is perfectly of the region and of herself. It is impossible to think of the one without the other, or to believe that Miss Smith could ever have been just her unique self anywhere else, . . . or that the place could have had so fortunate an interpretation without her."[45]

Smith extended her aesthetic sense of the Low Country's romance to the atmosphere of her city studio, where she offered tourists and prospective art buyers repose from the world outside its doors, as well as a little evocative drama. "To visit Miss Smith's studio in Charleston," a Savannah journalist wrote,

is to find oneself in an atmosphere as delicately tonal as her paintings are. . . . There is a garden enclosed by a wall next door at the side and the entrance to the studio opens on that pleasant greenery. Inside you seem to have taken a step or two down—perhaps you have—and you are in a square room, with many paintings, fragile aquarelles in gold frames on the walls, and the painter herself, in soft blues and grays, welcoming you. One after another she takes the watercolors from her big portfolios to show you, and their misty and harmonious colors, their subtle patterns, their radiance, even a soft brilliance that you feel in them, draw you into another world than that you have left clanging outside. This is the quiet world of the lonely cypress, of pink lotus blooming before the sun is well up, of birds singing in secret places, among woods and over water, of tropical flowers blossoming in unravaged beauty, of waterfowl meditating on sheltered ledges, watching a moon at dawn, or rising in rhythmical flight with their fellows.[46]

Smith did more than just offer refreshments and exhibit her works to her studio visitors; she re-created for them her keenly constructed world of Charleston gentility. One by one she would display each painting, describing in her soft accent the scene's historical circumstances, transporting the viewer to the time and the place in which the imagined scene took place.[47]

Smith's studio thus functioned not only as a clearinghouse for her art but also as a sort of "virtual history clinic" for interested tourists. It served both as the primary site for her invention of an aesthetic ideal of Charleston and as a place where the history of the Low Country could be "experienced" vicariously through Smith family lore. "As a result of my historical training by my Father, of our book on dwelling houses, and of my background and familiar knowledge of rice-plantations," she recalled, "my studio was frequented not only by visitors interested in my painting, but by those interested in these other matters."[48] Even in her rhetoric, Smith transformed the circumscribed space of her studio into a kind of imaginary rice field, declaring, "I was lucky. Instead of going away to garner grain I reaped it within my own four walls, and I had my Father at hand to arrange my happy findings into sheaves[,] for his daily visit to my studio was, indeed, the reason for so many visitors in their quest for interest and information."[49] As a result, for many tourists, Alice Smith's art studio became as important a stop as the city's well-advertised historic sites, such as the Old Exchange Building and the Colonial Powder Magazine.

Underneath her public persona as an aristocratic spinster lady of the Old South, Alice Smith was also a serious, modern businesswoman whose income contributed to the livelihood of her Church Street household. She was, in the words of one close friend, "a lily but a woman of steel" who profitably marketed both her image and her artworks.[50] Like other cultural producers in Charleston at the time, Smith was a paradox; she was by no means a dilettante "lady artist." Her business savvy and awareness of modern market forces were as well developed as her painterly technique. She networked with professionals in her field and supervised the selecting, packing, insuring, and accounting required to place her works on tour. The Baltimore Museum of Art, the Delgado Museum of Art in New Orleans, the Houston Museum of Fine Arts, the Milwaukee Art Institute, the Chicago Art Institute, the Pennsylvania Academy of Fine Arts, and the Brooklyn Institute for the Arts were among the country's notable museums and galleries eager to display her pictures.[51] Her sentimental and dreamlike renderings of the Low Country proved very marketable far beyond coastal Carolina.

Smith's sales figures from the decades between the world wars attest to her reputation as an interpreter of her region and to the efficacy of her seductive, studio-based sales method. At her peak earning in the late 1920s and early 1930s, she enjoyed significant commercial success. In 1926, she sold twenty-three paintings, over half purchased by Northerners, and many dozens of souvenir cards depicting the eighteenth-century rice plantation Middleton Place, for a total income of over $3,000, or the equivalent of over $30,000 in 2002 dollars.[52] The following year, as Charleston became an increasingly popular tourist destination, Smith more than doubled her income; even more non-Southerners bought her paintings, thirty-two out of forty-seven buyers, for a total return of over $6,500. In 1930, while the nation slipped deeper and deeper into the Depression, Smith enjoyed her most profitable year to date, earning over $9,000—the approximate equivalent of an astounding $93,000 in 2002 dollars—from art-related work.[53] For a time, wistful watercolors made Alice Smith a well-to-do woman, particularly by Charleston's standards.

Throughout the 1930s, a significant segment of Smith's clientele consisted of wealthy, predominantly urban, non-Southern whites who purchased her paintings at traveling exhibits or at the artist's Charleston studios during the peak tourist months while visiting from the colder climes of New York, Philadelphia, Boston, Chicago, Detroit, and even Montreal. Patrons included members of America's elite, such as Mrs. Marshall Field, Mrs. Solomon Guggenheim, and Victor and Marjorie Morawetz, all of New York, and Nicholas Roosevelt of Philadelphia.[54] It is significant that Smith's work appealed to white elites from urban areas of the nation that were in the throes of industrial and social turmoil in the 1920s and 1930s. An antidote for modernity—the frantic subways and skyscraper construction of New York, the racial unrest of Chicago, and the immigrant and labor struggles of Detroit—Smith's pastoral landscapes offered these viewers an alternative America. She fashioned in soft-focused pastels a world of men and women living a human-scale existence in apparent harmony with the natural order, which included, in Smith's view, African American deference to a white ruling class.

By the mid-1930s, the deepening Depression, her father's death, her sister Lili's severe illness and eventual death, and her focus on selling her rice book combined to lessen Smith's productivity and income. By the advent of the Second World War, her art business had slowed to a crawl as Charleston's transient population shifted from tourists to military personnel. Smith lamented, "The War destroyed any artistic business completely—Service men and civilian workers, or their wives do not, & cannot buy pictures, and Charleston was completely given up to the Armed services & the Navy Yard."[55]

Despite her very modern embrace of market forces, Smith was among the most socially conservative and philosophically antimodern contributors to Charleston's cultural revival. A self-described "sentimentalist" who believed she belonged to an earlier age, Smith consistently critiqued modernity in her writings and art.[56] In a 1930 interview with the *New York Evening Post* during a rare sojourn outside of Charleston, she expressed her anxieties about the hustle and bustle of the capital of American modernism: "You remember when Alice of Wonderland nibbled the mushroom? Well, when I come to New York and see all the great tall buildings and the people rushing about I feel as if I were eating the side of the mushroom that makes one grow smaller and smaller. . . . So I have to go back to Charleston and eat the other side of the mushroom and get to feel myself again."[57] In her "Reminiscences," Smith expressed her fear that she was "writing [her]self down as a complete reactionary," even as she extolled the virtues of Charleston's old ways. She warned her readers to beware the specters of ecstasy and experience held out by modernity, arguing that "one of the by-products of this marvelous machine age of ours and its scientific gains is a proportionate loss of thought. . . . The inventions of today seem not so important in comparison with the general character and fortitude that were the gifts of those [past] years."[58] Smith believed Americans needed to learn from the past, not disdain it in favor of sleek and shallow fashions. Even though her actions as a single, childless businesswoman transcended traditional boundaries for elite white Southern women of her day, Smith still saw herself as "a worshipper of the dictum that there is a good reason for every custom."[59]

A descendant of slave-owners on both sides of her family, Smith truly believed the nostalgic, paternalist version of the South's slave past and the concomitant certainty of African Americans as dependent and childlike charges in the modern South. In a 1916 article for *Art in America*, Smith wrote of idyllic relations between master and slave on colonial and antebellum plantations. She detailed a world where there were "such close interests between employer and the employed that the result was the happy family life so characteristic of

Southern establishments." Smith also credited the slave system with placing "the dominance of the man of civilization, of morals, and education, over the absolute savage."[60] Four decades later, Smith's attitude about the rightful place of African Americans in American society seemed unchanged. "When injustice to the African is talked of it seems to me that one of the worst examples is the present trend of teaching negroes to be ashamed of their past,—of their beginning—of their natural gifts. . . . The negroes are losing the old gullah touch, and many are learning to speak more or less good English."[61] Smith maintained her conviction that Low Country African Americans were special but inferior to whites and thus should not aspire to achieve a position in society contrary to their nature. In her view, it was best for South Carolina's blacks to exist in the local culture as uneducated exotics dependent on the noblesse oblige of whites.

Smith further reified this philosophy in her ambitious, memory-laden work *A Carolina Rice Plantation of the Fifties*.[62] This volume of thirty watercolors included a historical essay by her cousin, Herbert Ravenel Sass, and her father's memoirs of his plantation boyhood. Significantly, it was published *not* by a regional South Carolina press but by the national powerhouse the William Morrow Company of New York. It constituted the culmination of her artistic career.

Smith's magnum opus was, in her own words, "intended to be a laurel wreath for that great civilization, of the rice-planting era in South Carolina."[63] "Carolina Gold" rice had been a vital and ubiquitous feature of Low Country life for centuries. More than just a staple of the local diet and a pillar of the economy, rice made its way into the region's aesthetics; images of rice stalks could be found on everything from colonial paper money to the carved headboards of the wealthy.[64] And yet significant commercial rice cultivation had all but ended in South Carolina by the late 1910s. Thus, Smith, ever wary of change, sought to create a visual record of the historic importance and beauty of an extinct culture for future generations of Charlestonians and Americans to admire. "When my generation is gone," she realized, "there will be no one to pass it on pictorially."[65] The result was a series of paintings that can best be described as what Estill Pennington calls "landscapes of longing," images that merge objective, natural observation with moral intention. "Landscapes of longing" contain enough familiar visual elements of nature to lull viewers into believing the images are records of fact, thus obscuring the subjective imaginings and values conveyed in them.[66] Although Smith spent some time in her youth on the dying rice plantations of the Cooper, Pee Dee, and Santee rivers, in particular the Heyward family's Wappaoolah and Elizabeth Allston

Pringle's Chicora Wood, in her book she set out to replicate a slavery-based agrarian institution of which she had no firsthand experience. Nonetheless, Smith, and her patrons and critics, considered her imagined antebellum world an authentic reproduction.[67]

The "Fifties" of the book's title, of course, were the 1850s, a period in history during which Smith's father and grandmother lived on rice plantations but which predated Smith's birth by over twenty years. "I threw the book back to the Golden Age before the Confederate War," Smith noted years later, "so as to give the right atmosphere because in my days times were hard."[68] Smith believed she was a capable and legitimate spokesperson for this slavery-based plantation system because of her sincere love of the land, family associations, and inherited memories. She filtered those memories through her impressionistic painter's palette of vivid pastels and iridescent whites.

Not only were the subjects and scenarios represented by Smith based upon hand-me-down memory, but the actual technique she employed to produce the images also depended on mental invention. Throughout her career, Smith relied singularly upon a method of reproduction that she termed "memory sketches." "Memory sketches" comprised detailed, direct observation of a scene, accompanied perhaps by a few cursory pencil sketches, and then the recollection of that image in her mind and finally in paint back in the comfort of her Charleston studio. One reviewer described her "memoranda" work as follows: "When the artist is ready to do a picture, she does not recall a particular place or scene. She does not assemble the data of her sketches and create a synthetic landscape. None of the pictures is actually a picture of a particular place. . . . When the picture is to be painted the artist places herself once more in the remembered mood of the place and from the store of memory the assembled importances [sic] of a scene come into being."[69] Despite her obvious reliance on imagination, Smith defended her memory approach as a verifiable and near-scientific method: she was the accurate replicator, not the creative inventor, of her region's historical and physical contours. "I do not mean *guessing*," Smith argued of her technique in 1926, "I mean remembering. Just as there is no guessing at a history lesson or at mathematics—they have to be remembered."[70] The "history" Smith remembered, memorized at her ancestors' knees, merged with her encounters with the Carolina environment and her own sentimental longings about the past to create an art that claimed the authoritative weight of "history."

Smith's rice series, dedicated to her recently deceased father, preserved and promoted a nostalgic and paternalistic view of Charleston's past and its people. To their credit, the plates in Smith's book carefully detail the geography of the plantation and the processes involved in the cultivation of rice, from the preparation of the fields and the first seeding to the loading of the schooners for transportation of the finished product downriver to market. Her usually impressionistic watercolorist's brush outline with precision the fields, trunks, canals, and buildings of the plantation, and it is in these images that Smith excelled aesthetically. When depicting the plantation's human population, however, Smith's unbridled sentimentalism is inescapable and the final artistic result notably stiff.

In the opening image, titled *Sunday Morning at the Great House*, Smith re-constitutes in watercolors a familiar scene of the "moonlight-and-magnolia South." This plantation image — of a genteel world where relations between benevolent enslaver and appreciative enslaved played out graciously under moss-hung live oaks — was already deeply etched in white America's imagi-nation from novels and book illustrations of the late nineteenth and early twentieth centuries and from Hollywood films. Margaret Mitchell's epic novel *Gone with the Wind*, which appeared the same year as Smith's rice volume, further popularized the myth. In *Sunday Morning*, a group of brightly dressed, neatly aligned slaves greet their master and mistress before a stately planta-tion house on a glorious Carolina day. An air of mutual affection pervades the painting, underscored by a black mammy tenderly cradling a white infant in her arms, and friendly exchanges between white and black children. From the veranda, an elderly white woman, whose gray hair reminds the viewer of the plantation system's deep roots, gazes down approvingly at the gather-ing of her "extended" family. A similarly pleasant glimpse of a harmonious interracial community is conveyed in *The Stack-Yard*, in which white and black children romp on large stacks of rice stalks as the mistress and her smiling slaves converse. A young black girl offers a tribute to her white mistress's child, a hand-picked bouquet of flowers in a heartfelt gesture that Smith believed symbolized reciprocal respect inherent in the plantation system.

In several images, Smith visually credits African American slaves with the dignity, skill, and exertion necessary to bring a crop to fruition; even so, she persists in depicting these individuals as amorphous, faceless types, figures that tend to melt into the agricultural landscape. While this blurry effect is in keeping with Smith's aesthetic choices, it is notable that her white figures are generally much better defined and undeniably individual, even within the ste-reotyped confines of their pictorial roles as mistress and master, than the slave figures, who do not escape anonymity. Instead, they are situated as part of a nondescript mass of humanity whose life was spent, according to Sass's ac-companying "historical" essay, "working cheerfully and not too strenuously"

Part of a traveling exhibition of plantation watercolors, Alice R. H. Smith's *Sunday Morning at the Great House* promoted the artist's romanticized vision of the Low Country's slave society during "the Golden Age before the Confederate War." Gibbes Museum of Art/Carolina Art Association.

under the Carolina sun.[71] Throughout her visual tribute to the slave South, Smith omits the reality of heat, insects, exploitative labor, the slave patrol, and, above all, the repressive violence of black bondage. For Alice Smith, the line between the real and the remembered was entirely blurred. Smith even modified her revered father's recollections to suit her imaginings. All of the African American slaves she depicts, for example, are dressed in a variety of vivid colors, their clothing perfectly intact, while her father's memoirs recount that the slaves were dressed in coarse "blue or grey woolens" on annual allotment, which assuredly looked ragged by the season's end.[72] As John Bennett noted in 1937, Smith "has ever looked upon the past as though it were a land of rainbows and dreams, and has viewed it in her loving and loyal fancy in such colors as never were on sea or land. . . . It undoubtedly makes her happier to do so; to paint the past in colors dreamlike and fair, regardless of the facts."[73] The viewer is meant to leave Smith's rice series believing that, as Sass declared, "nowhere in America was slavery a gentler, kinder thing than in the Carolina Low Country."[74]

Smith effectively conveyed her particular vision of South Carolina's plantation culture to an art-interested American public through book sales and a multicity, two-year tour of her rice paintings. Critics across the country internalized Smith's claim about the authenticity and accuracy of her compositions, describing them as "valuable historical documents."[75] The *New York Times Book Review*, for example, observed that Smith "has rendered a special historical service" that elegantly convinced the reader that life "in the Low Country of this period was a really delightful one."[76] The *Washington Star* found Smith's paintings to be "without [romantic] exaggeration." "Her works," the critic continued, "are very subtle but very true; they perpetuate and make tangible the elusive and lovely."[77] Nationally renowned cultural critic Henry Seidel Canby of the *Saturday Review* emphasized the "real historical and sociological value" of Smith's work as "a contribution to the valid memorials of our rich American past." He concluded with a passage of nostalgia that Smith herself could have written: "Here was a culture which to a high degree developed an extraordinary sense of responsibility, and which encouraged the art of living, which has since been so generally lost. And it left its mark upon a countryside which these pictures commemorate."[78]

Smith donated her rice paintings to the Carolina Art Association, the managing body of the Gibbes Art Gallery, now called the Gibbes Museum of Art, where they, along with other artistic images from the 1920s and 1930s, continue to resonate with visitors today. Steven Dubin has argued that "museums are important venues in which a society can define itself and present itself publicly. Museums solidify culture, endow it with a tangibility, in a way few other things do."[79] Thus, when the Gibbes decided in the 1980s to reproduce a limited edition of eight images from Smith's rice book for sale in the museum's shop, it underscored the centrality of her vision to the city's public identity. Toward the end of her life, Smith boasted of her recall ability: "I can to this day, not just *remember* but put myself there in the past where I want to be."[80] Locating her privilege to speak for Charleston in the power of her bloodline, Smith transformed her personal, family-based memories into a body of accessible and material objects. Her enduring presence on the city's aesthetic map has allowed Alice Smith to retain, even in death, her position as a chief interpreter of her place and its past.

"We Have Made a Friend of Time in Charleston": Elizabeth O'Neill Verner's Charleston [81]

Smith's artistic influence on Charleston's public identity extended beyond her own watercolors and into the career of the city's most prolific etcher, Elizabeth O'Neill Verner. Elizabeth Verner's story provides a rich case study of the workings of historical memory and representational politics in cultural production on two fronts: first, in her hoped-for persona as a member of Charleston's elite white circle; and, second, in the romanticized aesthetic she expressed in her artwork depicting the city and its African American inhabitants, particularly black women. Verner occupied a position that was both secondary and central to the city's life. Because of her lack of significant familial and historical connections with elite society, Verner could not claim to belong to the inner circle of patricians. And yet, through her etchings, prints, pastels, public speaking, and publications, she was undeniably successful at creating and promoting an image of the city that echoed and confirmed elite historical memory, thereby convincing her art-buying public that she was an authentic representative of the much-coveted "insider" Charleston.

Elizabeth O'Neill Verner had absolutely no control over the most considerable barrier to her lack of insider status: the conditions of her birth. Born in 1883 and raised on Legare Street in what would become the historic district, Verner was a member of a large Irish Catholic family with a mercantile heritage. She was the third of Henry and Mollie O'Neill's twelve children, only nine of whom grew to adulthood. Given the family's relatively "new immigrant" blood —grandfather Bernard O'Neill emigrated from the "Old Sod" in the 1840s— as well as their devout Roman Catholicism—Verner was convent-educated —the O'Neills were never privy to the sanctum sanctorum of Charleston society, that tight circle of former slave-owning families who attended the annual Saint Cecilia Ball and, on Sundays, sat in age-old family pews at St. Michael's and St. Philip's Episcopal Churches.[82]

As if to compensate for this family "handicap" and to associate herself more intensely with the Low Country's past, Verner spoke and wrote about her family in exaggerated historical terms. In particular, she characterized her rice-broker father as a knightly figure, a remnant of what she described as "the gracious fifties when the whole South was affluent."[83] Unfortunately for Verner's attempts at fashioning pedigree, Henry O'Neill did not fight for the Confederacy; instead, his family sent him to France during the Civil War to be educated. In 1876, however, Henry joined the Charleston Light Dragoons and served as lieutenant colonel and aide-de-camp to Wade Hampton during the bloody and ultimately successful campaign by white South Carolinians to restore racial and political "home rule." The portrait of this uniformed officer occupied a central place in the family dining room of Verner's childhood home, as well as in her adult imagination. Verner latched on to her father's show of loyalty to the white South during the violent "red shirt days" of Reconstruction as proof that she belonged in Charleston and enjoyed a shared heritage with her elite counterparts. "Every Southern child felt that she had been a part of it," Verner contended in language similar to Alice Smith's. "The grown-ups said little about it, too bitter was the memory to wish it passed on to their children, but we could not escape the shadow." In her writings, Verner reveled in her childhood memories of interactions with the elite "George-town planters" who frequented the O'Neill home to discuss business with her father, "Mr. Henry."[84] By Verner's estimation, the mere proximity of these men of status lent a kind of vicarious legitimacy to her family name. Similarly, through a decision described by her biographer as "difficult and emotional," Verner effectively overcame another obstacle of birth, her Roman Catholicism, by adopting the Presbyterian faith of her husband in the early 1920s.[85]

As an adult, Verner continued this pattern of self-fashioning and sought out interaction with the city's elites, but her relationships with them were largely on the professional, not intimately social, level. In particular, she forged a strong cooperative professional relationship with her neighbor and mentor, Alice Smith. Although Verner had received two years of formal art education at the Pennsylvania Academy of Fine Arts, it was Smith who introduced her to etching in the early 1920s. In May 1923, Verner was among the nine artists, including Smith, Hutty, and Ohio-born writer and Poetry Society leader John Bennett, who established the Charleston Etchers' Club. The club purchased a press that they shared to "pull" their etchings, most of which depicted Charleston and Low Country scenes.[86] The Charleston Museum, under the direction of Laura Bragg, housed the large press and sponsored the club's annual public exhibitions. Over the course of its ten-year history, the Etchers' Club served as a central vehicle for Charlestonians' regionalist expressions, expanding its membership to include individuals who were active in other areas of the city's cultural revival such as Robert N. S. Whitelaw, later director of the Gibbes Art Gallery; historic preservationist and architect Albert Simons; and A. T. S. Stoney, a member of the Society for the Preservation of Negro Spirituals.[87]

In 1925, widowed with two children to support, the forty-two-year-old Verner needed to make a living. Smith encouraged her to forego the quick expediency of an office job or real estate work and to commit herself to a career as an artist and entrepreneur. Smith sent samples of Verner's work out with her own to galleries, museums, and art professionals across the country, in particular to Bertha Jacques of the Chicago Society of Etchers. Smith also ushered her clients across Atlantic Street from her studio to Verner's. "Until 1925," Verner recalled, "I merely had two hobbies, art and love of Charleston. I combined the two into a profession."[88] "Mother couldn't have done it without

[Smith]," Verner's daughter, Betty Hamilton, recalled. And yet, despite their open cooperation and mutual respect, the relationship had its insurmountable social limits. "It wasn't exactly a friendship." Hamilton noted, "It was more of a mentor-pupil relationship, although they had their funny times because they were so different."[89]

Through her cultural activism in the city and throughout the South, Verner allied herself with Charleston's white elites and promoted herself as a spokesperson for the city beyond its borders. A sincere interest in preserving the Charleston heritage that she so proudly and problematically acclaimed motivated Verner to became a founding and vocal member of the Society for the Preservation of Old Dwellings in 1920. She also joined the Poetry Society of South Carolina, whose membership was relatively democratic and open. Verner's leadership in the Southern States Art League further enhanced her effectiveness at promoting her city. Founded by Southern artists attending an "All-Southern Exhibition" in Charleston in 1921, and incorporated in 1922, the Art League was a collective response to criticisms from outside the South that the region was void of cultural merit. The all-white league sought "to encourage and promote art and its appreciation throughout the Southern States" via arts education and annual traveling exhibits of Southern artwork.[90] The organization encouraged Southerners to depict indigenous scenes, to "take advantage of the great beauty around them, and search for the romance and hidden mysteries of our section of America," before "foreign" non-Southerners did so.[91] In response, league artists often created nostalgic images of "the dead-and-gone" South, which perpetuated stereotypes of African Americans in historic and contemporary positions of servitude to whites, from the cotton-picking slave to the doting mammy.[92]

A charter member and one of five officers on the board of directors from 1922 to 1933, Verner embodied the league's combination of modern, aggressive organizational style and sentimental, racially paternalistic content. A description of the league in the June 1922 issue of the *American Magazine of Art* might just as well have been a characterization of Verner: "Indeed, the spirit of the old south for gallantry, courage and chivalry, high ideals and noble purposes seemed . . . blended with that of enterprise, energy and ambition which are the badge and watchword of the new south today."[93] As with many other cultural preservationists and artists in Charleston between the world wars, Verner, too, attempted to straddled the gap between the Old and the New Souths.

Verner sincerely feared that the historic and romantic Charleston she envisioned and that formed the bedrock of both her business and her personal identity might be ruined by unchecked innovation. And yet she was not opposed outright to change. Like her colleagues in the Society for the Preservation of Old Dwellings, Verner wanted change to "come gently" and with due consideration to the city's historic character. "We do not want the silhouette of chaste St. Michael's steeple hidden by skyscrapers nor blackened by the smoke of industry; nor her joyous bells drowned in the roar of traffic." In addition to historic tourism, from which she profited, Verner proposed bolstering the local economy by encouraging artisan-based industries, such as brickmaking, lace-making, tile and wrought-iron crafting, or even furniture and textile reproduction.[94] Verner argued for striking a balance in Charleston between the urge to preserve and the economic need for development. If this balance were achieved, she argued, "when America is wearied of too much industry, when her fingers are blistering from coupon clipping and her lungs blackened, she can leave her busy marts and come to our city—to live."[95]

In spite of her nostalgia for times gone by, Verner was also a very modern, practical businesswoman. She worked long hours, traveled extensively, exhibited and marketed her etchings shrewdly, and published two book-length tributes to the city. Over the course of her career, she produced over 260 images. "To sell I had to work 14 hours a day for 10 years and I did!" she later recalled.[96] By the early 1930s, the art business she single-handedly developed grew to such an extent that Verner hired a secretary to help administer it. Verner's national acclaim and professional savvy won her contracts to produce drawings of famous sites outside of Charleston, including a monument to modern capitalism, New York's Rockefeller Center, and a national shrine to the past, George Washington's home at Mount Vernon. She also received two honorary doctorates for her work, from the Universities of South Carolina and North Carolina, respectively.[97] Verner was not above commercializing her reputation and work, acting as spokeswoman for modern ventures ranging from life insurance to Florida real estate and lecturing across the country.[98] Likewise, more than any other Charleston artist of her day, Verner took advantage of modern technology to mass-produce her images. She recognized the reproductive possibilities of her medium and ordered thousands of copies of her most popular prints in postcard form, which she in turn sold for profit in the city's upscale hotels, boutiques, bookshops, and tearooms.[99] At the same time, aware of the economic and legal ramifications of her copyrighted images, Verner hired a lawyer to regulate uses of her compositions by the growing tourism market of the 1930s.[100]

Despite her professional gains, Elizabeth Verner was keenly aware that she would always be something of an outsider in Charleston's elite white social circles. No matter the economic success she or her father before her enjoyed, no matter how enthusiastically she toed the party line on preserving a particular race- and class-based version of Charleston's past, Verner was engaged in an uphill battle. She would never share in the privilege of Charleston's oldest families, whose descendants, bearing names such as Heyward, Pinckney, Ravenel, and Drayton, filled both the leadership and the rank-and-file posts in the city's growing cultural organizations. For instance, she would never be asked to join that most socially elite cultural organization of the interwar period, the Society for the Preservation of Negro Spirituals, whose roster comprised a roll call of these old-line former slave-owning families. And yet the Spirituals Society published four of her illustrations in its 1931 literary monument to the region's history and people, *The Carolina Low-Country*.[101] Professionally, these elites acknowledged Verner's considerable artistic contributions to the civic mythmaking process. Her claims to ancient Charleston ladyhood, however, could only reach so far—and could only be convincing, ultimately, to outsiders unschooled in the rigidities of Charleston's white social hierarchy.

Verner attempted to abide by elite customs, such as maintaining an acceptable period of mourning after her second husband's death—"These black clothes are hard to wear but Charleston wouldn't understand my not wearing them"[102]—but mere custom-adherence did not translate into a new social status. In what must have been a difficult moment of confession and defeat, in 1935 Verner noted this intractable situation in her personal journal: "The social lines [in Charleston] are clearly marked but they are lines of blood and breeding and have nothing to do with bank accounts. A bank account is very valuable . . . but it does not secure an invitation to a party no matter tho' it were a bank account with 10 figures if it brings no letters of introduction with it." And yet, in the same pages, the artist wrote lovingly of the city's eccentric older aristocratic women and mused wistfully, "When I am an old lady I want to be a Charleston old lady."[103] Clearly, Verner herself was conflicted about the limits and possibilities of her identification with Old Charleston.

Fortunately, the art-buying clientele who expanded Verner's own bank account did not necessarily master the nuances of Charleston's complex social order. Each tourist season, visitors streamed into the artist's studio and the area hotels, boutiques, gift shops, and tearooms where she exhibited her works to purchase a piece of the alluring "Old Charleston" they had come to consume—in this case, in the form of an etching, print, or pastel created by a real Charleston native. In buying Verner's art, tourists participated in a kind of economy of historical memory—owning an image informed by the artist's memory that in turn served to fix the visitor's memory of Charleston.

Elizabeth O'Neill Verner, in the courtyard of her studio, depicting in picturesque pastel one of the local flower women whose images were central to the artist's business and to the iconography of historic Charleston. From the Collections of the South Carolina Historical Society.

In a rather typical exchange between artist and tourist, for example, a visitor from New York wrote Verner in 1937: "It was my first visit [to Charleston], but the memory shall remain as green as your oaks. May I ask you to choose a bit of Charleston — for the enclosed check — and mail [it] to me?"[104] Verner's commercial success, even in the depths of the Depression, attests to the artist successfully associating herself with the romantic entity called "Historic Charleston."

The support of key Renaissance figures further enhanced Verner's claims to being a representative of "romantic and historic" Charleston. The advocacy of Alice Smith, whose position as the artistic embodiment of aristocratic Charleston went unchallenged, lent an air of authenticity to Verner's status among visitors. Likewise, Charleston writer DuBose Heyward credited Verner with producing an intimate and authentic vision of their native city. Her work, he argued, was more than mere "atmosphere"—it was suggestive of the real "glamour and faded aroma of the past." Heyward, Charleston's quasi-official public spokesperson of the 1920s and 1930s and a descendant of one of the most elite Low Country families, commented of Verner, "Only an artist who shares the traditions that form the spiritual background of his locale can hope to capture this illusive element. It is the hallmark of genuine autochthonous art."[105] In 1928, Heyward even selected Verner to provide local-color etchings for the special Charleston edition of his best-selling novel, *Porgy*. Six years later, for the introduction to the catalog of a Verner exhibit in Boston, Heyward provided his imprimatur yet again: "There is a quality to the etchings of Elizabeth O'Neill Verner that possesses the power to evoke an extraordinary response in one who knows the city intimately. They contain a certain element that cannot be contained by the hackneyed 'atmosphere.'"[106] Such commendations surely reinforced the artist's professional standing and validation among tourists. Elizabeth Verner may not have shared bloodlines with the city's most elite, but she invoked and actively promoted the elite conception of Charleston's physical beauty, historical worth, and racial hierarchy. In Charleston in the 1920s and 1930s, that was a crucial first step toward both belonging—and selling.

Verner's published writings also emboldened her professional reputation as a representative of the "real" Charleston. In her 1939 magnum opus, a collection of essays and etchings titled *Prints and Impressions of Charleston*, the artist described for her reading public the deep feelings of connection and personal memory that overwhelmed her while she etched various sites in her hometown. As she guided her knife into the metal plate, Verner ruminated about the "memories from earliest childhood associated with the spot" she chose to depict: "the people who have lived there, the stories passed on seep through; in time the house itself begins to speak, to tell amazing things."[107] She acknowledged the formative and often cathartic power over remembrance in her art production: "Now how can I know when I have finished [an etching] whether the tales the house has told me are fact or fancy. People who care too much about absolute fact must be fearfully unhappy; I want to be happy when I have finished an etching, for an etching is a labor of love."[108]

Verner articulated the voice of a woman claiming the ability to hear Charleston's stories, as well as the privilege to reproduce and represent its historical memories. In a poem published in a local paper, for example, Verner rhapsodized comically about better times:

> Do you remember the parties of an ante bellum day,
> When everyone was happy and you didn't have to pay? . . .
> Do you remember the feeling of being invited out
> To enjoy yourself alone, like everyone about,
> With plenty of provisions free to all the guests who came,
> And cards and pencils furnished and not fifty cents the game?
> . . . But oh! for one more party of the ante bellum time,
> When everyone was happy and you didn't bring a dime![109]

In her 1941 *Mellowed by Time: A Charleston Notebook*, Verner reinforced this position, citing her dedication to Charleston as an important requirement for her claiming the city as her own, thus overcoming her family's short historical association with the place. "What has caused this deep-rooted devotion to it is hard to define. Age and tradition are obvious reasons, but it is more complex than that," Verner observed. "Too many whose roots were transplanted here, as were my own, share this passion for the city. Three generations is too short a time to have lived here to count, if tradition be the only criterion."[110] Importantly, in positing affection for Charleston as a viable means of attaining social legitimacy, Verner offered her readers the possibility of belonging as well.

In the same way that Verner shaped a public persona for herself, she sifted through fantasy and reality — memory and fact — to construct mythical representations of Charleston. Although her etchings have been read by some critics as important social history documents, Verner herself warned against such an approach: "Artists and historians are diametrically opposed in the approach to life," she cautioned. "An historian is essentially a dealer in facts while the whole training of an artist is in the realm of fancy."[111] Urged on by her preservationist instincts, Verner recorded her city's architectural traits, selectively editing out evidence of the modern — streetcars, telephone poles, electrical wires, automobiles, the port — and stressing instead its ancient and, in her opinion, timeless character. "It is one of my deepest regrets," she lamented in 1939, "that I did not begin etching until 1923, for by that time so much which to my generation represented Charleston had disappeared. I would prefer having etched the Charleston of my childhood, with its horse-drawn streetcars"[112] and "the 'ground-nut cake woman' fanning her tooth-some ware with a palmetto fan."[113] Occasionally, Verner entirely reworked scenes to evoke a longed-for previous condition that she considered more picturesque. In *King Street*, for example, she envisioned from recollections the neighborhood between Broad and Tradd streets "before it was transformed from slums to prim little residences with glimpses of newly made gardens seen through iron gates."[114]

Informed by historical memory, Verner created a visual map of Charleston in such popular prints as *In the Bend of Church Street*, *Looking up Meeting Street*, *St. Philip's Portico*, and *Pineapple Gates*. Highlighting Charleston's buildings, their massive columns, piazzas, slanted roofs, and intricate wrought-iron detail, Verner's etchings reveal the artist's dedication to promoting an image of the city as genteel and aristocratic. Time's presence pervades each image. A crack in a wall, a horse-drawn carriage rattling over uneven cobblestone sidewalks, the long shadows cast by a massive live oak, a tilting carriage post create a sense of Charleston as a place of permanence, tradition, and history. To Verner, these antiquated elements were not evidence of the city's contemporary poverty or dilapidation. Instead, echoing DuBose Heyward's characterization of Charleston as "an ancient and beautiful city that time had forgotten before it destroyed," Verner considered this wear and tear a symbol of Charleston's "ancient grandeur."[115] "Better than the walls to me have been the shadows they cast," she explained in her writings, "better than the trees, their pattern on uneven flagstone." To her credit, Verner acknowledged her immersion in a world of illusion and her fetishization of ruin and romanticism, noting: "It is hard to separate the substance from the shadow, the legend from the fact. Often, to me, the legend is truer than the fact."[116] In this light, Verner's pieces can be considered in part a form of personal wish fulfillment. "Although so much of the old order has inevitably passed," she mused in 1939, "the patina of the city must be far more beautiful today than it ever could have been in its pristine glory."[117]

Verner extended this tendency toward mythmaking to her depictions of African Americans, finding in their "humble dwellings" something romantic and "amusingly individual."[118] In *Do-As-You-Choose Alley*, for example, she offers her curious white audience a glimpse of Charleston's "exotic" African American world. Emerging from her etcher's needle, the alley's black community occupies a quaint collection of picturesque and ramshackle shanties. Verner reduces the infamous lane—a place Charleston police officers would not enter at night—to just another charming city vista, without overt commentary on the very real plight of the city's African American population and their socially destabilizing potential.

Verner depicted African American Charlestonians with such frequency that they became a central component of her artistic reputation and her successful business. In most instances, her African American figures underscored her conception of racial hierarchy and "ancient grandeur." And yet she was not a mere reactionary who invoked the exaggerated visual vocabulary of the minstrel-based popular culture of her day. African Americans were, in the artist's own words, "an integral part of the beauty of Charleston,"[119] and her characterizations ranged from the paternalistic and picturesque to the realistic and dignified.

In most of her etchings, Verner's African American figures functioned as anonymous and quaint props that, like a mansion's balustrade or a church's steeple, contribute to the artist's goal of rendering picturesqueness. While she took great care to depict with precision the most minute of architectural details, the textured brick or the panels of a door, Verner typically rendered her urban black characters as featureless types — street hucksters, market workers, domestic servants, or female flower sellers. These were figures whose bodies merged with the lines of the buildings around them, whose faces were blurred, or whose physical proportions were made miniature in relation to the overwhelming majesty of the surrounding architecture. "The negro," Verner proclaimed in 1929, "is Nature's child; one paints him as readily and fittingly into the landscape as a tree or marsh."[120] As the title of her commercially popular print *In the Shadow of St. Michael's* implies, the African American woman balancing a basket of flowers on her head under the portico of Charleston's famous church cannot be considered separately from the monument to white planter society that literally frames her. She is both physically and figuratively within the dappled shadow of the culture that produced St. Michael's Church, under the presumed protection and limitations of its paternalistic traditions. This print was so effective at conveying a certain image of Charleston that the chamber of commerce, of which Verner was a member, presented it to President Franklin Delano Roosevelt as a souvenir of his visit to the city in 1935.[121]

In a few instances, however, Verner depicted the individuality and humanity of her black subjects, as in the keenly executed, well-defined portraits of *Cyrus, Sue of Combahee, The Brown Singer,* and *The Reverend Jenkins.* In each example, Verner's lines convey a very real sense of the sitter's personality and story. It is important to note, however, that only the latter two images depict

Elizabeth O'Neill Verner's *In the Shadow of St. Michael's*, circa 1930, etching on paper, 10 × 7¾ inches. In black and white, Verner displays the attitudes of Charleston's white elites: the oldest and most revered Episcopal church is rendered in great detail, while a black flower vendor in front of it is nearly faceless. Collection of the Greenville County Museum of Art, Museum purchase.

the reality of Charleston's thriving middle-class community and were not commercially reproduced. In the end, Verner, like her old-line counterparts, remained committed to presenting a selective and one-sided rendering of the local black population.

A staple image of this sort from Verner's visual idiom was the African American woman who sold flowers door to door and on the steps of the post office on Broad Street. Verner passed a great deal of time sketching these women. She claimed to know of the true poverty of some of her flower women models. "I had visited her cabin," Verner explained, and yet the artist felt no pity for her subject because "the face which I was trying to paint was carved deep around the eyes and mouth with lines of contentment. She had not complained; she seemed perfectly happy."[122] In the mid-1930s, Verner shifted from black-and-white etching to the vividly romantic shades of pastels and focused almost exclusively on depicting Charleston's "colorful" street peddlers. In the days of early grocery chains and booming department stores, these vendors successfully hearkened back to the simpler days that Verner and her patrons sought on Charleston's cobblestoned streets.

As an artist, Verner controlled the manner in which these women would be considered and remembered by her clientele; in 1944, Verner's influence over her subjects extended to include supervising who among them would be able to ply their trade. During the high point of the spring tourist season, the city received a series of complaints about noise, blocked sidewalks, litter, fighting, and overly aggressive sales tactics among the flower women who hawked their wares in the heart of the historic district. Local politicians, fearful of losing visitor dollars, considered a proposal to relocate the women from the post office sidewalk to the marketplace. Ironically, had the same city leaders who were so preoccupied with the presentation of "historic" Charleston actually studied more of Charleston's past, they might have discovered such a relocation plan to be a false solution and that aggressive sales tactics were, ironically, as historic as the city's architecture. In the 24 September 1772 issue of the *South Carolina Gazette*, a traveling Englishman complained of similar conduct among female African American peddlers in the "lower Market, where . . . constantly resort a great number of loose, idle, disorderly negro women, who are seated from morn 'til night, and buy and sell on their own accounts, what they please, in order to pay their wages, and get as much for themselves as they can."[123] In an undated manuscript written by Verner, the artist claimed the embattled flower women called upon her for help: "Bit by bit they poured out their misery. 'We can't sell no more flowers after next Wednesday.' . . . I promised (to help) and drove on." Elizabeth Verner turned politician and entered the debate. Perhaps these women struck a sympathetic chord within—here, too, were women working with the beauty of the Low Country, trying to support themselves and make their way in a changing world, as Verner herself had done (and was doing). Verner asserted the flower women's tourist appeal, not to mention their centrality in her own artistic affairs. "I wanted the flower women because I painted them and I needed them as models," Verner admitted. At the same time, she was well aware of their public-relations appeal for the city: "I pointed out [to the mayor] that Charleston had more free advertising in nationally known magazines than any other city in the country and that in every picture a flower woman was strategically placed to give local color."[124] Verner mobilized fellow Garden Club members in a successful protest. In response to this pressure, city officials endowed the artist with the authority to regulate the presence of the flower women on the streets through the issuing of a limited number of "good behavior" vendor licenses that the artist distributed from her studio at 38 Tradd Street.[125] "But now they think of me as their policeman, not as their protector," the artist lamented. "But I do not mind for they have given me so much."[126]

As their "supervisor," Verner also exercised some regulatory power over the physical appearance of the flower women, when, under the auspices of the Garden Club, she gave each woman a colorful "bit of pretty cloth" to wear on their heads.[127] Unfortunately, no evidence exists in the historical record to determine how the flower women themselves felt about this practice, but the local newspaper reveals some white dismay over this level of aesthetic control as "unnatural" or even comic. "Frankly," the News and Courier editorialized, "we don't like the idea of compulsory head bandannas. . . . Unless adopted by the Negroes themselves in their own original manner, items of costume suggested by the white folks have a way of looking out of place. . . . It reminds us of the guidebooks for certain European communities that have overplayed the tourist bait with their 'natives in colorful costume dancing in the market-place.'"[128] A letter to the News and Courier, written in faux Gullah speech and signed "Flower Woman's Friend," concurred: "We flower 'oomen wants to sell flower een ting, we dunkuh bout look like no befo' de wah picture."[129] Verner responded that the bandannas were merely a goodwill gesture, an incentive to induce the flower women to cooperate with the new ordinance. "The last thing the Garden Club of Charleston would wish," she defended, "is that these flower women be put in artificial costume."[130] Regardless of the motivation, the ordinance and the dispersal of colored head wraps to the flower women provided Verner with considerable control over the way in which these "local color" women could labor, and over the way they were represented in the Charleston landscape.

Throughout her life, Elizabeth Verner tried to cast off her outsider status through self-fashioning and artistic expression. While she remained on its social margins, Charleston's elite white society afforded Verner professional respect. Likewise, she achieved commercial success by convincing the tourists who comprised the core of her business that she, and by extension her artistic vision, represented authentic Old Charleston. Thus, just as consumers vicariously participated in the myth by purchasing art, Verner participated by producing art. Through a mix of fact and fantasy, of sincere chauvinism and market savvy that mirrored the mythmaking, devotion, and commercialism at the core of Charleston's elite white cultural productions of the 1920s and 1930s, Elizabeth Verner carved out a niche for herself in the city's public life. Like Smith's, Verner's images remain a staple part of Charleston's visual canon today.[131] "It is the mission of the artist," Verner wrote in 1939, "to make the untrained eye look at what it has always seen, for looking implies the act of will."[132] As an "act of will," Elizabeth O'Neill Verner and Alice Ravenel Huger Smith trained their eyes to see only certain aspects of Charleston that complemented their views on modernization, race, and preservation. Informed by a strong sense of historical memory, they contrived images based on their selective gazes that helped define Charleston's visual and historic identity in the years between the world wars. Smith's and Verner's personal lives, artwork, and public careers point to larger lessons beyond Charleston's borders. Public identities, and indeed history itself, cannot be separated from the politics of representation.

CHAPTER THREE

History Touches Legend in Charleston

THE LITERARY PACKAGING OF AMERICA'S MOST HISTORIC CITY

outh-Baiting' from now on is going to be more of a dangerous sport than formerly," Charleston's literary leaders declared in 1921. They staked their claim in the inaugural issue of the *Year Book of the Poetry Society of South Carolina*. Determined to defend their region's cultural vitality against long-standing critics such as H. L. Mencken, whom the Society likened to "a sort of literary General Sherman," a small group of aspiring writers and poets founded the Poetry Society of South Carolina (pssc) in October 1920.[1] An early manifestation of Southern literary regionalism, the Society was a starting point for the successful careers of several local authors whose publications reintroduced many Americans to Charleston and its people. The pssc helped successfully resuscitate, for a time, the city's former antebellum status as a cultural center, where men of letters and ideas, such as William Gilmore Simms, Henry Timrod, and Paul Hamilton Hayne and their *Russell's Magazine*, enjoyed national influence.[2] The poetry and novels of the pssc's leading writers, natives DuBose Heyward, Josephine Pinckney, and Beatrice Witte Ravenel and Northern-born residents Hervey Allen and John Bennett, reveal this common mission, as well as an urge to recall the past in print. A powerful historical memory shaped the published works of these individuals, most evidently in their characterizations of the region's agrarian commitments, its racial arrangements, and its relationship with modernity. By adding their history-laden expressions into the cultural mix at the very moment that other elite groups were doing likewise, Charleston's most productive literati effectively helped fashion a romanticized idea of the city as a place where, in the words of American poet Amy Lowell, "History touches legend."[3]

Although the PSSC was a pioneering organization in the cultural revival known as the Southern Literary Renaissance, its legacy and import have been largely overshadowed by the literary outpouring of the famed Vanderbilt Agrarians and authors such as William Faulkner and Eudora Welty.[4] Recent scholarship, most notably in the form of writer biographies and reissues of important novels from the period, has begun once more the work of recuperating Charleston's literary reputation.[5] Certainly, some significant works emerged from the PSSC group in the 1920s and 1930s, such as DuBose Heyward's best-selling 1925 novel, *Porgy*, and Julia Peterkin's 1929 Pulitzer Prize winner, *Scarlet Sister Mary*. And Charlestonians were in contact—even in competition—with the leading figures of the larger movement.[6] And yet, while uneasy about the potential encroachments of the modern age, such as industrialization and big government, most of Charleston's writers did not experience the degree of alienation, disgust, and disruption evident in the works of their counterparts elsewhere in the South.[7]

In order to make sense of the world around them, Charlestonians did not plumb the depths of their psyches or rebel against established literary styles. Rather, they seemed to believe that the salve for modernity's angst could be found in the way elite white Low Country South Carolinians had traditionally approached life rooted in the sanctity of land, family, and racial order. Instead of casting aside their community membership to achieve a kind of modernist, artistic distance from their literary subject matter, these elite white writers asserted their right to speak for Charleston *because* of their intimate associations with the city. PSSC members' overriding sense of belonging to their world and their commitment to continuity convinced them that theirs were the region's authentic cultural voices. This parochialism and intellectual complacency also guaranteed, as Michael O'Brien has argued, that Charleston's writers and poets of the interwar period were largely incapable of making significant original contributions to the history of ideas.[8] This may indeed be an accurate estimation based on the definition of "contribution" in intellectual history circles; for cultural historians, however, these poems and novels provide a rich opportunity to explore how one group's successful literary articulation of historical memory became the basis of a selective civic identity that claimed to speak for the entire community.

Charleston's literary impulse of the 1920s and 1930s was part of a regionalist movement of writers and artists in various parts of the nation who attempted to define themselves, their homelands, and their country in the tumultuous years from the end of the First World War through the Great Depression. Rooted in the late-nineteenth and early-twentieth-century local-color and folklore tradition established by writers such as Mark Twain and Mary Austin, regionalist literature sought to celebrate America's diverse local character and to elevate the lives of the "folk." Such work often critiqued the cultural costs that accompanied the modern quest for a standardized and streamlined society. From the Chicago poems of Carl Sandburg, to the prairie novels of Mari Sandoz and Willa Cather, to John McGinnis's Dallas-based *Southwest Review*, writers and poets across America considered regionalism a two-pronged opportunity—to chronicle and celebrate local culture and to offer an arts-based political solution to the problems of modernity. As historian Robert Dorman has argued in his sweeping examination of the American regionalist movement, proponents of this school of thought envisioned the region as "the utopian means for reconstructing the nationalizing, homogenizing, urban-industrial complex, redirecting it toward an accommodation with local folkways and local environments."[9]

Charleston's writers and poets shared with their regionalist counterparts a love of local traditions and environment, as well as a disdain for the mechanized and potentially alienating forces of modernization. Yet, with the exception of the hyperagrarian, pro–states' rights writings of Herbert Ravenel Sass, most Charleston writers did not consider regionalism an explicit political intervention bent on reconstructing America; nor did visions of an egalitarian utopia entice them. Unlike literary regionalists elsewhere in the nation, Charleston's poets and writers did not embrace democratic pluralism or populism as potential solutions to America's problems; instead, they celebrated in words the city's tradition-bound racial hierarchy. While Charleston in the 1920s and 1930s was by no means the polyglot immigrant hub of New York or Chicago, it was home to an array of ethnically identified peoples, including Greeks, Germans, Irish, Italians, and Jews, which added diversity to the city's majority Anglo-French-American and African American populations.[10] References to "ethnic" Charlestonians, however, are rarely found in the literature of the interwar period; where they exist, the image is generally derogatory. Likewise, when middle- and working-class white Southerners appear in the works of Charleston writers, they are generally depicted as corrupt and racist, providing stark contrast to elite white characters, who are presented as genteel, paternalistic, and, above all, "understanding" of the plight and nature of African Americans. While some writers, notably Heyward, Peterkin, and Bennett, exhibited a deep sensitivity toward African American culture and others, such as Pinckney, revealed momentary cracks in the generally seamless white aristocratic surface, none wrote to defend democracy. Rather, their works collectively preserved an elitist status quo, echoing a foundational conception of Charleston as a place of order and romance that was not significantly different from the world represented in the novels and poems of their nineteenth-century literary ancestors, such as William Gilmore Simms and Henry Timrod. They also did not veer far from the conventional depictions of turn-of-the-century writers such as Henry James, who rhapsodized that "the Past, that of vanished order," endured in the city;[11] or Owen Wister, whose very popular 1906 novel *Lady Baltimore* presented a genteel Charleston trapped in antebellum amber, where proper widows ruled over fiercely loyal servants, lamented change, and policed family manners and marriages as they embroidered during calling hours.[12] By keeping within the acceptable boundaries of literary tradition, the city's white poets and writers focused their gazes selectively on the history, landscape, and quality of human interaction that they believed lay at the heart of the region's character.

There were occasional departures from this norm. DuBose Heyward exhibited brief soul-searching about the correctness of tradition in his Civil War novel *Peter Ashley*. Likewise, his portrayal of working-class black Charlestonians in *Porgy* was considered radical by many critics in 1925, evidence perhaps of a white modernist fascination with the black "other." Similarly, Julia Peterkin's representation of African American life on her Lange Syne plantation, forty miles from Columbia, South Carolina, has been described by one scholar as a kind of "Gullah-inflected modernism." Peterkin was a PSSC member for only the brief period of 1925 to 1931, and she worked largely in isolation from her Charleston peers. Nonetheless, her treatment of black folk culture and linguistic and religious traditions situate her early works as a "bridge" between the South Carolina literary scene and the Harlem Renaissance.[13] Finally, Josephine Pinckney's poem "The Misses Poar Drive to Church" is an ironic and humorous treatment of the strength of custom among the city's patricians, as is her nuanced 1945 novel, *Three O'Clock Dinner*. In it, Pinckney provides a gentle bit deep critique of an old-line family's encounter with modernizing Charleston. Although the author claimed her novel was a "social comedy [in] the quaint tradition," critics and audiences recognized it as much more.[14] The *New York Times*, for example, applauded Pinckney's transcending mere regional concerns: "The fact that [her characters] are Southern is unimportant compared to the fact that they are human."[15] The Literary Guild chose to highlight the novel as a main selection, which sold in the hundreds of thousands, and MGM Studios purchased its movie rights, though the film version was never produced.[16] For the most part, however, Charleston writers working in the 1920s and 1930s avoided serious analysis of their culture and city. Indeed, Heyward best articulated his group's civic understanding in his famous opening lines of *Porgy*: Charleston was above all "an ancient, beautiful city that time had forgotten before it destroyed."[17]

Despite the lack of hard-hitting intellectualism in their writings, members of the so-called Charleston Group were serious about their literary endeavors and, most important, enjoyed varying measures of national professional success throughout the 1920s and 1930s. They published novels and volumes of poetry with major New York publishing houses such as Harper & Brothers and the MacMillan Company. They benefited from a brief post–World War I vogue in poetry that allowed them to print their verse in notable literary anthologies and journals, including *Braithwaite's Anthology*, *Contemporary Verse*, the *Bookman* and *Poetry*. National magazines, such as *Harper's*, *New Republic*, *Women's Home Companion*, the *Atlantic Monthly*, and *National Geographic*, carried their short stories and articles. The Literary Guild, which along with the Book-of-the-Month Club helped shape the tastes of the American reading public through their book membership program, designated certain Charleston novels as literary selections of the month.[18] Likewise, several novels were rewritten as plays and staged in major theaters throughout the country—some even optioned by Hollywood. The Charleston Group also acted as the publisher of works of major living poets through the annual *Year Book of the Poetry Society of South Carolina* and sponsored lectures in Charleston by some of the most renowned and even scandalous literary figures of their day, including Amy Lowell, Carl Sandburg, John Crowe Ransom, Henry Seidel Canby, Robert Frost, Stephen Vincent Benet, and Gertrude Stein. By 1932, Charleston's literary lights, in particular Heyward and Pinckney, carried enough artistic clout to host a convention of the biggest and brightest names in Southern literature in the city. Certainly, by the 1930s, the commercial success of several Charleston writers and the concomitant artistic reputation of the city had been re-established.

"The Town Is Beautiful with the Past": The Poetry Society of South Carolina[19]

The Poetry Society of South Carolina grew out of family connections, shared friendships, and literary interests among several prominent Charlestonians and three individuals who were not native residents of the city. Throughout 1919 and 1920, Charleston-born DuBose Heyward, a dissatisfied, thirty-five-year-old insurance agent and would-be poet, and Pittsburgh-born Hervey Allen, a thirty-year-old instructor of English at the local military school for boys and recently published poet, gathered on Wednesday nights at the Legare Street home of John and Susan Smythe Bennett.[20] John Bennett, the author of the acclaimed children's book *Master Skylark*, was born in Ohio in 1865 but in 1902 married into an old-line Charleston family. An active student of local folklore and history and a supporter of the city's many cultural institutions, Bennett quickly became an "adopted Southerner" and an ardent Charleston enthusiast. More than twenty years older than Heyward and Allen, Bennett served as a literary sounding board for the young men, offering them supper and evenings before the fire and poring over their poems with a professional eye.[21] During the course of these weekly literary "fang-fests," as Heyward called them, the three men developed a strong working relationship, which became the driving force behind the Poetry Society.[22] Meanwhile, a group of women from the men's social circle, including Helen von Kolnitz Hyer, Josephine Pinckney, and Elizabeth Miles, met regularly to discuss ideas and poetry at 7 Gibbes Street, the home shared by Isabelle Heyward and Laura Bragg, the Massachusetts-born director of the Charleston Museum. Bragg, a well-read intellectual, was in correspondence with leaders in the modern American poetry movement and exposed the women in her informal "salon" to the writings of some of the nation's contemporary lights, including Carl Sandburg, Vachel Lindsay, and Amy Lowell.[23] As friends, and in some cases relatives, the two groups of aspiring poets quickly recognized their mutual interests. Believing that "culture in the South is not merely an *ante bellum* tradition, but an instant, vital force, awaiting only opportunity to burst into artistic expression," they formed the Poetry Society in late 1920.[24]

The leaders of the PSSC realized that to revive the literary reputation of Charleston, as well as the cultural life of the South, they first had to cultivate an appreciative local audience who could identify personally with the group's endeavors. Likewise, as products of an insulated and self-obsessed community preoccupied with manners and caste, they were also well aware that their public actions required sanction from within their own social circle. In a city known more for its entrenched genteel parochialism than for its heady intellectual climate, this translated into the creation of an organization that was, as one member once described it, "one-tenth poetry and nine-tenths society."[25]

The scion of two of Charleston's oldest and most elite white families, Heyward understood the necessity of appealing to white Charleston's ego and value system when he became the Society's first secretary. His Heyward

An Ohio native who married into an old-line
Charleston family, author John Bennett mentored
DuBose Heyward and was a leader of the Poetry
Society of South Carolina. From the Collections
of the South Carolina Historical Society.

ancestors arrived in Charles Town in 1672, two years after the founding of
the fledgling colony during the reign of Charles II. Over time, his relatives
included a lord proprietor, king's officers, a soldier in the Yamassee uprising
of 1715, an early rice planter, a series of wealthy land- and slave-owners, and
Confederate officers. His great-great-great-grandfather, Thomas Heyward,
was a signer of the Declaration of Independence whose home, known as
the Heyward-Washington House, became a rallying point for historic preservationists in the late 1920s. On the DuBose side, Heyward claimed the
blood of seventeenth-century Huguenot settlers and succeeding generations
of prominent plantation owners and soldiers, including Revolutionary War

hero General Francis Marion.[26] Heyward used his social position to build up the pssc. He assured those receiving a letter of invitation that it was addressed "to a limited number only," who would have a hand in the vital job of "preserving the cultural heritage of the past" while enjoying the "stimulating intercourse" of renowned, and, he was quick to point out, English-speaking, poets and critics. Not all members had to be active poets, Heyward noted, but they had to be civic-minded and enlightened individuals "interested, in the broadest sense of the word, in furthering the art and appreciation of poetry in the community by bringing here in readings and critical addresses the best practitioners of the art." Admission to such lofty entertainment was "strictly confined to members of the Society," which would number only 250 persons, the seating capacity of the South Carolina Hall. To increase its exclusivity quotient further, the pssc established annual dues at the rather high rate of five dollars per year.[27] In no time, the membership list filled with the names of the city's most elite white families; belonging to the Society became, in the words of its first vice president, John Bennett, the "thing to do."[28]

To attract members, the Society drew heavily from the same well-established institutional, cultural, and familial networks as their peer organizations, the Society for the Preservation of Old Dwellings, the Charleston Etchers' Club, and the Society for the Preservation of Negro Spirituals. The same names — Frost, Smythe, Mazyck, Huger, Deas, Heyward, Pinckney, Smith, Pringle, Simons, Stoney, Waring — that formed the social register of Charleston blue bloods formed the backbone of the pssc. To ensure this elevated position within Charleston society, the pssc often elected as its (largely honorary) president a member from a prominent old-line family who enjoyed social clout and ties with the professional community but who rarely exhibited poetic aspirations. From its first president, Broad Street attorney Frank Frost, through newspaper editors Thomas R. Waring (*Charleston Evening Post*) and William Watts Ball (*News & Courier*), to architect Albert Simons, the Society's first decade of presidents were sometimes confused by their appointment to this allegedly literary assembly. While introducing John Crowe Ransom, the inaugural speaker for the 1928 – 29 season, Simons quipped, "It is indeed an almost overwhelming honor to greet you as President, though for what good reason I should be President, I am somewhat at a loss to understand. Being a Poetry Society, however, I suppose one should not expect rational interpretation and account for it on the grounds of poetic justice."[29]

This politic strategy resulted in an aesthetically conservative organization whose members were generally disinterested in writing and critiquing poetry, much less in engaging with the experimental trends of abstraction and free verse popular in American and European literary circles. Shortly after the Society's founding, the majority of the membership grew bored by meetings dedicated to poetry reading and criticism. Thus, in 1922, the PSSC created a small "study group" as a forum for "the writing, study, and practical criticism of verse" for the handful of members who considered themselves serious poets.[30] The PSSC's intellectual leaders—Hervey Allen, DuBose Heyward, and Josephine Pinckney—exhibited a willingness to address modern concerns over language and form, yet they did not wholeheartedly adopt modernist fashions in their own compositions. Although it possessed at its outset a potential for rebellion and far-reaching literary impact, the PSSC was part of what Daniel Singal has accurately described as a broader regionalist movement characterized by "genteel amateurism" that was "unable to free itself from the intellectual underpinnings that had controlled late nineteenth-century southern writing."[31] The PSSC could be compared to similar organizations in Richmond and Norfolk whose literary efforts were, in Singal's words, "more the last hurrah of the Tidewater culture than the actual advent of Modernism."[32] The membership's essentially traditional tastes—its affection for conventional lyric form and content—were in evidence in the program of and response to the PSSC's first season.

At its inaugural meeting on 25 January 1921, a crowd of about 200 persons listened intently as John Bennett, the town's established author and by this time a stately gray-haired gentleman in his fifties, outlined the state of contemporary American poetry and the tenets of the radical "New Poetry" movement.[33] Tellingly, the so-called New Poetry movement was, by 1921, over a decade old, but to the Charleston audience it was an innovation, and a potentially threatening one, that needed to be explained and demystified if the PSSC were to survive.[34] Bennett consoled the assembly, "Be at peace; they [the new poets] have found nothing new." Instead, he argued, the best of the new practitioners merely dealt in a fresh manner with the time-honored themes of love and tragedy that "have been the heritage of man from age to age since the beginning of time." At the same time, Bennett did not condone a wholesale retreat to established poetic traditions. He assailed the "verbose, academic, sentimental, insincere" poetry of the Victorian period, characterizing it as "like its furniture, void of taste, of beauty and of inspiration." And yet, in a literary world hastily discarding the past "and all its loveliness," Bennett warned his listeners to discriminate and to resist being seduced by the fashionable whims of a "loudly-trumpeted" revolutionary troubadour generally lacking in substance. He summed up the hopes of his fellow Society founders when he urged moderation and tolerance among its members: "Let us therefore be supremely careful not to forget the old while listening with open-hearted welcome to the voices of the new song." Finally, in a nativistic and Anglophilic appeal common among American literary regionalists of the period, Bennett concluded his talk with impassioned praise for the power of the English language to unite America, "a strange country, made of many strange people and races and nations as mingled together." "ALL the OLD POETS were NOT beautiful," Bennett declared; "ALL the NEW Poets are NOT Great; But ENGLISH POESY shall not perish while Two Great nations [the United States and Great Britain] SING."[35]

A *Charleston Evening Post* editorial by future Society president Thomas Waring welcoming the establishment of the PSSC echoed Bennett's sense of the importance of striking a balance between an appreciation for the old and an openness to the new in poetry: "The 'Imagists,' the 'Symbolists' and the writers of 'Free Verse' have been so widely advertised that they have entirely overshadowed the large number of sincere and talented writers who have been interpreting the spirit of today in the older, more musical forms. It will be the aim of the Poetry Society of South Carolina to introduce the work of this more conservative element, and at the same time to give the public an opportunity of deciding for themselves their attitude towards the new schools."[36]

The Society made good on its call for tolerance of poetry done well in whatever form, old or new, by hosting during its first season an impressive range of national literary figures, from the avant-garde to the mainstream. Beginning in February 1921 with a visit from Chicago poet Carl Sandburg, the man whom Bennett described as the "rudest of Radical," Charleston experienced a firsthand performance of "new poetry."[37] In typical understated fashion, the Society's *Year Book* commented that Sandburg's poetry reading, accompanied by his playing the guitar and singing "American ballads," as well as his "vivid personality," "aroused much healthy discussion and interest . . . [and] created a strong impression on his audience." In March, Harriet Monroe, editor of *Poetry*, one of the nation's leading journals of verse and a staunch supporter of the PSSC, spoke on "New Poetry." After two such evenings dedicated to the new, the Society's members were no doubt relieved to hear Jessie B. Rittenhouse, a founding member of the Poetry Society of America, present a lecture titled "Modern English and American Conservative Poets, the Personality and Work." As the *Year Book*'s editors noted, "While greatly interested in the radical poetry movement, Charleston looked forward to hearing Miss Rittenhouse lecture on the poets who write in an idiom with which the South is more familiar. Needless to say, Miss Rittenhouse made many friends for herself and her poetry."[38] And thus the pattern, attitude, and content of the PSSC was established—exposure to the new while embracing the familiar.

The PSSC attempted to cultivate a regionwide literary awakening through a variety of avenues, in particular its yearbooks. These annual publications contained poetry, editorials, commentary, news of membership activities, and Low Country illustrations by local artists and PSSC members such as Alice Smith, Alfred Hutty, John Bennett, and Elizabeth O'Neill Verner. Yearbooks also boasted advertisements for members' commercial works, such as Clelia McGowan's *Plantation Silhouettes and Other Poems*, Archibald Rutledge's novels "About the Real South," and Janie Screven Heyward's recitals of "the authentic dialect and folk lore of the Carolina Coast Negro."[39] Furthermore, to encourage poetic production, the Society offered prizes for the best poetry produced in an array of categories—from the local high school and college prizes, to the regional, including the Laura Bragg Prize for the best local color and the Southern Prize for works produced by "bona fide citizens" of the Southern states, to the quasi-international, namely, the $250 Blindman Prize, "open to any citizen of the United States and to any British subject speaking English as his or her native tongue."[40] Several major poets submitted works to these competitions. In 1923, for example, John Crowe Ransom's poem "Armageddon" beat runners-up Donald Davidson and William Alexander Percy to capture the Southern Prize. Tellingly, several prominent Society members considered Ransom's poetic depiction of a raucous encounter between Christ and Satan blasphemous and protested its promised publication in the 1923 yearbook. To resolve "this rather absurd and serious dilemma," the PSSC printed the poem in a separate limited-edition bibelot distributed to a select list of members and reviewers, "leaving," as Hervey Allen wrote President Thomas Waring, "both the Sadducees and the Bolsheviks happy."[41]

The Society's yearbooks were sent to all PSSC members and were also sold to locals and tourists in Charleston bookstores for fifty cents, but they had a wider intended audience as well. All Carnegie libraries, all South Carolina colleges, the state governor and legislature, most university libraries, major college English departments, publishing houses, select newspapers and magazines, literary figures, and other poetry societies throughout the country also received the yearbooks.[42] They served as a site for declaring publicly the PSSC's connectedness to the larger American community of letters. The yearbooks' savvy editors, for example, at times dedicated individual volumes to national literary powerhouses and patrons such as Harriet Monroe, Amy Lowell, and Mrs. Edward MacDowell, founder of the MacDowell Colony, an artists colony in Peterborough, New Hampshire.[43] Backed by such an effective mode of publicity, the Society also served as the model for the formation of several poetry societies in other Southern states, including Texas, Georgia, Maryland, Virginia, Florida, Louisiana, North Carolina, and Tennessee.[44]

From the outset, Charlestonians' impulse to organize the PSSC was motivated by a desire to defend the South's cultural potential from its detractors and to assert its rightful place in the national literary scene.[45] In an essay titled "The Worm Turns," in the inaugural yearbook (1921), for example, the organization launched a counterattack against H. L. Mencken's conception of the "Bozart" South. Written by Allen, the essay articulated two central themes of Charleston's literary regionalism: first, that the celebration and commemoration of the local was not sectional in nature but was rather a critical step toward the creation of a truly national culture; and second, that the promise of America's cultural future lay in the South.

Throughout its early years, the PSSC walked this fine line between regional and national interests. The ultimate goal of the Society was, after all, a regional revival and the resuscitation of the South's image in the eyes of the nation's cultural critics. Allen's essay, for example, asserted the literary and artistic potential of the South over that of other parts of the country, in particular the North and the West: "Despite the invasion of Northern industrialism, there is still a romance and a colorful life here which, if we have not written about it much, we love. . . . We predict that there is a literary future for the South when the cow-boy shall have been buried upon the lone prairie and the millionaire self-made hero of the industrial romance left for the admiration of Akronese."[46] To prove his point, Allen chronicled the South's contributions to national culture, including the writings of Poe and Twain, the Brer Rabbit tales, and African American spirituals and jazz music, proclaiming the region the only one in the country capable of producing a culture that was at once Southern and American. Likewise, in a statement hinting at the anti-immigrant rhetoric of the post–World War I period, he declared the South's relative lack of things foreign a boon for American arts and letters. "The North . . . is not producing anything characteristically Northern. The truth is, it is not homogeneous enough to do so," Allen contended. "Despite our color lines and our cleavages, which we notice do not grow better when shifted to the North, the South has been able to produce something peculiarly American, which no other section of the United States has been able to do, except a little corner of New England, Indiana and the now defunct western frontier."[47]

Although the Poetry Society presented itself as a vibrant vehicle for the creation of a new and "authentic" American culture, the poetry produced by its members betrayed their continued commitment to the picturesque elements of a past world as the perfect raw material for artistic expression. "Practically untouched by art, and within the memory of living men, the South has passed through three great phases replete with poetic material," the 1921 *Year Book* contended; "first, the colorful, romantic days 'before the war,' then the tragedies, the sacrifices, and the lifting courage of our rebirth, and now the surgent vital days of our own time, with their strong realism standing out in *bas relief* against a background of unbelievable color, charm and romance."[48] Thus, while poets and writers in other parts of the world, from T. S. Eliot to F. Scott Fitzgerald, were exploring man's internal self, Charleston poets were content to fix their collective gaze on the external world around them, depicting its history, natural life, legends, and local characters in uncritical fashion. Heyward scholar William Slavick associates this propensity for uncomplicated chauvinism and artistic convention with Charleston's tenacious social traditions and relative isolation from the challenges of modernizing America: "They were Charlestonians, and Charleston had substituted manners for education and art—particularly in its view of language. It rejected the new or foreign. It had not experienced the clash of values World War I, the New South and the Scopes Trial in nearby Dayton, Tennessee had provided the Vanderbilt community. Nothing changed so precipitously in Charleston as to become a crisis; nothing was so serious, complicated, or profound as what Faulkner saw in Yoknapatawpha, Tate in the Confederate Dead, and Ransom in the passage of life."[49]

Influenced by the strong presence of convention and manners, Charleston's poets directed their pens at representing, rather simplistically, what they considered to be the romantic character and historical drama of their region's past and present. In 1926, two articles written by Heyward, joined under the title "Contemporary Southern Poetry," appeared in one of the nation's most distinguished literary publications, the *Bookman*. With the success of the PSSC, Heyward became the virtual spokesman for the poetry revival in the South, and here he attempted to explain the South's, and particularly Charleston's, fixation on itself. "This tendency," he contended, "sprang from a traditional and almost passionate loyalty to environment, and the peculiarly haunting influence, at times almost hypnotic in its spell, of the landscape upon the temperament of the artist."[50] In addition to the region's natural beauty, its peculiar history of defeat created a conservative and discriminating generation of Southerners who grew to adulthood surrounded by the powerfully evocative remnants and ruins of their ancestors' vanishing way of life—their homes, their literature, their paintings: "Behind the garden walls and the shuttered windows, in many homes, for a generation the classics have been read, and Sullys and Romneys have been lived with, known, and valued with an almost passionate appreciation. The result," Heyward noted, "has been an aesthetic education, a little old-fashioned perhaps but certainly more genuine than that furnished in most of the expensive finishing schools."[51]

While some of the poetry written by non-Charlestonians and published in the yearbooks embraced a range of traditional topics, including love, death, time, and nature, in general, the poems written by native Charlestonian members emphasized three themes: a near genetic disposition toward cherishing the past; a fascination with the alleged "primitivism" of working-class African Americans; and a suspicion of things modern. The prize-winning poems for the Society's first year, for example, all embraced these three fundamental ideas. Founding member Helen von Kolnitz Hyer garnered the 1921 Poetry Society Prize for "Chat Île Plantation Deserted," her evocative chant to an abandoned rice plantation. Hyer deployed several standard images of the "vanishing splendor" of the rice civilization of Carolina's past when she described the plantation's jessamine-wrapped ruins and Spanish moss–draped oaks. Like the civilization that created it, Chat Île was "shrined in the magic of moonlight" apart from the realities and changes of modern times:

Thou art slumbering still in the somnolent shade of the
    moss-curtained oaks which conceal
The reasons of time that have torn the veil from thine altar of chivalry,
    Chat Île.[52]

The winner of the 1921 Caroline Sinkler Prize, Josephine Pinckney's "In the Barn," told the story of an elderly African American farm laborer named Scipio. At the end of a hard workday, Scipio patiently shucks corn to the rhythms of a plaintive spiritual, while "The home-bound negroes idle in the lane, / Gossiping as they go." Pinckney thus painted a portrait of African American life as carefree and simplistic, a picture rife with stereotypical cultural images, including the banjo and "the evil eye."[53]

Even critically acclaimed Beatrice Witte Ravenel, an early officer of the PSSC who generally worked in isolation from her Charleston peers, exhibited the same unconditional love affair with her hometown. This is not altogether surprising from the daughter-in-law of Harriott Horry Ravenel, author of the filiopietistic local history, *Charleston, the Place and the People*, published in 1906. And yet, of all the local poets affiliated with the PSSC, Ravenel was the closest in style and propensity to the moderns, in particular to imagists such as her friend Amy Lowell. The Radcliffe-educated Ravenel consistently deployed free verse, precise imagery, and an economy of language in her compositions.[54] Nevertheless, she passionately celebrated her region's history and environment and bemoaned its losses. In her three-part tribute to the Yemassee, a Native American tribe destroyed by white colonial settlers, Ravenel illustrated both her stylistic departure from and thematic similarity to her Charleston colleagues. In this ghost-haunted series, Ravenel constructed in language the same evocative landscape Alice Smith rendered in watercolor. Likewise, Ravenel drew on inherited conceptions of place and past, basing much of her understanding of the Yemassee on the Indian lore invented by Charleston novelist William Gilmore Simms in his 1835 work, *The Yemassee*.[55] The most evocative poem of her trilogy, "The Yemassee Lands," won the Poetry Society Prize for 1922. The verse follows an imagined historical memory of the Yemassee along the course of the Savannah River and the surrounding lands that the tribe once controlled. Ravenel constructs a landscape rich with the ghostly presence—"phantom mocassined tread," "invisible hunters," "hidden drums"—of this once warrior tribe. To the visitor on this sacred land, the past is inescapable: "Something follows and waits . . . And will not be appeased." The passage of time, Ravenel sings, only reinforces the Indians' hold upon the Low Country. Their spirit lurks in the earth and in the shadows—in the "Gossamer webs," "Cypress roots," and "undulant mists of the sunsets of summer"—and accosts the senses of the modern trespasser:

> After two hundred years
> Has the forest forgotten?
> Always the trees are aware
> (Significant, perilous, shaken with whispers of dread
>   and of welcome)
> Of the passage of urgent feet. . . .
>
> Ever and ever again
> The Red Man comes back to his own
> In the Yemassee Lands.[56]

Even Ravenel, the most stylistically unorthodox member of the Charleston Group, could not escape the historical commitments of her class and the notion of the region as, in the words of Amy Lowell, "beautiful with the past."[57]

As products of a world where the past imposed itself inescapably, DuBose Heyward and Josephine Pinckney, like Ravenel, necessarily filtered their understanding of the region through the lens of historical and familial associations, creating a body of poems imbued with intimacy, duty, and nostalgia.

Yet for a time, Hervey Allen, the war-weary veteran from the industrial city of Pittsburgh, also fell under elite white Charleston's hypnotic spell. Allen so thoroughly echoed the orthodox take on the city's past, and became so vitally connected to its leading lights, that he was asked to join the prestigious hereditary organization, the St. Cecelia Society.[58] These poets' most significant volumes of poetry, Allen and Heyward's *Carolina Chansons: Legends of the Low Country*, Heyward's *Skylines and Horizons*, and Pinckney's *Sea-Drinking Cities*, are thus particularly indicative of the poetic packaging of the region during this period. These volumes memorialize Charleston and the Low Country in voices rife with longing, awe, and unmitigated devotion. In particular, they celebrate three regional themes — natural beauty, social traditions and racial arrangements, and historic value — which became for Charleston poets the holy trinity of Low Country representations.

Heyward, Allen, and Pinckney describe, for example, the semitropical Low Country environment in alluring terms. They dot "this sun-drugged land of ours"[59] with images of palmettos, herons, "lush magnolia shade,"[60] and the "multi-colored sweeping marshes . . . [and] fluent silver of the sea."[61] Their whispering grasses and dripping mosses bestow a haunted, dreamlike aspect to the landscape, as do their urban images of shuttered mansions and "molten gardens mottled with gray-gloom, / Where lichened sundials shadow ancient dates, / And deep piazzas loom."[62] Appropriately, this rich atmosphere provides, as Allen and Heyward note in the preface to their 1922 volume *Carolina Chansons*, "a pensively melancholy yet fitting background" to the romantic dramas that they enact in their poems.[63]

These three poets depict Low Country blacks as primitives who proclaim their superstitions — of "Hag hollerin'" and the "evil eye" — and sing spirituals in the exotic Gullah tongue. The representation of blacks reflects the white poets' limited understanding of contemporary everyday African American life in Charleston. As passive objects of white invention, African Americans are passionate beings who are both wise and careless, almost always close to the land, and ever loyal to elite white residents. Most fit the mold of Pinckney's "John, the negro boy," who appears in her 1927 collection, *Sea-Drinking Cities*; it is John who keeps an old unreconstructed Sea Island rice planter company and "with dumb Admiration cushions him and completes his ease."[64] From the sage old black women who watch the world pass by from their porch in Pinckney's "The Old Women" to the gentle servants of Heyward's "Modern Philosopher," Charleston poets stereotyped Low Country blacks as servile and simple. They pass their days rather simply, singing street cries, selling flowers, loving freely, smoking corncob pipes, gambling, and "picking shrimp on the kitchen porch."[65] In most instances, either explicitly or implicitly, this construction of the African American presence served to buttress the weightier traditions of the elite white society. Heyward explains this age-old symbiotic relationship between black and white Charlestonians in "Modern Philosopher":

> They fight their battles for you every day,
> The zealous ones, who sorrow in your life.
> Undaunted by a century of strife,
> With urgent fingers still they point the way
> To drawing rooms, in decorous array,
> And moral heavens where no casual wife
> May share your lot; where dice and ready knife
> Are barred; and feet are silent when you pray.
>
> But you have music in your shuffling feet,
> And spirituals for a lenient Lord,
> Who lets you sing your promises away.
> You hold your sunny corner of the street,
> And pluck deep beauty from a banjo chord:
> Philosopher whose future is today.[66]

These oversimplified, earthy African Americans serve as foils to the noble white characters who inhabit the Charleston poems. All three poets turn a loving and at times slightly ironic eye to those tenacious older members of their society who, finding themselves in meager circumstances, nonetheless hold tight to rituals of the past. Pinckney's staid Misses Poar, for example, ride to church in an oxen buggy—"(They've had no horses since sixty-four / When the Yankees stopped at the house of Poar.)"—led by "the negro coachman in beaver hat, / Slightly nibbled by moth and rat." Dressed in their faded antebellum finery, they proudly take their places in the "square front pew" and follow the services "In dear Great-grand-papa's prayer book."[67] Similarly, Allen's "Miss Perdee" emerges from "the wrought-iron gate" in "the sleeves of 1888" to maintain her social rounds, strictly south of Broad Street. "The Perdees," the reader learns, "had blue blood in Adam's veins / When Adam had the rib he gave to Eve."[68] At times the portraits of these old-line Charlestonians are meant to be poignant. Pinckney's "On the Shelf" reveals the sacrifices some families made to maintain their centuries-old lifestyle. To feed his family, Mr. Skirling, a struggling rice planter in a "faded jacket / Of wine-red velvet," drives his "ancient double buggy" to a bookshop in town.

Once there, he fingers old volumes as if appraising them for purchase "to deceive Himself rather than anybody else." In reality, Skirling has come to sell a treasured volume of his family's "Abbotsford Edition" of Sir Walter Scott. In "a voice / Tuned to commanding negroes from a horse," the downtrodden Skirling hands over the volume and returns home to dine with his extended family. Changes in the local economy and the demise of the rice-planting regime, Pinckney tells the reader, have led to this sad occasion. But the Skirlings find comfort in the maintenance of their traditions and the continuity of their surroundings, such as "the chair that Lafayette sat in."[69]

The region's enduring historical character, found in its landscapes and its people, then, is the overarching message of these poems. By stressing the Low Country as a fervent custodian of the past, these poets also comment on the impact of modernity on the Low Country, suggesting that change is an unwelcome intruder. Allen and Heyward, for example, dedicated their collaborative work, *Carolina Chansons*, to their mentor, John Bennett, "in front of whose warming fire these stories took place."[70] The collection reflects the conservative artistic view of all three men, summed up in John Bennett's comments in a 1929 interview: "I have little patience with much of our modern literature. . . . We have allowed entirely too much debunking in this period. Debunking has become a fad; all the established institutions have been debunked as have practically all the heroes and heroines of history."[71]

Contrary to debunking the past, Heyward and Allen elevate history and its heroes to the realm of the noble in *Carolina Chansons*. They weave dramatic tales that are, as one reviewer noted, "just over that border line of romance that makes history palatable."[72] Their verse, peopled by drum-beating Native Americans, adventurous English, French, and Spanish settlers, and swashbuckling pirates and gallant Confederates, covers a wide chronological and thematic expanse of Low Country history. They laud specific romantic heroes, such as Lafayette and Edgar Allen Poe, both of whom spent time in the region, and heroines, such as Theodosia Burr, daughter of Vice President Aaron Burr and wife of South Carolina governor Joseph Alston, who drowned at sea in 1813. Through all of this, the poets seek to present what they call the authentic South—"to speak simply and carefully amid a babel of unauthentic utterance."[73]

While claiming to be legitimate voices of the South, Heyward and Allen admit that their works "do not pretend to exact historical accuracy. . . . [They are] impressionistic attempts to present the fleeting feeling of the moment, landscape moods, and the ephemeral attitudes of the past." At the same time, however, they defend the essential historicity of their poems, based on "much painstaking research and careful verification" of "legends and facts."[74] Likewise, they include lengthy endnotes to many of the poems to help ground them in historical detail. The resulting works, they argue, "are not local only, they are stories and pictures of a chapter of American history little known. . . . They may carry a decided interest to the country at large."[75]

Heyward and Allen situate the city of Charleston as a regal witness to a past that is slipping away — "sunstruck with old ghosts." "Sea Island winds sweep through Palmetto Town," Allen wrote in a poem of that name, "Bringing with piney tang the old romance / Of Pirates and of smuggling gentlemen; / And tongues as langourous as southern France." To Allen, the city is peppered with the remnants of the gay and dramatic past — from old sloops and ancient walled gardens to the rustling brocade skirts of ladies in their stately mansions. Even the turbaned African American flower women are vessels of a time gone by, as they bandy about "old English words now seldom heard."[76] Allen calls his readers to revel in the stories Charleston can tell, "Before they are gone."[77] He warns against the false promises of the present, where "the traffic streams" in favor of the real glory of the past as seen in the city's "cobbled shores" and "lingering trees": "Despise the garish presences that flaunt / The obvious possessions of today, / To wear with me the spectacles that haunt / The optic sense with wraiths of yesterday."[78] While highly reverent, Allen's poems tend to be more descriptive and episodic and less intimate and personal than Heyward's. Without the authority of ancestors to draw upon, Allen focused his poetic vision on rendering those aspects of Charleston, its legends, folklore, atmosphere, and environment, that were accessible to non-natives.

To insider Heyward, however, Charleston was more than a mere reliquary of historical episodes and individuals; it was a world where the past and present were deeply, even autobiographically, intertwined. His poems describe in intimate detail and possessive first-person tones *his* Charleston. "They tell me she is beautiful, my City," he rhapsodizes in "Dusk,"

> That she is colorful and quaint, alone
> Among the cities. But I, I who have known
> Her tenderness, her courage and her pity,
> Have felt her forces mould me, mind and bone,
> Life after life, up from her first beginning.
> How can I think of her in wood and stone!
>
> . . . these, my songs, my all, belong to her.[79]

Armed with this hefty sense of belonging and ancestry, Heyward offers his services as a guide to the real Charleston for the uninitiated tourist—"You who have known my city for a day. . . . Then laughed, and passed along your vagrant way."[80] In the poem "Silences," he moves his readers through the city streets "when the night flows deep and kind / Along these narrow ways of troubled stone" into the living memories of the Charleston's landmark churches and their "empire of forgotten things." Heyward believes that the city reveals its memories and its true self only to those who cherish it: "Then will the city know you of her own, / And feel you meet to share her sufferings; / While down a swirl of poignant memories, / Herself shall find you in her silences." To the rhythm of the church chimes, telling a "tale of golden years / Far less like bells than chanted memories," Heyward paints a vivid picture of white aristocratic life in the antebellum city:

> Once coaches waited tow on shining row
> Before this door; and where the thirsty street
> Drank the deep shadow of the portico
> The Sunday hush was stirred by happy feet,
> Low greetings, and the rustle of brocade. . . .

The Civil War interrupts this idyllic scene—"One after one / All lovely things went down the sanguine tide." Yet Heyward claims that the buildings, like "A prisoned spirit vibrant in stone," remember and call those who love them to do likewise: "but only in the singing rain / Flutters old echoes in the portico; / Those who can still remember love it so."[81]

Josephine Pinckney's poems also exhibit this intense sense of privileged intimacy with Charleston and the Low Country. Like Heyward, she was descended from major slave- and landowning families who played important roles in the history of South Carolina and Charleston. In addition to her father, a Confederate captain and Santee River rice planter, Pinckney's ancestors included Thomas Pinckney, the Revolutionary War hero, early governor, and George Washington's appointed American ambassador to the court of St. James. She was also related to two signers of the Declaration of Independence.[82] Not surprisingly, then, Pinckney's poems often venture into the most intimate sanctuaries of the city's elites—into the private homes protected by closed gates and high walls designed to keep outsiders in their place. Through these works, Pinckney transports her readers through time and space and into a protected sanctuary that "preserved and framed"[83] the charm of the past—where "Tall panes of glass wall out the common street, / Wall in ancestral echoes bewailing change." In these immense, shadowy rooms deco-

Poet and author Josephine Pinckney. From the Collections
of the South Carolina Historical Society.

rated with "brocaded curtains" and "carved chair-backs," Old Charleston
endures, as if frozen in time, set apart from the "Tides of new people [who]
froth about" outside.[84] Even "uninterrupted dust" enshrines the memories
of previous generations in these private temples to the past.[85]

Inherent in these odes to the endurance of tradition is a critique of what
Heyward, Allen, and Pinckney considered the forces of modernity that threatened Charleston's righteous way of life. Allen's earliest published character
portrait of an old-line Charlestonian, "The Old Judge," for example, draws
a direct connection between the advent of the New South and the demise of
the sights, sounds, and power structure of the Old South:

> And now the new South quickens, in the square
> The huge trucks thunder and the motor blare.
> The park oaks droop with Spanish moss and age,
> The *jedge* no longer now is *marss* but *boss*,
> And all the old things suffer change and loss.[86]

Clearly, to these poets, the passing of old ways was lamentable.

Heyward's 1924 volume *Skylines and Horizons* contains his most explicit call
for cherishing Old Charleston and staving the tide of change. In his long
sonnet "Chant for an Old Town," African American workers discover "a

mouldy chest" containing Blackbeard's treasure while they are digging up the city's "ancient flagged pavements" to build skyscrapers and streets "like Pennsylvania Avenue, Canal Street, Riverside Drive, / All asphalt and uniform concrete." Heyward decries this so-called march of progress and the modern sensibility that values the homogeneous and reduces all actions to the rational world of profits. This dangerous intruder challenges the city: "Can you prove by mathematics / Why you should survive?" When Charleston has only "a crooked, moss-hung tree / A century old" to show for itself, "The engines come" and begin to "Shatter! Shatter! Shatter!" the world that once was. Heyward begs developers to "pause before the ruin is complete." He indicts them as insensitive to the values of the past and ignorant of the shallow contours of a future without reverence for the things that came before it: "Trading new lamps for old, you storm the street. / Then, heedless of the magic in the old, / You leave them strewn in fragments at our gate. / For that which stands have pity, and withold [sic]. / Leave for your sons these walls inviolate." In the end, the ghostly pirates return to the city to claim their booty, leaving the empty city to face the "steel-throated" engines alone and to mourn without protection.[87]

   Carolina Chansons, Skylines and Horizons, and *Sea-Drinking Cities* were all produced by major New York publishing houses, and all received positive notice in newspapers and journals throughout the country.[88] An excerpt from one representative review suffices to convey the general appreciation for and internalization of their particular characterization of Charleston. In evaluating Pinckney's volume, the *Washington Post* noted appreciatively, "This is poetry—its essence and its spirit, American, too, in mold, whispers from our ancient cities, our Charleston. . . . Through these poems rise a vista of galleried mansions with huge colonial pillars beautified by Virginia creepers, wild honeysuckle and wisteria sleeping out their destinies within the sound of the Atlantic's many-toned voice. And the people who live in them; manor lords and ladies, left over from a gentler age to teach the age that courtesy can exist, even in a world where women vote."[89]

   Through their poetry, Heyward, Allen, and Pinckney effectively constructed and conveyed an alluring identity for the Low Country—its landscape, people, and history. The poetry and career trajectories of these three central figures of Charleston's literary effort illustrate two important facets of regionalism: first, its effectiveness as a force for constructing a civic identity; and second, its limitations in providing sustainable artistic satisfaction for individuals, such as Allen, for whom the regionalist endeavor was not autobiographical.

   The 1927 publication of Pinckney's *Sea-Drinking Cities* can be considered the last significant volume of poetry produced by a member of the Poetry Society of South Carolina. A few years earlier, as the national fascination with poetry faded, the Society experienced a major managerial crisis that left it floundering. In 1924, the recently married DuBose Heyward gave up his insurance practice to dedicate himself to full-time prose writing. The economic imperative of making a living forced Heyward to abandon Charleston. Heyward divided his time between writing at his home in Hendersonville, North Carolina, lucrative speaking tours across the country, and brief visits to his hometown, all but ignoring his duties as PSSC president. "I gave the best of my enthusiasm to the work when in Charleston, and I would continue to do so if I could also earn a living out of literature in the blessed old city, but I cannot stay there and starve," he complained to Bennett in 1925.[90] Ironically, Heyward supplemented his income through vehement lectures about his pet topic, the revival of Southern letters, even as the literary organization that helped stimulate it under his leadership faltered.[91]

At the same time, Hervey Allen's commitment to the Low Country and to regionalist writing weakened: "La renaissance de sud est fini[e]," he wrote John Bennet's wife, Susan.[92] In 1924, he accepted a position teaching English at Columbia University and, like Heyward, began to shift his energies to prose writing. With Allen's departure, the Society received another blow. In 1926, W. Van Whithall, Allen's friend and the patron of the Blindman Prize, the Society's most prestigious award, withdrew his sponsorship.[93] For his part, Allen never again lived in Charleston, nor did he write local-color verse, with which he had grown increasingly disillusioned after the publication of *Carolina Chansons*.[94]

By spring 1925, a full-blown leadership crisis followed these departures, which were seen by some, especially Bennett, as desertions. Bennett, who with Pinckney had stepped in to fill the void, chastised Heyward: "I am sick to death of carrying other peoples' affairs. . . . If you cannot find it possible to look after your orphan child . . . make some arrangement by which the Society's opening in the Fall will function."[95] Concern, dismay, and panic filled the correspondence between Allen, Bennett, and Heyward during the late spring of that year. "It is rather heart-breaking to feel the driving power that we have put behind the constructive end flagging," Heyward asserted, "but we might as well realize that part of it did not give a tinker's dam except to a few devoted souls in the membership."[96] With his "Absentee Presidentism . . . a poetical practical failure," Heyward resigned the position in late April 1925.[97]

In the following years, Bennett and Pinckney shouldered much of the burden of maintaining the PSSC. This included what Pinckney called the "grand

The city's most celebrated author and poet, DuBose Heyward, pictured here with his wife, Dorothy, and Poetry Society guest speaker Gertrude Stein (center) in front of the upscale hotel Villa Magherita in 1935. From the Collections of the South Carolina Historical Society.

scrambulation" of arranging the annual programs and editing the yearbooks, despite health and time concerns and increased disinterest on the part of the membership.[98] By 1934, financial straits related to the Depression and lack of suitable poetic material caused the Society to cease publication of the *Year Book*. The PSSC decided to dedicate the little monies at its disposal to bringing speakers of note to the city. For example, during the 1934–35 season, over which Heyward presided in a onetime return to the presidency, both Edna S. Vincent Millay and Gertrude Stein were featured; characteristically, the latter spoke to a rather perplexed local audience about the "difference between poetry and prose, why she preferred the period to colons, and why she tried to avoid nouns."[99] By the mid-1930s, much of the administrative leadership of the PSSC had shifted to a group of individuals affiliated with the English department of the local military college, the Citadel. Professor James G. Harrison, who served several terms as PSSC president during the 1930s and 1940s, described this era as a period "of hard times and eventual moribundity."[100] The creative fire of the organization had dissipated. It left, however, several notable legacies — as an undeniable catalyst to what became known as the Southern Literary Renaissance; as a launching pad for Heyward's successful career as a novelist; and finally, as the engine behind the literary foundations of Charleston's romantic and historic identity.[101]

"A Cul-de-Sac in Time and Place": *Transmitting the Elite Ideal through Prose*[102]

Beginning in the mid-1920s, poetry gave way to prose (fiction and nonfiction) as the main vehicle for constructing Charleston's literary identity. Local and nonlocal writers working in fiction and nonfiction covered a range of themes from the region's history and politics to its social and racial customs. Several followed in the footsteps of local historians, such as Harriet Horry Ravenel and Daniel Elliott Huger Smith, and chronicled what they considered to be Charleston's central role in the American narrative.[103] Eola Willis, Harriet Kershaw Leiding, and William Watts Ball, for example, produced pages of text concerning topics as varied as eighteenth-century theater and Southern political theory.[104] For her first novel, Josephine Pinckney also turned to historical fiction as an appropriate vehicle for memorializing the region. In *Hilton Head*, she recounts the adventures of her ancestor, Dr. Henry Woodward, the man credited with bringing the first rice seeds to the Carolina Low Country from Madagascar, thus stimulating the growth of the region's plantation empire.[105] Likewise, both DuBose Heyward and nature-adventure writer Herbert Ravenel Sass penned novels about Charleston during the antebellum and Civil War periods in an attempt to cash in on the American reading public's interest in the South of those eras. Written in the early 1930s, Heyward's *Peter Ashley* and Sass's *Look Back to Glory* predated, though never outsold, Margaret Mitchell's classic Old South tale, *Gone with the Wind*. Nonetheless, promotional materials for Heyward's *Peter Ashley* described the story in familiar terms: "Duels, horse races, the St. Cecilia Ball — and Peter Ashley himself, the gallant young South Carolinian, hero of an age of chivalry that has passed forever."[106] Similarly, in *Look Back to Glory*, Sass constructed a wistful romance, complete with "the old paraphernalia" — chivalrous planters, docile slaves, charming belles, and magnificent homes.[107] Through antebellum Low Country culture, Sass argued against President Roosevelt's increased centralization of the American government and in favor of the supposed agrarian states' rights and the limited-democracy policies of the Old South.[108]

Similarly, the manners and mores of old-line white Charlestonians and the modern challenges to the maintenance of their customs became a subject of interest to writers and readers during the Depression. Some non-native authors capitalized on the appeal that aristocratic Charleston held in the American imagination. In popular mysteries, such as *Plantation Murder* and *Road to Folly*, for instance, stereotyped images of the region's genteel decay and the nobility of its white gentry dominated the story lines.[109] A few native writers handled the characterization of tradition and the clash between old and new in a more nuanced fashion, Pinckney's 1945 *Three O'Clock Dinner* being the most sophisticated.[110] Katherine Ball Ripley, daughter of PSSC president and newspaper editor William Watts Ball, published an intimate and complex portrait of a typical Old Charleston family in her 1936 novel, *Crowded House*. Although the protagonist Robb family boasts a great-great-great-grandfather who was a colonial governor—"The Robbs lying under the moss-grown stones in St. Michael's churchyard had been important people"—the twentieth-century family finds itself in reduced financial and strained personal circumstances.[111] To support his six children, John Robb sells insurance and tries to instill in his brood a reverence for tradition. The modern generation, however, generally fails to uphold these communal values and grows alienated from the family. Instead of marrying well and within her caste as tradition dictates, for example, one Robb daughter falls in love with a middle-class German baker; another marries a wealthy "Yankee" just to escape the stifling pressures of home; and yet another defies the norms of Southern womanhood and chooses not to marry, becoming instead an academic who also lives in the North. Even Vee Robb, who pursued the age-old pattern of marrying a Low Country man with a good name and an old plantation house, finds herself alone. She is the victim of her husband's adherence to another, less talked about, white Southern tradition—a sexual liaison with an African American woman.[112] In general, only the African American "members" of the Robb household, the "Dah" and their valet, Peter, remain cheerfully constant—protective and proud of the old ways.[113]

Along with white gallantry, the idea of Low Country blacks as the strongest remaining vestige of a vanishing civilization was permeates Charleston prose. The city's literati had long been preoccupied with the character, language, and culture of the region's African American population. This interest was part of a national fascination, on the part of blacks and whites alike, with African American and African culture. For many individuals, from sociologists at the University of North Carolina to the novelists of Harlem, African American life became a focus of research and literary output.[114] In New York, African American writers and artists told the story of their own race; in Charleston, however, the perspective was all elite white.[115] Individuals such as John Bennett, Sam Stoney, and members of the Society for the Preservation of Negro Spirituals collected and appropriated local black folklore and linguistic traditions. In their literature and songs, they attempted to replicate and preserve the rich Africanisms resonant in the Gullah language spoken in the street cries and the animal tales and Bible stories of the region's former slaves and their descendants.[116] Gullah became such an important staple of the Low Country literary diet that some white writers strived to establish their credibility in the language. In *Black Genesis*, Sam Stoney drew on the weight of his ancestry, his plantation childhood, and "a familiarity with such stories that antedate his conscious memory." Apparently, Stoney's spoken Gullah was so impressive that Columbia University asked him, instead of a native-speaking Low Country African American, to record the dialect for its library collection.[117] At times, writers tried to outdo each other as the definitive Gullah authority. John Bennett, whose multivolume notebooks testify to years of field research, and Ambrose Gonzales, author of the first major Gullah volume, *The Black Border: Gullah Stories of the Carolina Coast*, vied for the title of "expert."[118] The incontestable result was a public, literary conception of the Gullah people and language that was completely filtered and controlled by elite whites.

Of all the writers who emerged from Charleston in the 1920s and 1930s, none was more professionally successfully or more consistently linked in the American imagination with the region than DuBose Heyward. He built on his celebrity as the cofounder and chief propagandist of the PSSC with the 1925 publication of his best-selling novel, *Porgy*. Beginning with this slim volume, Heyward expanded his commercial appeal with American, and even international, audiences through the late 1930s. The savvy author serialized his works in popular magazines, turned them into plays for Broadway, and had them translated for foreign-language markets; he even passed a short stint as a screenplay writer in Hollywood. Despite his ambition and professionalism, Heyward remained, in the words of his biographer James Hutchisson, "a gentle patrician still very much connected to the traditions of southern art. He knew when to push and when to stand pat, always mindful of his image. . . . [He was] a gentleman who didn't ignore the inbred code of taste and manners in [his] quest for commercial success—a code absolutely crucial to the cultural makeup of Charleston."[119]

Heyward's personal commitment to enshrining his vision of Charleston in literary form—a devotion that eventually provided him with a lucrative income—was rooted in a web of thick family associations. He was born in 1885 to the marriage of two patrician South Carolina families, the DuBoses and the Heywards. As with many of Charleston's once wealthy white plantation families, the Heywards and DuBoses fell on hard times after the Civil War. Still considered an aristocrat in a city that valued birth and blood over pocketbook, Heyward's father, Ned, nonetheless had to work in the local Bennett rice mill on the Ashley River to support his growing family. A machinery accident in the mill claimed Ned's life when DuBose was only two years old.[120] The death of one parent meant the young DuBose would be raised by his mother, Janie Screven DuBose Heyward, who "knew the history of South Carolina from A to Izard," and by an extended family of grandparents, who filled his young ears with family stories relating to Charleston's past.[121] As with his artistic compatriot Alice Ravenel Huger Smith, DuBose Heyward's childhood experiences and worldview were deeply shaped by the values and memories of his ancestors. Years later, Heyward dedicated his volume of poems *Skylines and Horizons* to his mother and noted her immeasurable influence over him as a thinker and writer. In "Your Gifts," Heyward thanked his struggling widowed mother, who replaced the toys she could not afford to buy with "the little shining word" of "wild, fantastic legends of long ago."[122] A deeply rooted historical memory was his inheritance and his literary legacy.

Ned Heyward's sudden death also left his family in a dire economic position. To make ends meet, Janie Heyward took in sewing and rented a beach property to what elite white Charleston delicately referred to as "paying guests." Most important for the cultural education of her son, she was also an active poet and amateur folklorist who began publishing volumes of her work as early as 1912 with "Songs of the Charleston Darkey." In "Songs," Heyward articulated her sense of Charleston's historicity and of the picturesqueness of its African American citizens, which her son, DuBose, later echoed in his poetry and prose. Her poem titled "Charleston" sings reverently of a "charming city, bathed in sunshine," where one finds "the meeting of Old ways with the new." As a witness to history, Janie Heyward declares, the city earned protection from modernity's potentially crushing force: "She has bravery and beauty, / And a past to waken pride, / Her's the joy of well-done duty, / And a future from the tide." Heyward also turned her artistic attentions to the rhythms of black daily life in the city, recording the street cries of the shrimp seller—"Shrimpy, Shrimpy; raw, raw Shrimpy!"—and the bedtime stories and melodies of a turbaned black plantation nurse singing her white charges to sleep.[123] Undoubtedly, young DuBose grew up listening to these Gullah-inspired stories, songs, and more.

A widow with two children to support, Janie Heyward made a solid career for herself as a raconteur of African American life in South Carolina. In drawing rooms, college auditoriums, and hotel parlors across the South, tourists and locals paid to hear her present poems, stories, street cries, superstitious tales, and jokes in her own version of the "Unique Dialect of the Disappearing Type of Negro."[124] Heyward always stressed the "authenticity" of her performances, explaining that she gathered her material from her intimate, daily contact with blacks. In particular, she credited the influence of "Maum Sina," the "old time darkey" slave who raised her on the DuBose family's cotton plantations and to whom she dedicated her recitations: "Of unusual intelligence, keen insight, and an unfailingly devoted heart, she stood as a fine example of HER type which has now passed from our civilization, going out with those conditions which produced it."[125] Heyward considered her art a form of both historic preservation and race education. Speaking from "my heart and memory,"[126] she told her audiences, "in giving you these sketches, my desire has been to record for the coming generations, the feeling which existed between the old-time Darkey, and his Master."[127] She characterized antebellum plantation interactions between slave-owner and enslaved as rich with "loving sympathy," "loyalty," and a "spirit of mutual kindness." In a poem titled "Silhouette," for example, Heyward sung longingly of "the old plantation days" of "courtly" masters and courteous, "imitative" slaves:

> Such close contact between the races
> Brought a love, with reverence blent;
> And the black folks loved the white folks,
> Viewing them as heaven sent.[128]

To cement her conception of the harmonious, paternalistic slave South, Heyward often concluded her program with a verse titled "What Mauma Thinks of Freedom," in which the former slave pines for the days when her master provided her with food, shelter, warm clothes, and medicines:

> I wish Mass Lincoln happy man,
> Wherebber he may be;
> But I long foh deh ole, ole days,
> Befo deh name of "Free."[129]

In Janie Heyward's world, both whites and blacks longed for the past, and even for slavery.

DuBose Heyward inherited not only his mother's family name and her predisposition toward storytelling but also her fascination with Low Country African American life.[130] Heyward grew up among his family's household servants, but, unlike most members of his caste, the contact did not stop there. From his first job with an insurance company collecting "burial money" from tenants in the city's black slums to the three summers he spent supervising black field hands on an aunt's plantation, Heyward's early exposure to Gullah culture was extensive.[131] At age twenty, he became a cotton-checker and warehouse timekeeper, passing full days in the company of the black stevedores who worked the waterfront along the Cooper River.[132] Through them, he saw a side of black Charleston he had never known existed — the dramatic "negro underworld," as he called it, of dope dealers, beggars, and grieving widows.[133] During the First World War, Heyward visited a wide array of African American community sites in the area, rallying blacks to buy liberty bonds.[134] These cumulative experiences altered Heyward's inherited, aristocratic sense of African Americans as stock characters. He later recalled, "I grew to see the primitive negro as neither a professional comedian nor an object for sentimental charity, but a racially self-conscious human being, living out his destiny beside us, and guided by a code, which while it has as yet accepted little of the law of the white man, represented a definite surge upward."[135]

After the war, Heyward continued to sell insurance, with his partner, Harry O'Neill, brother of the soon-to-be artist Elizabeth Verner, but his encounters with the region's working-class black population had left an indelible mark on his imagination, as did the resounding voice of his mentor John Bennett, who encouraged Heyward's exploration of black themes. A serious student of Gullah culture, Bennett broke important ground by writing about African American Charleston's complex web of color lines and family ties in his 1921 "legend," *Madame Margot*. In the story of a successful black milliner, "with a shop above the bend in King St," Margot makes a deal with the Devil so her very fair-skinned daughter could become white and eventually marry a wealthy white planter in New Orleans. Much of white Charleston disapproved of Bennett's work, in particular of the idea that a white man could fall in love with a woman with African blood. Bennett's claim that the tale was at once a fantastic legend and a drama based upon actual historical events only exacerbated the negative local response.[136] With Bennett urging him forward, Heyward turned his literary eye toward exploring that "hidden" black world, "this life which was going on within your own, yet was apart from it."[137] During the writing of *Porgy*, he became, in his own words, "quite obsessed with the material."[138] Until his death in 1940, Heyward wrote many novels, short stories, and, with his wife, Dorothy, successful plays about a variety of subjects. Yet he remained, as a contemporary once described him, "Haunted by darkies."[139] "He [the African American] is authentic southern atmosphere," Heyward wrote in 1931, "and, as such, has something to sell in a limited, but rich and highly specialised [*sic*] market."[140] Heyward's most popular "negro work," *Porgy*, illustrates the historical and racial understandings of this man who contributed so significantly to a popular, literature-based conception of Charleston.

Porgy is essentially an all-black tale of the passion, love, violence, and fortitude of the "negro underworld." Set to the rhythms of the Low Country seasons, the narrative follows the tumultuous love affair between Porgy, a crippled, black beggar, and Bess, a struggling drug addict and former prostitute who "belongs" to the powerful and brutal stevedore Crown. During a heated crap game and fueled by corn whiskey, Crown murders a respectable working-class African American named Robbins and flees to the Sea Islands to escape the white law. Bess moves in with the unlikely lover Porgy, and, for a time, the two are happy together. Their peace is short-lived, however, when summer arrives and Bess and Porgy join their friends for a picnic on "Kittiwah" Island. There, in the sultry heat, the fugitive Crown seduces Bess. When Crown returns to Charleston to "claim" his "'oman" Bess, Porgy kills him. Because of the protective measures of Porgy's community, the white police never find the murderer, and they certainly do not suspect the withered and weak Porgy of committing the crime. In the end, as Porgy sits in jail for contempt after refusing, out of fear, to identify Crown's corpse, Bess leaves him for promises of a sweeter future downriver in Savannah.

From the first paragraph of *Porgy*, Heyward venerates Charleston as a site that retains the patina of a prior age and is somehow set apart from the forces molding other American cities. He characterizes early-twentieth-century Charleston as "an ancient, beautiful city" caught in a sacred moment between the hallowed traditions of the past and the impending changes of the modern age. To Heyward, Charleston's "golden age" is real; it cannot be dismissed as "legendary" or as "the chimerical era treasured by every man past middle life, that never existed except in the heart of youth."[141] Heyward reinforces this idea throughout his novel in his nostalgic descriptions of the city's grand architecture and of its enduring system of elite, white paternalism. Much of the novel's action occurs at "Catfish Row," for example, a crowded and dilapidated African American waterfront tenement. Concerned about the "authenticity" of his local color and incapable of escaping the urge to make personal and historical associations with his work, Heyward modeled his setting after the real-life Cabbage Row. Once a grand building at 89–91 Church Street, Cabbage Row was next door to Heyward's ancestral home, the Heyward-Washington House, which would be the focus of later historic preservation efforts. The Row was also near his private residence in 1924 at 76

Church Street.[142] Where African Americans now cavorted "within the high-ceilinged rooms, with their battered colonial mantels and broken decorations of Adam designs in plaster," Heyward writes dreamily, "governors had come and gone, and ambassadors of kings had schemed and danced."[143] Porgy's adventures on the cobblestone streets of the Battery, Charleston's most elite residential neighborhood, reinforce this notion of the city as "a land of such beauty that he [Porgy] never lost the illusion that it was unreal." Heyward rhapsodizes: "No one seemed to work in that country, except the happy, well-clothed negroes who frequently came to back gates when he passed, and gave him tender morsels from the white folks' kitchens. The great, gleaming houses that looked out at him with kindly eyes that peered between solid walls of climbing roses. Ladies on the deep piazzas would frequently send a servant running out to give him a coin and speed him on his way."[144]

This variety of patrician kindness and generosity toward blacks extends throughout the novel. While most of Heyward's "po' buckra," or nonelite white characters—his cops and store owners and their rough bill collectors—come across as brutish, hostile, and insensitive, Archdale, the most prominent elite white character, is a pure gentleman and, thus, a "friend" to Porgy.[145] When asked why he intercedes with the law on behalf of a Row resident unjustly accused of murder, Archdale explains the system of white paternalism still operative in Charleston decades after emancipation: "Why, I am the Rutledge's [*sic*] lawyer; and I look after their colored folks for them. I think they must have owned half the slaves in the county."[146] In both physical and racial terms, then, Porgy's Charleston is, as one scholar has accurately described it, a kind of "cul-de-sac in time and space."[147]

From its early dramatic scene—a crap game that ends in the wail of spirituals as the Row mourns Robbins's death—to its closing moments, which find Porgy and his goat hopefully reestablished in their common begging place—"alone in an irony of morning sunlight"[148]—Heyward quite remarkably attempts to look beyond the superficial white understanding of African Americans in Jim Crow Charleston. In what he called his "experamental [*sic*]"[149] novel, Heyward departs at times from the traditional tropes of white-authored fiction about blacks. First, he situates a self-contained black community, complete with its own rules, entertainments, and rituals, at the center of his tale; and second, he treats his characters as human beings, possessing a degree of individuality and dignity—unprecedented among white Southern writers. Instead of replicating a literature of black-faced, banjo-strumming field hands and stern but lovable mammies, Heyward focuses his novel on Catfish Row's universally human struggles for happiness, hope, and survival.

So different was Heyward's treatment that rumors even circulated that Heyward was African American. Many readers believed a white man, particularly of Southern patrician breeding, was incapable of writing such a "realistic" work about an "alien" race. The *Baltimore Sun* reported, for example, that "on one occasion he [Heyward] walked into the lecture hall of a certain university a few minutes before his talk was to begin, and picking up a program read: 'We have great pleasure in presenting this evening, Mr. Dubose Heyward, who is not only a member of Harlem's intellectual colony, but who is also a Southern Negro of the old tradition.'"[150] Eventually, his friend and pssc cofounder Hervey Allen was compelled to pen a brief biography of Heyward "to stop any questions as to Heyward's color and quality."[151]

Despite his admirable and decidedly modern attempts at social realism, in the end, the Low Country scion failed to escape fully the central assumptions of his own racial and class heritage. His black characters lead largely undisciplined lives, rife with ignorance, alcohol, drugs, loose sexual relations, and violence, and thus prove somewhat pitiful and helpless as human beings. At their core, Heyward's African Americans are still exotic primitives who are alternately comedic or dangerous. Heyward describes the outrageous strains of a parade by "The Sons and Daughters of Repent Ye Saith the Lord Lodge" as "crash[ing] through the slow, restrained rhythm of the city's life like a wild, barbaric chord."[152] The pageant's participants provide whimsical foil to old white Charleston—"Out of the fetters of civilization this people had risen, suddenly, amazingly. Exotic as the Congo, and still able to abandon themselves utterly to the wild joy of fantastic play, they had taken the reticent, old Anglo-Saxon town and stamped their mood swiftly and indelibly into its heart." Their "barbaric" presence reminds aristocratic onlookers of the slavery-based genteel civilization that is no more: "Then they passed, leaving behind them a wistful envy among those who had watched them go,—those whom the ages had rendered old and wise."[153]

Heyward further conveys the idea of blacks as primitives in his detailed descriptions of his characters' bodies. Porgy, who is almost "Eastern and mystic" in looks, is "black with the almost purple blackness of unadulterated Congo blood."[154] He is able to "doze lightly under the terrific heat, as only a full-blooded negro can."[155] Crown's physical portrait—"the great muscles of his torso flickered and ran like the flank of a horse"—extends this idea of African Americans as near-savage animals.[156] With the "body of a gladiator," "gleeming teeth," and "low snarl," Crown impales Robbins on his cotton hook, and together, "Down, down, down the centuries they slid," back to the ways, the reader is to understand, of the jungle.[157]

While sympathetic to the plight of African Americans in a modernizing world, Heyward's work was not a radical form of social protest calling for change. He did not use his book as a rostrum for addressing the prevailing "Negro Question" of his day. He protested that his book was not "a vehicle for propaganda or discussion of the race problem, or for a meretricious type of Negro humor, but as I saw him, solely as subject for art."[158] In response to a letter from a Chicago woman asking why he characterized blacks as being incapable of being "civilized," Heyward replied characteristically, "Why in Heaven's name, must the writer have 'motives and messages' wished on him? If I have discovered anything about the Southern Negro at all it is simply that, because he is still at heart a primitive, because he has resisted American standardization and has retained a native delight in color and song, he is a more fruitful subject for art than his conventionalized white neighbor."[159]

The closest Heyward ever came to delineating publicly his early views on the race question was in a 1923 article titled "And Once Again—the Negro." He described with admitted envy what he considered the simple and happy life of Low Country blacks, generally unencumbered with the restrictions of white civilization. He also mourned what he saw as the imminent passing of this carefree existence:

> Are they an aeon behind, or an aeon ahead of us? Who knows? But one thing is certain: the reformer will have them in the fullness of time. They will surely be cleaned, married, conventionalized. They will be taken from the fields, and given machines. Their instinctive feeling for the way that leads to happiness, saved as it is from selfishness, by humor and genuine kindness of heart, will be supplanted by a stifling moral straitjacket. . . . I can only be profoundly sorry for him, for there he sits in the sunshine unconsciously awaiting his supreme tragedy. He is about to be saved.[160]

For Heyward, changing the racial status quo was undesirable for blacks but sadly inevitable.

Heyward best reveals this attitude through his modern "New Negro" character from *Porgy* named "Sportin' Life." Unlike his Charleston-bred counterparts, Sportin' Life, a fast-talking, fancily dressed mulatto from New York, has no respect for traditions. He dismisses the inhabitants of Catfish Row as "dese old-fashioned lamp-oil nigger what have no adwantage." When he fails to adhere to the local customs by admiring the "good-lookin' white girls in dis town," one local black warns Sportin' Life of Jim Crow's ever-present violent possibilities: "Don't yuh try any Noo Yo'k'in' around dis' town. . . . Yas, my belly fair ache wid dis Noo Yo'k talk. De fus t'ing dat dem nigger fuhgit is dat dem is nigger. Den dem comes tuh dese decent country mens, and fills um full ob talk wut put money in de funeral ondehtakuh pocket."[161] Through this Catfish Row resident who is educated in the ways of white paternalism, Heyward expresses his views on the reasonableness and self-policing of Charleston's racial system: "Dis county aint nebber yit see a black man git lynch. Dese nigger knows folks, an' dey knows nigger. Fer Gawd' sake keep yuh mout' off w'ite lady. Yuh gots pleanty ob yuh own color fut talk 'bout. Stick tuh dem, an' yuh ain't git inter no trouble."[162] Significantly, it is Sportin' Life, with his modern promises of freedom, who contributes to the dismantling of Porgy's happiness by luring Bess back into cocaine addiction.

Heyward's willingness to straddle the fence between a realistic and an exotic depiction of African Americans — between a modernistic and a nostalgic stance — rendered his novel appealing and nonthreatening to both Southern and non-Southern white audiences. Heyward originally believed "with almost certain knowledge that it would never be a paying book. The American public will not buy a book that takes the negro seriously, they want him only as a comic."[163] And yet, during Heyward's lifetime, *Porgy* enjoyed great success. Major contemporary newspapers and scholarly journals North and South sung its praises. *The New York Times* declared *Porgy* "a noteworthy achievement in the sympathetic and convincing interpretation of Negro life by a member of an 'outside' race."[164] In the *Virginia Quarterly Review*, James Southall Wilson declared, "No more beautiful or authentic novel has been published in America for a decade."[165] Heywood Broun's *New York World* review expressed well Northern white readers' enthusiastic reception: *Porgy* was "among the most fascinating of recent books. . . . I was fully prepared for another of those condescending books about fine old black mammies and such like. But this is not the book. . . . Mr. Heyward takes a step beyond the usual attitude of white writers in the South who deal with Negro life."[166] Even future first lady Eleanor Roosevelt loved *Porgy*. She sent Heyward her copy of the book, asking him to sign it: "I cannot tell you how much the book has interested us all. It is a permanent inhabitant in our library."[167] NAACP leader W. E. B. DuBois, however, sounded a slightly more critical and socially insightful note: "DuBose Heywood [*sic*] writes 'Porgy' and writes beautifully of the black underworld. But why does he do this? Because he cannot do a similar thing for the white people of Charleston, or they would drum him out of town."[168]

Porgy's vigorous nationwide book sales catapulted Heyward to a new financial bracket and to a permanent career as a professional writer. Heyward's income from writing and lecturing leapt from $1,358 in 1925 to $10,243 the

The cover from the sheet music of *Porgy and Bess* makes
use of stock Charleston images from the period, such
as a palmetto tree, a tenement house, and a black
street huckster. From the Collections of the
South Carolina Historical Society.

year after *Porgy* was published. Until the great stock market crash and subsequent Depression several years later, Heyward and his wife continued to
earn a significant combined professional salary from their works, hitting an
astounding high point in 1929 of over $50,000 (equal to approximately half a
million dollars in 2002).[169]

Heyward's images of Charleston, its history and its people, were further
popularized by the stage version of *Porgy*, which opened to enthusiastic crowds
at the New York Theatre Guild in October 1927. To reinforce the play's "authentic" flavor, the New York producers brought from Charleston the all-
black Jenkins Orphanage Band to perform in the pageant/parade scenes.[170]
The play's program alerted viewers that it was "the original band" that was
"part of the actual aggregation described in the lodge parade of Mr. Heyward's
novel." Likewise, the playbill contained lyrics to the spirituals sung in the play
and thanked Charleston's all-white Society for the Preservation of Negro

Spirituals for their "assistance in securing and recording the spirituals used in the play."[171] Dorothy Heyward, coauthor of the play, noted in a *New York Times* article that her husband, along with fellow Charlestonian Sam Stoney, "undertook to give a lesson in Gullah to our Northern actors."[172] Thus, even though critics praised the production for employing a black cast instead of white actors in blackface, the actors' understanding of Gullah and of the life-style of the Low Country African American, and by extension the audience's understanding, was nonetheless filtered through the sensibility of elite white Charlestonians.[173]

Popular and critical praise for the play—its rich atmospheric scenery, passionate spirituals, and vivid storyline—ran high.[174] Percy Hammond praised the "dilapidated grandeur of the Catfish Row setting" in the *Herald Tribune*.[175] The New York *American* marveled at "the fervor, the hysteria, the emotionalism, and the curious abandon" of the spirituals. "All the colored 'folks' raised their voices, gesticulated, gyrated, as they joined the volcanic choruses. It was something new to most of us—may I say to all of us."[176] *New York World* drama critic Alexander Woolcott called its first night "an evening of new experience, extraordinary interest and high startling beauty. . . . Except for the isolated masterpiece 'The Emperor Jones,' this 'Porgy' is the first good job the American theater has done with the Negro. . . . The subscription list was overjoyed by the entertainment."[177] After its popular New York run, *Porgy* went on a long road trip and played in packed houses across the country and abroad. *Porgy* even reached nontheater audiences when America's most popular blackface vaudevillian, Al Jolson, performed an adapted version of the play on radio.[178] The play's success and storyline also attracted Broadway lights when George and Ira Gershwin collaborated with Heyward to create the opera *Porgy and Bess*. From its opening in 1935 until today, audiences have embraced Porgy's Charleston as a world where "the livin' is easy."[179]

Subsequent to *Porgy*, Heyward's position as a social critic evolved. In his 1929 novel *Mamba's Daughters* and 1931 play *Brass Ankle*, for example, he moved in more progressive directions, exploring controversial themes of the "race question," such as intermarriage, miscegenation, and hierarchies within the black community. However, because *Porgy* was his most successful work and the literary work most often associated with Charleston, these developments had little impact on popular conceptions of the city's character. And yet, despite the national identification of the handicapped beggar's tragic tale with Old Charleston, a theatrical version of the novel was not mounted in the city of its birth for many decades. In 1954, the same year the U.S. Supreme Court struck down segregation in its *Brown v. Board of Education* ruling, Charleston's

Dock Street Theatre and a local black troupe, the Stagecrafters, attempted to stage a performance. In keeping with local customs, the theater aisle would have divided the audience, blacks to one side, whites to the other. After a protest from the national black weekly *Jet* and the NAACP, the Dock Street Theatre canceled the production.[180] It was not until forty-five years after the novel's original publication that *Porgy and Bess* opened in Charleston as part of the city's tricentennial celebration in 1970.[181]

CONSIDERED WITHIN THE larger literary post–World War I literary scene, Charleston's literary productions drew upon and also helped fuel white America's ongoing love affair with the so-called romantic South. This myth, first articulated, arguably, in the antebellum period and reinforced after the Civil War with the popular writings of Joel Chandler Harris, Thomas Nelson Page, and Thomas Dixon, endured into the Hollywood era through films such as *The Birth of a Nation, Jezebel,* and *Gone with the Wind*.[182] Following this trend, throughout the 1920s and 1930s, an increased number of novels, mysteries, plays, and popular magazine articles and stories took as their subject the South and, even more specifically, the South Carolina Low Country.

Despite its productivity and contemporary success, the Charleston Group today is little known. Its members' works rarely appear in regional literary anthologies, which tend to include instead more intellectually complicated and original works by William Faulkner, Eudora Welty, Robert Penn Warren, and Thomas Wolfe. DuBose Heyward's name is sometimes recognized, but mostly in connection with his collaboration with the Gershwins in the writing of *Porgy and Bess*. While knowledge of the Charleston Group's contribution to the American literary scene of the 1920s and 1930s has faded, its cultural productions have had an enduring impact on the city about which its members wrote. Their poems, novels, and folktales were central material and intellectual expressions of the historical identity and public culture that elite whites constructed for the city during the interwar years.

CHAPTER FOUR

Here Came Remembrance

STAGING RACE AND PERFORMING THE PAST

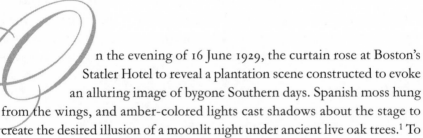

O n the evening of 16 June 1929, the curtain rose at Boston's Statler Hotel to reveal a plantation scene constructed to evoke an alluring image of bygone Southern days. Spanish moss hung from the wings, and amber-colored lights cast shadows about the stage to create the desired illusion of a moonlit night under ancient live oak trees.[1] To complete the picture, some forty white Charlestonians, dressed in elaborate antebellum costumes, stood in a semicircle facing the audience. "The menfolk wore tuxedos and broad bow ties of the cavalier days, and the women, Southern belles who lived up to the southern tradition of beauty, in crinoline dresses."[2] The silence broke as the members of this "historical" tableaux began to sing the low, rhythmic tones of an African American spiritual. To the swaying of colored hoop skirts and the clapping of white hands, the singers beckoned their listeners to escape on the wings of song to the presumably simpler, romantic days of the Old South. "Come Come en Go Wid Me," they intoned in their version of the Gullah language common to African Americans in the South Carolina Low Country: "Ef yuh wan tuh git tuh Heben, Jus' come en go wid me."[3] Through a rousing ovation and flowers thrown onto the stage, the Northern white audience expressed its delight at the musical journey to the "Heben" known as the plantation past.[4]

Founded in 1922 by a group of slave-owner descendants in Charleston, the Society for the Preservation of Negro Spirituals (SPS) presented this peculiar brand of heritage display to enthusiastic audiences throughout the South and North in the years between the world wars. Their public concerts comprise a rich and complicated example of the staging of race—of blackness and whiteness—in 1920s and 1930s America, as well as the mobilizing of historical authority to legitimate contemporary political and social structures. A formidable player in Charleston's culture-preservation machine, the work of the Spirituals Society also provides an opportunity to consider the way racial beliefs and historical memory can be constructed and transmitted bodily. Anthropologist Paul Connerton has argued that social memory is essentially performative in nature—that individuals create commemorative rituals to give shape to the myths and values that have meaning to them. The ritual SPS performances might be best understood as the "ceremonially embodied form" of the idealized memories and traditions of the Low Country slave plantation, as understood by the singers themselves.[5] Through song, movement, staging, and costume, the SPS "preserved" the voice and beliefs of a mythic "old-time" African American that served as a counterpart to the Society's simultaneous performative construction of Southern whites as genteel and paternalistic. The final product was an entertaining "history" lesson for concertgoers.

The success of SPS performances drew from a range of established racist stereotypes in American culture, from Joel Chandler Harris's late-nineteenth-century tales of the nurturing Uncle Remus to the more menacing rapist Gus in D. W. Griffith's landmark silent film, *The Birth of a Nation.* Blackface images long permeated the world in which the SPS operated. Blackface minstrelsy, for example, originated in the early-nineteenth-century North when white circus performers projected onto the stage their imagined sense of the world of black folk to amuse their largely working-class white audiences. Throughout the century, blackface gained popularity through the theatrical practices of white performers, such as Daniel Decatur Emmett, the Ohio-born singer considered by many to be the composer of "Dixie," and Thomas Dartmour Rice, the creator of the standard minstrel character, "Jim Crow." In time, blackface became such a common cultural practice that even some black performers, such as Charles Callendar's "Georgia Minstrels," began to apply burnt cork to their faces and to participate in the popular commercial craze.[6] Minstrelsy's central format of burlesque, jokes, songs, and dances, its themes, and the antics of comedic, wily, or childlike blacks extended into the early twentieth century as a standard feature of vaudeville programs. From the late 1880s on, the emerging consumer culture increasingly adopted black caricatures—the smiling, kerchief-wearing Mammy; the grinning, watermelon-eating pickanninny; the loyal, pipe-smoking Uncle Mose—to adorn salt and pepper shakers,

Dressed in their stage costumes, Spirituals Society members gathered in a
Charleston garden for a photo promoting their first northern tour in 1929.
From the Collections of the South Carolina Historical Society.

cookie jars, spoon rests, souvenirs, advertisements, postcards, sheet music,
toys, banks, and household bric-a-brac; the best-known example of this
character in popular material culture, of course, is the pancake-making Aunt
Jemima.[7] The fiction of a nurturing, devoted Southern black Mammy became
so ingrained in the American imagination that in 1923 Congress debated a
proposal to erect a statue in "her" honor on the mall in Washington, D.C.[8]
Although the monument resolution failed to pass, the ideal of the Mammy
did not go away. Hattie McDaniel's Academy Award–winning version of
the character in the 1939 blockbuster film *Gone with the Wind* testified to the
figure's primacy in American popular culture. Always on the pulse of national
tastes, Hollywood consistently depicted blackface on screen, making it central
to the action of the nation's first "talkie" production, *The Jazz Singer* in 1927.
Not to be outdone, radio (and later television) programs such as *Amos 'n Andy*
continued the minstrel tradition in American entertainment. By the time the
Society for the Preservation of Negro Spirituals took to the stage, then, racist
notions of blacks fully permeated white popular culture.[9]

At first glance, SPS performances might be misconstrued as a mere continuation of the long-standing blackface minstrel tradition in American entertainment history. Once understood predominantly as a visual form of racial domination, blackface is currently being reinterpreted by scholars of American culture. Eric Lott and Michael Rogin, for example, see in the "racial masquerade" of blackface an unstable process of white racial and political identity formation.[10] Following this understanding, blackface functions as a fluid and creative phenomenon for its predominantly working-class and ethnic/immigrant white audience. For Lott, nineteenth-century blackface presented a space for negotiating racial conflict as working-class whites crossed the "rigidly bound" color line and "safely" explored their contradictory feelings of repulsion and desire for things black.[11] Rogin, on the other hand, argues that the racial humor of blackface in twentieth-century cinema provided a vehicle for the "Americanization" of European immigrants, who were able to define themselves in opposition to African Americans, thus moving "settlers and ethnics into the melting pot by keeping racial groups out."[12] In each case, blackface served in part as a white forum for temporary "identity exchange."[13]

While the Spirituals Society shared with blackface the appropriation of African American cultural forms—language, music, and movement—that helped perpetuate white-conceived racial stereotypes of blacks, the specifics of the Society's concerts render them largely incompatible with these current scholarly understandings of minstrelsy as, in Rogin's words, "a form of racial cross-dressing."[14] First and foremost, SPS members were elites who performed for other white elites. Rhetorically, the SPS infused performances with the language of noblesse oblige and cultural stewardship in an attempt to distance themselves self-consciously from the racial burlesque of blackface and the vulgar racism of the resurgent Ku Klux Klan of the 1920s. Spirituals Society members did not "cross-dress" under the cover of burnt cork and the tattered or dandified costumes common to minstrel productions. Instead, they donned the costume of the slave-owner, not the slave, to underscore racial hierarchy and to declare visually their role as representatives of the Old South in modern-day America. Thus, Society members did not seek to inhabit an alternative, fantasy persona of blackness, nor did they experiment with notions of disorder through their performances, a common trope of blackface minstrelsy. The Spirituals Society did not test the power structure in their performances but rather sought to reinforce it.[15] Unlike their blackface counterparts, then, there was no mistaking the essential whiteness and elitism of

Charleston's Society for the Preservation of Negro Spirituals. For sps singers, color and class lines were fixed, not fluid, and were to remain that way.[16]

The Spirituals Society, then, was something altogether different on the American entertainment scene of the 1920s and 1930s. Its members were were not interested in letting go of their elite white propriety and escaping into an "exotic" black world, as did the fur-wearing white clientele who flocked to the jazzy, high-energy, and free-footed all-black spectacles of establishments such as Harlem's Cotton Club and Connie's Inn.[17] Nor can they be considered simply a white version of the formal all-black choirs who brought such fame to Fisk and Hampton Universities in the late nineteenth and early twentieth centuries by touring the United States (and abroad) and performing religious hymns for largely white audiences.[18] Yet the Society shared with other modernist-era ventures, such as the Harlem Renaissance and John Lomax's development of an archive of American folklore at the Library of Congress, the widespread white fascination with African American culture.

As a highly successful form of the kind of historical masquerade and pageantry popular in the early part of the twentieth century, the Spirituals Society concerts gave dynamic, performative shape to idyllic myths and memories about Charleston's past, its present, and, by extension, its future.[19] Basing the correctness of its worldview on authority claims rooted in family ties and selective historical memory, the sps presented its elite white audiences with a prescription for the angst of modern America, in particular, the dislocation of traditional agrarian-based values brought on by the violent disorder of industrialization, urbanization, immigration, unionization, and, most especially, African American politicization. The Society's answer: reclaim a social heritage rooted in the land, kinship networks, and, above all, rigid racial hierarchy. Their speaking for and thus depoliticizing a "vanishing" people through their concerts, then, was an attempt to recast both history and culture in the interest of negotiating these cultural changes and positing an answer to the so-called Negro problem. The result was a therapeutic performative commodity that elite whites around the country eagerly consumed, thus further eroding sectional feelings under the banner of white supremacy.

"A Memorial to Other Days": Spirituals as a Bridge to the Past [20]

On a warm Friday afternoon in May 1923, the Society for the Preservation of Negro Spirituals appeared for the first time in public at a benefit concert for St. Philip's Episcopal Church in Charleston. Twenty or so singers assembled at 9 East Battery Street, an antebellum mansion fronting Charleston harbor, to conduct a spiritual "shout" for a paying audience.[21] During the performance, a thirty-six-year-old white woman named Panchita Heyward Grimball stepped forward from her fellow chorus members and explained her organization's main purpose: to collect and preserve African American spirituals. The group was not interested in just any spirituals, only those identified with a specific time and place—spirituals "that were sung in slavery days and the 25 years immediately following in the Carolina coast country." Such a specific historical focus, Grimball explained, bolstered the Society's goal of maintaining "as much as possible of the pure African wildness and beauty of tone, only touched by the religion of the Anglo-Saxon, not as the negro of today sings the Baptist, Methodist and Episcopal hymns, merely varied by the African love of syncopation."[22]

The Society's interest in the musical expressions of former slaves and their descendants was rooted not only in a sincere aesthetic appreciation for the spirituals' beautiful melodies and lyrics but also in intimate associations between these songs and the white singers' family histories. Most Society members were descended from slave-owners; some had even been raised on decaying postbellum plantations by African American nurses and thus had extensive exposure to Gullah and spirituals during their lifetimes. For the SPS, spirituals were valuable and worthy of preservation because they represented an aspect of the elite white birthright and a vital link to a personalized version of Carolina's past. The Society sought to pass down to posterity more than just the songs themselves; it saw spirituals as a powerful vehicle for promoting a particular historical understanding of the past that was shaped by the contemporary erosion of racial traditions that had once been rooted in, as Grimball described it, "the slave's love for this Master and our undying love for our Maumas."[23] The Spirituals Society's activities, then, illustrate more about the fears and hopes of its white participants than they do about the actual cultural practices of African Americans.

For months prior to this inaugural concert, a group of elite white friends and family members had been meeting casually at each other's homes to sing spirituals for pleasure and to reminisce about their lost plantation childhoods. One day in 1922, over lunch at Wappaoolah, the Heyward family plantation on the Cooper River, Grimball and several others present discussed forming their group into "a society."[24] At the time, Charleston had a full-blown case of organizational fever, hosting an astonishing array of newly founded elite cultural associations bent on preserving and memorializing the region. Both the Poetry Society of South Carolina and the Society for the Preservation of Old Dwellings, for example, had been established two years earlier, and the birth of the Charleston Etchers' Club was only a year away. In keeping with this general enthusiasm, in the fall of 1922, at Grimball's Colonial Street home in Charleston's Battery neighborhood, elites formed the Society for the Preservation of Negro Spirituals. In the beginning, the Society professed three main goals: "the preservation of Negro Spirituals and Folk Songs, the education of the rising generation in their character and rendition, and the maintenance of a social organization for the pleasure of the members."[25] In 1927, the Society added organized charitable work — "to relieve the distress of the old time negro and his people" — to their mission.[26]

Of all the elite white cultural organizations established in Charleston in the interwar years, none was more socially exclusive than the Spirituals Society.[27] Relative to the SPS, the Poetry and Preservation Societies had nearly open memberships; likewise, the Etchers' Club, with non-blue-blooded members such as artists Elizabeth Verner and Alfred Hutty, was more democratic. By contrast, only the very select few were invited to join the Spirituals Society. The requirement that all members be "Charleston people who were born and reared on plantations nearby or who were reared under plantation traditions" guaranteed its elitist and somewhat incestuous character.[28] During the 1920s and 1930s, the truly active core of this organization generally numbered around fifty persons, many of whom were related by blood or marriage.[29] Most of these amateur singers were young, married professionals — bankers, lawyers, architects, writers. Their surnames — Porcher, Smythe, Stoney, Grimke, Ravenel, Heyward, Huger, Hutson, Sass, Rutledge, Drayton — constituted a familiar roll call of the oldest and once powerful slave-owning families in the Low Country.[30]

Of course, none of the Society's charter members had experienced first-hand the world they memorialized in song — life on a slave plantation. Most members, in fact, were born after 1876, the year in which Wade Hampton's terrorist band of "red shirts" rampaged across the state restoring white supremacy from what white South Carolinians considered the dark days of "Negro Rule" during Reconstruction. Regardless of their distance from the antebellum past, SPS members declared as their birthright full allegiance to their ancestors' world; indeed, they brought it "back to life" in the public performance of spirituals. "We love these wonderful primitive songs which come from the soul of an alien race," SPS president Alfred Huger explained in 1930. "When we sing them they are really sung in our own hearts with a reverence and sympathetic understanding of [their] significance to the old South, of which, I am happy to say, all of us are a part."[31] Yet not every member of the

SPS was, indeed, a Southerner. Mrs. William Elliott (Katherine C.) Hutson, for example, who served for years as the group's prolific executive secretary and supervised the Society's field recordings of spirituals in the mid-1930s, claimed Mount Vernon, Ohio, as her birthplace.[32] Apparently, that regional handicap could be largely overcome by a "good marriage," in this case to an old-line plantation family like the Hutsons, and by the attendant unconditional devotion to the city and its elite white heritage. Through blood, marriage, a strong sense of inherited historical memory, and a desire to reinvent their past and present realities, this generation of singers felt inextricably tied to antebellum plantation culture and compelled to celebrate a past they never knew.[33] Not surprisingly, the SPS did not publicize their occasional non-Southerner member. Instead, the Society cultivated a reputation as a group comprised *exclusively* of the children of former slave-owners, who, they claimed, "all know and understand the negro character, probably as well as any white man ever does."[34] Thus, SPS members positioned themselves as authentic representatives of the plantation past.

Through spirituals, the Society sought to preserve their portrait of a particular type of Low Country African American they called "the old-time darkey."[35] This "type" was either a former slave or a free African American bred in a mythical tradition that dictated dependency on and contented deference to whites. The favored "old-time darkey" was generally a poor and illiterate laborer or former house servant who lived in the countryside and maintained the linguistic tradition of the Gullah-speaking people. The Gullahs had their roots in the many thousands of slaves and their descendants who forged on the rice plantations of the South Carolina Sea Islands a language and folk culture that mixed African and European forms. Key to this community development was the absence of the slave masters who preferred to spend their days off the plantations in the white society of Charleston.[36] In the face of this absenteeism, and with the power of sheer numbers on their side, the Gullah created what historian and folklorist Charles Joyner calls a strong "symbolic group identity . . . for themselves [that] was impressed most powerfully upon the generations to come."[37]

Several historical developments contributed to the Society's concern about the imminent "extinction" of this type of African American. First, beginning in the 1910s, a steady stream of blacks left the South hoping to escape the oppression of Jim Crow and to secure better-paying jobs in the North, especially as American industry reoriented itself toward producing materiel for World War I. Part of this "Great Migration" also included the movement of blacks from the countryside to cities within the South, such as Charleston, thus destabilizing what SPS members called the blacks' "country" culture.[38] The "civilizing effect of city life" contaminated the authentic primitivism of the "old time darkies in their country churches."[39] Second, improved educational opportunities for blacks in Charleston, such as the 1920 victory of the local NAACP branch in securing black teachers in black city schools, signaled an increasingly vocal black population interested in civil rights and middle-class cultural norms.[40] The visible and vocal presence of a "New Negro" leadership in the city owed much to the Avery Institute, an all-black school founded after the Civil War under the auspices of the American Missionary Association. Eugene C. Hunt, an African American native of Charleston and Avery graduate, described white attitudes toward black education at his alma mater during the 1930s:

> As far as the whites in the city were concerned I don't think they had a very great affection for Avery. I believe that they had some of that old attitude that here was a school that was educating the Negroes to be smart alecks and I don't think that they had any fondness whatsoever for Avery which was teaching blacks that they were the equal of anybody and need not apologize to anybody. . . . I think this is why the whites did not like us so because we did not accept the fact that we were inferior in any way and we carried ourselves as well even though we had to obey the laws at the time.[41]

Third, growing black literacy and urbanity contributed to the increased use of printed religious hymnals among black congregations wishing to distance themselves from anything associated with slavery and jeopardized the survival of spirituals.[42] "The negro of today," longtime SPS president Alfred Huger noted in 1927, "has no use for the unprinted hymns and the old religious songs of the plantation negro are fast becoming unknown or forgotten by his own race."[43] SPS member DuBose Heyward explored this very real black middle-class prejudice and the generational tensions against the ecstatic singing of spirituals in his 1929 Charleston novel, *Mamba's Daughters*. Says one educated black character in the novel, "Oh, that's all right for these ignorant negroes, I suppose, but where'd we be if we stopped at that? We've got to go beyond it. We've [*sic*] living in a civilised [*sic*] community."[44] With the future of traditional, spontaneous spirituals thus endangered among the very people who created them, SPS members decided it was their duty as historical stewards to preserve slavery's musical legacy.

The SPS was neither the first nor the only group of white individuals intrigued by the art of Africa American spirituals after the Civil War. In Thomas

Wentworth Higginson's 1867 *Atlantic Monthly* essay, "Negro Spirituals," the former Massachusetts abolitionist and colonel of the First South Carolina Volunteers, the first federally authorized African American regiment of the Civil War, reproduced thirty-five songs, many garnered from his time in the Low Country. "There is no parallel instance of an oppressed race thus sustained by the religious sentiment alone," he wrote. "These songs are but the vocal expression of the simplicity of their faith and the sublimity of their long resignation."[45] That same year, three Northern white authors published the music and lyrics of over 130 spirituals in a volume titled *Slave Songs of the United States*. Presaging the concerns SPS members voiced fifty years later, the authors lamented the disinterest in spirituals on the part of the Emancipation generation: "It is, we repeat, already becoming difficult to obtain these songs. . . . The 'spirituals' . . . are going out of use on the plantations."[46] As the decades passed, spirituals began appearing more regularly in folk collections, such as Thomas P. Fenner's *Cabin and Plantation Songs* of 1892 and H. E. Krehbiel's 1914 *Afro-American Folk Songs*.[47] African American interest in spirituals sung in a formal manner was also manifested in the choirs of Fisk and Hampton Universities, each of which published several volumes of their folk songs.[48] The singing and compositions of conservatory-trained Henry T. Burleigh, an early popularizer and publisher of spirituals, as well as the later stage performances of Paul Robeson, Roland Hayes, and Marian Anderson, brought black folk music into mainstream America. By the 1920s, the fascination with black folklore in white academic circles, such as the social scientists and early folklorists working with Howard W. Odum at the University of North Carolina, and certain "reawakened"[49] race-conscious black circles was very real. In 1925, James Weldon Johnson, the NAACP national leader and composer of the "Negro National Anthem," "Lift Ev'ry Voice and Sing," declared spirituals a national "vogue."[50] Johnson, who the same year coauthored the *Book of American Negro Spirituals*, saw particular political significance to this trend for his people: "This reawakening of the Negro to the value and beauty of the Spirituals was the beginning of an entirely new phase of race consciousness."[51] Of course, members of Charleston's SPS would argue that the spirituals' real value lay in quite the opposite idea of American blackness.

Shortly after its inception, the Society established two committees to expedite the collection and preservation of "authentic" spirituals. The Committee on Expeditions, for instance, arranged excursions into the surrounding countryside "to hear negroes sing," while the Committee on Research and Preservation, headed by Katherine C. Hutson and local poet/author Josephine Pinckney, reflected the growing contemporary interest in social-scientific approaches to culture. Its mission was to ascertain "the locality, origin and history of each spiritual" and to create a permanent record of each spiritual's lyrics and melodies.[52] To achieve these ends, sps members traveled to remote plantations and island churches in the Low Country to hear African Americans singing and conducting religious services.

These expeditions, much like the singing of spirituals in concert, provided sps members with an opportunity to experience vicariously residual elements from the past they imagined so vividly. In a local newspaper article, Hutson conveyed her sense of the exotic aspect of these ventures during a visit to a marshy coastal plantation "wrapped in the witchery" of a summer night. She called her reader to "imagine yourself" in a landscape haunted by time: "On the one hand, an abandoned rice field stretches itself into obscurity through the fast fading twilight, and on the other a negro grave yard in a protecting grove of moss hung oaks, raises its wooden 'tombstones' like 'hants' into the night; the silence unbroken save for the occasional bellow of an alligator in the rive field bog." From the shadows, Hutson continued seductively, you hear "a low wailing song accompanied by the dull monotonous thud of a tom-tom, beating out its tatoo into the night air . . . defining the measures of a primitive plantation spiritual . . . and gradually, as one stirring from a dream, we realize that we have come upon a plantation praise house, the place where spirituals are born. Could any one fail to thrill at such a disclosure?"[53] Spirituals Society members and their loyal audiences could not.

With such rare "free access"[54] to "authentic" Gullah performances, the sps quickly became a sort of clearinghouse for information on spirituals. After all, it had supplied the spirituals for the 1927 Broadway opening and subsequent national tour of DuBose Heyward's successful play *Porgy*.[55] This public status as experts is not surprising given the proprietary manner in which the sps spoke of "owning" the spirituals they sang, effectively transforming regionally potent spirituals into a national consumer product.[56] In 1931, for example, a woman living in New York City who described herself as "a southern girl—from Georgia," wrote the sps: "I understand that you are now selling Spirituals and I would very much love to have some—I collect and sing them so of course welcome any opportunity for new ones."[57]

As the Society's stature grew, a wide array of individuals and groups from across the country deferred to the Society for guidance about spirituals. Women's clubs, students, and teachers requested reading recommendations for the preparation of lectures and research papers on spirituals. Representatives of religious and civic groups likewise sought aid in designing educational and entertainment programs. A folksinger in Saskatchewan, Canada, appealed to what he considered the SPS's experience-based authority: "I have never lived among our colored people and lack the understanding that must be possessed by those of you who have been giving such effective interpretations to their songs."[58] Even some civil servants working in Roosevelt's New Deal government programs, such as the Works Progress Administration's Writer's Project and the Civilian Conservation Corps, corresponded with the SPS. The Society also received letters asking permission to use "their" spirituals in performances and in publications, including the highly nationalist *Girl Scout Songbook*[59] and a children's textbook. In the latter case, the Society insisted on "the privilege of proofreading both for music and Gullah" to assure its "correctness" and "authenticity."[60]

In the face of this increase in renown, the SPS adopted a more serious and professionalized approach to the collection and preservation of spirituals. In the beginning, members simply listened carefully to the words and rhythms of the spirituals during their country excursions, and then attempted to reproduce those sounds by memory during rehearsals back in the comfort of their Charleston parlors. Likewise, early on, the Society resisted publishing spirituals because it considered printed hymnals the harbinger of cultural decline. The SPS wished instead to preserve in the oral tradition the music's primitivism and spontaneity, thus avoiding possible "misinterpretation by persons not familiar with the 'gullah' language they were composed in."[61] In the late 1920s, many individuals—in particular academics in folklore, sociology, and musicology—were publishing volumes of African American songs and stories.[62] In 1931, the Society formally entered this national conversation with the publication of forty-nine spirituals in their volume *The Carolina Low-Country*. Meanwhile, continuing their desire to control the "correct" presentation of Gullah, the SPS contemplated recording spirituals, "so that their true form will be preserved for future generations."[63] Responding to market demand and alluring new technology, the seemingly antimodern SPS eventually turned from written transcription to the thoroughly modern method of audio recording.

Walter Garwick, a New York purveyor of recording instruments, visited Charleston in 1936 to secure recordings of local African American folk music and dialect for a collection being developed for Columbia University by English professor George W. Hibbitt.[64] The Spirituals Society members who escorted Garwick around town and to outlying churches to facilitate his work were excited by the new technology.[65] The following year, in the midst of the Depression, the Society purchased from Garwick a $575 electrograph recording instrument that could be operated from the engine of a car or boat,

A photo of a group of African Americans, most likely taken during one of the Spirituals Society's excursions to the country-side to hear and record Gullah singing. From the Collections of the South Carolina Historical Society.

allowing the Society to make field recordings.[66] Armed with this new device, Garwick declared, the Society could "preserve a distinct and important division of American history" while becoming "better known everywhere for this work." Garwick also pointed out the potential commercial possibilities of Gullah recordings to a folk-interested American public: "I believe those street calls could be made into records that will return a sufficient profit . . . [and] should sell to every college and library."[67]

The Society put the machine to good use, creating its own rich yet selective audio history of African American life in Low Country South Carolina. Drawing upon their elite white network of "'key' people in the various river and plantation sections of the low country," they recorded examples of "endangered" African American sermons, prayers, and spirituals from Collins Creek on the Santee River south to Edisto Island.[68] In some regards, the belief that these Gullah expressions were "fast vanishing" reflected more than mere nostalgia and resulted in the Society's very real ethnographic contribution to the preservation of American folklore.[69] On one occasion, for example, the SPS operated its electrograph in the pews of "Crumble Alley" Church on Cromwell Alley in Charleston shortly before the building was destroyed and its long-established black congregation disbanded to make way for the construction of an all-white public housing project, the Robert Mills Manor.[70] The Society also recorded the sing-songy entrepreneurial calls of Charleston's

African American street hucksters—"Yes Ma'm, I got flowers" and "Porgy walk with a knife and fork"[71]—whose methods were a throwback to an earlier form of merchandising that predated establishments that lined King Street, Charleston's main commercial thoroughfare. As Garwick promised, the SPS street cries record sold for $1.50 to tourists, educational associations, and through the Gramaphone Shop, a New York–based record distributor.[72] In July 1937, Harold Spivacke, the acting chief of the Division of Music at the Library of Congress, took an interest in the Society's collection and solicited the SPS to deposit its recordings in the nascent Archive of American Folk-Song.[73]

The collection, preservation, and recording of spirituals constituted a significant aspect of the SPS members' understanding of themselves as paternalists acting in the mode of their planter ancestors. Because compulsory education was "ruining" country black folk and their music, the Society's logic went, and because African Americans failed to recognize this as a tragedy, the ladies and gentlemen of the SPS had to follow the tradition of generations of elite whites by protecting African Americans from their own worst tendencies. At times, this meant whites attempting to educate African Americans about the value of spirituals. In 1936, for example, during a recording trip to Bethel Church in the small coastal shrimping village of McClellanville, the SPS encouraged blacks to avoid the temptations of modernity and adhere instead to their ancient traditions. SPS member Major Hugh McGillvary appealed to the all-black congregation to preserve their spirituals "in spite of the white man's organ and hymn book." He flattered the assembly, praising their "gift of song, melody and rhythm" and noting "that the white man cannot compete with the negro on those grounds, no matter how he may try."[74] At a 1929 concert held at Charleston's Victory Theater for 2,500 delegates of the South Carolina Teachers' Association, Alfred Huger, SPS president at the time, recounted another example of the SPS educating blacks on the value of spirituals. Huger introduced the group's traditional closing number, "Primus Lan'," with an eerie tale of white stewardship and untimely death. One rainy day while searching for spirituals up the coast near Beaufort, several SPS members waited out a storm by sharing a farm shed with a group of African American tomato pickers. When Huger and his companions discovered that the laborers did not know the spiritual "I'll Meet Yuh in de Primus Lan'," they proceeded to teach them the words and music. Shortly thereafter, Huger told his captivated audience, the rain stopped and the African Americans began to row home across a small river. "Something went wrong in connection with the craft, which capsized. The two women, who had recently been singing of meeting in the 'Primus Land,' were both drowned."[75] Had the SPS members not "out-Negroed the Negro" in this instance, these two poor laborers might have died without having praised their maker accordingly.[76]

In 1927, after several years of concert success and increased regional celebrity, the SPS extended its paternalism beyond mere cultural stewardship into actual charitable contributions benefiting Low Country blacks.[77] "As descendants of plantation owners and slave owners," President Huger explained to a Philadelphia woman in 1929, "we feel that the money we get from singing these songs which we have learned from the negroes themselves on the plantation[s] hereabouts should be spent in the preservation of this music and in the relief of suffering and disease among the race which created the music."[78] Accordingly, the Society's Relief Committee wrote checks to city welfare agencies earmarked "colored relief," which was especially needed during the desperate years of the Depression.[79] In keeping with their "planter" paternalism, the members turned their attention most often to Charleston's outlying areas where the "old time negro and his people" could still be found.[80]

Through word of mouth and subsequent home visits, the Relief Committee selected as worthy of aid a particular type of "old time negro." The Society placed a premium, for example, on the recipient's status as a former slave or servant of a prominent white Low Country family or, as in the case of seventy-one-year-old Tina Armstong, a "cook in the Confederate War."[81] Case files describing these individuals stressed the docile character traits — "loyal," "hard worker," "faithful," and "uncomplaining" — that Society members felt lacking in the "modern" black.[82] The SPS Committee dispensed traditional forms of charity — food, clothing, firewood, medicine, grocery money, crutches, even funerary clothes — in a manner not dissimilar to the dispersal of new clothes and increased food rations to slaves during Christmas on the antebellum plantation. Select "old time" blacks undoubtedly benefited from this largesse.

From the late 1920s to 1940, the Society allocated thousands of dollars of their concert earnings to help individual Low Country African Americans, in some cases supporting "regulars" until their deaths.[83] In certain instances, the SPS coordinated its charity efforts with local relief agencies to avoid redundancy.[84] In doing so, the Society occasionally stepped in to help individuals and families who might have fallen through the cracks of FDR's New Deal — those who lived, as the local paper described them, "in remote settlements deep in the recesses of the country where the forgotten man has not yet been remembered save by those who penetrate the wilderness."[85] Through its charitable work, the Spirituals Society achieved two ends. It made a material difference in the lives of some struggling blacks during the Depression and reinforced its public and private image as a paternalistic institution carrying on an endangered Charleston tradition.

In addition to charitable works, SPS members reinforced their private and public personae as benevolent paternalists through their publicity materials. The cover drawing of a 1928 Spartanburg, South Carolina, concert program, for instance, depicts two older men facing each other in profile—one white and one black—before a small rural house. Standing upright, and elegantly dressed, the white man smiles from beneath his hat. As he reaches into his pocket as if to offer financial assistance, the white gentleman pats the old, slouched and graying black man on the shoulder comfortingly. It is a scene where the etiquette of racial hierarchy and noblesse oblige interact unmistakably.[86]

"It Is History Reenacted": Performing the Past through Song[87]

The public concert, of course, constituted the Spirituals Society's primary forum for producing and conveying its historical memory. In its early years, the Society's concerts were predominantly small-time local affairs. Occasionally, their performances were part of a larger program displaying "native" talent, such as the "Original [Gullah] Dialect Readings" of Janie Screven Heyward, DuBose Heyward's mother, or the Charleston Orchestra's performances of traditional "plantation melodies" to set the appropriate mood.[88] The audiences at these early recitals were composed mainly of elite white locals—often the friends and families of Society members who were sympathetic to the SPS's worldview—as well as a smattering of elite white tourists. Charleston newspaper editor William Watts Ball evaluated the exclusive "quality" of one such audience in 1924, noting, "We do not suppose that it would have been possible to assemble an audience more capable of passing judgment upon the rendering of spirituals."[89]

Over time, the Spirituals Society became a "headliner" act and expanded its sphere of influence beyond local elites through live national radio broadcasts and tours across the region and major cities in the North. Subsequently, it adopted a more sophisticated and calculated approach to performances, including elaborate costumes and scenery, as well as professionally printed programs and publicity materials. As the Society changed, its role in shaping Charleston's historical memory landscape also evolved. Its local concerts became more and more civic-minded affairs, self-consciously mounted during the tourist and convention seasons, often at the request of the chamber of commerce, with the intent of advertising the city's "historic charm." What began as a very private, entirely voluntary, and largely social organization in

1922 quickly transformed into a professional-minded association with a large stake in its identity as a public representative of Low Country culture.

The 1923 St. Philip's benefit kicked off eighteen years of concerts in packed school auditoriums and civic halls throughout South Carolina and Georgia. For a percentage of the door receipts, a group of at least twenty male and female SPS members, in full antebellum costume, would sing about fifteen spirituals in the Gullah dialect. During a typical program, under a canopy of Spanish moss, one voice in a minor key might begin, "Who buil' duh Aa'k?" evoking the response from the other singers, "Norah, Norah Lawd."[90] The singers would begin to sway gently, then clap quietly, then increase their bodily movements to include foot stomping that matched the quickening rhythm and growing volume of their harmonizing. After completing one spiritual, the chorus would wait silently until the applause died down, only to start up again, stomping as they declared, "Somebody een yuh, it mus' be Jedus."[91] The hoped-for result was a replica of the "Negro shout."

In addition to singing and "shouting," the typical SPS performance included commentary by various members about the origin and meaning of the spirituals and the character of the antebellum society that produced them. Not surprisingly, the Society did not understand spirituals to be, as Frederick Douglass claimed, "the prayer and complaint of souls boiling over with bitterest anguish."[92] Nor did they consider spirituals anything like what W. E. B. DuBois described as "the music of an unhappy people, of the children of disappointment,"[93] or what James Weldon Johnson saw as the artistic outpourings of a slave "far from his native land and customs, despised by those among whom he lived, experiencing the pang of separation of loved ones on the auction block, knowing the hard task master."[94] Instead, Society members stripped the spirituals of their inherent critiques of slavery's oppression—"I gwine t' res' from all my labuh w'en I dead."[95] Lyrics such as "Keep uh runnin' Fiah gwine tuh obuh tek you"[96] and "Gottuh Tek Duh Chillun Outuh Pharaoh Han'"[97] were not, the Society claimed, "originally or even generally the expression of the negroes longing for freedom."[98] Rather, the SPS packaged Low Country spirituals as simple devotional songs—"primitive" black versions of "white camp meeting songs."[99] In his essay in *The Carolina Low-Country*, Robert W. Gordon further articulated the Society's official take on the origins and meaning of spirituals. He argued that since so few of the songs actually contained references to physical slavery any reading of them as oppression or work songs lacked force.[100] The end result, then, was a conception of slavery cleansed of its brutality and instead celebrated as a benevolent antebellum system.

Neither the elites of the SPS nor their white concert audiences chose to recognize the possible double meanings hidden in the spirituals' lyrics.[101] SPS members exhibited no awareness of their ironic status as descendants of planters triumphantly singing of the slave's toil: "Doin' my Maussah wu'k . . . Dis ole wurl' ain't muh home. Chill muh body not muh soul . . . Walkin' on duh borruh lan' . . . my Lawd."[102] Instead of expressions of labor exploitation, SPS president Louis T. Parker described these words in a radio concert as "a good example of the plaintive, woeful type as sung in a minor key and expressing the old time negro's philosophy on life."[103] Similarly, the meaning of a black person praying hopefully for liberation from enslavement and Christian salvation through death—"'Cause w'en I cross dat siporatin' line I'm gwine lebe dis wurl' behin'"[104]—became, in the Society's rhetoric, merely the blacks' "joyful anticipation of going to heaven."[105] There was no place in the Society's performance of the past for the essential violence of slavery and African Americans' profound religious resistance to it.

Just as the Society made sure to communicate its particular understanding of the spirituals' meanings to their audiences, so, too, did it work to distance performances from the blackface minstrel tradition. As early as May 1923, the fear of being misconstrued as "a burlesque on the religious practices of the negroes, or the catch-penny mimicry of the familiar 'black-face comedian,'" led Society secretary Arthur J. Stoney to suggest "that before an uninitiated audience, it would be advisable . . . to dispense with the ecstatic and rhythmic motions employed by the negroes."[106] Although the Society vetoed Stoney's proposal, it adopted the practice of explaining why and how their performance was fundamentally different from vaudeville minstrelsy. Before each concert, a representative singer informed the audience that although the Negro's "way of expressing himself, even in religion, is often amusing," the Spirituals Society members approached "their subject sincerely with only respect and love for the oldtime negro as they know him . . . to reproduce his voice, pronunciation and actions while singing, but never to ridicule him."[107]

Occasionally, white audiences failed to make the distinction. Crowds sometimes exploded with laughter at the Society's "shouting" or, as evidenced by a 1930 *Philadelphia Ledger* headline "Ancient 'Coon Songs' Brought to Philadelphia by Charlestonians," continued to comprehend the Society's performance within the language of minstrelsy. Even if these audiences understood SPS claims that its work was "in no sense a caricature of the negro,"[108] the Society's performances nonetheless perpetuated a derogatory stereotype of African Americans as essentially "primitive" and musical people.[109]

The almost immediate and steady increase in concert requests after the

Society's debut indicates that its particular brand of Low Country cultural performance was a hit. At its first appearance outside of Charleston, at the Savannah Theatre in February 1924, for example, the Society sang before a capacity crowd. According to the local paper, all 1,200 people in attendance thrilled at the "absolute fidelity" of the performance.[110] Even critics of the Society's low-quality amateur singing—"the hearts of the Society are often better attuned than their ears"—nevertheless commented on the "authenticity" of their productions.[111] Many white Southerners appreciated the Society's work and empathized with its concerns over what Alfred Huger called "the 'demoralising' reforms of civilization" on Southern blacks.[112] After a 1930 concert in his city, for example, the editor of the *Augusta Chronicle* bemoaned the fact that Uncle Remus tales and the spirituals "which we of the older generation heard with wide open eyes in the far off days of our childhood are no longer told to children by their second mother—the dark-skinned Maumma." The editor lauded the Society's work in trying to preserve the songs of the "primitive negro . . . in a state uncontaminated by the outside world."[113] As stewards of the past, members of the Society became known in certain regional circles, in the words of one enthusiast from Mississippi, as "true Southerners."[114]

While undoubtedly expressing a regional identity, the SPS also claimed spirituals as part of "the art of the whole country."[115] The Society's productions were aimed at and appealed to non-Southerners as well, who became a mainstay of local concerts from the mid-1920s on. At a 1924 Charleston concert, the *News & Courier* reported that "the enthusiasm of the natives of the coast was fully shared by visitors from a distance. . . . [S]everal ladies from New York . . . declared that this recital alone would have been more than worth the trip."[116] Over the years, several tourists donated money to the Society to encourage its endeavors.[117] When "A Yankee who appreciates your work" gave a "substantial check" to an SPS member in 1929, the Society's sense of itself as both an American and a Southern institution was reinforced. The SPS saw such largesse, bestowed "within the shadow of Fort Sumter," as a powerful sign of sectional reconciliation, abetted by a shared racial sensibility: "May I not say," the SPS member responded to the donor, "that . . . your gift . . . makes the grandson of a Naval Captain killed while serving in the Confederacy, feel the more strongly what I have always felt, that the war between the States was a mistake of the mind and not of the heart."[118]

Recognizing the national impact the SPS could have on luring tourists to Charleston, local newspapers and city government touted the Society's performances as not-to-be-missed opportunities to experience a part of America's

Low Country past. "They afford the visitor a glimpse into the very heart of the old South," wrote the *News & Courier*, "the South of the romantic and colorful plantation era, which has left so many monuments in this region in the shape of fine old plantation houses, beautiful gardens and stately live oaks."[119] As the Society hoped, some audience members embraced its performance of historical memory as a window into the country's literal history. A reviewer from the *Atlantic Monthly*, for example, noted the power of the Society's costumes and staging in recreating the past: the ensemble "might, without any violent demand upon the imagination, have come together in the fifties of the last century out of the stately houses . . . [of] the Battery."[120] After a "complimentary" concert for the Thirty-fourth Annual United Daughters of the Confederacy Convention in Charleston in 1927, Matthew Andrews Page, a historian from Baltimore, enthused, "Never in my life have I enjoyed anything as more, if as much. It is history reenacted in a most charming and delightful fashion. . . . In my opinion, the negroes themselves could not do so well before an audience."[121] Likewise, commenting on a private SPS performance at Fenwick Hall, a plantation restored by Northern cultural philanthropists Victor and Marjorie Morawetz, internationally renowned composer and music critic Walter Damrosch rhapsodized, "I think the whole thing reflects the spirit of the cultural history of the old South. . . . It is something that should be perpetuated. You people must not let it die."[122]

As tourists from the North and Midwest took their experiences of SPS concerts home with them, the Society's celebrity increased beyond its immediate region. As a result, in 1929, in 1930, and again in 1935, the Society launched tours outside the South, which provided them with fruitful occasions to transmit their idealized vision of Charleston to the nation and to ensure that their "legacy of memory" lived on.

In the spring of 1929, the Society received an invitation from the governor of Massachusetts and the mayor of Boston to sing before the Sixteenth Biennial Conference of the National Federation of Music Clubs.[123] The federation represented over 4,500 music clubs and 300,000 members from across the United States,[124] offering the Society an unprecedented opportunity to promote its work and to forge "national contacts" to further its publication goals.[125] Aware of the tourist appeal of such a concert, Charleston's civic and business leaders threw their full weight behind the Society's trip north. The chamber of commerce sent out to prominent newspapers throughout the South and North hundreds of photographs of Society members, in full costume, arranged picturesquely around a garden pond.[126] Over fifty local businesses, from the Carolina Floral Store to the Southern Ice Company, purchased advertising space in the program for the Society's 23 March local fund-raising concert.[127] The SPS commissioned a poster especially for this event, designed by local artist Ned Jennings, that became a staple of the group's publicity for years to come. Jennings's graphics incorporated all the standard elements of the romantic Southern past that the SPS sought to evoke on stage. Echoing the SPS's concert scenery, the poster featured seven figures in antebellum finery, silhouetted before a glowing full moon, under a large live oak, its protective branches draped with Spanish moss. One male figure bows chivalrously and presents a flower to a seated woman, her hand placed delicately on her hoop skirt, while another couple gaze lovingly at each other, their hands clasped tenderly. In the background, a Greek Revival plantation house, replete with ionic columns and surrounded by blooming azaleas, looms large over a group of four well-kept slave cabins, each of which emits a cozy stream of smoke from its chimney.[128] The geography of this imagined ancestral scene is ordered, beautiful, and nurturing. The institution central to this visual myth makes it presence known not in the persons assembled—no black figure graces the poster—but in the highly symbolic yet anonymous little cabins. The absence of African Americans from this poster speaks legions about their silencing through SPS performances. This local concert was a rousing financial success. Coupled with a $1,000 loan from a local bank, funds raised enabled the Society to send forty-six singers to Boston in June 1929.[129]

As seen in the Jennings poster, the SPS's fantasy production functioned in part as a highly interpretive historical act with therapeutic value for the performers and audience members and as a living tourist brochure for the mythic Old South lingering in Charleston's streets. Promising that the modern American could travel through time to this city where living remnants of an ordered and hierarchical society persisted, SPS fare proved a seductive offering to Northern audiences. The city of Boston, for example, accorded the Spirituals Society a hero's welcome. When buses carrying the Society arrived at the Massachusetts state line on 15 June 1929, "a special escort of motorcycle policemen met [them and] . . . they were given the right of way through the dense traffic of the Boston streets to the Sheraton Hotel [on the Charles River]."[130] Upon their arrival, Massachusetts governor Frank Allen hosted a reception for the singers at the capitol building, posing with these esteemed dignitaries for a throng of newspaper photographers waiting on the statehouse steps.[131]

The Society's three Boston-area concerts were similarly well-received. At Ames Hall in Salem on 15 June, audiences "shook the hall" with appreciative applause.[132] The following day, the crowd at the Boston Repertory Theater

The Southern Club of Boston sponsors the

First Appearance in Boston
of
The Society
for the
Preservation of Spirituals
of

CHARLESTON, SOUTH CAROLINA

Representing the most distinguished families of the old aristocracy of the South

REPERTORY THEATRE
Monday Evening :: June 17, 1929

Tickets $3.00, $2.00, $1.50, $1.00

Tickets at Repertory Theatre, Herrick's and at Room 916, 45 Milk St., Tel. Lib. 2747.

This moonlight and magnolia image of the antebellum South became a standard of the Spirituals Society's concert programs and posters. From the Collections of the South Carolina Historical Society.

expressed its delight at the Society's presence on stage through a series of "involuntary" oohs and aahs. That night, before hundreds of delegates of the National Federation of Music Clubs at the elegant Statler Hotel on the Boston Common, the reaction was similar. "Imagine," the *Boston Transcript* marveled at the scene, "the old song which Miss Jenkins and Mrs. Hutson learned from their mammy nurse, sung by a perfectly groomed debutante!"[133] Reviews consistently attested to the "authenticity" of the spirituals, noting the Society's refusal to sing songs that were not sung by South Carolina blacks. "It is of course impossible," the *Transcript* reporter contended, "for the casual listener to judge of this authenticity, but he feels it so strongly that never a doubt exists in his mind."[134] The collective fantasy was complete.

Back home, Charleston newspapers kept locals abreast of the Society's Boston adventures, happily noting its effect on the former stronghold of abolitionism. The *News & Courier* boasted, "For hundreds of Bostonians Southern scenes of by-gone years were limned, not on canvas, but through the voices of Charleston men and women. . . . Memory of their concerts in Boston will long stay green."[135] The *Charleston Evening Post* delighted at the thought of "stuffy" New Englanders responding so vigorously to "shouting": "These southerners had broken the sternness of a spirited New England demeanor, filled it with a wine of 1850 vintage from a Charleston vineyard, made it smile and live."[136] Clearly, the agrarian and racial values embodied in the antebellum culture commemorated by the SPS were not so regional after all.

After "intoxicating" Boston audiences, the Society stopped briefly for a very exclusive performance near Wilmington, Delaware. Outside the city, at the DuPont family estate, Longwood, the SPS held an open-air garden concert for 400 elite members of society from up and down the East Coast.[137] In only four days above the Mason-Dixon line, the Spirituals Society of Charleston had successfully conveyed its peculiar conception of the Low Country to an expanded and influential constituency.

Less than seven months after its Boston/Wilmington tour, the Society, led by Vice President Augustine T. Smythe, took to the road once more. For this second tour, the Charleston Chamber of Commerce arranged for an Associated Press reporter to accompany the singers, thus assuring publicity "over a wide field."[138] At the request of Victor and Marjorie Morawetz, the SPS arrived in New York City in January 1930 to sing to the Thursday Evening Club.[139] SPS president Alfred Huger accepted the invitation, opining that the organization constituted for the SPS "a proper New York audience."[140] In the select Thursday Evening Club, founded in 1878 and comprised of conservative intellectuals, as well as the old-line society of Washington Square, the

Spirituals Society found its Northern social equivalent.[141] Marjorie Morawetz described the club's membership to Huger as "conservative, cultivated and representative—perhaps a little more of the past than the present."[142] An evening of exchange between like-minded elite individuals was sure to result.

On 9 January 1930, luminaries such as former first lady Mrs. Woodrow Wilson, music critic Walter Damrosch, and former Democratic presidential nominee John W. Davis and guests such as Archie Roosevelt, Thomas Aldrich Bailey, and Mrs. Charles Dana Gibson filled the Junior League Auditorium with applause and approval at the Society's so-called Gullah spirituals.[143] The concert also featured a special performance by Rene Ravenel Jr., the president of the Junior Spirituals Society, which had been formed a few months earlier and was comprised of the children of SPS members. Through this offshoot, the SPS hoped to perpetuate the organization and its particular historical memory into the next generation.[144] In this moment, then, three levels of historical memory were operating. The concert recast mythic recollections of the past to create educational entertainment in the present and a legacy for the benefit of the future. For the concert's program, the SPS recycled the Jennings plantation scene used for its 1929 fund-raising concert. The Society's romantic packaging of the past left an indelible imprint on its New York spectators. Damrosch noted, "From all over the room one heard exclamations of delight."[145] Mrs. William Proctor, of Proctor and Gamble, wrote Marjorie Morawetz from her Park Avenue home after the concert: "Those charming people, their sincerity and simplicity and their lovely art, created an atmosphere that I can't throw off, even if I wanted to!"[146]

After an enthusiastic reception at a concert in Philadelphia's Bellevue-Stratford Hotel the following evening, the Spirituals Society returned to Charleston, where their contribution to the city's celebrity status was duly recognized. "A group of amateurs," the editor of the *News and Courier* proclaimed, "is bringing to Charleston a quality of advertising that is beneficial . . . [in] spreading Charleston's fame afar."[147] Accordingly, national magazines, such as the *Atlantic Monthly* and the *Etude*, carried features on the SPS.[148] Requests for concerts from all over the country flooded SPS offices. Groups in cities such as Spokane, Cincinnati, Nashville, Grand Junction (Colorado), Ironwood (Michigan), and Shippensburg (Pennsylvania) all wanted to share in the Spirituals Society experience.[149] With the economic strain of the Depression, however, the Society declined all offers from outside of the South.

The Society continued to perform regionally, functioning as an important element of Charleston's public trade in historical memory. A concert by the

Spirituals Society became a signature element of any visitor's experience of the Low Country. "For this Society is famous now," the local newspaper explained, "much more than perhaps its members now fancy, and of course from that is a degree of obligation—many visitors are disappointed if they have no opportunity to hear a concert of the society while they are in Charleston."[150] The SPS gladly entertained visiting dignitaries in small concerts at local plantations, such as automobile industrialists Henry Ford and Harvey Firestone and their wives at Magnolia Gardens.[151] The Society also expanded its audience by broadcasting several concerts over local and national radio during the late 1920s and early 1930s. Using technology to popularize their historical understanding of place, the SPS, as one radio announcer intoned, provided listeners with "vivid glimpses into the life of a past and a present Charleston."[152]

The SPS also performed at special occasions. In December 1931, members decided to sing a free concert at the Academy of Music for Charlestonians in appreciation of their support over the years. When the question of African American attendance at this concert was raised, the Society decided to pursue two paths that further accentuate its paternalistic character. First, the Society agreed that blacks could attend the concert for free, as long as they sat in the "Third Gallery," the traditional place in theater for African Americans living in the segregated South. Second, the SPS opted not to advertise that the concert would be open to local blacks. Instead, just as they turned to the "old time darkies," especially the "Maums" and nurses of their childhood memories, for inspiration in their singing, so, too, did SPS members seek to ensure the presence of only the "right" kind of African American audiences, certainly not NAACP types. Thus, the Society "adopted a suggestion that each member should inform his family servants to pass the word among their friends that they would be admitted."[153] In the end, even this "free and open" concert would be kept "in the family," safe from possible critique.

In another instance, the SPS performed locally in March 1930 to raise money for the restoration of Stratford Hall, the birthplace of Robert E. Lee. A natural affinity existed between the preservation of historically significant structures, a cause that many SPS members actively supported at home, and the Society's collection and memorialization of spirituals. Again, the illustrations employed to publicize the concert reveal much about the mind-set of the performers. Designed by A. T. S. Stoney, the Lee concert poster represents a radical departure from standard SPS images. First, it lacks any hint of white presence in the image, and second, it makes blatant visual references to blackface. Under a banner declaring "NEGRO SPIRITUALS," two black females—with broad noses,

Negro Spirituals

A Concert by the
Society for the Preservation
of Spirituals
For the Benefit of the
Robert E. Lee Memorial Foundation
ACADEMY of MUSIC
Friday–March 7 at 8:15
Tickets now on sale at the Box Office

Although they typically tried to distance their performances from the blackface minstrel tradition, the Spirituals Society deployed Mammy caricatures to publicize a local concert for the preservation of Robert E. Lee's Virginia home. From the Collections of the South Carolina Historical Society.

wide white lips and teeth, pierced ears, and turbaned heads — smile enthusiastically.[154] While the broadside seems to promise African American performers, the SPS cast was, in fact, all white. Perhaps the Society's persistent claims to the authenticity of their production allowed them in this particular instance to present themselves to this audience as either surrogate "old time darkies" or, more likely, their stewards. In either case, the actual Gullah people were effectively silenced, and in their stead, the voices of a Southern white elite worldview were made to be heard.

The Lee benefit concert, the Society's singular public affiliation with the Lost Cause, raised approximately $850 "to honor the memory of our beloved Confederate leader"[155] and to help make "a national shrine" of his Virginia estate.[156] The day before the concert, the local Charleston newspaper, always sensitive to the national demographics of the city's tourists, downplayed Lee's Confederate identity, describing him instead for potential ticket-buying visitors as "a great American."[157] And yet, during the concert's intermission, in another rare display of the Society's connection with the rebel cause, young white Charleston women sold small Confederate flags to the audience to supplement the concert's proceeds.[158] In this celebration, any potentially divisive political fires of former sectionalism were squelched by the common white desire to laud the plantation past.

Throughout the 1930s, the Society also regularly took to the stage to entertain visiting conventioneers as diverse as the National Council of Catholic Women, the American Ornithologists Union, the American Bar Association, and the Association of Edison Illuminating Companies.[159] With support of the city council and then-mayor Thomas Stoney, the SPS was also directly involved in bringing the annual convention of the National Federation of Music Clubs to Charleston in 1930.[160] Likewise, the Society worked closely with the local chamber of commerce, appearing during its "Golf Week"[161] and in a 1932 promotional film of the city, titled *An Old City Speaks*.

In addition to its annual springtime concerts and convention performances, the most important civic-minded SPS appearance was at the chamber of commerce's tourism spectacle, the Azalea Festival. Beginning in the mid-1930s, the Society performed at this yearly event designed to boost tourism dollars. Although the Society claimed to stand for the preservation of African American spirituals, in at least one festival appearance, the SPS felt threatened by the presence of actual "negro farm hands" who might sing while presenting a "plantation scene" to the tourists.[162] After some deliberation, the Society agreed to perform. It informed the event organizers that the Society singers would appear only "with the understanding that there will be no other group singing Spirituals in connection with the Azalea Festival."[163] The SPS monopoly on representing "authentic" plantation culture was not to be challenged, and their concert went ahead as scheduled. The popular association of the SPS with Gullah spirituals was so complete that the organization became the first choice of white festival organizers outside the city as well. After being repeatedly turned down in her requests that the SPS perform at the 1935

National Folk Festival in Chattanooga, its director, Sarah Gertrude Knott, posed a potentially acceptable alternative. If the Society could not participate, she asked, could they send along "a few of the Gullahs"?[164]

In 1935, despite economic hardship, the Society received invitations from two institutions — the Robert E. Lee Memorial Foundation, once more, and the Roosevelt White House — which carried enough weight in the members' view to warrant another trip north, this time to Washington, D.C. On Saturday, 19 January, at the height of the Depression, audience members paid a phenomenal five dollars each to hear the Society sing for the Lee restoration. The scheduled afternoon concert sold out so quickly that the Society willingly offered to sing again in the evening to meet the demand.[165] The following day at 4 o'clock, the Society re-created "the chants of the slaves"[166] at the White House. Over 200 people, including Franklin and Eleanor Roosevelt, several of their grandchildren, and many prominent members of the cabinet and Congress, sat in the audience.[167] During the closing number, the forty-six SPS singers, including some of Charleston's leading cultural activists — DuBose Heyward, Albert Simons, Josephine Pinckney, and Herbert Ravenel Sass — departed briefly from their established theatrical tradition. In a moment of communalism with their assembled audience, the singers walked off the stage and "while singing, filed along the front row, clasping the hands of the President and Mrs. Roosevelt."[168] The Roosevelts were so "very enthusiastic about the whole presentation" that they gave the Society photographs of themselves in appreciation, in frames made of wood from the 1817 reconstruction of the White House, effectively exchanging one artifact for another.[169] Upon hearing reviews from the D.C. concerts, the Charleston Chamber of Commerce thrilled at the "good advertisement" the SPS constantly generated for the city.[170]

Additional public notice for Charleston's historic identity came in the form of the Society's 1931 "Memorium to the Old South," *The Carolina Low-Country*.[171] Originally intended as a published collection of SPS spirituals, the project expanded to include poetry, essays, and illustrations that together best encapsulated the group's views on history, nationalism, and race through meditations on South Carolina's "golden age" of plantations.[172] "Interest in the book," Alfred Huger explained to his Northern publishers at the prestigious New York firm MacMillan, "is, of course, due . . . to a feeling that somehow or other in some intangible manner the negro spirituals and the negro character unite us of this generation with the civilization which went down in 1865."[173] As with so many local endeavors in this period, the volume was a collaborative effort that relied upon the participation of prominent individuals across Charleston's cultural scene, from local-color artists Alice Ravenel Huger Smith and Elizabeth O'Neill Verner and preservation architect Albert Simons, to writers DuBose Heyward and Josephine Pinckney, to newspaper editor Thomas R. Waring. Augustine T. Smythe best expressed the collective motivation for creating what Heyward wistfully called "our valedictory—our requiem for a lost yesterday"[174]: "to express in one book, the feelings of the members of the Society and of all others of similar heritage, towards the songs themselves, and the black people who sing them, and towards the region in which they live, its natural aspects, its history, its triumphs, defeats, despairs and recoveries, and its tremendous hold upon the hearts, lives and thoughts of those who call it home."[175]

The authors of *The Carolina Low-Country*, whose writings alternated in tone between eulogy and travelogue, sought a national audience. Sectional language is generally absent from the text. Instead, the essayists characterize the region as a cradle of national heroes and as an important site of American history, adventure, and romance. They dedicate numerous pages to detailing the Low Country's role in colonial settlement, Revolutionary warfare, and the construction of "the gentlest, the most humane, the most chivalric civilization that America has ever known."[176] Not surprisingly, slavery is discussed only delicately as an institution that developed "naturally" from the agrarian economy and characterized by "affection and mutual understanding"[177] between master and slave: "In the Negro cabin in the Quarters are contentment, abundant rations, the sounds of banjos and of singing."[178] This book-length tribute to the national values of the Low Country downplayed the divisive events of the Civil War and Reconstruction, which appear only as an "inexpressible tragedy"[179] for the nation and, more important, as "the death-knell"[180] for South Carolina's plantation civilization, its "glamour and romance."[181] Tellingly, the sps historical timeline presented in *The Carolina Low-Country* ends with this defeat. *Charleston Evening Post* editor Thomas R. Waring best summarized this historical sensibility in his contribution to the book, titled "Charleston: The Capital of the Plantations": "Here came the harpies of Reconstruction. Here came the end of an era, and here came remembrance."[182]

With *The Carolina Low-Country*, as well as their concerts at home and in the North, the Society for the Preservation of Negro Spirituals successfully packaged their revisionist historical memory and paternalistic racism in a form that was both appealing to and easily consumed by white audiences. Through song, movement, costuming, and a racialized/classist rhetoric, the sps entered into the public debate about the meaning of "Americanness" that raged in 1920 and 1930s America. In the process, they posited a critique of modernity and articulated a counterargument to the NAACP's vision of "blackness" around which white Americans, even in the former strongholds of abolitionism, could rally. With the Society's help, by the late 1920s, the promotion of a sanitized history-based tourism had become as much a part of the Charleston landscape as St. Michael's steeple.[183]

CHAPTER FIVE

Where Mellow Past and Present Meet

SELLING HISTORY BY THE SEA

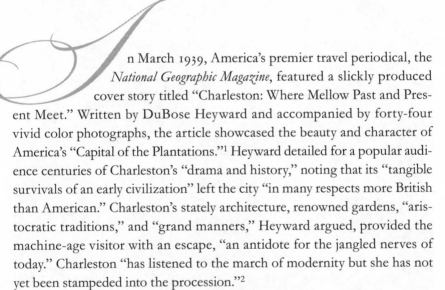

n March 1939, America's premier travel periodical, the *National Geographic Magazine*, featured a slickly produced cover story titled "Charleston: Where Mellow Past and Present Meet." Written by DuBose Heyward and accompanied by forty-four vivid color photographs, the article showcased the beauty and character of America's "Capital of the Plantations."[1] Heyward detailed for a popular audience centuries of Charleston's "drama and history," noting that its "tangible survivals of an early civilization" left the city "in many respects more British than American." Charleston's stately architecture, renowned gardens, "aristocratic traditions," and "grand manners," Heyward argued, provided the machine-age visitor with an escape, "an antidote for the jangled nerves of today." Charleston "has listened to the march of modernity but she has not yet been stampeded into the procession."[2]

At the same time, Heyward contended that Charleston was also a "one hundred percent American" city, which boasted not only national heroes and patriots but also progressive urban facilities, such as highways and airports. Though steeped in tradition, the city was not a retrograde "museum piece."[3] Instead, Heyward painted a portrait of a booming industrial center with fine hotels, sophisticated transportation facilities, manufacturing plants, a deep-water port, and an expanding U.S. naval yard. *National Geographic*'s wide read-

A 1939 *National Geographic Magazine* photo of the interior of the Porgy Shop, an antiques store on Church Street that catered to tourists and capitalized on the success of Heyward's novel and the subsequent opera, *Porgy & Bess*, by George and Ira Gershwin. B. Anthony Stewart/NGS Image Collection.

ership, then, encountered a city of contradictions—American and foreign, traditional and modern.

Heyward's public characterization of Charleston in 1939 illustrates well the tensions present in the city's self-conscious development of a history-based tourism industry between the world wars. Cultural preservationists and city officials agreed that Charleston would benefit from increased tourism. Both groups depended upon luring outside capital to the region to support their ventures, and thus both served to profit from tourism. Yet at times they could not agree on how best to attract visitors, or, more pointedly, how best to define the city's public identity. For their part, artists, writers, and preservationists enthusiastically celebrated the region's historical artifacts and physical beauty, emphasizing in the process the city's time-worn, nostalgic, and "exotic" aspects. Local politicians and business leaders, meanwhile, tended to stress Charleston's modern amenities, recreational facilities, and thoroughly progressive spirit. In 1929, for example, historic preservationists considered the widening and paving of downtown flagstone sidewalks a threat to the city's "Old World charm," while boosters saw it as a necessary improvement for encouraging business and travelers.[4] By committing to historical tourism, Charleston's leadership discovered an industry that would support their sometimes overlapping and sometimes contradictory agendas. Together, these constituencies embarked on a delicate balancing act that attempted to maintain the "authentic" historic charm that was the object of tourists' consumption and to develop the modern conveniences—the roads, hotels, and dining and entertainment establishments—that those same visitors demanded. By the early 1930s, as Charleston sank deeper and deeper into economic depression—at one point, so bankrupt it paid its city government workers in scrip—this partnership became vital to the city's fiscal survival.[5] Historical tourism became, as Heyward described it, "an economic 'back log' against evil days."[6]

While Heyward's economic assertion here is correct—tourism undoubtedly began the decades-long infrastructural transformation of Charleston from dilapidated Southern backwater to polished destination city—he presents only a partial explanation of the impact of Charleston's historical tourism. As James Sears has shown, tourism plays a "powerful role in America's invention of itself as a culture."[7] Similarly, Charleston's heritage trade was an ideological construct that enabled a small group of elite whites to perpetuate their selective historical memories and peddle them to eager tourists in a highly consumable form.

"A City Imagined from a Civic Consciousness":
"America's Most Historic City" Is Born[8]

Charleston's tourist industry did not spring forth spontaneously in the 1920s, nor was it without regional precedents. The city had long been considered a scenic stop on a tour of the American South. Mention of its beauty and historic merit appear in travelogues and novels throughout the nineteenth and early twentieth centuries, depicting it as a quaint, quiet town still living in the past.[9] And yet Charleston's leadership never successfully exploited this position to develop a significant tourism industry until after World War I. Visitors might have passed a quick day in the city and then opted to spend the bulk of their vacation dollars at nearby beach or sporting locales. Area beaches along the Sea Islands, for example, which had historically drawn planters and their families away from the city during the sickly summer season in antebellum days, attracted wealthy Northern patrons. Other beach attractions, such as the resorts at Myrtle Beach near the North Carolina border, drew more middle- and working-class crowds. Just east of Charleston, the Isle of Palms Hotel and Dancing Pavilion, called "the Coney Island of the South"[10] by one promotional brochure, and the Atlantic Beach Hotel on Sullivan's Island also lured visitors to their sandy shores with dances, entertainment, and spectacles. In 1896, for example, the Atlantic Beach Hotel amused spectators with a rather bizarre "five mile dash between the black cyclist Jim Moore and Mr. Reedy's horse, Miss Madred," the horse grabbing the win.[11] Likewise, for several decades, the town of Aiken, South Carolina, situated between Charleston and Augusta, Georgia, enjoyed status as a "Health and Pleasure Resort" for individuals seeking the "recuperative qualities of dry, pure atmosphere."[12] Aiken also boasted a rigorous winter racing and polo season that catered to the affluent Northern and Southern horse set, including millionaires such as William K. Vanderbilt and Augustus F. Goodwin.[13]

Despite these highly coordinated area examples of cultivating a formal tourist trade, Charleston never followed suit, much to the chagrin of local boosters, who consistently tried at the turn of the century to make it into a tourism and convention town. Tourism advocates did celebrate two short-lived victories when the city hosted the national Confederate veterans' reunion in 1899 and the South Carolina Inter-State and West Indian Exposition in 1901–2; the latter even brought President Theodore Roosevelt to town.[14] And yet these episodes were never sustained long enough to sufficiently resuscitate Charleston's long-stagnant post–Civil War economy. A chamber of commerce publication from 1904 bitterly complained of local complacency with the status quo: "The conservatism which has characterized Charleston, has hitherto prevented her merits as a winter resort from becoming so widely known as they should be. Consequently, while many other places with less to recommend them have grown in public favor, attracting crowds of visitors and even permanent residents, Charleston has remained comparatively but little known to the outside world."[15] In response, droves of ambitious young men left the city in the early twentieth century, leaving in their wake what novelist Owen Wister described as a "visible sadness" — "belated" and "retrospective."[16] In 1907, Henry James called Charleston a city of ruins and widows — "of gardens and absolutely of no men — or of so few that, save for the general sweetness, the War might still have been raging and all the manhood at the front."[17] Tens years later, one travel writer declared, "Charleston is perhaps the only city in America that has slammed its front door in Progress's face and resisted the modern with fiery determination."[18]

As America entered the First World War, however, the economic tide in Charleston changed momentarily, giving local boosters a glimmer of hope that a new day might be dawning. The U.S. Navy yard had expanded to meet wartime needs, but the city's once thriving antebellum port remained in 1921, in the words of New York–based ports consultant Edwin J. Clapp, "wholly useless save as an historical artifact."[19]

Former staple industries such as large-scale farming and shipping would not be the answer to Charleston's economic slide; instead, a nascent tourist-based economy encouraged by wartime factors slowly emerged.[20] With Europe eliminated as a vacation spot, Americans of the leisure classes took to their beloved automobiles and traveled within their own country, often on the newly built highways and rails south to Florida.[21] Along the way, they "discovered" Charleston's mild climate and what a 1913 guidebook called the "potent charm of a most distinctive southern town."[22] In the years immediately following the war, wealthy Americans, among them John D. Rockefeller Jr. and former lieutenant governor of Rhode Island Z. W. Bliss, continued this practice of domestic tourism that often involved passing parts of the winter and early spring in Charleston's mild climate.[23]

By the mid-1920s, as the cultural activities of Charleston's artists, writers, and preservationists gained attention beyond the city limits and as high-class "winter colonists" streamed into the city each year for "the season," civic leaders acknowledged the potential profitability of an enlarged tourist trade. The attraction for visitors now was more than just climate. Charleston presented an opportunity to explore and possibly to associate oneself with a glamorized heritage. Although the chamber of commerce's "Tourist and Convention Department"[24] and the city council's "Sub-Committee on Marking of Historical Places"[25] had operated from the late 1910s on, it was not until the election of Mayor Thomas Stoney in 1923 that the city government began to pursue tourism with coordinated enthusiasm. Stoney's immediate predecessor, John Patrick Grace, a second-generation Irish American who was raised in the city, expressed only a limited interest in developing tourism. Instead, he focused the bulk of his energies on urban improvements to stimulate industry and commerce.[26] Stoney, on the other hand, was a young lawyer from an old-line former slave-owning family who grew up on an area plantation. With eighteenth-century roots in prominent Low Country families, such as the Gaillards and Porchers, Stoney was a blood relative of many of Charleston's leading cultural preservationists and an eventual member of some of their societies.[27] Perhaps his personal associations with the region's past, coupled with his desire to resurrect the local economy, made Stoney more sympathetic than Grace to celebrations of the elite past through tourism.

In his inaugural address to the city council on 17 December 1923, Stoney proclaimed tourism a top priority of his administration: "There is every reason to believe that Charleston will soon develop into a great tourist resort; and it will be my great effort to promote this development in every way practicable."[28] The following year, Stoney faced a massive civic debt and rising unemployment as the city's short-lived postwar prosperity waned. The once-booming navy yard, for example, had cut thousands of civilians jobs.[29] In response, the mayor put the full force of his political machine, the elite "Broad Street Ring," behind the development of a tourist trade. He hoped to capitalize on the growing popularity of Florida's resorts among Northern travelers. Thus, in his "Annual Review" of 1924, Stoney declared Charleston "America's Most Historic City" and, ironically, pushed for modern improvements to stimulate the trade, such as more paved roads, electric street lighting, recreational centers, and a new rail passenger station to facilitate visits to the city.[30] Stoney asked his culturally conservative constituents to adopt "the right mental attitude" by considering development an asset to Charleston's historical heritage. "We have to sell Charleston to the outside world," he declared, "and the first step in this direction is to sell Charleston to Charlestonians."[31]

While the economic impact of Stoney's words was not immediate, they roused considerable support from figures in key corners of Charleston's public life. Local newspaper editors William Watts Ball (*News & Courier*) and his brother-in-law Thomas R. Waring Sr. (*Charleston Evening Post*), who together held a virtual monopoly on the city's presses, made tourism advocacy a family affair. They dedicated hundreds of pages to articles and editorials praising the city's cultural and environmental assets and encouraging locals to join in the boosterism. Ball and Waring also supported the growing historic preservation movement, as well as the activities of the city's artists, writers, and Spirituals Society. At the same time, they looked to Florida's prosperous tourist trade as a model for Charleston's economic recovery. They pushed for a range of improvements, including the planting of trees to beautify the city's approaches, the bolstering of the area's seaside resorts, such as Folly Beach and the Isle of Palms, and the allocation of public monies for advertising Charleston as a tourist and convention site.[32] In 1926, for example, Ball's *News & Courier* produced and nationally distributed 100,000 copies of a special edition map indicating tourist routes to Charleston via federal and coastal highways.[33] Like their mayor, Waring and Ball also tried to convince their readers that the development of tourism was the personal responsibility of every good citizen. In a 1925 editorial, Waring encouraged locals to solicit visitors, arguing that "all Charleston concerns that have extensive correspondence outside of town can do effective community advertising in their ordinary mail" by writing positively of the city's features.[34] Throughout the 1920s and 1930s, both newspapermen remained steadfast in their civic chauvinism, supporting any improvements that might aid in the development of an economically viable tourist trade.

Similarly, Charleston's business organizations, in particular the chamber of commerce, increasingly shared the mayor's vision. In 1924, chamber manager Meigs Russell declared, "There is no source from which new money can be brought in here except through the medium of tourists."[35] That same year, chamber representatives successfully entertained the conventioneers of the Traveling Passenger Agents of the Northeastern and Canadian Railroads as they were en route to their annual meeting in Florida. "These men," the chamber's annual report declared, "have more influence in the routing of tourists than any other group of men in North America."[36] The chamber also established in its downtown offices a hospitality center featuring a "Reading and Rest Room" as an information clearinghouse and meeting place for visitors.[37] Through its Tourist and Convention Bureau, the chamber paid for the production and placement of historical markers on structures throughout Charleston[38] and facilitated the publication of articles about the city in major national travel and feature magazines, such as the *American Motorist*.[39] The bureau also distributed promotional brochures to railroads and steamship companies, travel agencies, and newspapers and magazines in the United States and Canada and sponsored the strategic placement of a visitor welcoming sign near the city's steamship docks, as well signs advertising Charleston's attractions along regional highways, north to Washington, D.C., and west to Knoxville.[40]

With such significant support in place, Mayor Stoney supervised a spate of urban improvements, many aimed directly at cultivating tourism, during his two terms as mayor (1923 – 31). In 1925, for example, he ordered the paving and lighting of the section of Queen Street that approached the arrival platform for passenger steamships of the Clyde Lines. The mayor also pushed for the development of a municipal golf course, a modern airport, and a yacht basin to lure wealthy patrons.[41] Personal aesthetic choices occasionally influenced Stoney's decisions. In an ongoing campaign to clean up the worn old town, for example, he dispatched city lawyers to sue for the destruction of a "disgraceful looking shed" near the steamship arrival platform that Stoney considered "a bad advertisement for 'Historic Charleston.'"[42]

As the promising potential of tourism took hold in the local imagination, Charleston witnessed the building of two major downtown luxury hotels that joined the already established Villa Margherita, Argyle, Timrod, and Charleston as popular venues for white visitors. The Francis Marion Hotel, at the corner of King and Calhoun streets, opened its 312 luxury rooms to the public on 7 February 1924, at the beginning of the increasingly popular "garden season," when the exotic flora of area homes and plantations were in full and shockingly colorful bloom. Financed by a group of local citizens, the twelve-story "fireproof" structure was the largest hotel in South Carolina. It boasted modern ventilation, lighting, and dining features, touting itself "a Modern Hotel in an Atmosphere of Tradition."[43] Even its interior decoration walked the fine line between past and present, coupling furniture "of the most modern design" with paintings and statues of Francis Marion, the local Revolutionary War hero after whom the hotel was named.[44] Three months later, the 350-bed Fort Sumter Hotel formally opened for business in a prime location that overlooked the Battery and Charleston Harbor with the original fort in clear view. While fully appointed with modern comforts and a rooftop garden, the Fort Sumter emphasized its waterfront location as an entrée into Charleston's heady past. The hotel's publicity materials described the colonial-era White Point Gardens that began at the hotel's front door as "Beautiful as a Dream: Tinged with Romance, Consecrated by Tradition, Glorified by History . . . Like a Fairy Garden created by the enchanter's wand."[45] Such an ideal setting offered Fort Sumter's visitors a chance to "slip back into the days gone by, recalling to mind the fabric of the history of this old city" through the "century-old oaks" and "stately old homes" surrounding the Battery.[46] Whereas at the old Fort Sumter, shots were fired that bitterly divided the nation, at the new, the violent past was erased and Northern occupants were more than welcome to stay as long as they liked.

Tourist demand for short- and long-term housing, increased by the presence of improved sleeping accommodations, kept Charleston's luxury hotel registers full during the winter and spring months. In September 1925, for example, the Francis Marion reported a 20 percent increase in business over the previous year. At times, demand even outstripped capacity. During the following two years, faced with a "heavy influx" of inquiries from Charleston's 79,000 visitors,[47] the chamber of commerce urged local citizens who owned furnished apartments to list them for rent with the chamber free of charge.[48] Eventually, this list expanded to include rooms to let in private homes.[49] Within a decade after the end of the First World War, Charleston had become established as a tourist post worthy of at least an overnight stay. More and more locals were actively participating in this new economy, which had become by the 1929–30 season the city's largest industry, generating $4 million of income for Charleston businesses.[50]

In addition to hotels, Stoney's administration oversaw the construction of two modern bridges, one spanning the Ashley River to the west and the other the Cooper River to the east. Connecting the peninsular city with its surrounding regions, each bridge facilitated automobile traffic between the city and its outlying attractions, plantations, gardens, and beaches. The Cooper River Bridge, in particular, was a monument to the hoped-for modernization of Charleston—but it was also a byway for tourists looking to steep themselves in the traditional relics of the old city. Backed by former mayor Grace and financed in part by outside capital, the $6 million, two-mile-long metal structure towered at its highest point 270 feet above the river's deep waters, replacing a ferry shuttle that had been the main mode of crossing the river since colonial times.[51] The bridge served as a vital, direct link to Route 40, the state highway that ran up the coast and joined the Atlantic Coast Highway, thus shortening the automobile route between the Northeast and Florida, via Charleston.[52] The *News & Courier* heralded the bridge's opening on 8 August 1929 as an "occasion for rejoicing, for congratulations, for renewed faith and confidence in the assured upbuilding of one of the garden spots of this earth."[53] National newspapers also covered the opening and its attendant three days of city-financed festivities and fanfare. The *New York Times Magazine* described the affair as a kind of coming-out party for the reticent, traditional town: "Aloof Charleston Calls Outer World," its headline declared. With the bridge in place, the *Times* concluded, "The present-day Charleston is a fascinating mixture of Old World culture and modern progressivism."[54]

As if to further underscore the push-pull of the old and the new in Charleston, just months before the dedication ceremonies of this "complicated spider web of steel,"[55] Stoney pushed a measure through the city council that counterbalanced this development trend. Drawing on the Society for the Preservation of Old Dwelling's nine-year battle to protect Charleston's historic landscape, the city on 23 April created a planning and zoning commission "to look to the regulating of building so that the original colonial atmosphere of the community will not be lost."[56] The commission's purview quickly expanded to include the supervision of a professional survey of the city's pre–Revolutionary War structures with the encouragement of preservation in mind. Many civic leaders recognized that tourists and their pocketbooks came to Charleston largely to enjoy the atmosphere its historic buildings afforded.[57] Professional tour guide William G. Sheppard detailed this reality in the local newspaper. Tourists, he explained, wanted to experience in Charleston "things of historical interest and architectural beauty that they have not seen the like [of] the world over." He cited visitors asking him to avoid modern Charleston and instead to highlight the town's ancient relics.[58] "Without her visible background," resident artist Alfred Hutty echoed in a local newspaper, "Charleston would have little to offer her discriminating visitors."[59] On 13 October 1931, in a bold maneuver to preserve this profitable architectural heritage, the city created the country's first planning and zoning ordinance, designating a twenty-three-block area in the downtown as the "Old and Historic District."[60] When Stoney signed the act into law on 19 October, he and the city government finally recognized formally what the Preservation Society had urged all along: historic buildings were an asset to the city's economy.[61]

Stoney often found himself caught in the middle of the delicate debate over preservation versus development. In August 1929, for example, Laura Bragg, the director of the Charleston Museum, protested the proposed construction of a filling station on the corner of Meeting and Chalmers streets, which would require the demolition of three houses dating from the late eighteenth and early nineteenth centuries. Bragg, whose home abutted the potential building site, appealed to the mayor's investment in tourism when she echoed "the words of many visitors that 'a filling station so near St. Michael's [Church] will be a crime,' and . . . that the station would be 'a disgrace' and that Charleston 'would be accused of having lost its traditional culture and good taste' if the station were allowed."[62] At the same time, the manager of the popular St. John Hotel nearby on Meeting Street ("Located Nearer than Anything to Everything of Interest in Historic Charleston"[63]) encouraged the mayor to replace "dilapidated buildings, now occupying the corner" with a contemporary gas station to serve his automobile-traveling clientele. In the end, the parties involved struck a bargain whereby the Esso filling station was built but in a rather oxymoronic "modern colonial style," designed by Albert Simons.[64]

The balancing act between protecting the particular historic character of Charleston and meeting the needs of the tourists who increasingly supported the local economy persisted throughout Stoney's term. Visitors demanded that the city fulfill broad guidebook promises of an "old-world atmosphere and romantic charm amidst up-to-date surroundings and modern conveniences."[65] At times, however, what passed for either "quaint" or "modern" during the day annoyed visitors by night. In 1929, for instance, the management of the Francis Marion Hotel complained to the mayor and the city council about "the striking of the quarter-hours by St. Matthew's Clock during the night annoying the guests."[66] During the day, guests might have enjoyed the bells as a charming feature of an old-time city following slower rhythms of life, but after a hard day of sightseeing, the bells became an anachronistic nuisance to tired and paying hotel guests. Similarly, these same guests demanded taxis by day to transport them to the region's historic sites, and yet by night they complained of the "'noise, hollering, whistling, loud talking and rowdyism' about the taxi stands across the street from the hotel."[67] Charleston's relationship with its visitors was clearly not without its problems and contradictions.

Small businesses that sprang up to capitalize on the presence of tourists in the city sometimes dismayed preservationists, especially during the terms of Stoney's successor, another old-line elite Charlestonian named Burnett Rhett Maybank, who was mayor from 1931 to 1938.[68] The commercialization of Church Street provides a rich example of this growing entrepreneurial impulse and its reception in some circles. To increase the potential value of old buildings, and thus to encourage their preservation, Charleston's zoning ordinance allowed for "the use of a part of existing dwellings or their accessory buildings, if constructed prior to 1860, as studios, tea rooms; gift, antique, book and handicraft shops; and other similar purposes having a relation to historic interest; provided the principal use of any dwelling so utilized is maintained as a dwelling."[69] Accordingly, the portion of Church Street south of Broad, a popular tourist thoroughfare that featured both the Heyward-Washington House and Cabbage Row, witnessed the birth of an array of new businesses catering to tourists. Several of these establishments—such as Caroline Rutledge's Stoll's Alley Annex and Mrs. M. W. Rhett's Old Ironsides Coffee House—were operated by ladies from "'the quality,'" or Charleston's "first families," indicating, in the words of the 1941 Works Progress Administration guide to South Carolina, "the compromise that Charleston has been forced to make with the formerly abhorred 'trade.'"[70] To further supplement their meager Depression-era incomes, some of these savvy women also rented rooms in their homes to tourists "when the hotels are crowded, at $4 and $6 a day"[71] and even served as "lady guides" providing walking tours of the city for a two- or three-dollar fee.[72]

A variety of establishments along entrepreneurial Church Street sold souvenirs of "Historic Charleston"—"books, and prints of houses and little tables and anything they could spare"[73]—to tourists. Elizabeth Verner's etching studio, for example, stood at the corner of Tradd and Church streets, while the Brewton Inn, at number 75, catered to visitors with "excellent luncheon and dinner in an attractive courtyard garden."[74] Across the street at number 76 stood the Porgy Book Shop, which capitalized on the success of DuBose Heyward's novel, and the real estate offices of Elliman, Huyler & Mullally, "formed to meet the increasing demand for Plantations, Town Houses, Shooting Preserves and Sea Islands among discriminating non-residents and sportsmen from every part of the country."[75] Real estate customers could then call upon the services of Emily Compton Barker, the interior decorator at number 77, to furnish their new homes in an approved Charleston style. By 1934, over twenty tourist-related establishments existed on the short, three-block stretch of Church Street.[76]

Not everyone welcomed this burst of commerce. During a 1933 visit to the city, Clement Wood, a native Alabamian and assistant historian general of the Sons of Confederate Veterans, and his author wife, Gloria, lamented "the commercialism of Charleston's charm." They pointed in particular to the transformation of Cabbage Row, the black slum setting of *Porgy*, into "a high class residence"[77] called the Briggs Apartments. In the mid-1920s, New York landscape architect Loutrel Briggs, best known for restoring many of Charleston's historic gardens, had saved Cabbage Row—"a veritable rookery, crumbling, leaking, the windows stuffed with rags, the out-buildings roofless, and the main buildings crowded with poverty-stricken tenement dwellers"—from the wrecking ball.[78] In response to the Woods' public "shock," Briggs defended his renovation of the property, which had for years posed health and crime problems in the neighborhood. In a 1922 petition to the city council, for example, thirty-seven white residents of nearby Church Street and St. Michael's Place called for the immediate eviction of the Row's all-black inhabitants. They detailed illicit and violent behavior "in and around the premises," including the prostitution of black women to white sailors and civilians, knife and gun fights, deplorable sanitary conditions, and the continual usage of "the most vile, filthy, and offensive language" by tenants.[79] In restoring the property, Briggs had to contend judiciously with the image of the Row in Heyward's novel, which had done so much to popularize Charleston in the American tourist's imagination.[80] "DuBose Heyward, with an artistry, to which my unskilled pen cannot do justice, has preserved for posterity the picturesque life of 'Catfish Row,'" Briggs wrote in a local paper, "and I have attempted to reclaim, with as little external change as possible, the building and restore it to something of its original state in revolutionary time."[81] For the Row to be successful, then, Briggs had to embrace that schizophrenic balance between colonial authenticity and contemporary "quaint" styles — between picturesque and commercial — that came to characterize Charleston's tourism industry in the interwar years.

Occasional dissent from the Church Street "renewal" resounded from preservationist circles as well. Susan Pringle Frost, real estate agent and cultural watchdog, protested to the city's Board of Architectural Review (BAR) the transformation of Church Street "into a business section." The founder of the Preservation Society feared that the once illustrious residential neighborhood would soon "rival King Street," the city's main commercial artery, if restaurants such as the Tavern and the Dixie Belle and retail establishments such as the French Hat Shop were not restricted.[82] At the same time, however, Frost asked Albert Simons, the leading member of BAR, to keep her role in the criticism quiet. Frost was a chamber of commerce member who did not want to alienate her business peers, particularly given the fact that she had benefited personally from the ordinance's flexibility when she established her real estate office in her King Street home and simply rechristened it a "studio."[83]

On the other side of the debate were prodevelopment Charlestonians who publicly expressed their displeasure at the mayor's preservationist policies. Not surprisingly, the same man who served as president of Cooper River Bridge, Incorporated, criticized what he called his opponents' "mania for mummies." Like elite white preservationists, Mayor Grace also turned to the past for inspiration for the city's future. In doing so, he invoked a very different historical memory for Charleston, one of a thriving port and entrepreneurial spirit. He argued that the ancestors' of elite whites did more than build beautiful homes; they created a city based on bustling commerce and energetic business enterprise. "Instead of selling the ruins of what they built," Grace argued in May 1929, "why not build something ourselves?"[84] Four months later, city alderman Adolph C. Leseman, representing the working-class Ward 6, similarly complained that the mayor's preoccupation with preserving the city's

Charleston also presented a modern commercial face to visitors, as seen in the neon lights and street traffic of this Christmas 1938 photograph of the popular local movie house, the Garden Theatre on King Street. Courtesy of the Charleston Museum, Charleston, South Carolina.

historic landmarks drained resources necessary to attract desperately needed industries and manufacturing to Charleston. Before the city council, Leseman "declared that uppermost in his mind is an 'Industrial Charleston' rather than an 'Historic Charleston.'"[85] Even some individuals involved in cultural preservation activities, such as Spirituals Society member Dick Reeves, called for balanced development in the city: "In our pride over 'Historic Interest', 'priceless gems of architecture', 'beautiful gardens', 'culture and refinement' and all the other Tourist-attracting phrases[,] we have somewhat overlooked the unlimited industrial possibilities and have imagined these heritages will build a city with no effort on our part." Reeves entreated his fellow citizens, "Let's adopt two slogans: 'Charleston—America's Most Historic City' and 'Charleston Offers Opportunities.'"[86]

The debate raged on throughout the 1930s. Nearly a decade after the passage of the first zoning ordinance, one Charleston resident blasted the preservation movement's sentimentality in what the writer called an "Open Letter to our Literary Below-Broad Belles": "Personally, I think it would be a greater compliment for Charleston to be called 'America's Most Sanitary or Most Progressive City' rather than 'America's Most Historic City.'"[87] Defending the city's historic heritage in 1938, artist Alice Smith spoke up for the preservationist side, pressing for continued vigilance in the face of modernity: "Changes that are often useless and unnecessary make it harder each day for a Charlestonian to say that this is 'America's Most Historic City,' yet it is on the basis of that [that] one of the important businesses depends. Do any of us want to make that statement fake, and turn away the trade it attracts?"[88] In the end, both preservation and its "modernized" infrastructure endured, as hundreds of thousands of tourists from all over the country journeyed to the Low Country during the Depression years to experience the Charleston mystique in comfort and convenience.

"Please God, Send Us the Yankees": The Content and Consumption of Historic Charleston[89]

During the 1920s and 1930s, the notion of Charleston as a vital repository of the nation's (not the section's) glorious past became fixed in the American imagination, not only through the writings and promotional endeavors of Charlestonians, but also through national tourist materials. In the 1910s, travel writers depicted Charleston as charming but generally rundown. Said one, "It is old and rusty in every way."[90] Similarly, earlier accounts written by outsiders tended to place the city's Confederate character on par with its colonial features. In 1913, for example, a *Travel* magazine writer discussed Charleston as a regional oddity; it was "The Real South" tinged with "the memory of tragedy."[91] By 1929, however, as Charleston's vividly reconstructed civic identity flourished, the same magazine declared it a national icon in an article titled "Charleston — Queen of Colonial America."[92] This is not surprising, given the ways city leaders touted the locale's early American historical import. To capitalize on the national obsession with things colonial, for instance, in 1926 the city sponsored an elaborate patriotic program celebrating the 150th anniversary of the battle of Fort Moultrie during the Revolutionary War. Events included a "Colonial exhibit" at the Charleston Museum and a reenactment of the battle by National Guardsmen, army regulars, and marines in "colonial costume."[93] Similarly, a 1932 "talkie" film made about Charleston, titled *An Old City Speaks*, further erased past sectional divides by describing the birthplace of secession as "a storybook of the past, a treasure house of the present, a heritage of patriotism for the future."[94] Playing in theaters across the country, it showcased for national audiences the region's colonial and Revolutionary landmarks, such as Fort Moultrie, as opposed to those from the Civil War. The film also featured the by-now-traditional canon of Charleston images: old mansions, African American street vendors, churchyards, gardens, and even a closing shot of the Spirituals Society singing in full costume. This, too, is not surprising when one considers that many of Charleston's most prominent elite white cultural activists aided director Lorenzo del Riccio in the production of his film by identifying and gaining access to worthy material. Among those who guided the camera's lenses around the old city were the omnipresent cultural stewards Susan Pringle Frost, Nell Pringle, Alice Ravenel Huger Smith, Elizabeth O'Neill Verner, Albert Simons, DuBose Heyward, Josephine Pinckney, Samuel Gaillard Stoney, Robert N. S. Whitelaw, Panchita Grimball, Alfred Huger, Katherine Hutson, Dick Reeves, Herbert Ravenel Sass, A. T. S. Stoney, and Thomas R. Waring Sr., all members of one or more of the city's preservationist and artistic associations.[95] Pleased with the final product, city officials believed the picture would "undoubtedly be the means of attracting many visitors here."[96]

In addition to celebrating Charleston's newly minted "all-American" nature, the country's periodicals and major newspapers also featured articles that replicated another myth concocted by local elites: Charleston was "anything but a commercial city"; it remained "untouched by present day influences"[97] and therefore served as an effective antidote to "frenzied twentieth-century realism."[98] "In a world of change," the *Chicago Tribune* alerted its readers, "Charleston changes less than anything. . . . Serene and aloof, and above all permanent, it remains a wistful reminder of a civilization that elsewhere has vanished from earth."[99] Charleston, then, offered the tourist an opportunity to explore a nonsectional, national heroism and elitist heritage while providing a retreat from the aches of modern life.

When necessary, however, Charleston did change. The tourist machinery occasionally adjusted the city's assets to suit the shifting needs of its consumers for something modern or traditional, foreign or American, colonial or antebellum. For some 1920s tourists, "Doing Charleston" was less about admiring colonial artifacts than about the footloose dance that took the country by storm in the mid-1920s.[100] The dance introduced many Americans to the name of the city, and, briefly, locals debated the benefits of capitalizing on its popularity. Some found association with the black dance offensive, while others applauded it. "For every hundred people who knew where Charleston was before this wonderful dance came out, there are ten thousand people asking where she is at today," one resident wrote the local paper, describing the fad as an economic asset. After all, he concluded, "We can't eat iron gates."[101] In February 1926, the Tourist and Convention Bureau held a local Charleston dance contest to coincide with the national dance finals held at Chicago's Trianon Ballroom.[102] In the end, however, the city found greater profit in exploiting the region's history than the nation's latest dance fad. Still, it remained flexible. In the mid-1930s, for example, as the colonial revival loosened its grip on American aesthetics, Charleston was able to satisfy white America's growing taste for antebellum culture.[103] On the heels of novels and films celebrating the Old South, Charleston became a source of inspiration for popular magazines. In March 1939, *House & Garden* devoted twenty-three pages to the architecture, interiors, and even cuisine of Charleston and the Low Country. Readers were promised access "Inside Plantation Houses" to learn the "Charleston way" to decorate a home or plan a garden. *House & Garden*'s advice, its editors assured their readers, was based on actual experience in the city, drinking up its ambience like an "aromatic liqueur." Editors "walked its streets and wandered about the outlying plantations—until they were saturated with the Charleston atmosphere."[104] Six months later, the same magazine further sated its audience's desire with double the number of pages devoted to the "Old South," complete with instructions on how to decorate like Scarlett O'Hara.[105] The following year, the Charleston Museum sponsored a popular "Gone with the Wind" exhibit that drew over 23,000 visitors between 19 January and 15 April, during the winter and garden seasons.[106]

The tourist encounter with Charleston was generally redolent with nostalgia for a genteel American past. With the Civil War troubles long behind the nation, this new annual "army" of visitors, *Travel* magazine opined in 1929, came "not to plunder, but to revere."[107] Most embarked on what became a near-standardized pilgrimage of the city's most "sacred" spots. For a few dollars, visitors could travel by bus or car to view the plantation gardens of the Ashley River: Magnolia, "The Most Beautiful Gardens in the World,"[108] and Middleton Place, the home of a signer of the Declaration of Independence and the "Oldest Landscape Gardens in America."[109] In the early 1930s, tourists could also take a boat ride, "silently propelled by a negro boatman," through the eery, moss-hung "mirrored mazes" of Cypress Gardens, a swamp park constructed on the plantation property owned since 1909 by Mr. Benjamin Kittredge of New York.[110] A walking tour of the city, accompanied perhaps by a paid guide or at least one of the many new guidebooks available for purchase, was also a necessary part of anyone's itinerary. Typical visitors might begin their stroll at two pre-Revolutionary sites, the Old Exchange Building and the restored Colonial Powder Magazine. Taking advantage of the Gateway

Walk, created by the women of the Garden Club of Charleston in 1930, visitors could pass through the cemetery of St. Philip's Church, viewing the grave of yet another of Charleston's four signers of the Declaration of Independence, and then stop at the Gibbes Art Gallery to take in some works by local-color artists, such as Smith and Verner, before continuing on to the see rare volumes at the Library Society and bask in the evocative, Spanish moss–hung church-yard of the Unitarian church.[111] Visitors heading eastward toward the Cooper River along Broad Street could view more American patriots' tombstones at St. Michael's churchyard on Meeting Street.

After visitors bought some flowers from one of the famed African Ameri-can "flower women" (popularized by Verner), a stop at Cabbage Row, *Porgy*'s now-famous haunt, and then some browsing in the antique shops on Church Street were de rigueur. On this bustling retail street, tourists might just find an authentic piece of Charleston's history to take home with them to Ohio, Massachusetts, or Georgia. Some of this consumerism came at the expense of preserving Charleston's antiquities. The Preservation Society and its sup-porters long bemoaned the sale of bits and pieces of Charleston's heritage to the highest outside bidder, and yet, ironically, they also benefited from the cash brought into the city by these same artifact-hungry tourists. Beleaguered by financial strains, especially during the Depression, many blue-blooded residents took advantage of the desires of tourists to lay claim to Charleston and put family heirlooms on the market. Declaring the city "the antique lov-ers dream come true," one 1931 *Resort Life* writer rather unsympathetically counseled readers, "In the numerous shops and studios there may be found many rare things, long treasured in the homes of Charleston's old families."[112] Apparently, some of these new Yankees did plunder. Of course, if an artifact of the "folk" was preferred, just a few blocks north at the Market, Sea Island grass baskets handmade by Gullah women were on sale. If by some chance the visitor forgot to purchase one of these woven souvenirs during his or her stay, they were also available for purchase, in a strange marriage of folk art and modern business principles, by mail order through Clarence Legerton's Sea Grass Basket Company.[113] After shopping Church Street and visiting the eighteenth-century Heyward-Washington House, under whose roof both a signer of the Declaration of Independence and George Washington slept, tourists could wander down to the Battery to view the mansions of former planters and Fort Sumter in the distance, perhaps stopping for lunch at the Villa Margherita. Finally, these pilgrims might return to their room at the Fort Sumter Hotel, pausing in the lobby to view and perhaps purchase etchings and watercolors produced by local artists. If visitors had timed their vacation correctly, the stay would likely include an evening concert of the Society for the Preservation of Negro Spirituals. Regardless of the available golf, beach, and sailing outings, "history," as packaged by Charleston's elite white civic and cultural leaders, was the main commodity of the trip.

While the city boasted many historical venues, the possibility of gaining access inside an old-line family's private residence was alluring to many visitors seeking that elusive but purportedly even more "authentic" Charleston experience. "People coming to Charleston are perennially unsatisfied," Laura Bragg explained in the early 1930s, "unless they are able to penetrate what seems to them the heart of Charleston life; that is, the interior of its homes."[114] The 1940 *WPA Guide to the Palmetto State* echoed this idea: "[T]he city exhibits an old-fashioned courtesy even in its casual contact with visitors, but the real Charleston is seldom touched or discovered by the stranger. There are few commercial places of entertainment and social life is centered in the homes of the people to a degree rarely found in America today."[115] The Preservation Society took advantage of this interest and held successful house and plantation tours annually to raise funds for their cause, while the Charleston Museum opened the Heyward-Washington and the Manigault Houses to curious, and paying, visitors. The Miles Brewton/Pringle House at 27 King Street also provided a "glimpse into the past" for those willing to pay the one-dollar admission. Susan Pringle Frost, ever the entrepreneur, and her sister Mary opened their ancestral home to the public to help defray its maintenance and restoration costs, to help support the household, to meet market demand, and to promote their celebration of an idealized colonial past. In an afternoon event they called "The Meaning of a House," the Frost sisters guided tourists through the mansion's halls, recounting in romantic detail the family legends and the house's history, which included serving as headquarters to the invading British (1780) and Union (1865) armies.[116] One photograph from the era, portraying the sisters dressed in colonial ladies' costumes as they await visitors, suggests that the Frosts knew very well how to embody the past for their patrons.[117] The thousands of signatures of tourists from all over the country and abroad that filled the guest books during the 1920s and 1930s indicate the heavy traffic at this site and the Frosts' success.[118]

Some elite visitors passed parts of the winter season as boarders in the Miles Brewton/Pringle House, soaking up the history lessons of its owners. "Did you ever sleep in the Louvre or the British Museum? Well, try the Pringle House," a Pittsburgh reporter mused in 1921. "If you are recommended by royalty . . . you may be received as a guest and permitted to sleep and eat in this marvelous house."[119] For these guests, Mary and Susan Frost served as

Realtor, preservationist, and entrepreneur Susan Frost (left) and her sister
Mary dressed in period costumes and offered paying visitors guided tours
of their home at 27 King Street. Courtesy of the Charleston
Museum, Charleston, South Carolina.

conduits of the living past in this house filled with evocative relics. "I came to *see* Charleston and I go having *felt* Charleston deeply," one female visitor wrote the sisters, "in the spirit of her people, who like you have made Charleston and her history."[120] Another from New York gushed to her hostesses about "the memories and realities we recalled there or that you described for us so vividly —they seemed our own experiences."[121] For many, an overnight at 27 King Street constituted time travel. "Within these classic doorways dwelt those to whom the past was the present and the future," one Rhode Island woman remarked wistfully. "Here were the chairs and sofa and mirrors acquired and cherished by men who made our history. Here the gowns and hangings and rugs of an earlier century still showed much of their former splendour. Here the coals still glowed in their old-time grates, tended by Georges and Sarahs as in the days of yore." Notably, this guest concluded that 27 King Street, as showcased by the Frosts, "speaks for all Americans."[122]

While the majority of the leisured classes who traveled to Charleston stayed in hotels,[123] the wealthiest and most elite minority purchased stately Low Country properties in which to pass the season. Beginning in the mid-1920s, the South Carolina coast, of which Charleston was the urban capital, experienced a real estate boom. "Indeed," editor William Watts Ball wrote to a friend in the spring of 1929, "the odor of genteel Yankee wealth, while not suffocating, is pervading Charleston."[124] Taken with the region's climate, sporting opportunities, historical aspects, and depressed land prices, wealthy elites from the North and Midwest began acquiring ancestral estates that, in many cases, had been in the same old-line Low Country families for centuries. From the northern Georgetown County south to Beaufort, along the region's many rivers and across its Sea Islands, America's monied elite—millionaires such as Solomon Guggenheim, Nicholas Roosevelt, Henry Luce, and A. Felix Dupont—became what architect Albert Simons described as "Wall Street Planters."[125] Other powerful men who had made their fortunes in commerce, manufacturing, or finance followed the fashion, including department store founders C. W. Kress and Archer Huntington (A&P), J. W. Johnson of Johnson & Johnson, "Bromo Seltzer King" Isaac Emerson, stationery magnate Z. Marshall Crane, and stock market gurus E. F. Hutton and South Carolina–born speculator Bernard Baruch.[126]

The Church Street real estate firm of Elliman, Huyler & Mullally conducted many of these transactions between the old Charleston aristocracy and the new monied classes. In 1927, for example, the Heyward family sold their ancestral plantation and the inspiration for many of Alice Smith's rice paintings, Wappaoolah, to a pair of New York businessmen. The new owners renovated the property, under the direction of Albert Simons, and quickly resold it to a couple from Cleveland for $70,000.[127] Similarly, in March 1930, the Stoney family sold its clan's "unifying and rallying place," Medway Plantation,[128] to newlyweds Mr. & Mrs. Sidney Legendre. Mr. Legendre was the Princeton-educated scion of an old New Orleans family and his wife was the heiress of New York State's largest carpet manufacturing family. The Legendres encountered Medway, "the oldest house in South Carolina of record,"[129] during a visit to their friend Benjamin Kittredge Sr. of New York and Dean Hall Plantation/Cypress Gardens. Gertrude Legendre, whose affluent family wintered in Aiken, South Carolina, during her childhood, recalled in her memoirs the alluring psychological effect of first seeing the isolated and romantically decrepit Medway: "[W]e spread our picnic by the pond and tried to imagine plantation life. . . . Something about it haunted us both."[130] Medway captivated the Legendres, who made it their permanent home during half the year. They expanded the grounds to 7,600 acres and added electricity, running water, and formal gardens to this colonial estate that had served as the setting for John Bennett's novel, the *Treasure of Peyre Gaillard*.[131]

In 1924, others from America's highest economic and social echelons built the Yeamans Hall Club, just inland from Charleston. Situated on a former colonial Landgrave estate,[132] this very modern development of private homes, a luxurious clubhouse, and an eighteen-hole golf course boasted a membership of which "perhaps half are Yale men, many of them Scroll and Key men to boot."[133] Every winter, these elites arrived by private rail car or yacht, accompanied by a retinue of friends and celebrities. By the early 1930s, these "absentee landlords"[134] collectively owned tens of thousands of Low Country acres as a private playground. Longtime Spirituals Society president Alfred Huger served as vice president of this development.[135]

In addition to historical allure and sporting opportunities, the Low Country offered America's leisured class a refuge from the turmoil of modern urban life. The author of a January 1932 *Country Life* article titled "The Renaissance of the Plantation" explained the appeal: "There is no part of America more remote from the pressure salesmanship and its philosophy of hurry and shove; there is no place where the sound of a stock ticker would seem so ill-suited to the surroundings. Any one stopping for a few minutes beside a silent coastal stream, or gazing at a majestic oak, can understand the love of the Northerner for the balmy silence of the old rice scenes."[136]

The Tourist and Convention Bureau of the chamber of commerce touted the region's claims more concretely; it advertised the city as a haven of good labor and race relations, as opposed to the strike- and riot-plagued North and Midwest. Appealing to American nativism and racism, the chamber in 1926 boasted "a high percentage of native born population" in a state that "is predominantly of pure Anglo-Saxon race." In addition to highlighting the minimal numbers of southern and Eastern European immigrants, the bureau characterized the city's demographic benefits as follows: "The Jewish element is in the eighth or ninth generation in Charleston . . . [and] Colored labor is of high quality and class. The low country Negroes are good tempered, courteous and industrious. There have been no race clashes, lynchings or riots since the reassertion of the white rule in 1877."[137] Ironically, even Solomon Guggenheim, a first-generation American Jew who owned both an area plantation and a city mansion at 9 East Battery, concurred with this estimation of Charleston as a true American town: "European immigration with its various 'isms' have made no impression upon it."[138]

The historical mythology of the region also provided the cultural parvenus among the "Wall Street Planters" — those with relatively recent middle-class or "ethnic" backgrounds — with an opportunity to remake themselves as Anglo-Saxon Protestant aristocrats. For these monied newcomers, as in American culture at large, plantation homes were intimately attached to ideas about pedigree, status, taste, legitimacy, and power. As one critic of Historic Charleston noted in 1944, "The damyankees [sic] have . . . come because of the legends and have stayed to try to make some of them real."[139] By owning such a home in the storied Charleston region, men like Victor Morawetz and Solomon Guggenheim could expand their "cultural capital" and stake a claim to a heritage not their own.[140] More than just a refuge from the strains of modernity, Charleston fulfilled the rising social pretensions of this class, enabling its members to melt more effectively into both elite echelons and the American mainstream. "The noblesse, the Yankees," author Josephine Pinckney mused, "are drawn to C[harleston] by the desire of those who come up in the world to emulate the Southern tradition — the gentleman farmer, the sportsman, the aristocrat."[141]

Bernard Baruch provides an excellent case in point. Born a Jew in Camden, South Carolina, to a German immigrant father and raised and educated in New York City, Baruch made millions as a Wall Street broker and served as chairman of Woodrow Wilson's War Industries Board. Although wealthy and very well positioned among the Northern business elite, this adviser to presidents nonetheless returned to his native state in 1905 to make a highly symbolic purchase: Hobcaw Barony. Baruch developed twelve thousand acres of this original colonial land grant into a hunting preserve where he entertained powerful guests from the North and abroad.[142] One such visitor, First Lady

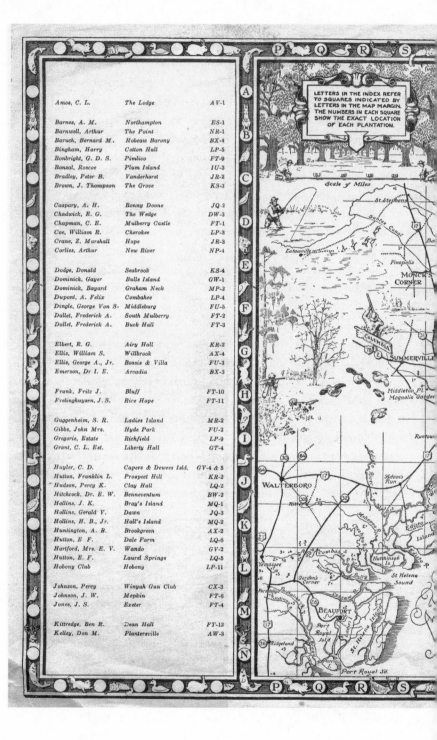

LETTERS IN THE INDEX REFER TO SQUARES INDICATED BY LETTERS IN THE MAP MARGIN. THE NUMBERS IN EACH SQUARE SHOW THE EXACT LOCATION OF EACH PLANTATION.

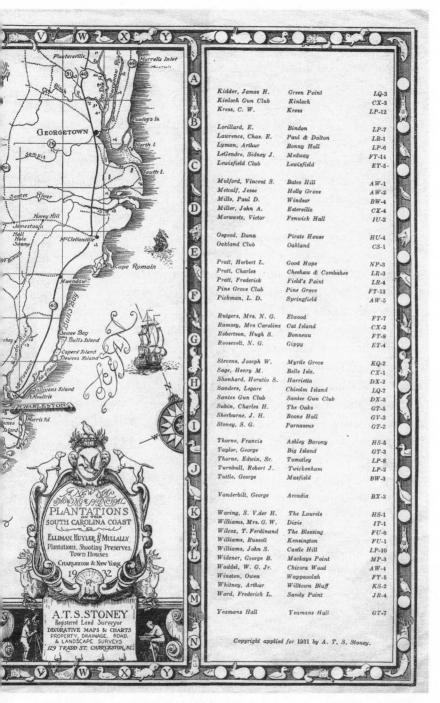

This 1932 map, drawn by A. T. S. Stoney for a local real estate company, indicates the principal plantations of the Low Country and, in many instances, their new ownership by wealthy Northerners. From the Collections of the South Carolina Historical Society.

Edith Wilson, even referred to her host as "My dear Baron," an honorific that must have thrilled him. What Baruch's lack of bloodlines and family status refused him in the South Carolina of his birth, his fortune captured in the changing marketplace of his adulthood.[143]

While some newcomers, such as President Theodore Roosevelt's cousin Nicholas G. Roosevelt of Philadelphia and Gippy Plantation, attempted to cultivate their long-abandoned fields, most millionaires passed their time in the leisurely pursuits of hunting, dining, riding, decorating, entertaining, and surveying their acreage.[144] In the hands of new owners, many plantations became the sites for a whirl of social activity as visitors from the North descended upon their landed gentry friends to hunt, golf, and taste the local flavor. Sidney Legendre of Medway lamented the compulsory social scene in a 1940 diary entry: "The spring season is the open season on plantation owners for anyone that has a car and is tired of the big city, or who does not want to motor to the North from Florida without breaking the trip en route."[145]

Surrounded by fine antiques, hired black servants, and plenty of land, many estate owners attempted to project an imagined "planter" persona.[146] The theatrical possibilities of the Low Country setting were not lost on writer Clare Boothe Luce and her publishing magnate husband, Henry. Dinners at Mepkin, their 7,200-acre holding, featured Mrs. Luce "often dressed as a Southern belle, in full-skirted, turquoise tafetta, with short, puffed sleeves, pearls or lapis lazuli jewelry and velvet bows in her hair."[147] Likewise, in a burst of paternalistic largesse, Isaac Emerson erected a brick church for the African American residents of his Arcadia Plantation. There, he, his wife, and "several guests from the north" comprised the benevolent "white folks" at a wedding ceremony in 1929: "The wedding presents from the Emersons were magnificent and numerous indeed," the local newspaper reported, "including among other things, 'envelope most bursting wid money[,]' as one darky expressed it."[148]

In exchange for sharing their cultural heritage, even if at times begrudgingly, Charleston's elite whites benefited in very real ways from this "Second [Yankee] Invasion."[149] *News & Courier* editor William Watts Ball best expressed local elite concerns about this development when he confided to a friend that "nothing is more dreadful than tourists, whether grasshoppers, boll weevils, or money-bagged bipeds. They will make Charleston rich or ruin her."[150] While not quite "making her rich," capital did pour into the otherwise depressed region via what Ball's newspaper dubbed "the establishment of a new aristocracy, moneyed and with a taste for the things which the old planters loved."[151] For example, Yeamans Hall—"whose members are eminently representative of the wealth, brains, and prestige of the nation"[152]—represented "a total investment of $2,000,000" in 1931.[153] Large sums of money flowed into Charleston through the restoration and annual maintenance of old properties by winter colonists as well. Even though Albert Simons complained to Sam Stoney in 1929, "I am getting quite fed up on millionaires," the architect's business boomed as a result of these nouveau Charlestonians' desire to acquire an architectural status symbol. "Outside of the winter colonists," Simons continued, "there is little local work."[154]

Winter colonists also brought with them a sense of sophistication and worldliness and a commitment to the region's aesthetic treasures that bolstered the cultural activism of local elites.[155] In its fund-raising efforts, for instance, the Society for the Preservation of Old Dwellings targeted preservation-minded winter colonists for donations.[156] Victor and Marjorie Morawetz of New York, owners of Fenwick Hall and several city properties, sponsored the Spirituals Society concert in New York. Solomon Guggenheim, meanwhile, allowed the Gibbes Art Gallery to be the first institution in America to exhibit his nonobjective modern art collection.

For some, however, the relationship between old heritage and new money was not without its problems. "These money bloated individuals actually want to rob us of our last heritage," a friend warned writer Herbert Ravenel Sass.[157] Not all newcomers were enthusiastically welcomed. Although she poured much of her fortune into the restoration of Medway, for example, Gertrude Legendre recalled her generally chilly reception from most local elites: "To Charlestonians, we weren't simply outsiders, we were something much worse—merchants."[158] But, overall, the relationship between the Low Country and the "millionaire planters" was mutually beneficial. As "an old lady of Charleston" remarked to a *Fortune* magazine reporter in 1933, "In 1865, the Devil sent the Yankees. . . . Today, God sends them."[159]

In the mid-1930s, Mayor Burnet Rhett Maybank wanted to attract even more Yankees, as well as Southerners, to the city to bolster the economy. In particular, he hoped to extend Charleston's appeal beyond America's more elite reaches to the motoring middle classes. Toward this end, the future South Carolina governor and senator created a city historical commission in March 1933. The commission officially opened its offices—decorated with the omnipresent artwork of Alice Smith, Elizabeth Verner, and Alfred Hutty—at 92 East Bay Street in January 1935. In addition to distributing tour maps to hotels, placing historical markers around the city, and soliciting tour groups from across the country, the commission, of which Herbert Ravenel Sass was a longtime member, also dramatized "history" in new forms for decidedly popular consumption. In 1935, for example, it broadcast a reenactment of the trial and execution of colonial patriot Colonel Isaac Hayne for local radio.[160]

Maybank further advanced his populist tourist vision by enthusiastically supporting the city's first Azalea Festival in March 1933.[161] A spectacle lasting several days, scheduled at the height of the garden season, the festival featured attractions designed to entertain a more general cross section of the traveling American public. Unlike the millionaires whose private yachts, personal train cars, and planes brought them to stay in their recently purchased city residences and area plantations, Azalea Festival customers most likely drove themselves and their families into town and stayed at local hotels or in one of the growing number of nearby tourist motor camps.[162] For the event's first incarnation, the city mounted a grand parade with elaborate floats, a beauty pageant, a golf tournament, a horse show, a dress parade of the Citadel cadets, a nighttime fireworks display, a water pageant off the Battery, a dance at the Isle of Palms pavilion, a fashion show, music recitals, and a street carnival "planned to rival New Orleans' famous Mardi Gras."[163] The *News & Courier* and the *Charleston Evening Post* published jointly a five-cent "Azalea Festival Edition" to help visitors negotiate the entertainments, as well as the city's historical landmarks, shopping and dining facilities, and local byways.[164] Over the years, the festival expanded to include full-costume historical pageants, including the reenactment of "a plantation scene" with "negro farm hands from Edisto Island,"[165] an antebellum lancing tournament "conducted under the rules of the days of knighthood,"[166] and the hanging of "gentleman pirate" Stede Bonnet on the Battery.[167] Thousands of people thronged to view these and other attractions that breathed life into the region's historical mythology. Deemed a success, the Azalea Festival became a popular annual event throughout the Depression and into the postwar era, luring tens of thousands of visitors to the city.

The festival also showcased a selective array of local African American talent to provide curious white visitors with "glimpses into negro life in the Low Country."[168] At Hibernian Hall, for example, fifty "genuine Gullah" singers from nearby Wadmalaw Island, including four former slaves, performed spirituals and reenacted a religious service at an evening titled "Plantation Echoes."[169] Similarly, the newspaper sponsored a "Contest of negro street criers,"[170] including vegetable, shrimp, and flower vendors "from the old school,"[171] who delighted audiences assembled at the Battery. Many of these black hucksters also competed in a footrace along White Point Gardens, once again cheered on by a swarm of visitors. Over the years, one of the most popular events proved to be a demonstration of rice preparation by black

The Azalea Festival attracted middle- and working-class visitors to Charleston during the Depression. In this 1938 photograph of the festival parade, the Fox Movietone cameraman films the City of Georgetown float, as well as the racially segregated audience. Courtesy of the Charleston Museum, Charleston, South Carolina.

Onlookers line the Battery to watch local black street merchants compete for the top huckster's title during the 1938 Azalea Festival. Courtesy of the Charleston Museum, Charleston, South Carolina.

farmhands from the Combahee River plantation of Theodore Ravenel, "the last of the large-scale rice planters in South Carolina."[172] (Tellingly, several years earlier, in 1927, Ravenel had sold some of his plantation holdings to New York investment banker E. F. Hutton.[173]) Sponsored by the Charleston Museum, the flailing and husking of rice by Ravenel's African American laborers to the rhythms of their traditional work songs enthralled audiences. In two weeks in 1937, over 11,000 visitors watched the demonstration.[174] One spectator, Mary L. Jobe Akeley, described by the *News & Courier* as an "African explorer" and teacher of American history at Hunter College, found the event "reminiscent of the jungles of the Belgian Congo." "She said she could shut her eyes," the newspaper reported, "and imagine herself back in the Congo, among the savages more primitive than those she visited on her last trip."[175]

Much as they benefited from the presence of wealthy winter colonists, savvy local cultural groups worked closely with the festival committee to capitalize on and educate the city's new tourists. Just because the festival attracted a different class of clientele to Charleston was not cause enough for elites to refuse a piece of the pie. The Society for the Preservation of Old Dwellings, for example, held house and plantation tours during the festival to raise money for the continued preservation and maintenance of the Heyward-Washington House. In 1934, the Society cleared $700 from these efforts.[176] That same year,

SELLING HISTORY BY THE SEA

African American women demonstrate the dying art of rice husking to white youths in a popular exhibit at the Charleston Museum (1937). Courtesy of the Charleston Museum, Charleston, South Carolina.

the Gibbes Art Gallery mounted an exhibition of Charleston artists "to show [visitors] the artists' conceptions of scenes in the city and nearby country."[177] Tourists could often purchase these images or similar ones at the artists' studios in town. And although at least one member of the Spirituals Society privately called it "that horrible Azalea Festival,"[178] in 1936 the group happily substituted their version of black spirituals for the "Plantation Echoes" performance. Introduced by DuBose Heyward and Mayor Maybank, the SPS broadcast this concert from the Academy of Music over national NBC radio.[179] Its rendition of Gullah songs was heard across the country and enthusiastically received by listeners from as far away as Toronto, Canada.[180]

Without a doubt, the success of the Azalea Festival, along with nearly every other tourist enterprise in Charleston by the early 1930s, relied heavily on the foundational cultural work of the city's white elites. Without preserved homes, *Porgy*, picturesque etchings, or folk music concerts, the self-conscious entity known as "Historic Charleston" would not have emerged as it did. White cultural elites shaped its content, form, and meaning and then publicized and commodified it effectively in the modern marketplace. They translated their personal and small-group memories into easily consumable forms that fixed a public idea of Charleston—genteel, ordered, historic, romantic—in the American imagination. Certainly, occasional critics dissented from the legendry that Charleston elites offered. "There is no such place as the utterly beautiful, charming, gracious old city that the romantics, the wishful thinkers, the fabulists say there is," Edward Twigg wrote in the January 1940 issue of *Forum* magazine. "Remote from that great day of hers is the real Charleston—poor, uncourtly, apathetic, and having as little to do with her own brilliant past as she has with the American present."[181] For the most part, however, white American tourists traveling to Charleston before World War II would have disagreed, as would city officials who always attempted to balance their commitment to this lucrative heritage crusade with simultaneous demands for commercial and industrial development.

In its "official" public rhetoric, then, Charleston became a place where ancient traditions and modern efficiency coexisted peacefully; where a tourist could journey through time without having to sacrifice modern comforts. In 1939, city leaders further highlighted this characterization when they chose the content for a time capsule to be opened in 2039. As part of their legacy for posterity, they included copies of DuBose Heyward's 1939 *National Geographic* essay, as well as the Spiritual Society's *Carolina Low-Country*. The goal was, in the words of then-mayor Henry Lockwood, "to hand over to future generations a city that is ever new at the same time that it is ever old."[182]

More than sixty years later, this compromise between the old and the new continues to profit the city. In 2003, 4.6 million tourists visited the Charleston area, leaving in their wake a total positive economic impact of $5.1 billion.[183] Mayor Lockwood would be pleased that his "Message to Charleston of the Future" in the 1939 time capsule had not fallen on deaf ears: "The community is more determined than ever that the priceless Old Charleston which is treasured by the whole United States shall be preserved, that its heritage from the past shall be passed in tact to the future."[184] Selling history by the sea remains Charleston's main vocation.[185]

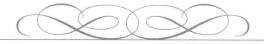

Afterword

To articulate the past historically does not mean to recognize it "the
way it really was." . . . It means to seize hold of a memory as it flashes
up in moments of danger. —Walter Benjamin, *Illuminations*

On 26 November 1937, 500 of Charleston's most prominent
white citizens and visiting dignitaries passed under an intricate wrought-iron balcony and across the threshold of the newly
restored Dock Street Theatre. Two years earlier, Mayor Burnet Maybank, a
staunch New Deal supporter, had secured $350,000 from the WPA to resurrect
the eighteenth-century playhouse at the corner of Queen and Church streets
from its decayed state as a "flophouse."[1] Given its status as America's oldest
theater, it is not surprising that the project involved the active participation
of many of Charleston's prominent cultural producers. The building's shell,
for example, comprised part of the nineteenth-century Planters Hotel, a landmark that had been safeguarded from destruction for many years by Susan
Frost and her Society for the Preservation of Old Dwellings.[2] Albert Simons,
president of the Carolina Art Association, which eventually administered
the completed building, and his architecture partner oversaw the building's
restoration. The Charleston Museum, under the direction of E. Milby Burton,
and the city council donated for the theater's decoration the interior of an old
city mansion where luminaries such as William Gilmore Simms and Robert E.
Lee had been entertained.[3] Local artist William Halsey painted the frescoes
surrounding the fountain in the courtyard behind the theater.

City newspapers, as well as national publications, heralded opening night with vivid descriptions of celebrity, ceremony, and Charleston's glory. Harry L. Hopkins, head of the Federal Emergency Relief Administration and a good friend of Maybank, came to town especially to dedicate the newly re-built theater. Echoing elite whites' rhetoric of the past two decades, Hopkins enthusiastically pointed to the Dock Street as evidence of Charleston's success in escaping "the ruthless march of the industrial system" and congratulated lo-cals for recognizing the value of "a proud heritage."[4] After Hopkins's speech, DuBose Heyward introduced the evening's highlight: the presentation of "The Recruiting Officer," the same play that had opened the theater in 1736, this time performed by the local acting troupe, the Footlight Players.[5] As was so often the theme in Charleston's public performance of its civic identity, Heyward proclaimed the enactment of George Farquhar's eighteenth-century comedy a "bridging of the gap between the present and the past."[6] As if to underscore further the hoped-for continuity between historical and contem-porary Charleston, after the curtain fell on the play's final scene, the voices of the Society for the Preservation of Negro Spirituals filled the theater to continue the evening's celebration.[7] In many respects, the Dock Street's 1937 opening represented the culmination of nearly two decades of self-conscious cultural production and historical performance in Charleston.

David Lowenthal has argued that "dismay at massive change stokes de-mands for heritage,"[8] and in Charleston, white elites responded to perceived threats to their way of life by turning to each other and a powerful notion of a shared past for comfort and empowerment. Drawing on extensive kinship networks and institutional affiliations, they developed a vibrant network of cultural and preservation organizations that provided the machinery for con-structing a public identity for "America's Most Historic City." Through these associations, elites translated their profoundly selective personal, familial, and status-group memories into power, embodied in concrete and exceedingly marketable heritage totems that claimed collective meaning: preserved plant-ers' homes, dreamy watercolor landscapes, picturesque local-color literature, and Gullah spirituals concerts. These entities formed the basis of the city's increasingly lucrative tourist industry, which in turn further enabled elites to convey their politicized memories to an expanded audience.

Out of their ancestors' past, white elites selected, reshaped, and packaged a historical memory for Charleston that was simultaneously a force of domi-nation, a way to impose their hegemony on the local scene, and a force of resistance, a way to critique the contemporary course of American culture. As a corrective to rampant industrialization, elites celebrated agrarian traditions.

The restoration of the nation's oldest theater, the Dock Street Theatre, shown here in its earlier, dilapidated state, marked the culmination of the pre–World War II stage of Charleston's historic preservation efforts. From the Collections of the South Carolina Historical Society.

To counteract African American political and economic mobilization, elites offered black dependence and primitivism. In response to political federalism, elites lauded Charleston's states' rights heritage while removing from it all traces of sectional hostilities. In the process, elites created a hierarchy of values that they considered worthy of commemoration and emulation for all Charlestonians, as well as for all Americans. Theirs was a historical memory carefully crafted to straddle the fence between nationalism and regionalism.

Although constructed to address white elites' specific social, economic, and political anxieties of the 1920s and 1930s, the "Historic Charleston" these individuals created has enjoyed a hearty afterlife in the post–World War II era. Its essential content—romantic, historic, aristocratic—has changed very little. Even the main organizations from the interwar cultural revival are still in operation. In the early 1950s, for example, the Society for the Preservation of Negro Spirituals recorded an album of their singing. The cover notes indicate that the Society's paternalistic racial understanding had not altered from its founding: "The colored man of a generation or so ago was a very interesting and in many ways attractive person. He was cheerful, he was contented, he was utterly improvident, he was reasonably diligent under supervision, he was basically—with certain exceptions—honest, and he was essentially, unfailingly, instinctively courteous."[9] Today's Society members are the children, grandchildren, and great-grandchildren of its originators. These descendants carry on tradition as they perform annual concerts of Gullah spirituals at the height of the tourist season, still dressed in the costumes of the antebellum plantation master class.

After the war, the Poetry Society of South Carolina also endured, but under new leadership from the English department faculty at the Citadel.[10] It continues to hold regular meetings and to encourage local literary expression. Even so, like Williams Simms before him, PSSC cofounder DuBose Heyward now remains the most touted of Charleston's writers in the public imagination. Certainly, the continued international success of the opera *Porgy and Bess* has helped ensure Heyward's prominence.

Reflecting the truism that the city's historic landscape was its core asset in the 1920s and 1930s, historic preservation efforts redoubled after the war and have further professionalized in recent decades. While the Preservation Society remains an important advocacy group today, the founding of the Historic Charleston Foundation (HCF) in 1947 signaled the city's permanent commitment to and expansion of an activist preservation agenda. The foundation adopted an innovative concept called the revolving fund to finance restoration projects more directly, and enlarged its mission to protect entire neighborhoods and a wider range of structures from demolition, including those outside the boundaries of the original historic zone.[11] The Historic Charleston Foundation is currently headquartered in the renovated former Esso service station on Meeting and Chalmer streets that was the source of great controversy for city preservationists in the early 1930s.[12] In addition to the HCF and Preservation Society, the Charleston Museum and the federally supported National Trust for Historic Preservation are prominent players in Charleston's historic landscape. They administer several historic structures in the city and the surrounding Low Country. Finally, the city government–sponsored Board of Architectural Review, established in 1931, still regulates exterior restorations and renovations, as well as new constructions, in the historic district, which the city has enlarged significantly in recent decades.

Aesthetically, the imprint of the 1920s and 1930s can still be seen on the city's art scene. While the Etchers' Club and the Southern States Art League are no longer extant, the Gibbes Museum remains a vital venue for the dissemination of local images, including those from the interwar years. Likewise, the creative sensibilities expressed by Alice Ravenel Huger Smith and Elizabeth O'Neill Verner and their peers continue to influence the kinds of images that are available on the local art market. A quick stroll down one of Charleston's streets in March or April reveals sidewalk artists displaying watercolors, drawings, and photographs of by-now stock Low Country images: ancient live oaks, street hucksters, and plantation columns, to name just a few.

At the base of all of this cultural activity there is tourism, which remains the largest industry of this city of 90,000 people. The recent construction of a waterfront park on the Cooper River and a high-tech Visitor Reception Center reflects the city's investment in tourism, as does its hosting of the annual Spoleto Festival USA, an international performing arts extravaganza that is a far cry from Maybank's Azalea Festival.[13] As in the 1920s and 1930s, most tourists today come to Charleston to visit its historic attractions, including its early preservation ventures, the Manigault and Heyward-Washington houses.[14] Many tourists, like Rhett Butler in the closing scene of the 1936 runaway best seller *Gone with the Wind*, seek in Charleston "the calm dignity life can have when it's lived by gentle folks, the genial grace of days that are gone."[15] Visitors find it in the material and ideological legacy left by the city's elite white cultural producers from the interwar years. Their historical memory endures.

Organizational Memberships and Select Authorship of
Major White Cultural Leaders in Charleston, 1920–1940

Hervey Allen
Poetry Society of South Carolina
Carolina Chansons: Legends of the Low Country (with DuBose Heyward, 1922)

John Bennett
Poetry Society of South Carolina; Society for the Preservation of Old Dwellings; Etchers' Club
Madame Margot: A Grotesque Legend of Old Charleston (1921)

E. Milby Burton
Charleston Museum; Society for the Preservation of Old Dwellings

Laura Bragg
Charleston Museum; Poetry Society of South Carolina

Alston Deas
Society for the Preservation of Old Dwellings; City Planning and Zoning Commission

Susan Pringle Frost
Society for the Preservation of Old Dwellings; Poetry Society of South Carolina

Panchita Heyward Grimball
Poetry Society of South Carolina; Society for the Preservation of Negro Spirituals

Dorothy Kuhns Heyward
Poetry Society of South Carolina; Society for the Preservation of Negro Spirituals
Porgy, the play (with DuBose Heyward, 1927)

DuBose Heyward
Poetry Society of South Carolina; Society for the Preservation of Negro Spirituals
Carolina Chansons: Legends of the Low Country (with Hervey Allen, 1922); *Skylines and Horizons* (1924); *Porgy* (1925); *Mamba's Daughters* (1929); *The Carolina Low-Country* (contributor, 1931); *Porgy and Bess* (with George and Ira Gershwin, 1935)

Alfred Huger
   Society for the Preservation of Negro Spirituals; Poetry Society of South
      Carolina; Yeamans Hall Proprietor
   The Carolina Low-Country (contributor, 1931)

Alfred Hutty
   Etchers' Club; Poetry Society of South Carolina; City Planning and Zoning
      Commission
   American Etchers, Alfred Hutty (1929)

Burnet Rhett Maybank
   Mayor, city of Charleston; senator, state of South Carolina
   City Planning and Zoning Commission; Society for the Preservation of Old
      Dwellings
   Elizabeth Maybank (wife): Poetry Society of South Carolina

Josephine Pinckney
   Poetry Society of South Carolina; Society for the Preservation of Negro
      Spirituals
   Sea-Drinking Cities (1927); *The Carolina Low-Country* (contributor, 1931)

Nell Pringle
   Society for the Preservation of Old Dwellings; Poetry Society of South Carolina

Beatrice Witte Ravenel
   Poetry Society of South Carolina
   The Carolina Low-Country (contributor, 1931)

R. Goodwin Rhett
   Mayor, city of Charleston
   Yeamans Hall Proprietor; Poetry Society of South Carolina
   Charleston: An Epic of Carolina (1940)
   Blanche S. Rhett (wife): Society for the Preservation of Old Dwellings

Herbert Ravenel Sass
   Poetry Society of South Carolina; Society for the Preservation of Old Dwell-
      ings; Society for the Preservation of Negro Spirituals; Historical Commis-
      sion, city of Charleston
   The Carolina Low-Country (contributor, 1931); *Look Back to Glory* (1933); *A Carolina
      Rice Plantation of the Fifties* (introduction, 1936)

Albert Simons
   Poetry Society of South Carolina; Board of Architectural Review; Society for
      the Preservation of Old Dwellings; Carolina Art Association; Charleston
      Museum; Society for the Preservation of Negro Spirituals; Regional Planning
      Committee/Civic Services Committee (*This Is Charleston*); Etchers' Club; City
      Planning and Zoning Commission
   The Early Architecture of Charleston (with Samuel Lapham, 1927); *Plantations of the
      Carolina Low Country* (with Samuel G. Stoney and Samuel Lapham, 1938)

Alice Ravenel Huger Smith
Etchers' Club; Poetry Society of South Carolina; Regional Planning Committee/
Civic Services Committee (*This Is Charleston*)
The Dwelling Houses of Charleston (with Daniel E. Huger Smith, 1917); *The Carolina
Low-Country* (contributor, 1931); *A Carolina Rice Plantation of the Fifties* (1936)

Augustine T. Smythe
Society for the Preservation of Negro Spirituals; Poetry Society of South
Carolina
The Carolina Low-Country (contributor, 1931)

A. T. S. Stoney
Society for the Preservation of Negro Spirituals; Etchers' Club

Samuel G. Stoney
Regional Planning Committee/Civic Services Committee (*This Is Charleston*)
Black Genesis: A Chronicle (with Gertrude Shelby Mathews, 1930); *Charleston:
Azaleas and Old Bricks* (with Bayard Wootten, 1937); *Plantations of the Carolina
Low Country* (with Albert Simons and Samuel Lapham, 1938)

Thomas P. Stoney
Mayor, city of Charleston
Society for the Preservation of Old Dwellings

Elizabeth O'Neill Verner
Etchers' Club; Society for the Preservation of Old Dwellings; Poetry Society
of South Carolina
The Carolina Low-Country (contributor, 1931); *Prints and Impressions of Charleston*
(1939); *Mellowed by Time: A Charleston Notebook* (1941)

Thomas R. Waring
Carolina Art Association; Board of Architectural Review; Poetry Society of
South Carolina
Charleston Evening Post (editor-in-chief); *The Carolina Low-Country* (contributor,
1931)

Robert N. S. Whitelaw
Carolina Art Association and Gibbes Art Gallery, director; Etchers' Club
Patricia Whitelaw (wife): Poetry Society of South Carolina; Society for the
Preservation of Old Dwellings

Abbreviations

ARHSF   Alice Ravenel Huger Smith File
ARHSP   Alice Ravenel Huger Smith Papers
ARHSSR   Alice Ravenel Huger Smith Sales Recordbooks
CCA   Charleston Chamber of Commerce Archives, Charleston, S.C.
CCPL   Charleston County Public Library, King Street Branch, Charleston, S.C.
CCRMD   City of Charleston Records Management Division, Charleston, S.C.
CM   Charleston Museum, Charleston, S.C.
COC   Robert Scott Small Library, Special Collections, College of Charleston, Charleston, S.C.
Duke   Rare Book, Manuscript and Special Collections Library, Duke University, Durham, N.C.
EONVF   Elizabeth O'Neill Verner File
EONVP   Elizabeth O'Neill Verner Papers
Gibbes   Gibbes Museum of Art, Charleston, S.C.
HCF   Historic Charleston Foundation
LC   Library of Congress, Washington, D.C.
PSC   Preservation Society of Charleston, Charleston, S.C.
PSSC   Poetry Society of South Carolina
SCHS   South Carolina Historical Society, Charleston, S.C.
SCL   South Caroliniana Library, University of South Carolina, Columbia, S.C.
SHC   Southern Historical Collection, University of North Carolina, Chapel Hill, N.C.
SPOD   Society for the Preservation of Old Dwellings/Preservation Society
SPS   Society for the Preservation of Negro Spirituals

Introduction

1. Henry James, *The American Scene* (New York: Harper & Brothers, 1907), 401–2.

2. Ludwig Lewisohn, "South Carolina: A Lingering Fragrance," *The Nation*, 12 July 1922, 36.

3. On the city's distinctive early architectural developments, see Bernard L. Herman, "The Embedded Landscapes of the Charleston Single House, 1780–1820," in

Exploring Everyday Landscapes, ed. Annmarie Adams and Sally McMurray, Perspectives in Vernacular Architecture, no. 7 (Knoxville: University of Tennessee, 1997), 41–57; and Carl Lounsbury, "The Dynamics of Architectural Design in Eighteenth-Century Charleston and the Lowcountry," in ibid., 58–71.

4. For information on Charleston's colonial and early American eras, see Peter A. Coclanis, *Shadow of a Dream: Economic Life and Death in the South Carolina Low Country, 1670–1920* (New York: Oxford University Press, 1989); Peter H. Wood, *Black Majority: Negroes in Colonial South Carolina, 1670 through the Stono Rebellion* (New York: Knopf, 1974); George C. Rogers Jr., *Charleston in the Age of the Pinckneys* (Norman: University of Oklahoma Press, 1969); and Walter J. Fraser, *Charleston! Charleston! The History of a Southern City* (Columbia: University of South Carolina Press, 1991). On the political battles behind the movement of the state's capital, see Matthew A. Lockhart, "'Under the Wings of Columbia': John Lewis Gervais as Architect of South Carolina's 1786 Capital Relocation Legislation," *South Carolina Historical Magazine* 104 (3) (July 2003): 176–97.

5. On the Stono Rebellion, see Wood, *Black Majority*. On Denmark Vesey, see Fraser, *Charleston! Charleston!* 187, 200–202; and Edward A. Pearson, ed., *Designs against Charleston: The Trial Record of the Denmark Vesey Slave Conspiracy of 1822* (Chapel Hill: University of North Carolina Press, 1999).

6. Coclanis, *Shadow of a Dream*, 120; William H. Pease and Jane H. Pease, *The Web of Social Progress: Private Values and Public Styles in Boston and Charleston, 1828–1843* (New York: Oxford University Press, 1985), 9–11, 70.

7. John Radford, "Identity and Tradition in the Post–Civil War South," *Journal of Historical Geography* 18 (1) (1992): 100.

8. Rogers, *Charleston in the Age of the Pinckneys*, 161.

9. Some historians argue that early-nineteenth-century Charleston was not so intellectually provincial and conservative. See, for example, Michael O'Brien and David Moltke-Hansen, eds. *Intellectual Life in Antebellum Charleston* (Knoxville: University of Tennessee Press, 1986); see also David Moltke-Hansen, "Southern Genesis: Regional Identity and the Rise of the 'Capital of Southern Civilization,' 1760–1860" (Ph.D. diss., University of South Carolina, 2000).

10. Louis D. Rubin Jr., *Seaports of the South: A Journey* (Atlanta: Longstreet Press Inc., 1998), 4.

11. Sidney Andrews, *The South Since the War* (1866; Boston: Houghton Mifflin, 1971), quoted in John P. Radford, "Culture, Economy and Urban Structure in Charleston, South Carolina, 1860–1880" (Ph.D. diss., Clark University, 1975), 225.

12. Dawson quoted in Paul M. Gaston, *The New South Creed: A Study in Southern Mythmaking* (Baton Rouge: Louisiana State University Press, 1970), 38.

13. See ibid., 38; Stephen Kantrowitz, *Ben Tillman and the Reconstruction of White Supremacy* (Chapel Hill: University of North Carolina Press, 2000); and Fraser, *Charleston! Charleston!* 365.

14. Fraser, *Charleston! Charleston!* 299.

15. Radford, "Culture, Economy and Urban Structure," 221. Radford's analysis of Charleston's urban structures and residential patterns from 1860 to 1880 suggests that Reconstruction did not significantly alter the city's social life or power base.

16. J. C. Hemphill, "A Short Story of the South Carolina Inter-State and West Indian Exposition," *Yearbook, City of Charleston* (1902), 107–71; William D. Smith, "Blacks and the South Carolina Interstate and West Indian Exposition," *South Carolina Historical Magazine* 88 (October 1987): 211–19; Bruce Harvey, "Architecture for the Future at the Charleston Exposition, 1901–1902," in Adams and McMurray, eds., *Exploring Everyday Landscapes*, 115–30; Anthony Chibbaro, *The Charleston Exposition* (Charleston: Arcadia, 2001).

17. Fraser, *Charleston! Charleston!* 359–60, 365; Jim McNeil, *Charleston's Navy Yard* (Charleston, S.C.: CokerCraft Press, 1985), 64–65, 77.

18. For more information on John Grace and attempts at progressive reform in Charleston, see John Joseph Duffy, "Charleston Politics in the Progressive Era," (Ph.D. diss., University of South Carolina, 1963); Doyle W. Boggs, "John Patrick Grace and the Politics of Reform in South Carolina" (Ph.D. diss., University of South Carolina, 1977); and Fraser, *Charleston! Charleston!* 365–66.

19. Fraser, *Charleston! Charleston!* 360.

20. Walter Edgar, *South Carolina: A History* (Columbia: University of South Carolina Press, 1998), 481.

21. Fraser, *Charleston! Charleston!* 363; Edgar, *South Carolina*, 481.

22. Fraser, *Charleston! Charleston!* 364.

23. Don Doyle, *New South, New Cities, New Men: Atlanta, Nashville, Charleston, and Mobile, 1860–1910* (Chapel Hill: University of North Carolina Press, 1990), 188. While many old-line white families continued to live in the city's upper sections, Charleston's Broad Street, a commercial thoroughfare lined with professional offices, churches, and shops, demarcated the northern boundary of the city's most elite neighborhood by the early twentieth century. See also Blaine A. Brownwell, *The Urban Ethos in the South, 1920–1930* (Baton Rouge: Louisiana State University Press, 1975), 199.

24. James Hagerty to the *Charleston Evening Post*, 11 January 1926, Thomas R. Waring Sr. Papers, SCHS.

25. See Elizabeth O'Neill Verner, Artist's Sketchbook, [pre–1 August 1935], property of David Verner Hamilton, The Tradd Street Press, Inc., Warrenton, Virginia.

26. Frederick Cople Jaher, *The Urban Establishment: Upper Strata in Boston, New York, Charleston, Chicago and Los Angeles* (Chicago: University of Illinois Press, 1982), 9. See also ibid., 320.

27. Rogers, *Charleston in the Age of the Pinckneys*, 22.

28. Lorri Glover, *All Our Relations: Blood Ties and Emotional Bonds among the Early South Carolina Gentry* (Baltimore: Johns Hopkins University Press, 2000), xv.

29. Jaher, *Urban Establishment*, 419. See also Pease and Pease, *Web of Social Progress*, 216–24.

30. Ibid., 9.

31. Ibid., 7. Nancy Press has argued that these patterns of class behavior among old-line Charleston descendants persisted into the late twentieth century as well. See Nancy Press, "Cultural Myth and Class Structuration: The Downtown Group of Charleston, South Carolina" (Ph.D. diss., Duke University, 1986).

32. See Mary Pringle Fenhagen, "Descendants of Judge Robert Pringle," *South Carolina Historical Magazine* 62 (July 1961): 151–64; (October 1961): 221–36. For the

Stoney/Maybank/Simons connection and others, see Emma B. Richardson, "Dr. Anthony Cordes and Some of His Descendants," *South Carolina Historical Magazine* 42 (1942): 133–55, 219–42; and 44 (1943): 17–42, 115–23, 184–95, reprinted in *South Carolina Genealogies*, vol. 2 (Spartanburg, S.C.: Reprint Company, 1983).

33. John Bodnar, *Remaking America: Public Memory, Commemoration, and Patriotism in the Twentieth Century* (Princeton: Princeton University Press, 1992), 15.

34. Pierre Nora, "Between Memory and History: Les Lieuxs de Memoire," *Representations* 26 (Spring 1989): 9. On the autobiographical nature of historical memory, see David Glassberg, "Public History and the Study of Memory," *The Public Historian* 18 (2): 7–24.

35. There has been a recent explosion in scholarship that focuses on the workings and manifestations of historical memory. For an interesting analysis of emerging "memory" paradigms, see Kerwin Lee Klein, "On the Emergence of *Memory* in Historical Discourse," *Representations* 69 (Winter 2000): 127–50.

Some of the studies that have influenced my analysis of Charleston include Bodnar, *Remaking America*; W. Fitzhugh Brundage, "No Deed but Memory," and essays by other authors in W. Fitzhugh Brundage, ed., *Where These Memories Grow: History, Memory, and Southern Identity* (Chapel Hill: University of North Carolina Press, 2000); David W. Blight, *Beyond the Battlefield: Race, Memory, and the American Civil War* (Amherst: University of Massachusetts Press, 2002); John R. Gillis, ed., *Commemorations: The Politics of National Identity* (Princeton: Princeton University Press, 1994); Richard R. Flores, *Remembering the Alamo: Memory, Modernity, and the Master Symbol* (Austin: University of Texas Press, 2002); David Glassberg, *Sense of History: The Place of the Past in American Life* (Amherst: University of Massachusetts Press, 2001); Charlene Mires, *Independence Hall in American Memory* (Philadelphia: University of Pennsylvania Press, 2002); Gary B. Nash, *First City: Philadelphia and the Forging of Historical Memory* (Philadelphia: University of Pennsylvania Press, 2002); Barry Schwartz, *Abraham Lincoln and the Forge of National Memory* (Chicago: University of Chicago Press, 2000); Sanford Levinson, *Written in Stone: Public Monuments in Changing Societies* (Durham, N.C.: Duke University Press, 1998); Kirk Savage, *Standing Soldiers, Kneeling Slaves: Race, War, and Monument in Nineteenth-Century America* (Princeton: Princeton University Press, 1997); Paul Connerton, *How Societies Remember* (New York: Cambridge University Press, 1989); Eric Hobsbawn and Terence Ranger, eds., *The Invention of Tradition* (New York: Cambridge University Press, 1983); "Memory and American History," special edition of *Journal of American History* 75 (March 1989); Michael Kammen, *Mystic Chords of Memory: The Transformation of Tradition in American Culture* (New York: Knopf, 1991); David Lowenthal, *The Past Is a Foreign Country* (New York: Cambridge University Press, 1985); and Patrick Wright, *On Living in an Old Country: The National Past in Contemporary Britain* (London: Verso, 1985).

36. For other instances of this phenomenon, see Benedict Anderson, *Imagined Communities: Reflections on the Origin and Spread of Nationalism* (London: Verso, 1983); Ian Donnachie and Christopher Whatley, eds., *The Manufacture of Scottish History* (Edinburgh: Polygon, 1992); Edward Muir, *Civic Ritual in Renaissance Venice* (Princeton: Princeton University Press, 1981); and Edward Said, *Orientalism* (New York: Pantheon Books, 1978).

37. Brundage, "No Deed but Memory," 11.

38. See, for example, James C. Scott, *Weapons of the Weak: Everyday Forms of Peasant Existence* (New Haven: Yale University Press, 1985); Partha Chatterje, *The Nation and Its Fragments: Colonial and Postcolonial Histories* (Princeton: Princeton University Press, 1993); Homi K. Bhabha, ed., *Nation and Narration* (New York: Routledge, 1990); Ian McBride, ed., *History and Memory in Modern Ireland* (Cambridge: Cambridge University Press, 2001); Bodnar, *Remaking America*; Margaret Kelleher, "Hunger and History: Monuments to the Great Irish Famine," *Textual Practice* 16 (2): 249–76; David Lowenthal, *The Heritage Crusade and the Spoils of History* (New York: Cambridge University Press, 1998), 227–50; and Kathleen Clark, "Celebrating Freedom: Emancipation Day Celebrations and African American Memory in the Early Reconstruction South," in Brundage, ed., *Where These Memories Grow*, 107–32.

39. Bodnar, *Remaking America*, 14.

40. David Thelen, "Memory and American History," *Journal of American History* 75 (March 1989): 1119. Maurice Hawlbachs asserted the importance of memory shaped in communion with others in his pioneering 1925 book, *The Collective Memory*, trans. Francis Ditter Jr. and Vida Yazdi Ditter (New York: Harper & Row, 1980).

41. On these controversies, see essays in Mike Wallace, *Mickey Mouse History and Other Essays on American Memory* (Philadelphia: Temple University Press, 1996); Randy Roberts, *A Line in the Sand: The Alamo in Blood and Memory* (New York: Free Press, 2001); Flores, *Remembering the Alamo*; Holly Beachley Brear, *Inherit the Alamo: Myth and Ritual at an American Shrine* (Austin: University of Texas Press, 1995); Edward T. Linenthal and Tom Englehardt, eds. *History Wars: The Enola Gay and Other Battles for the American Past* (New York: Metropolitan Books, 1996); and Richard Handler and Eric Gable, *The New History in an Old Museum: Creating the Past at Colonial Williamsburg*, (Durham, N.C.: Duke University Press, 1997).

42. At first glance, elite white Charlestonians' fascination with so-called African American primitivism might have placed them in the company of their modernist contemporaries in America's urban centers. This grouping, however, would be both awkward and inaccurate. White Charlestonians' interest in the black "folk" was not a form of experimental, "exotic" release, as has been posited about the experience of elite whites who frequented Harlem's nightclubs. Instead, Charlestonians used what they perceived to be black primitivism to reinforce their belief in white gentility and the necessity of a racial system based on paternalism and white control. See Ann Douglas, *Terrible Honesty: Mongrel Manhattan in the 1920s* (New York: Farrar, Straus, and Giroux, 1995); and David Levering Lewis, *When Harlem Was in Vogue* (New York: Oxford University Press, 1981).

43. Robert L. Dorman's *Revolt of the Provinces: The Regionalist Movement in America, 1920–1940* (Chapel Hill: University of North Carolina Press, 1993) provides an excellent discussion of American regionalism, but he, too, focuses on the standard proponents of Southern regionalism, Faulkner, the Agrarians, Howard Odum, W. T. Couch, and W. J. Cash. A recent volume of essays on Charleston's cultural scene in the 1920s and 1930s goes a long way toward addressing this bias. See James M. Hutchisson and Harlan Greene, eds., *Renaissance in Charleston: Art and Life in the Carolina Low Country, 1900–1940* (Athens: University of Georgia Press, 2003).

44. T. J. Jackson Lears also warns against this oversimplification in his study of American antimodernism, *No Place of Grace: Antimodernism and the Transformation of American Culture, 1880–1920* (New York: Pantheon Books, 1981), xiii–xvii, 303–4. Charleston's story extends the pertinence of Lears's observations both chronologically, beyond the immediate post–Word War I era, and geographically, into the American South, a region untouched by his study.

45. Ian McKay, *The Quest of the Folk: Antimodernism and Cultural Selection in Twentieth-Century Nova Scotia* (Montreal: McGill-Queen's University Press, 1994), 35.

46. Discussions of Southern identity locate its origins in either internal factors, such as family, religion, and land, or external factors, such as the region's history. Texts such as C. Vann Woodward's germinal article "The Search for Southern Identity" and Carl N. Degler's *Place over Time* helped set the parameters for arguments about Southern distinctiveness. More recently, this line of inquiry continues in volumes such as *The Encyclopedia of Southern Culture* and the serial *Southern Cultures*. See John Shelton Reed, *The Enduring South: Subcultural Persistence in Mass Society* (Lexington, Mass.: Lexington Books, 1972); Carl N. Degler, *Place over Time: The Continuity of Southern Distinctiveness* (Baton Rouge: Louisiana State University Press, 1977); C. Vann Woodward's "The Search for Southern Identity," in C. Vann Woodward, *The Burden of Southern History*, rev. ed. (Baton Rouge: Louisiana State University Press, 1968), 3–25; Charles Reagan Wilson and William Ferris, eds., *The Encyclopedia of Southern Culture* (Chapel Hill: University of North Carolina Press, 1989); and the periodical *Southern Cultures* (Chapel Hill: University of North Carolina Press).

My examination is more in line with contemporary studies that consider the phenomenon of "Southernness" and regional identity as an integral part of a national identity. See, for example, Nina Silber, *The Romance of Reunion: Northerners and the South, 1865–1900* (Chapel Hill: University of North Carolina Press, 1993).

47. Thomas P. Stoney, "Mayor Stoney's Annual Address," *Year Book, City of Charleston* (1924), liv.

48. Robin D. G. Kelley, "'We Are Not What We Seem': Rethinking Black Working-Class Oppression in the Jim Crow South," *Journal of American History* 80 (June 1993): 75–112.

49. Doyle, *New South, New Cities, New Men*, 310; Susan V. Donaldson, "Charleston's Racial Politics of Historic Preservation: The Case of Edwin A. Harleston," in Hutchisson and Greene, eds., *Renaissance in Charleston*, 189.

50. For more on the Southern Literary Renaissance and the Harlem Renaissance, see Richard H. King, *A Southern Renaissance: The Cultural Awakening of the American South, 1930–1955* (New York: Oxford University Press, 1980); Louis D. Rubin Jr., *The Writer in the South: Studies in a Literary Community* (Athens: University of Georgia Press, 1972); Daniel Joseph Singal, *The War Within: From Victorian to Modernist Thought in the South, 1919–1945* (Chapel Hill: University of North Carolina Press, 1982); Nathan Irvin Huggins, *The Harlem Renaissance* (New York: Oxford University Press, 1971); and Lewis, *When Harlem Was in Vogue*.

51. Because I believe the term "Charleston Renaissance" overstates the qualitative caliber of Charleston's cultural output, confusing it with the more critical and complicated Harlem and Southern Literary Renaissances, and because it lacks significant

historical resonance with the central figures of the city's cultural scene, I avoid using the term in this work. There is only occasional reference to the term "renaissance" in the primary sources. In scholarly sources, the earliest mention I found of the term "Charleston Renaissance/Renascence" was in a 1958 dissertation that deals only with the Poetry Society of South Carolina: Headley M. Cox Jr., "The Charleston Poetic Renascence, 1920–1930" (Ph.D. diss., University of Pennsylvania, 1958). According to Martha Severens, curator of the Gibbes Museum of Art in Charleston, South Carolina, from 1979 to 1990, the term "Charleston Renaissance" was first applied publicly to the 1920s/1930s interdisciplinary revival in the arts, literature, and historic preservation in 1985. Severens argues that the label was deployed by the staff of the Gibbes Museum as an efficient marketing tool for the 1985 art exhibition "Charleston in the Age of Porgy and Bess," which celebrated the sixtieth anniversary of the publication of DuBose Heyward's novel *Porgy* and the fiftieth anniversary of the premiere of *Porgy and Bess*, George Gershwin's American opera based on Heyward's work. Today, the Gibbes Museum devotes a permanent exhibition space, the Charleston Renaissance Gallery, to works of art from the 1920s and 1930s. For its ease and drama, the term has become firmly ensconced in scholarly and popular vocabulary (Martha Severens, interview by author, 18 October 1993, Gibbes Museum of Art, Charleston, S.C.). Subsequently, the term has been put to frequent use in recent years. See, for example, Hutchisson and Greene, eds., *Renaissance in Charleston*; Frank Q. O'Neill, "Light on the Water: The Golden Age of Charleston's Art," *Kiawah Islands Legends* 2 (Spring/Summer, 1991): 28–36; Boyd Saunders and Ann McAden, *Alfred Hutty and the Charleston Renaissance* (Orangeburg, S.C.: Sandlapper Publishing Company, Inc., 1990); and Martha R. Severens, "Charleston in the Age of Porgy and Bess," *Southern Quarterly* 28(1) (1989): 5–23.

52. Allen Tate, "The Profession of Letters in the South," quoted in Michael O'Brien, *Rethinking the South: Essays in Intellectual History* (Baltimore: Johns Hopkins University Press, 1988), 157.

53. Mrs. St. Julien [Harriott Horry] Ravenel, *Charleston, the Place and the People* (New York: MacMillan Company, 1906); Alice R. Huger Smith and D. E. Huger Smith, *The Dwelling Houses of Charleston* (Philadelphia: J. B. Lippincott Company, 1917).

Chapter One

1. The Charleston city motto is in Latin: *Aedes mores juraque curat.* Translation from Walter J. Fraser, *Charleston! Charleston! The History of a Southern City* (Columbia: University of South Carolina Press, 1989), 170. For a detailed description and history of Charleston's city seal and motto, see David C. Heisser, "'The Warrior Queen of Ocean': The Story of Charleston and Its Seal," *South Carolina Historical Magazine* 93 (July/October 1992): 167–95.

2. The Society for the Preservation of Old Dwellings (SPOD), established in 1920, predated both preservation projects: Williamsburg, Virginia (1924), and Greenfield Village in Dearborn, Michigan (1926). As one of the earliest examples of organized historic preservation, SPOD and Charleston's historic zoning ordinance served as the model for cities across the country, including efforts in New Orleans, Natchez, and

Alexandria, Virginia. See Charles B. Hosmer, *Preservation Comes of Age: From Williamsburg to the National Trust, 1929–1949* (Charlottesville: University Press of Virginia for the National Trust for Historic Preservation, 1981), for a detailed treatment of these early restoration/preservation projects in the United States, including Charleston's influence.

3. For more on the role of architecture and monuments in shaping public identity in the Southern context, see Catherine Bishir, "Landmarks of Power: Building a Southern Past in Raleigh and Wilmington, North Carolina, 1885–1915," in W. Fitzhugh Brundage, ed., *Where These Memories Grow: History, Memory, and Southern Identity* (Chapel Hill: University of North Carolina Press, 2000), 139–68.

4. Organized interest in collecting Americana and folk arts and in preserving and fostering regional culture began in the late nineteenth and early twentieth centuries. In the 1920s and 1930s, in part in response to the increased modernization, urbanization, and industrialization of the First World War and later to the crises of the Great Depression, many Americans celebrated local history and folk culture as they grappled with the question of what it meant to be an American. Michael Kammen presents an excellent and expansive analysis of this general phenomenon in *Mystic Chords of Memory: The Transformation of Tradition in American Culture* (New York: Knopf, 1991). See also Robert L. Dorman's *Revolt of the Provinces: The Regionalist Movement in America, 1920–1940* (Chapel Hill: University of North Carolina Press, 1993); and David E. Whisnant, *All That Is Native and Fine: The Politics of Culture in an American Region* (Chapel Hill: University of North Carolina Press, 1983).

5. See discussion of elite kinship networks in introduction.

6. Kenneth Severens, *Charleston: Antebellum Architecture and Civic Destiny* (Knoxville: University of Tennessee Press, 1988), 20.

7. Membership announcement, [1920], SPOD Papers, PSC.

8. For a description of the first SPOD meeting and the subsequent financial struggle of the Pringle family over the Manigault House, see J. Holton Fant, "Tea and Talk: A Preservation Memoir," *Preservation Progress* (Fall 1990): 1–4, 17.

9. Sidney R. Bland, *Preserving Charleston's Past, Shaping Its Future: The Life and Times of Susan Pringle Frost* (Westport, Conn.: Greenwood Press, 1994), 16–19, 46.

10. Ibid., 29; Mabel Pollitzer interview transcript, 19 September 1973, Southern Oral History Project, SHC.

11. Wendy Temple, "Susan Pringle Frost: Charleston's First Lady of Preservation, 1873–1960," *East Cooper Magazine* 2 (11), article clipping in Susan Pringle Frost File, SCHS. See also Bland, *Preserving Charleston's Past*, 91; and speech notes, 5 May 1920, Minutes File, SPOD Papers, PSC.

12. Alice R. Huger Smith and D. E. Huger Smith, *The Dwelling Houses of Charleston* (Philadelphia: J. B. Lippincott Company, 1917), 375.

13. Membership announcement, [1920], SPOD Papers, PSC.

14. Speech note, 5 May 1920, in Minutes File, SPOD Papers, PSC.

15. Minutes, 21 April 1920; and membership announcement, [1920], SPOD Papers, PSC; see also Susan P. Frost to Messrs. Logan & Grace, 22 May 1925, Susan Pringle Frost File, CCRMD.

16. Membership announcement, [1920]; and Minutes, 14 February 1925, SPOD Papers, PSC.

17. And yet Frost's biographer, Sidney R. Bland, asserts, "Debts, not profits, highlight Susan Frost's real estate career. Interest, taxes and mortgages overshadowed sales, especially in the 1920s and 1930s . . . and she rarely paid income taxes inasmuch as losses usually outweighed gains." Nonetheless, Frost stayed in business. Likewise, with her two sisters, she managed to generate income by opening their family home, the Miles Brewton/Pringle House at 27 King Street, as lodgings for "paying guests" and as a historic house museum for tourists throughout the period. With this model in mind, Frost reasoned that the Manigault House, and later the Heyward-Washington House, could produce enough door receipts to maintain the properties. See Bland, *Preserving Charleston's Past*, 99. See also meeting announcement, 16 June 1920, Minutes File, SPOD Papers, PSC; Mabel Pollitzer interview transcript; and M. M. Pringle to [May Rhett], 19 February [no year], reprinted in Richard N. Cote, "Guide to the Alston/Pringle/Frost Manuscript Collection," SCHS.

18. The heritage activities of these groups, including the Natchez (Mississippi) Garden Club, often propagated highly sectional views of the past. For a broader discussion, see James M. Lindgren, *Preserving the Old Dominion: Historic Preservation and Virginia Traditionalism* (Charlottesville: University Press of Virginia, 1993), 6–9, 240–48; James M. Lindgren, *Preserving Historic New England: Preservation, Progressivism and the Remaking of Memory* (New York: Oxford University Press, 1995); George Willson Newell and Charles Cromartie Compton, *Natchez and the Pilgrimage* (Kingsport, Tenn.: Southern Publishers, 1935); Hosmer, *Preservation Comes of Age*, 306–13; Bland, *Preserving Charleston's Past*, 111–12; and Jack E. Davis, *Race against Time: Culture and Separation in Natchez Since 1930* (Baton Rouge: Louisiana State University Press, 2001), 60.

19. [Susan Pringle Frost] to *News & Courier*, 11 May 1828, SPOD Papers, SCHS.

20. This notion of using the past to mediate change by no means originated with SPOD. See, for example, Gaines Foster's study of the rise of the Confederate tradition in the post–Civil War South, *Ghosts of the Confederacy: Defeat, the Lost Cause, and the Emergence of the New South, 1865 to 1913* (New York: Oxford University Press, 1987). Foster provides a brilliant example of how Confederate veterans negotiated the difficult transition from the Old to the New South through collective attempts to remember and memorialize the past. For Southern women's commemorative activism concerning the Lost Cause, see essays in Cynthia Mills and Pamela H. Simpson, eds., *Monuments to the Lost Cause: Women, Art, and the Landscapes of Southern Memory* (Knoxville: University of Tennessee Press, 2003).

21. Meeting announcement, 5 May 1920, SPOD Papers, PSC.

22. Ibid.

23. Meeting announcement, 12 April 1920, SPOD Papers, PSC.

24. Meeting announcement, 5 May 1920, SPOD Papers, PSC.

25. Minutes, 16 June 1920, SPOD Papers, PSC.

26. The scholarship on white women's presuffrage voluntarism and political activism is substantial. For a sampling of the germinal texts, see Paula Baker, "The Domestication of Politics: Women and American Political Society, 1780–1920," *American*

Historical Review 89 (June 1984): 620–47; Estelle Freedmen, "Separatism as Strategy: Female Institution Building in American Feminism, 1870–1930," *Feminist Studies* 5 (1979): 512–29; Nancy A. Hewitt, *Women's Activism and Social Change: Rochester, New York, 1822–1872* (Ithaca, N.Y.: Cornell University Press, 1984); Linda Kerber, *Women of the Republic: Intellect and Ideology in Revolutionary America* (Chapel Hill: University of North Carolina Press, 1980); Suzanne Lebsock, *The Free Women of Petersburg: Status and Culture in a Southern Town, 1784–1860* (New York: W. W. Norton and Co., 1985); Anne Firor Scott, *Natural Allies: Women's Associations in American History* (Urbana: University of Illinois Press, 1991); Darlene Rebecca Roth, *Matronage: Patterns in Women's Organizations, Atlanta, Georgia, 1890–1940* (Brooklyn, N.Y.: Carlson Publishing, Inc., 1994); Kathryn Kish Sklar, *Catherine Beecher: A Study in American Domesticity* (New Haven: Yale University Press, 1973); and Marjorie Spruill-Wheeler, *The New Women of the New South: The Leaders of the Woman Suffrage Movement in the Southern States* (New York: Oxford University Press, 1993).

African American middle- and upper-class women also invoked domesticity as an imperative for public activism. Interracial coalitions, however, were rare, and black and white women's efforts at reform remained, for the most part, separate enterprises. For an overview of the National Colored Women's Club movement, see Dorothy C. Salem, *To Better Our World: Black Women in Organized Reform, 1890–1920* (Brooklyn, N.Y.: Carlson Publishing, Inc., 1990). See also Elsa Barkley Brown, "Womanist Consciousness: Maggie Lena Walker and the Independent Order of Saint Luke," *Signs* 14 (3): 610–33.

27. Ann Pamela Cunningham was from the up-country of South Carolina, but her initial letter of appeal to save George Washington's home was published in the *Charleston Mercury* in December 1853. See Dwight Young, "How the Perseverance of Miss Ann Pamela Cunningham Helped Give Birth to a Movement," *Preservation* (July/August 1996): 116; Elswyth Thane, *Mount Vernon Is Ours: The Story of Its Preservation* (New York: Duell, Sloan and Pearce, 1966); and Robert P. Stockton, "Charleston's Preservation Ethic," *Preservation Progress*, special ed. (Spring 1993): 11–12.

28. During the 1920s and 1930s, the restored Powder Magazine served as the South Carolina state headquarters for the National Society for the Colonial Dames in America and was a popular tourist site. See Ellen Parker, "Historical Sketch and Catalogue of the Old Powder Magazine, 79 Cumberland Street, Charleston, South Carolina," 3d ed. (Charleston, S.C.: The South Carolina Society of Colonial Dames, 1946).

29. Frost's obituary notes, "She [Frost] chose the original name to include 'dwelling' because as used in the Bible, the word implied a permanent residence passed down from generation to generation" ("Rites Set Today for Miss Frost," *News & Courier*, 8 October 1960); see also William Henry Hanckel, "The Preservation Movement in Charleston, 1920–1962" (M.A. thesis, University of South Carolina, 1962), 11; and Michael Kevin Fenton, "'Why Not Leave Our Canvas Unmarred?': A History of the Preservation Society of Charleston, 1920–1990" (M.A. thesis, University of South Carolina, 1990), 5.

30. Minutes, 16 June 1920 and 6 February 1931, SPOD Papers, PSC.

31. Ernest H. Pringle to G. Corner Fenhagen, 16 April 1932, Manigault House Papers, SCHS.

32. Manigault House guest book, Manigault House Papers, SCHS; Miles Brewton House guest book, SCHS; Miles Brewton House guest books, Peter Manigault private collection, 27 King Street, Charleston, South Carolina. For more on women's preservation efforts, see W. Fitzhugh Brundage, "White Women and Historical Memory" in *Jumpin' Jim Crow: Southern Politics from Civil War to Civil Rights*, ed. Jane Dailey, Glenda Elizabeth Gilmore, and Bryant Simon (Princeton: Princeton University Press, 2000), 115–39.

33. "Miss Frost Tells History of Her Preservation Work," *News & Courier*, 24 February 1941. See also Susan Pringle Frost to Nell Pringle (12 May 1931, Manigault House Papers, SCHS), in which she writes: "I myself have had very heavy losses in business of various kinds; first in the florist business, I lost eight thousand besides all the accrued interest; I have not been able to pay either as yet but still hoping; I have lost heavily on Tradd St.; the public thinks I made money and it makes little difference to me what the public thinks; my books will show that on almost every restored house sold I made big losses."

34. Alston Deas, "They Shall See Your Good Works," *Preservation Progress* 7 (May 1962): 1.

35. Fraser, *Charleston! Charleston!* 373.

36. Bland, *Preserving Charleston's Past*, 49.

37. See Susan Frost to William Watts Ball, 8 June 1916, William Watts Ball Papers, Duke (emphasis is mine); see also Bland, *Preserving Charleston's Past*, 48, 50.

38. Bland, *Preserving Charleston's Past*, 51–52; see also Mabel Pollitzer interview transcript.

39. Bland, *Preserving Charleston's Past*, 10.

40. Susan Pringle Frost to "Nina [Pringle]," 21 January 1919, quoted in Cote, "Guide to the Alston/Pringle/Frost Manuscript Collection," 70, SCHS.

41. See the detailed discussion of the Miles Brewton/Pringle House as a tourist site in Chapter 5.

42. Margaretta Pringle Childs, interview by author, 22 November 1993, Charleston, S.C. See also Susan Pringle Frost, "Highlights of the Miles Brewton House" (Charleston, S.C.: Privately published, 1944). In this pamphlet, Frost presented her personal memorial to the house and its inhabitants, including African American servants and family pets, through prose, poetry, and photographs.

43. Ernest recalled one of his earliest jobs as a boy selling newspapers to help raise money for the Colonial Dames' restoration of the Powder Magazine, in which his mother participated. See Pringle to Fenhagen, 16 April 1932, Manigault House Papers, SCHS.

44. Ibid.; see also Bland, *Preserving Charleston's Past*, 15.

45. Childs interview.

46. Pringle to Fenhagen, 16 April 1932, Manigault House Papers, SCHS.

47. Childs interview.

48. "Society Restores Manigault House, Mrs. Ernest Pringle is Leader in Work of Preserving City's Beauty," *News & Courier*, 25 February [1931/32], newspaper clipping, SPOD Scrapbook 1932–45, SPOD Papers, SCHS.

49. Manigault House guest book, May 1929, Manigault House Papers, SCHS.

50. Nell McColl Pringle, untitled short story, [1930], Susan Pringle Frost File, SCHS.

51. Ibid.

52. A handwritten note on the first page of the story says, "This is my good description of the mental anguish I have gone through about the Manigault house [*sic*] — It was submitted & refused by House Beautiful & others" (ibid.).

53. Guest book entry, 22 November 1928, Manigault House guest book, SCHS.

54. See Fant, "Tea and Talk," 1–2; and Pringle to Fenhagen, 16 April 1932, Manigault House Papers, SCHS.

55. Nell McColl Pringle, untitled short story, [1930], Susan Pringle Frost File, SCHS.

56. "Asks Public to Save National Shrines," *New York Times*, 6 April 1932, newspaper clipping in Albert Simons Papers, SCHS.

57. In 1937, Standard Oil jumped on Charleston's preservation bandwagon and gave their portion of the Manigault property to the Charleston Museum, which was then under the direction of former SPOD president E. Milby Burton. See Selby F. Paul, "Society Restores Manigault House, Mrs. Ernest Pringle is Leader in Work of Preserving City's Beauty," *News & Courier*, 25 February 19[31], newspaper clipping, in SPOD Scrapbook, 1932–45, SPOD Papers, SCHS; and Hosmer, *Preservation Comes of Age*, 247–48.

58. See Jennie Holton Fant, "The Princess of Tides," *Charleston Magazine*, August/September 1993, 34–37, 62–63.

59. Mike Wallace, *Mickey Mouse History and Other Essays on American Memory* (Philadelphia: Temple University Press, 1996), 9–16. See also Hosmer, *Preservation Comes of Age*, and Lindgren, *Preserving the Old Dominion*.

60. Pringle to Fenhagen, 16 April 1932, Manigault House Papers, SCHS.

61. "Thanks to Mrs. Pringle Society Praises Her Work for Manigault House," *News & Courier*, 5 May 1933.

62. Albert Simons and Samuel Lapham Jr., *The Early Architecture of Charleston* (New York: Press of the American Institute of Architects, Inc., 1927); Samuel Gaillard Stoney, Albert Simons, and Samuel Lapham Jr., *Plantations of the Carolina Low Country* (1938; Charleston, S.C.: Carolina Art Association, 1964); Bayard Wootten and Samuel Gaillard Stoney, *Charleston: Azaleas and Old Bricks* (Boston: Houghton Mifflin, 1937); Beatrice St. Julien Ravenel, *Architects of Charleston* (Charleston, S.C.: Carolina Art Association, 1945).

63. Elise Pinckney, "Samuel Gaillard Stoney: An Ardent Charlestonian," *South Carolina Magazine*, March 1951, article clipping, Samuel Gaillard Stoney File, SCHS.

64. Wootten and Stoney, *Charleston*, 25.

65. Albert Simons to Mr. A. Lawrence Kocher, Chairman, Committee on Preservation of Historic Monuments and Natural Resources, New York City, 12 April 1928, Albert Simons Papers, SCHS.

66. For examples of antique-stripping and demolition of historic structures in Charleston, see Albert Simons to Mr. Sedgwick, 5 July 1922; Albert Simons to Mr. Rivers, 8 May 1928; and Albert Simons to Fiske Kimball, May 24 1928, Albert Simons Papers, SCHS; Alston Deas to Mayor Thomas P. Stoney, 29 April 1929, SPOD Papers,

SCHS; Albert Simons to Colonel Aiken Simons, T. Grange Simons, Esq., W. Lucas Simons, Esq., and Lt. Condr. R. Bentham Simons, 10 February 1931, Box "CAA Correspondence (1916–1935)," Thomas R. Waring Sr. Correspondence File, 1931, Gibbes; William Watts Ball to Fitz McMaster, 8 March 1929, William Watts Ball Papers, Duke; "Display of Colonial Interiors as Museum Trophies Assailed," *New York Herald Tribune*, 27 November 1932; "Two Rooms of Stuart House: Bit of Early Charleston Shown in Minneapolis Institute of Arts," unnamed Charleston newspaper clipping, [1931], SPOD Scrapbook, SPOD Papers, SCHS; and "Preserving Historic Buildings Intact," *Old-Time New England: The Bulletin of the Society for the Preservation of New England Antiquities*, 21 (October 1930), article clipping, SPOD Papers, SCHS. See also Meyric R. Rogers, "The American Rooms," *Bulletin of the City Art Museum of St. Louis* 16 (October 1931), "Charleston pamphlets," Gibbes, for description of a Charleston room taken from the second floor of 61 Tradd Street and installed in the St. Louis museum as part of the period-room craze among museums and collectors.

67. Albert Simons to Colonel Aiken Simons et al., 10 February 1931.

68. Albert Simons to A. Lawrence Kocher, 12 April 1928, Albert Simons Papers, SCHS.

69. Simons claimed that members of the "mechanic class" were particularly susceptible to buyers. "These people are naturally rather dazzled by the extravagant sums that are paid for the interiors of some of our old houses by some of our winter visitors through the high pressure salesmanship of the antique dealers that infest this city" (Simons to Horace W. Peaslee, 6 July 1931, Albert Simons Papers, SCHS).

70. Albert Simons to John Mead Howells, 5 July 1928, and Howells to Simons, 13 July 1928, Albert Simons Papers, SCHS. See also Hosmer, *Preservation Comes of Age*, 243.

71. "Keep Charleston Charleston," *News & Courier*, 29 November 1932.

72. Albert Simons to James J. Morrison, Esq., College of Law, Tulane University, 29 May 1939, Albert Simons Papers, SCHS.

73. Albert Simons to T. R. Waring, 26 September 1931, Box "CAA Correspondence (1916–1935)," Thomas R. Waring Sr. Correspondence File, 1931, Gibbes.

74. Albert Simons to T. R. Waring, 27 July 1933, Albert Simons Papers, SCHS.

75. Albert Simons to Samuel G. Stoney, 6 May 1929, Albert Simons Papers, SCHS.

76. "Selections from the Work of Simons and Lapham, Architects, 42 Broad Street, Charleston, S.C.," [1930], brochure, Gibbes.

77. Hanckel, "Preservation Movement," 17–18.

78. "The Preservation and Restoration of Old Charleston of National Significance," [1929/30], unnamed newspaper clipping, SPOD Scrapbook, SPOD Papers, SCHS.

79. Of course, wealth alone was not grounds for membership. While considering the Morawetzes' candidacy, for example, the Society wrote to friends in New York to determine whether the couple was Jewish. See Albert Simons to John Mead Howells, 24 November 1926, Albert Simons Papers, SCHS; and William Watts Ball to [D. F.] Houston, 22 October 1937, William Watts Ball Papers, Duke.

80. See Simons and Stoney, *Plantations of the Carolina Low Country*.

81. Frances W. Emerson, Cambridge, Massachusetts, to Albert Simons, 23 April 1928, Albert Simons Papers, SCHS.

82. Hosmer, *Preservation Comes of Age*, 245.

83. Deas succeeded Frost as SPOD president in 1927. See Certificate of Incorporation, 7 November 1928, SPOD Papers, PSC. The name "Society for the Preservation of Old Dwellings" was officially changed to "The Preservation Society of Charleston" in 1927. See Corporation document, 22 March 1957, SPOD Papers, PSC.

84. See, for example, Alston Deas, "Aspects of Charleston—Epitaphs," *News & Courier*, [1929], newspaper clipping, Alston Deas File, SCHS; and "Heyward House Restoration To Begin, Funds Are Secured," unnamed Charleston newspaper clipping, 18 April 1929, Heyward-Washington House File, SCHS.

85. Bernard S. Groseclose Jr., "Tribute to Preservationist: Col. Alston Deas," *News & Courier*, 25 January 1985.

86. Hosmer, *Preservation Comes of Age*, 245.

87. "Heyward House Tournament Today," *News & Courier*, 23 January 1938.

88. Mary Ralls Dockstader, "The Heyward-Washington House, Charleston, South Carolina," undated essay, Heyward-Washington House File, SCHS.

89. *News & Courier*, 11 May 1928, as quoted in Hosmer, *Preservation Comes of Age*, 243.

90. John Patrick Grace to William Watts Ball, 9 May 1929, William Watts Ball Papers, Duke.

91. Thomas P. Stoney, Mayor, to Alston Deas, 21 May 1928, and Alston Deas to Mayor Burnet R. Maybank, 30 May 1932, SPOD Papers, SCHS; Hosmer, *Preservation Comes of Age*, 238–42, 254–60.

92. *Year Book, City of Charleston, South Carolina* (1929), 320–21.

93. Alston Deas, "Charleston First Zoning Ordinance," *Preservation Progress* 27 (January 1983): 3.

94. Hosmer, *Preservation Comes of Age*, 240; Robert P. Stockton, "Historic Preservation in Charleston," undated essay, Historic Preservation File, SCHS.

95. Albert Simons, lecture notes, 1949–50, Albert Simons Papers, SCHS.

96. Hosmer, *Preservation Comes of Age*, 240.

97. Albert Simons to Marjorie Morawetz, 5 July 1932; and Albert Simons to Delos Smith, 10 August 1933, Albert Simons Papers, SCHS.

98. Albert Simons to T. R. Waring, 15 September 1932, Albert Simons Papers, SCHS.

99. Simons and Lapham to Lippincott, 10 November 1924, as quoted in Eugene Waddell, "The Only Volume in the Octagon Library," in James M. Hutchisson and Harlan Greene, eds., *Renaissance in Charleston: Art and Life in the Carolina Low Country, 1900–1940* (Athens: University of Georgia Press, 2003), 117.

100. The Charleston Museum, "A Project for a Hall of Charleston Architecture for the Charleston Museum," [1934–35], Albert Simons Papers, SCHS.

101. "Old Books Tell of Architecture," *News & Courier*, 6 May 1934.

102. Marjorie Morawetz to Albert Simons, 24 June 1932, Albert Simons Papers, SCHS. See also Helen McCormack to Laura Bragg, 1 January 1936, Laura Bragg

Papers, SCHS, in which McCormack writes, "The Wagner house on Broad Street has been done over and all the ginger-bread taken off. It looks infinitely better."

103. Fraser, *Charleston! Charleston!* 254.

104. Albert Simons to James J. Morrison, New Orleans, 29 May 1939, Albert Simons Papers, SCHS.

105. Albert Simons to John Bennett, 22 March 1934, Albert Simons Papers, SCHS.

106. Mamie Garvin Fields, *Lemon Swamp and Other Places: A Carolina Memoir* (New York: Free Press, 1983), 194.

107. Fraser, *Charleston! Charleston!* 366.

108. T. J. Woofter Jr., "Charleston Negro Housing," [1926], Albert Simons Papers, SCHS; Albert Simons to J. M. Hamilton, 7 September 1933, Albert Simons Papers, SCHS; photographs, Robert Mills Manor File, CCRMD. See also Fields, *Lemon Swamp*, 194–96. Shabby, dilapidated houses, both white- and black-occupied, were commonplace in downtown Charleston from the end of Civil War until long after the Second World War. For more descriptions, see Owen Wister, *Lady Baltimore* (New York: Macmillan Company, 1906); and Henry James, *The American Scene* (New York: Harper & Brothers, 1907). Photographer Frances Benjamin Johnston also captured Charleston's ramshackle housing conditions in her photographs from the 1930s. See Frances Benjamin Johnston Collection, Division of Photographs, LC.

109. Susan V. Donaldson, "Edwin A. Harleston and Charleston's Racial Politics of Preservation," in Hutchisson and Greene, eds., *Renaissance in Charleston*, 187. See also Walter B. Hill, "Family, Life and Work Culture: Black Charleston, South Carolina, 1880–1910" (Ph.D. diss., University of Maryland, 1989), 412; and Bernard E. Powers, *Black Charlestonians: A Social History, 1822–1885* (Fayetteville: University of Arkansas Press, 1994), 246.

110. Fields, *Lemon Swamp*, 19.

111. John P. Radford, "Culture, Economy and Urban Structure in Charleston, South Carolina, 1860–1880" (Ph.D. diss., Clark University, 1975), 106–13. Charleston's racially integrated neighborhoods grew out of the slave-era tradition of black domestics living in quarters adjacent to white homes. A lack of significant residential segregation persisted into the mid-twentieth century. A housing study in 1910, for example, found that Charleston had no concentrated "Negro district" (ibid., 111–13).

112. Albert Simons, Report of meeting with Robert D. Kohn, Director of Public Housing, Bureau of Public Works, Department of the Interior, 20 October 1933, Albert Simons Papers, SCHS; Albert Simons to Burnet Rhett Maybank, 29 November 1934, Albert Simons Papers, SCHS.

113. Marvin Leigh Cann, "Burnet Rhett Maybank and the New Deal in South Carolina, 1931–1941" (Ph.D. diss., University of North Carolina at Chapel Hill, 1967), 104–6; Josiah E. Smith, "The Housing Authority of the City of Charleston," *Year Book, City of Charleston* (1940), 184.

114. Josiah E. Smith, "The Housing Authority," *Year Book, City of Charleston* (1938), 177.

115. Mrs. B. E. Smith to Albert Simons, 4 January 1934, Albert Simons Papers, SCHS; see also Mrs. B. A. Shuler to Albert Simons, 3 January 1934; Mrs. Ewing Steinberg to Albert Simons, 5 January 1934; and Cord Steinberg to Albert Simons, 6 January 1934, Albert Simons Papers, SCHS.

116. Carrie T. Pollitzer to Mayor Burnet Rhett Maybank, 1 January 1934, Albert Simons Papers, SCHS.

117. "Residents at Site of Manor Grumble at Having to Move," *News & Courier*, [1938], newspaper clipping, Housing Authority File, CCRMD.

118. Josiah E. Smith, "The Housing Authority of the City of Charleston," *Year Book, City of Charleston* (1939), 168. This report includes before and after photographs of the Cromwell Alley neighborhood, which was demolished to construct the Robert Mills Manor.

119. "Society in Favor of Keeping Jail," *News & Courier*, 4 March 1938; "Citizens Asked to Sign Petition," *Charleston Evening Post*, 2 July 1938.

120. Fraser, *Charleston! Charleston!* 384; see also *Year Book, City of Charleston, 1938* (c. 1940).

121. Josiah E. Smith, "The Housing Authority," *Year Book, City of Charleston* (1938), 177–78.

122. Minutes, 24 January 1940, SPOD Papers, SCHS. See also Minutes, 1 February 1940, SPOD Papers, SCHS; and "Cleanup in Archdale Street Endorsed," *News & Courier*, 2 February 1940.

123. Robert Whitelaw to Frederick Keppel, 30 November 1939, City Plan, Director's Correspondence, 1939–42, HCF.

124. Samuel Stoney, *This Is Charleston: A Survey of the Architectural Heritage of a Unique American City*, 3d ed. (Charleston, S.C.: Carolina Art Association, 1964), 5.

125. Hosmer, *Preservation Comes of Age*, 256, 260–61.

126. Ibid., 262.

127. Albert Simons, foreword to Stoney, *This Is Charleston*, vii.

128. Stoney, *This Is Charleston*, 4–5.

129. Albert Simons, quoted in Hosmer, *Preservation Comes of Age*, 274.

Chapter Two

1. Alice R. Huger Smith, *A Carolina Rice Plantation of the Fifties* (New York: William Morrow and Company, 1936).

2. "Miss Alice R. Huger Smith Speaks at Mount Holyoke," unnamed Charleston newspaper clipping, 17 October 1937, ARHSF, SCHS.

3. Estill Curtis Pennington, *Look Away: Reality and Sentiment in Southern Art* (Spartanburg, S.C.: Saraland Press, 1989), 12.

4. Mary H. Phifer, "Southern Personalities: Elizabeth O'Neill Verner, Etcher," *Holland's: The Magazine of the South*, October 1929, 15, clipping, EONVP, SCHS.

5. Selby F. Paul, "Artists Find Charleston Inspiration to Fine Work," *News & Courier*, 26 February 1930, newspaper clipping, EONVP, SCHS.

6. Leila M. McCauley, "Renaissance in the South," *Chicago Evening Post*, 17 April

1928, as quoted in "Charleston Entitled to Honors as One of Chief Art Centers of Country," *News & Courier,* 29 April 1928, newspaper clipping, EONVP, SCHS.

7. See *Charleston City Directory* (1923 and 1928).

8. Associated Artists of Charleston, Minutebook, 1927–41, Gibbes. Neither Smith nor Verner was a member of this group.

9. John Bennett, letter to the editor, *News & Courier,* 6 November 1939. For more on Charleston's visiting artists, see Martha R. Severens, *The Charleston Renaissance* (Spartanburg, S.C.: Saraland Press, 1998); and Martha R. Severens, "To Sell the City of Charleston: The Visual Arts and the Charleston Renaissance," in James M. Hutchisson and Harlan Greene, eds., *Renaissance in Charleston: Art and Life in the Carolina Low Country, 1900–1940* (Athens: University of Georgia Press, 2003), 35–56.

10. Alfred Hutty, quoted in Boyd Saunders and Ann McAden, *Alfred Hutty and the Charleston Renaissance* (Orangeburg, S.C.: Sandlapper Publishing Company, Inc., 1990), 13.

11. For more on the Carolina Art Association, see Harold A. Mouzon, "The Carolina Art Association: Its First Hundred Years," *South Carolina Historical Magazine* 59 (July 1958): 125–38; and *Selections from the Collection of the Carolina Art Association* (Charleston, S.C.: Carolina Art Association, 1977).

12. Duncan Philips, *American Etchers, Alfred Hutty,* vol. 2 (New York: T. Spencer Hutson, 1929), introduction, n.p.

13. Hutty's Charleston career has been thoroughly delineated in Saunders and McAden, *Alfred Hutty and the Charleston Renaissance.* Therefore, it is not detailed in this chapter, which focuses instead on the native articulation of Charleston's identity in the fine arts by Smith and Verner. For more information concerning Hutty's Charleston-based images and career, see Saunders and McAden, *Alfred Hutty and the Charleston Renaissance.* See also Martha R. Severens, "Charleston in the Age of *Porgy and Bess*," *Southern Quarterly* 28 (Fall 1989): 5–23; Birge Harrison, "Old Charleston as Pictured by Alfred Hutty," *The Magazine of American Art* 12 (November 1922): 479–83; and Alfred Hutty File, SCHS.

14. For more information on Charleston's nonobjective art exhibits, see Robert N. S. Whitelaw, "Solomon R. Guggenheim Collection of Non-Objective Paintings," exhibition catalog, 1 March 1936; Baroness Hilla Rebay, "Solomon R. Guggenheim Collection of Non-Objective Paintings," third enlarged exhibition catalog, 7 March 1938, in Anita Pollitzer Papers, SCHS; Elie C. Edson, "Charleston Dared," press release, Anita Pollitzer Papers, SCHS; Robert N. S. Whitelaw to Solomon Guggenheim, 2 March 1936, and Whitelaw to W. S. Budworth, 17 March 1936, Exhibition Files, Gibbes; and articles and letters to the editor in *News & Courier* and *Charleston Evening Post,* March through April, 1936 and 1938.

15. C. Vann Woodward, "The Search for Southern Identity," in C. Vann Woodward, *The Burden of Southern History,* rev. ed. (Baton Rouge: Louisiana State University Press, 1968), 23.

16. Matthew Baigell, *The American Scene: American Painting of the 1930s* (New York: Praeger Publishers, 1974), 13–18; see also William H. Gerdts, *Art Across America: Two Centuries of Regionalist Painting, 1710–1920,* vol. 2 (New York: Abbeville Press Publishers,

1990); and Robert L. Dorman, *Revolt of the Provinces: The Regionalist Movement in America, 1920–1940* (Chapel Hill: University of North Carolina Press, 1993), xi–xiii.

17. In addition to Gerdts, *Art Across America*, and Baigell, *American Scene*, see Wanda M. Corn, *Grant Wood: The Regionalist Vision* (New Haven: Yale University Press, 1983), and Erika Doss, *Benton, Pollock, and the Politics of Modernism: From Regionalism to Abstract Expressionism* (Chicago: University of Chicago Press, 1991). For fine discussions of the relationship between modern identity and primitivism through imagery and folklore, see Leah Dilworth, *Imagining Indians in the Southwest: Persistent Visions of a Primitive Past* (Washington, D.C.: Smithsonian Institution Press, 1996); and Ian McKay, *The Quest of the Folk: Antimodernism and Cultural Selection in Twentieth-Century Nova Scotia* (Montreal: McGill-Queen's University Press, 1994).

18. Henry Louis Gates Jr., "The Face and Voice of Blackness," in *Facing History: The Black Image in American Art, 1710–1940*, ed. Guy C. McElroy (Washington, D.C.: Bedford Arts, Publishers, 1990), xxix.

19. For more on Charleston's long-standing black middle class, see Edward Ball, *The Sweet Hell Inside: A Family History* (New York: William Morrow, 2001); Wilbert Jenkins, *Seizing the Day: African Americans in Post–Civil War Charleston* (Bloomington: Indiana University Press, 1998); Bernard E. Powers, *Black Charlestonians: A Social History, 1822–1885* (Fayetteville: University of Arkansas Press, 1994); Edmund L. Drago, *Initiative, Paternalism, and Race Relations: Charleston's Avery Normal Institute* (Athens: University of Georgia Press, 1990); and Mamie Garvin Fields, *Lemon Swamp and Other Places: A Carolina Memoir* (New York: Free Press, 1983).

20. Anne Dewees Kelley, interview by author, 18 November 1993, Charleston, S.C.; see also *Charleston City Directories* (1920–40) for information on locations of black-owned businesses in the city.

21. For more information about these artists, see Jeanne Moutoussamy-Ashe, *Viewfinder: Black Women Photographers* (New York: Dodd, Mead & Company, 1986): 34–39; and Michael Francis Blake Papers, Duke.

22. See W. Burke Harmon, president, Harmon Foundation, New York, to Edwin Harleston, 7 March 1931, Harmon Foundation Papers, LC. For a full-scale biography of Edwin Harleston and his family, see Ball, *Sweet Hell Inside*; Maurine Akua McDaniel, "Edwin Augustus Harleston, Portrait Painter, 1882–1931" (Ph.D. diss., Emory University, 1994); and Susan Donaldson, "Charleston's Racial Politics of Historic Preservation," in Hutchisson and Greene, eds., *Renaissance in Charleston*, 176–98.

23. Correspondence, Edwin Harleston File, CM; Edwin Harleston Papers, SCHS; "African-Americans in the Permanent Collections of the Gibbes Museum of Art/CAA," including catalog of recent Harleston exhibit, "Painter of an Era," Gibbes.

24. Elizabeth Verner Hamilton, interview by author, 30 November 1993, Charleston, S.C. Atlantic Street was the closest thing Charleston had to a small art colony, housing at one point Alice Smith's studio at number 8, Elizabeth Verner's at number 3, Anna Heyward Taylor's at number 4, and Leila Waring's at number 2. In the 1930s, Verner moved her studio two blocks up the peninsula to 38 Tradd Street, where other artists, including Alfred Hutty (46 Tradd Street), Anna Heyward Taylor (79 Church Street), and Alice Smith (69 Church Street), lived and operated studios at

that time. See *Charleston City Directories* and Elizabeth Verner Hamilton, "Four Artists on One Block and How They Got Along," unpublished ms., CCPL.

25. Hamilton, "Four Artists," 9; Leila Waring, quoted in *Alice Ravenel Huger Smith of Charleston, South Carolina: An Appreciation on the Occasion of Her Eightieth Birthday from Her Friends* (Charleston: Privately published, 1956), 27.

26. For a treatment of the Reconstruction period in general, and the situation in South Carolina in particular, including the Hamburg riots, see Eric Foner, *Reconstruction: America's Unfinished Revolution, 1863–1877* (New York: Harper & Row, 1988); Julie Saville, *The Work of Reconstruction: From Slave to Wage Laborer in South Carolina* (New York: Cambridge University Press, 1994); Stephen Kantrowitz, *Ben Tillman and the Reconstruction of White Supremacy* (Chapel Hill: University of North Carolina Press, 2000); and Richard Zuczek, *State of Rebellion: Reconstruction in South Carolina* (Columbia: University of South Carolina Press, 1996). See also Claude G. Bowers, *The Tragic Era: The Revolution after Lincoln* (Cambridge, Mass.: Houghton Mifflin, 1929); and correspondence between newspaper editor William Watts Ball and Bowers, 18 and 19 June 1929, in William Watts Ball Papers, Duke.

27. Alice Ravenel Huger Smith, "Reminiscences," in *Alice Ravenel Huger Smith: An Artist, a Place, and a Time*, by Martha R. Severens (Charleston, S.C.: Carolina Art Association, 1993), 71.

28. Ibid., 73.

29. Old homes and massive trees figure prominently in the art work of Smith and Verner. Michael Kammen (*Meadows of Memory: Images of Time and Tradition in American Art and Culture* [Austin: University of Texas Press, 1992], 133–81) has argued that these elements are symbolic of history, time, and memory in American painting, especially since the late nineteenth century. In particular, Kammen contends that houses in various stages of ruin function as vessels for memory while trees represent living witnesses to time and memory.

30. Smith, "Reminiscences," 82.

31. Ibid., 83.

32. Ibid., 71.

33. Ibid., 82–83; 68–69.

34. Ibid., 93.

35. Marietta Neff, "A Painter of the Carolina Lowlands," *American Magazine of Art*, [1923], 406, article clipping, ARHSP, vol. 4, Gibbes.

36. For more on Smith's artistic development and influences, see Severens, *Charleston Renaissance*, 1–7.

37. Alice Ravenel Huger Smith to Mrs. Meyer, 6 April 1915, ARHSP, SCHS.

38. Alice R. Huger Smith, *Twenty Drawings of the Pringle House on King Street* (Charleston, S.C.: Lanneau's Art Store, 1914). See also Alice R. Huger Smith, "Doorways, Gateways and Stairways of Quaint Old Charleston," *Art in America* 4 (August 1916): 296.

39. Elizabeth Allston Pringle [Patience Pennington], *A Woman Rice Planter* (New York: Macmillan Company, 1922).

40. Alice R. Huger Smith, "Charles Fraser," *Art in America* 23 (1) (December 1934):

22–34; Herbert Ravenel Sass, "Carolina Marshes," *Country Life*, January 1930, 34–38; Herbert Ravenel Sass, *Adventures in Green Places* (New York: G. P. Putnam's Sons, 1935).

41. Alice Ravenel Huger Smith to Mrs. Ruby Warren, Orlando Art Association, 22 November 1926, ARHSP, SCHS.

42. "Her Work," *Smith: An Appreciation*, 39; see also "Reminiscences," 123, in which she writes, "I say 'this country' and feel that I am a true sister and contemporary of Jane Austen, who frequently tells of a heroine moving into 'another country,' which meant, perhaps, twenty miles off." By age seventy-three, when Smith wrote her "Reminiscences," she had left the confines of the Low Country only six times ("Reminiscences," 86).

43. Author unknown, "Charm of Charleston, S.C. Stirs Its Visitors to Keen Appreciation: Past and Present of Southern City Commingle in an Atmosphere of Kindliness and Culture," *Christian Science Monitor*, 12 March 1926, article clipping, ARHSPS, Gibbes.

44. "Charleston Painter Invited by Chicago Artists' Community to Attend Display of Her Work," *Chicago Post*, 13 November 1928, newspaper clipping, ARHSPS, Gibbes.

45. H. B., "Art in Charleston," *The State* (Columbia, S.C.), 14 December 1930.

46. Jane Judge, "Painter of Lowlands Interprets South's Beauty," *Savannah Morning News*, 23 October 1927, newspaper clipping, ARHSPS, Gibbes.

47. William Halsey, interview by Robert Cuthbert, 13 July 1974, Charleston, S.C., in Robert Cuthbert Papers, SCHS.

48. Howard Carraway, "Artist Cites Memory, Vocabulary As 'Musts' for Aspiring Painters," *Florence Morning News*, 19 May 1946, newspaper clipping, ARHSPS, Gibbes.

49. Smith, "Reminiscences," 95.

50. Anna Wells Rutledge, interview by author, 29 June 1993, Charleston, S.C.

51. ARHSSR, "Bills Payable," 1923–38, Gibbes.

52. To compute historical dollar conversions, see *Columbia Journalism Review*, "Inflation Calculator," ⟨http://www.cjr.org/tools/inflation⟩, accessed 13 August 2004.

53. ARHSSR, Gibbes. To compute historical dollar conversions, see *Columbia Journalism Review*, "Inflation Calculator," ⟨http://www.cjr.org/tools/inflation⟩, accessed 13 August 2004.

54. ARHSP, vol. 1, Gibbes; ARHSSR, "Bills Payable," 1923–38, Gibbes. The latter includes useful information on exhibition sales.

55. ARHSP, vol. 1, Gibbes.

56. Alice Ravenel Huger Smith to Herbert Ravenel Sass, 30 October 1933, Herbert Ravenel Sass Papers, SCHS.

57. Marion Clyde McCarroll, "Alice Ravenel Huger Smith Wanted to Be an Artist, but She Was Too Homesick to Leave Charleston to Study," *New York Evening Post*, 26 November 1930, newspaper clipping, ARHSP, Gibbes.

58. Smith, "Reminiscences," 70.

59. Ibid., 65.

60. Smith, "Doorways, Gateways and Stairways," 296.

61. Smith, "Reminiscences," 103.

62. Smith, *Carolina Rice Plantation.*

63. Smith, "Reminiscences," 97.

64. See James Henry Tuten, "Time and Tide: Cultural Changes and Continuities among the Rice Plantations of the Lowcountry, 1860–1930" (Ph.D. diss., Emory University, 2003), ch. 8.

65. Alice Smith quoted in "Watercolors by Local Artist Shown at Gibbes Art Gallery," *Charleston Evening Post,* 14 December 1936, newspaper clipping, ARHSPS, Gibbes.

66. Pennington, *Look Away,* 112–47.

67. Smith, "Reminiscences," 97–106.

68. Ibid., 97.

69. Henry Bellamann, "Art in Charleston," *The State,* 1931, as quoted in Severens, "To Sell the City of Charleston," 37.

70. Alice Ravenel Huger Smith to Mrs. Ruby Warren, Orlando Art Association, 22 November 1926, ARHSP, SCHS.

71. Herbert Ravenel Sass, "The Rice Coast: Its Story and Its Meaning," in Smith, *Carolina Rice Plantation,* 13.

72. See D. E. Huger Smith, "A Plantation Boyhood," in Smith, *Carolina Rice Plantation.*

73. John Bennett to J. T. Gittman, 27 October 1937, John Bennett Papers, SCHS, quoted in Severens, "To Sell the City of Charleston," 55.

74. Sass, "Rice Coast," 42. Sass argues that slavery in the South Carolina Low Country was an exceptionally benevolent familial institution: "'Slavery' is not a good name for the institution as it existed on the plantations of the Carolina Low Country. The planters did not speak of his negroes as slaves; he called them his 'people' and as he spoke of them so he thought of them—they were his people, not his chattels, and many of them were his loved and devoted friends" (ibid., 39).

75. "Southern scenes," *New York Herald Tribune,* 29 November, 1936, newspaper clipping, ARHSPS, Gibbes.

76. C. McD. Puckette, "Life on Carolina' Rice Plantations," *New York Times Book Review,* 3 January 1937, newspaper clipping, ARHSPS, Gibbes.

77. "Watercolors of a Carolina Rice Plantation to be exhibited," *Washington Star,* 9 January 1937, newspaper clipping, ARHSPS, Gibbes.

78. Henry Seidel Canby, "The Rice Coast in Art," *Saturday Review,* 5 December 1936, ARHSP, Gibbes.

79. Steven C. Dubin, *Displays of Power: Memory and Amnesia in the American Museum* (New York: New York University Press, 1999), 3.

80. Smith, "Reminiscences," 98.

81. Elizabeth O'Neill Verner, *Mellowed by Time: A Charleston Notebook,* 3d ed. (Charleston, S.C.: Tradd Street Press, 1978), 81.

82. For biographical information on Verner and the O'Neill family, see Marlo Pease Bussman, *Born Charlestonian: The Story of Elizabeth O'Neill Verner* (Columbia, S.C.: The State Printing Company, 1969), 4–7.

83. Elizabeth O'Neill Verner, "A Portrait of Father: Henry John O'Neill," undated pamphlet, EONVP, SCHS.

84. Ibid.

85. Bussman, *Born Charlestonian*, 24.

86. "By-Laws of the Etchers' Club of Charleston," John Bennett Papers, SCHS.

87. Gwen Shepherd Davis, "The Charleston Etchers' Club and Early South Carolina Printmaking" (M.A. thesis, University of South Carolina, 1982), 23–28.

88. Elizabeth Verner quoted in "Charleston Artists of the Twenties," pamphlet, 1986, EONVF, SCHS.

89. Hamilton interview.

90. Southern States Art League, "Aims and History," [1925], EONVP, SCHS.

91. Louise B. Clark, second-vice-president of league, quoted in Amy Kirschke, "The Southern States Art League: A Regionalist Artists' Organization, 1922–1950," *Southern Quarterly* 25 (Winter 1987): 17.

92. Kirschke, "Southern States Art League: A Regionalist Artists' Organization," 10.

93. Amy Kirschke, "Elizabeth O'Neill Verner and the Southern States Art League," in Lynn Robertson Myers, ed., *Mirror of Time: Elizabeth O'Neill Verner's Charleston* (Columbia, S.C.: McKissick Museum, University of South Carolina, 1983), 28; see also Kirschke, "Southern States Art League: A Regionalist Artists' Organization," 4; and "Southern States Art League," *American Magazine of Art* 13 (June 1922): 188.

94. Elizabeth O'Neill Verner, *Prints and Impressions of Charleston* (Columbia, S.C.: Bostick & Thornley, Inc., 1939), 16–17.

95. Ibid., 17.

96. Elizabeth Verner to Clara Verner, 21 November 1961, Archives of American Art, Smithsonian Institution, roll 3589, quoted in Severens, "To Sell the City of Charleston," 42.

97. Lynn Robertson Myers, "Doing and Creating: A Biographical Sketch," in Myers, ed., *Mirror of Time*, 12, 14.

98. "Equitable [Life Assurance Society of the United States] Agency Items," pamphlet, 21 January 1935, EONVP, SCHS; "An Artist's Impressions of Hollywood By-the-Sea in Words and Pictures" (Hollywood, Fla.: The Home Seekers Realty Company, 1926), pamphlet, EONVP, SCHS.

99. For information on Verner's postcards business, see Elizabeth Verner to The Albertype Company, New York, 19 October 1934 and 6 February 1940, EONVP, SCHS.

100. Louis M. Shimel to deMerrell's Studio, 8 January 1935; and Louis M. Shimel to The Francis Marion Hotel, 8 January 1935, EONVP, SCHS.

101. Augustine T. Smythe, Herbert Ravenel Sass, Alfred Huger et al., eds., *The Carolina Low-Country* (New York: MacMillan Company, 1931).

102. Elizabeth O'Neill Verner, Diary (1934–37), EONVP, SCHS.

103. See Elizabeth O'Neill Verner, Artist's Sketchbook, [pre–1 August 1935], property of David Verner Hamilton, The Tradd Street Press, Inc., Warrenton, Virginia. DuBose Heyward, a true insider, had articulated a similar notion of the Charleston white elite in his 1928 novel *Mamba's Daughters*, when the wealthy Atkinsons, new in town, come up against the same subtle discrimination.

104. Frances M. Frost to Elizabeth O'Neill Verner, 9 April 1937, EONVP, SCHS.

Until spring 2002, Verner's former studio at 38 Tradd Street operated as a museum and clearinghouse for visitors seeking a souvenir of her artistic rendition of Charleston. Today, Verner's grandson, David Verner Hamilton, continues to operate his grandmother's business from his home in Warrenton, Virginia.

105. Heyward quoted in typescript biographical essay attributed to *Town and Country Magazine*, [circa 1934], EONVP, SCHS. DuBose Heyward's connection to Verner predated her ascension as a noted Charleston etcher; he and Verner's brother, Harry O'Neill, were business partners for several years in their own insurance firm before Heyward decided to become a professional writer in 1924.

106. Introduction by DuBose Heyward, *Elizabeth O'Neill Verner*, exhibition catalog (Boston, 1934), as quoted in Myers, "Doing and Creating," 13.

107. Verner, *Prints and Impressions*, 12.

108. Ibid.

109. Bussman, *Born Charlestonian*, 22.

110. Verner, *Mellowed by Time*, 8.

111. Ibid., 1.

112. Verner, *Prints and Impressions*, 2–3.

113. Ibid., 5.

114. Ibid., 9.

115. DuBose Heyward, *Porgy: A Novel* (Charleston, S.C.: The Tradd Street Press, 1985), 5; Verner, *Prints and Impressions*, 10.

116. Verner, *Prints and Impressions*, 11.

117. Ibid., 6.

118. Elizabeth O'Neill Verner to *News & Courier*, 15 March 1948, as quoted in Bussman, *Born Charlestonian*, 77.

119. Verner, *Mellowed by Time*, 33.

120. Elizabeth O'Neill Verner, "Spirituals of the Low Country," *News & Courier*, 29 April 1929.

121. Severens, *Charleston Renaissance*, 56.

122. Verner, *Mellowed by Time*, 28.

123. *South Carolina Gazette*, 24 September 1772.

124. Elizabeth O'Neill Verner, undated manuscript, SCHS, as quoted in Myers, "Doing and Creating," 14. To support her claim, Verner could have pointed to the color photographs of Charleston's "flower women" that accompanied DuBose Heyward's March 1939 *National Geographic* article, "Charleston: Where Mellow Past & Present Meet."

125. Hamilton interview.

126. Elizabeth O'Neill Verner, undated manuscript, SCHS, as quoted in Myers, "Doing and Creating," 14.

127. Elizabeth O'Neill Verner, letter to the editor, *News & Courier*, 5 March 1944; see also "61 Flower Women Register; Will Wear Bright Bandannas," *News & Courier*, 1 March 1944.

128. "A Happy Conclusion," *News & Courier*, 2 March 1944.

129. Letter to the editor, *News & Courier*, 5 March 1944.

130. Elizabeth O'Neill Verner, letter to the editor, *News & Courier*, 5 March 1944.

131. Until its closing in 2002, Elizabeth Verner's Tradd Street studio, for example, served as a combination museum/gift shop and was a standard stop on most walking tours of the city. Likewise, today the Gibbes Museum displays Verner's images in a gallery dedicated to works from the 1920s and 1930s.

132. Verner, *Prints and Impressions*, 1.

Chapter Three

1. [Hervey Allen], "The Worm Turns," *Year Book of the Poetry Society of South Carolina* (Charleston, S.C.: The Society, 1921), 14.

2. See David Moltke-Hansen, "The Expansion of Intellectual Life: A Prospectus," in Michael O'Brien and David Moltke-Hansen, eds., *Intellectual Life in Antebellum Charleston* (Knoxville: University of Tennessee Press, 1986). This volume presents an excellent overview of the city's expanding intellectual climate and national influence in the first half of the nineteenth century, of which PSSC members were well aware. See also the anthology of ordinary Charleston writers from the period, William Gilmore Simms, ed., *The Charleston Book: A Miscellany in Prose and Verse* (Charleston, S.C.: Samuel Hart Sr., 1845), reissued by the Reprint Company Publishers, Spartanburg, S.C., 1983, with an introduction and biographical notes by David Moltke-Hansen and biographical notes by Harlan Greene.

3. Amy Lowell, quoted in *Year Book of the Poetry Society* (1921), 17.

4. For treatments of the phenomenon called the Southern Literary Renaissance, see Daniel Joseph Singal, *The War Within: From Victorian to Modernist Thought in the South, 1919–1945* (Chapel Hill: University of North Carolina Press, 1982); Richard H. King, *A Southern Renaissance: The Cultural Awakening of the American South, 1930–1955* (New York: Oxford University Press, 1980); Richard Gray, *The Literature of Memory: Modern Writers of the American South* (Baltimore: Johns Hopkins University Press, 1977); and Michael O'Brien, *The Idea of the American South, 1920–1941* (Baltimore: Johns Hopkins University Press, 1979). While each author proposes his own understanding of the origins and meaning of the Southern Literary Renaissance, all emphasize the centrality of the Southern writer's struggle to reconcile the traditions of the region's past with doubt-provoking challenges of the present.

5. See, for example, Josephine Pinckney, *Three O'Clock Dinner* (1945; Columbia: University of South Carolina Press, 2001); DuBose Heyward, *Mamba's Daughters* (1929; Columbia: University of South Carolina Press, 1995); James M. Hutchisson and Harlan Greene, eds., *Renaissance in Charleston: Art and Life in the Carolina Low Country, 1900–1940* (Athens: University of Georgia Press, 2003); Mary Crow Anderson, *Two Scholarly Friends: Yates Snowden–John Bennett, Correspondence, 1902–1932* (Columbia: University of South Carolina Press, 1993); Harlan Greene, *Mr. Skylark: John Bennett and the Charleston Renaissance* (Athens: University of Georgia Press, 2001); James M. Hutchisson, *DuBose Heyward: A Charleston Gentleman and the World of Porgy and Bess* (Jackson: University of Mississippi Press, 2000); and Susan Millar Williams, *A Devil and a Good Woman Too: The Lives of Julia Peterkin* (Athens: University of Georgia Press, 1997).

6. For a discussion of this relationship through the correspondence of Josephine

Pinckney and Donald Davidson, see Barbara Bellows, "The Lowcountry Lady and the Over-the-Mountain Man: Josephine Pinckney, Donald Davidson and the Burden of Southern Literature," in Hutchisson and Greene, eds., *Renaissance in Charleston*, 19–34.

7. See Introduction for a discussion of the term "Charleston Renaissance" to describe the city's literary output in the period.

8. Michael O'Brien, "'The South Considers Her Most Peculiar': Charleston and Modern Southern Thought," *South Carolina Historical Magazine* 94 (April 1993): 119–33. O'Brien skillfully situates the conventional outlook of Charleston writers in relation to the more artistically intellectual convictions of the Fugitives/Agrarians of Vanderbilt. William H. Slavick (*DuBose Heyward* [Boston: Twayne Publishers, 1981], 38–43) also discusses in detail the Fugitive poets' estimation of Charleston poets as nonintrospective, wed to tradition and continuity, overly sentimental, and generally lacking in profundity. For the basic conservatism of the prevailing literary forms, attitude, and content of Charleston poetry, see also Cox, "The Charleston Poetic Renascence, 1920–1930" (Ph.D. diss., University of Pennsylvania, 1958), 74–78.

9. Robert L. Dorman, *Revolt of the Provinces: The Regionalist Movement in America, 1920–1940* (Chapel Hill: University of North Carolina Press, 1993), xvii.

10. See *Charleston City Directory*, 1920–40.

11. Henry James, *American Scene* (New York: Harper & Brothers, 1907), 403. Of his encounter with Old Charleston and its black inhabitants James wrote: "Prismatically, none the less, they had shown me the 'old' South; in one case by the mere magic of the manner in which a small, scared, starved person of colour, of very light colour, an elderly mulattress in an improvised wrapper, just barely held open for me a door through which I felt I might have looked straight and far back into the past. The past, that of a vanished order, was hanging on there behind her" (403).

12. Owen Wister, *Lady Baltimore* (New York: MacMillan Company, 1906).

13. Judith Giblin James, "Gullah-Inflected Modernism: Julia Peterkin's Scarlet Black Madonna," in Hutchisson and Greene, eds., *Renaissance in Charleston*, 142–54. See also Susan Millar Williams's excellent biography of Peterkin, *A Devil and a Good Woman Too.*

14. Josephine Pinckney, "Notes," [1940s], Josephine Pinckney Papers, SCHS.

15. Orville Prescott, "Books of the Times," *New York Times*, 21 September 1945.

16. See Marshall A. Best, Viking Press, to Herbert P. Shippet, University of South Carolina, 16 October 1975, Josephine Pinckney Papers, SCHS. Pinckney also wrote an insightful essay examining Southern provincialism, titled "Bulwarks against Change," in W. T. Couch, ed., *Culture in the South* (Chapel Hill: University of North Carolina Press, 1934). Alongside the Agrarians' *I'll Take My Stand, Culture in the South* debated the issue of Southern identity in modern America. See Twelve Southerners, *I'll Take My Stand: The South and the Agrarian Tradition* (New York: Harper, 1930).

17. DuBose Heyward, *Porgy: A Novel* (Charleston: Tradd Street Press, 1985), 5. The book was originally published in 1925; the Charleston edition, illustrated with etchings by Elizabeth O'Neill Verner, was published in Garden City, New York, by Doubleday, Doran & Company, Inc., in 1928.

18. That poetry was fashionable in postwar America is evinced on the local level

in Charleston by the reams of poor-quality but earnest verse sent to local newspaper editors for possible publication. See the Thomas Waring Sr. Papers, SCHS. For more on the role of book clubs in shaping of popular literary tastes, see Janice A. Radway, *A Feeling for Books: The Book-of-the-Month-Club, Literary Taste, and Middle-Class Desire* (Chapel Hill: University of North Carolina Press, 1997).

19. Amy Lowell, quoted in *Year Book of the Poetry Society* (1921), 17.

20. For biographical information on Hervey Allen, see clippings in Hervey Allen File, SCHS.

21. See Josephine Pinckney, "Charleston's Poetry Society," *Sewanee Review* 38 (January– March 1930): 54; Cox, "Charleston Poetic Renascence," 16–18; Frank Durham, *DuBose Heyward: The Man Who Wrote Porgy* (Columbia: University of South Carolina Press, 1954), 21–25; and Greene, *Mr. Skylark*, 147–58.

22. DuBose Heyward to John Bennett, 4 July 1921, John Bennett Papers, SCHS; see also John Bennett to W. Van R. Whithall, 18 October 1921, ibid.; Hutchisson, *DuBose Heyward*, 22–24; and Harlan Greene, "Mr Bennett's Amiable Desire: The Poetry Society of South Carolina and the Charleston Renaissance," in Hutchisson and Greene, eds., *Renaissance in Charleston*, 57–75.

23. Cox, "Charleston Poetic Renascence," 16–17; Drayton Mayrant [Katherine Drayton Mayrant Simons], "'If Any Man Can Play the Pipes': A Sketch of the Poetry Society of South Carolina," *South Carolina Magazine* 14 (September 1951): 9; John Bennett, lecture notes, 21 July 1939, John Bennett Papers, SCHS. For more on Bragg as a force in Charleston, see Louise Anderson Allen and James T. Sears, "Laura Bragg and Her 'Bright Young Things': Fostering Change and Social Reform at the Charleston Museum," in Hutchisson and Greene, eds., *Renaissance in Charleston*, 155–75; and Louis Anderson Allen, *A Bluestocking in Charleston: The Life and Career of Laura Bragg* (Columbia: University of South Carolina Press, 2001).

24. "Foreword," *Year Book of the Poetry Society* (1921), 5.

25. Pinckney, "Charleston's Poetry Society," 52.

26. For DuBose Heyward genealogical information see James B. Heyward, "The Heyward Family of South Carolina," *South Carolina Historical Magazine* 61 (1958): 143–58, 206–23; and Dorothy Kelly MacDowell, *DuBose Genealogy* (Columbia, S.C.: R. L. Bryan Co., 1972).

27. Heyward to Marshall, [1920], DuBose Heyward Papers, SCHS. See also "Constitution of the Poetry Society of South Carolina," Albert Simons Papers, SCHS.

28. John Bennett, lecture notes, [late 1930s], John Bennett Papers, SCHS. Memberships lists published in the PSSC yearbooks attest to the popularity of the organization and its quick shift from an almost entirely local composition to a more regional and national one. In 1920, the group consisted of 220 individuals, including only 13 non-Charlestonians, a mere 2 of whom were non-Southerners. By 1923, as its reputation spread via self-promotion, the yearbooks, and Heyward's traveling lectures, the PSSC found it necessary to establish a "non-resident membership" to accommodate those interested in affiliating with this up-and-coming literary organization. That same year, the rolls boasted 260 resident members, with 66 nonresident members, some from as far away as South Dakota, California, and Puerto Rico. Among those listed for 1923 is African American author "Mr. Jean Toomer, Washington, D.C.,"

whose race presented a significant problem to the leaders of the all-white PSSC. Unfortunately, only one letter, from John Bennett to DuBose Heyward, exists that discusses this dilemma, albeit in rather frantic tones. In the end, in an effort to avoid bringing attention to the issue and to keep from alienating both their orthodox Southern and more liberal Northern audiences, the PSSC leaders decided to print Toomer's name on the membership lists for 1923 without special designation or public discussion. See John Bennett to DuBose Heyward, 19 August 1923, John Bennett Papers, SCHS; and Frank Durham, "The Poetry Society's Turbulent Year: Self-Interest, Atheism, and Jean Toomer," *Southern Humanities Review* 5 (Winter 1971): 76–80.

29. Albert Simons, speech, 4 December 1928, Albert Simons Papers, SCHS. As newspaper editors, Waring and Ball deployed their journalistic connections to publicize the Society's activities in Southern newspapers. In 1930, for example, Ball sent out a mass mailing to Southern editors in nearly every Southern state asking them to print a paragraph in their newspapers soliciting entries for the PSSC poetry prizes (William Watts Ball to [Southern editors], 1 January 1930, William Watts Ball Papers, Duke).

30. *Year Book of the Poetry Society* (1922), 12.

31. Daniel Joseph Singal, *The War Within: From Victorian to Modernist Thought in the South, 1919–1945* (Chapel Hill: University of North Carolina Press, 1982), 84.

32. Ibid. Singal identifies several attributes of modernism that have helped me situate Charleston writers generally outside of the movement, despite occasional superficial manifestations of the modernist impulse. These characteristics include a willingness to explore the irrational aspects of the conscious; a perception of the universe as "turbulent and unpredictable" and of conflict as positive and virtuous; "an ability to live with uncertainty"; and, finally, "a critical temperament uninhibited by considerations of formal manners: gentility gives way to the necessity of making contact with 'reality,' no matter how ugly or distasteful that reality might be" (ibid., 8). See also Daniel Joseph Singal, "Towards a Definition of American Modernism," *American Quarterly* 39 (1): 7–26. For discussion of the Cavalier myth in Southern Victorian culture, see Singal, *War Within*, 11–33, and William R. Taylor's seminal study, *Cavalier and Yankee: The Old South and American National Character* (Cambridge: Harvard University Press, 1979).

For an overview of modernism as an aesthetic movement and its particular manifestation in the movement's American capital, New York City, see Ann Douglas, *Terrible Honesty: Mongrel Manhattan in the 1920s* (New York: Farrar, Straus, and Giroux, 1995), 3–28. For a discussion of the difficulties of defining literary modernism, see C. Barry Chabot, *Writers for the Nation: American Literary Modernism* (Tuscaloosa: University of Alabama Press, 1997), 6–14. For specific aspects of modernist ideas in the interwar period and their effects on literature, citizenship, and labor, see Clive Bloom and Brian Docherty, eds., *American Poetry: The Modernist Ideal* (New York: St. Martin's Press, 1995), 1–9; Walter Benn Michaels, *Our America: Nativism, Modernism, and Pluralism* (Durham, N.C.: Duke University Press, 1995); and Michael Denning, *The Cultural Front: The Laboring of American Culture in the Twentieth Century* (New York: Verso, 1996), 28–29.

33. Proponents of "New Poetry," including Ezra Pound, Carl Sandburg, Amy

Lowell, and Robert Frost, sought to free themselves from the strictures of the late-nineteenth-century "genteel tradition" of poetry and to create a democratic art form. Contemporary literary scholar Louis Untermeyer (*The New Era in American Poetry* [New York: Henry Holt & Company, 1919], 9–10) described this passionate state of American poetry in 1919 as "powerful and introspective . . . human racy and vigorous; it is not only closer to the soil but nearer to the soul. Our poets have shaken themselves free, first of all from the pontifical rhetoric, the tag-end moralizing of our literary doctors and doctrines. And as they have rid themselves of the tradition of didacticism, they are growing clear of the tradition of routine romanticism."

34. Notably, Charleston poet Beatrice Witte Ravenel wrote most of her compositions in free verse, even though their content conformed to the regionally chauvinistic and romantic tendencies of her colleagues. Her work is discussed later in this chapter. See Louis D. Rubin Jr., ed., *The Yemassee Lands: Poems of Beatrice Ravenel* (Chapel Hill: University of North Carolina Press, 1969).

35. John Bennett, ["Poetry in America"], speech, 25 January 1921, John Bennett Papers, SCHS. The capitals are Bennett's.

36. "The Poetry Society," *Charleston Evening Post*, [no date], newspaper clipping, DuBose Heyward Papers, SCHS.

37. Bennett, ["Poetry in America"], speech. For nativism in regionalism, see Michaels, *Our America*. North Carolina literary critic Archibald Henderson echoed this sense of the South as the cradle of English-language culture in "The New South in Letters and Art," in the *New York Herald* "Books" section, 18 March 1923: "The population [of the South] is extraordinarily homogeneous. There is no immigrant problem. The people are native to the soil upon which they have dwelt in many cases for three centuries. 'In the South,' says Virginia Frazer Boyle, 'is the purest Americanism and the purest English speech in America.' In the Southern mountains survive among the people the ballads of the spacious days of Elizabeth" (*Herald* newspaper clipping, John Bennett Papers, SCHS). For an analysis of American Anglophilia and the "discovery" of Appalachian folkways, see David E. Whisnant, *All that is Native and Fine: The Politics of Culture in an American Region* (Chapel Hill: University of North Carolina Press, 1983).

38. "Activities of the Past Year," *Year Book of the Poetry Society* (1921), 8.

39. *Year Book of the Poetry Society* (1922), [no page number].

40. Ibid. (1923), 28, 26.

41. Hervey Allen to Thomas R. Waring, 13 June 1923, John Bennett Papers, SCHS. See also John Bennett to DuBose Heyward, 13 June 1923, ibid.; DuBose Heyward to Hervey Allen, [1923], DuBose Heyward Papers, SCHS; and Durham, "Poetry Society's Turbulent Year," 76–80.

42. Cox, "Charleston Poetic Renascence." 46; Marjorie Elizabeth Peale, "Charleston as a Literary Center, 1920–1933," (M.A. thesis, Duke University, 1941), 25; Pinckney, "Charleston's Poetry Society," 53.

43. Both Heyward and Allen spent productive summers at the MacDowell Colony, where they wrote and networked with the rising literary stars of their day, as well as with publishers in Boston and New York. Heyward met his future wife, Ohio-born playwright Dorothy Hartzell Kuhns, at MacDowell. The colony was named after

American poet and composer Edward MacDowell and administered by his wife. The colony's philosophy of encouraging regional artists complemented the goals of the PSSC. MacDowell, for example, was described as a man "intensely loyal to America and American traditions. . . . He wanted Americans to encourage their own men in Music, Art and Literature, and not to respect a third rate artist simply because he came from a foreign country having traditions of culture" (Louis A. Springer, "The Life and Work of Edward MacDowell," *New York Herald*, 27 August 1922, newspaper clipping, DuBose Heyward Papers, SCHS).

44. "The Allies," *Year Book of the Poetry Society* (1923), 69–75; Frank Durham, "South Carolina's Poetry Society," *South Atlantic Quarterly* 52 (April 1953): 277–85.

45. "Foreword," *Year Book of the Poetry Society* (1921), 6.

46. [Hervey Allen], "Worm Turns," 14, 15.

47. Ibid., 16.

48. "Foreword," *Year Book of the Poetry Society* (1921), 5.

49. Slavick, *DuBose Heyward*, 43. See also Cox, "Charleston Poetic Renascence," 75.

50. DuBose Heyward, "Contemporary Southern Poetry: The Poets," *The Bookman* 63 (March 1926): 53.

51. DuBose Heyward, "Contemporary Southern Poetry: The Audience," *The Bookman* 62 (January 1926): 563.

52. Helen von Kolnitz Hyer, "Chat Île Plantation Deserted," *Year Book of the Poetry Society* (1921), 33.

53. Josephine Pinckney, "In the Barn," *Year Book of the Poetry Society* (1921), 32.

54. See Curtis Worthington, "Beatrice Ravenel: Avante-Garde Poet of the Charleston Renaissance," in Hutchisson and Greene, eds., *Renaissance in Charleston*, 76–95; and Susan V. Donaldson, "Songs with a Difference: Beatrice Ravenel and the Detritus of Southern History," in *The Female Tradition in Southern Literature*, ed. Carol S. Manning (Urbana: University of Illinois Press, 1993), 175–92.

55. Rubin, *Yemassee Lands*, 16.

56. Beatrice Witte Ravenel, "The Yemassee Lands," *Year Book of the Poetry Society* (1922), 43–45.

57. Amy Lowell, quoted in *Year Book of the Poetry Society* (1921), 17.

58. Bellows, "Lowcountry Lady," 213.

59. DuBose Heyward, "Horizons," in *Skylines and Horizons* (New York: MacMillan Company, 1924), 57.

60. Hervey Allen, "Palmetto Town," in DuBose Heyward and Hervey Allen, *Carolina Chansons: Legends of the Low Country* (New York: MacMillan Company, 1922), 50.

61. DuBose Heyward, "The Pirates," in Heyward and Allen, *Carolina Chansons*, 25.

62. Allen, "Palmetto Town," 50.

63. Heyward and Allen, preface to *Carolina Chansons*, 9.

64. Josephine Pinckney, "An Island Boy," in Josephine Pinckney, *Sea-Drinking Cities* (New York: Harper & Brothers, 1927), 42.

65. Josephine Pinckney, "Hag!" in Pinckney, *Sea-Drinking Cities*, 27.

66. DuBose Heyward, "Modern Philosopher," in Heyward and Allen, *Carolina Chansons*, 72.

67. Josephine Pinckney, "The Misses Poar Drive to Church," in Pinckney, *Sea-Drinking Cities*, 73.

68. Hervey Allen, "Beyond Debate," in Heyward and Allen, *Carolina Chansons*, 111.

69. Josephine Pinckney, "On the Shelf," in Pinckney, *Sea-Drinking Cities*, 65–68.

70. Heyward and Allen, inscription to Bennett in *Carolina Chansons*, in Winifred Rothermel, "Charleston Poet as Teacher," *Birmingham News* (Alabama), 27 January 1929, newspaper clipping, John Bennett Papers, SCHS. Early working titles for *Carolina Chansons* included "Familiar Songs and Scenes of the Dear, Sunny Southland" (DuBose Heyward to John Bennett, 14 May 1921, John Bennett Papers, SCHS) and "Voices Old and New" (DuBose Heyward to Hervey Allen, 31 May 1921, DuBose Heyward Papers, SCHS).

71. John Bennett interview, quoted in Rothermel, "Charleston Poet as Teacher."

72. Beatrice Ravenel, *The State*, 17 December 1922, quoted in Peale, "Charleston as a Literary Center," 102.

73. Heyward and Allen, preface to *Carolina Chansons*, 9.

74. Ibid., 10.

75. Ibid.

76. Allen, "Palmetto Town," 50–51.

77. Allen, "Seance at Sunrise," 19.

78. Hervey Allen, "Presences," in Heyward and Allen, *Carolina Chansons*, 23–24.

79. DuBose Heyward, "Dusk," in Heyward and Allen, *Carolina Chansons*, 117–18.

80. Ibid., 118.

81. DuBose Heyward, "Silences," in Heyward and Allen, *Carolina Chansons*, 20–22.

82. For Pinckney genealogy, see Mabel L. Webber, "The Thomas Pinckney Family of South Carolina," *South Carolina Historical and Genealogical Magazine* 39 (January 1938): 15–35; "Funeral Tomorrow for Miss Pinckney," *News & Courier*, 6 October 1957; and "Do You Know Your Charleston: Birthplace of Josephine Pinckney," *News & Courier*, 24 December 1945, Josephine Pinckney File, SCHS.

83. Josephine Pinckney, "Thread Flowers," in Pinckney, *Sea-Drinking Cities*, 31.

84. Josephine Pinckney, "Through a Window-Glass," in Pinckney, *Sea-Drinking Cities*, 3–4.

85. Pinckney, "Thread Flowers," 31.

86. Hervey Allen, *Wampum and Old Gold* (New Haven: Yale University Press, 1921), 49–50.

87. DuBose Heyward, "Chant for an Old Town," in Heyward, *Skylines and Horizons*, 65–71.

88. Cox, "Charleston Poetic Renascence," 104. For a sampling of reviews, see newspaper clippings (1922–24), DuBose Heyward Papers, SCHS; and "Reviews" notebook, 1927–28, Josephine Pinckney Papers, SCHS.

The publication of a special "Southern Number" of Harriet Monroe's *Poetry: A Magazine of Verse* (April 1922), coedited by Allen and Heyward, undoubtedly helped publicize their collaborative volume. Monroe had visited Charleston the previous year and had been taken in by what she called the city's "wealth of historic tradition and as-sociation." She congratulated the city on the formation of the PSSC, drawing a picture of Charleston that Society members undoubtedly approved and believed true. "What Charleston wills she does," Monroe wrote in *Poetry*, "not in the bravura Chicago manner, by a bubbling-up of helter-skelter democratic forces; but by a haughty wave of her queenly hand, the grand gesture of the assured aristocrat who never dreams of denial. Today she wills the arts." See Harriet Monroe, "Southern Shrines," *Poetry: A Magazine of Verse* 18 (May 1921): 92–93. For their part, the Nashville Agrarians were furious that Charleston's conception of the South—the aristocratic seaboard—won out in this national publication, which appeared the same month as the first issue of their journal, *Fugitive*. Even though they pursued a common goal—the resuscitation of Southern letters—the Charleston and Nashville groups held competing visions of what constituted the authentic South, the tidewater or the inland agrarian. Allen Tate characterized the Charleston-edited number as "a saccharine orgy of feminine emotion." See Bellows, "Lowcountry Lady," 20.

89. "Sea-Drinking Cities Grips Book Lovers," *Washington Post*, 15 January 1928, newspaper clipping, "Reviews" notebook, Josephine Pinckney Papers, SCHS.

90. DuBose Heyward to John Bennett, 11 April 1925, John Bennett Papers, SCHS. Just a year and a half earlier, Heyward's enthusiasm for the PSSC was at its height and his dreams of literary grandeur for himself and his city were bold. In July 1923, for example, he proposed donating five acres of land to establish outside of Charleston "The DuBose Heyward Colony" for artists, modeled along the lines of the MacDow-ell Colony. The colony was never built. See DuBose Heyward to Hervey Allen, 13 July 1923, and DuBose Heyward, "General plan for colony" [1923], DuBose Heyward Papers, SCHS.

91. According to a professional pamphlet advertising his services as a lecturer and "interpretive" reader of contemporary poetry, Heyward spoke on three subjects: "The New South Through Her Poets," "The Southern Mountaineer in Poetry" (read-ings from *Skylines and Horizons*), and "Romance in the Native Legend" (readings from *Carolina Chansons*). Heyward's extensive travels during his early years as a professional writer-lecturer contributed to his status as a national spokesperson and evangelist for Southern high culture. His winter/spring tour of 1924–25, for example, included not only Southern destinations but also points North, including Illinois, Michigan, Mas-sachusetts, and Washington, D.C. See "DuBose Heyward," professional brochure, [1925/26], DuBose Heyward Papers, SCHS; and Durham, *DuBose Heyward*, 44–45.

92. Hervey Allen to Susan Smythe Bennett, 24 May 1924, John Bennett Papers, SCHS.

93. On establishment of the Blindman Prize, see John Bennett to W. Van R. Whithall, 18 August 1921, John Bennett Papers, SCHS. Whithall took the money from the PSSC's Blindman fund to create a poetry scholarship at the MacDowell Colony (ibid., 14 October 1926).

94. For Allen's views on the limits of regionalism as a sustainable force for literary inspiration, see Hervey Allen, "Amy Lowell as a Poet," *Saturday Review of Literature*, 5 February 1927, 557–58, 568; and Hervey Allen, "Author's Note," in *New Legends* (New York: Farrar & Rhinehart, 1929), vii.

Bennett biographer Harlan Greene suggests that allegations of Allen's sexual impropriety with several of his young male students at the High School of Charleston led to his quick departure from the city. See Greene, *Mister Skylark*, 193–95.

95. John Bennett to DuBose Heyward, 9 April 1925, John Bennett Papers, SCHS.

96. DuBose Heyward to John Bennett, 11 April 1925, John Bennett Papers, SCHS.

97. John Bennett to Hervey Allen, 15 May 1925, John Bennett Papers, SCHS. Heyward's resignation letter is dated 24 April 1925 (see Heyward to PSSC Executive Committee, John Bennett Papers, SCHS). On membership apathy and shrinkage, see Josephine Pinckney to John Bennett, 15 July 1928; John Bennett to Thomas R. Waring, 1 February 1931; and Executive Board to PSSC membership, 15 October 1941, all John Bennett Papers, SCHS.

98. Josephine Pinckney to John Bennett, 15 July 1928, John Bennett Papers, SCHS.

99. James G. Harrison, "The Poetry Society of South Carolina, 1934–1950," PSSC pamphlet, 1972, SCHS. For characterizations of contemporary audience reactions to Stein's lecture, which range from "pleased, mystified and infuriated" to "never completely spellbound . . . never completely amused," see Thomas L. Johnson, "Charleston Was Charleston," *State Magazine*, 17 February 1985, 12–13; see also Glenn Allan to John Bennett, 31 October and 18 November 1935, John Bennett Papers, SCHS.

100. James G. Harrison, "South Carolina's Poetry Society: After Thirty Years," *Georgia Review* 7 (Summer 1953): 205.

101. The Poetry Society of South Carolina continues to function on a small scale in Charleston today.

102. Slavick, *DuBose Heyward*, 61.

103. D. E. Huger Smith and Alice R. Huger Smith, *The Dwelling Houses of Charleston* (Philadelphia: J. B. Lippincott Company, 1917); Mrs. St. Julien [Harriet Horry] Ravenel, *Charleston, the Place and the People* (New York: MacMillan Company, 1906). Ravenel also wrote biographies of two major eighteenth-century Low Country figures titled *The Life and Letters of Eliza Lucas Pinckney* (New York: Charleston Scribner's Sons, 1896) and *The Life and Times of William Lowndes, 1782–1822* (Boston: Houghton Mifflin, 1901).

104. See Eola Willis, *The Charleston Stage in the Eighteenth Century, with Social Settings of the Times* (Columbia, S.C.: The State, 1924); Harriet Kershaw Leiding, *Charleston: Historic and Romantic* (Philadelphia: J. B. Lippincott Company, 1931); William Watts Ball, *The State That Forgot: South Carolina Surrenders to Democracy* (Indianapolis: Bobbs-Merrill Company, 1932). Ball was not a Charlestonian by birth but married into an old Charleston family and made the city his home for most of his life as editor of the *News & Courier*.

105. Josephine Pinckney, *Hilton Head* (New York: Farrar & Rhinehart, 1941).

106. Advertisement for *Peter Ashley*, 1932, DuBose Heyward Papers, SCL.

107. John Bennett to DuBose Heyward, 20 October 1933, John Bennett Papers, SCHS. Herbert Ravenel Sass, *Look Back to Glory* (Indianapolis: Bobbs-Merrill Com-

pany, 1933). Sass and Heyward capitalized further on the growing national interest in American history by quickly producing a volume titled *Fort Sumter* (New York: Farrar & Rinehart, 1938), which excised the chapters in *Peter Ashley* (New York: Farrar & Rhinehart, 1932) and *Look Back to Glory* that detailed the 1861 and 1863 attacks on Fort Sumter.

108. Herbert Ravenel Sass to John Bennett, 12 February 1933, John Bennett Papers, SCHS.

109. Christine Noble Govan, *Plantation Murder* (New York: Houghton Mifflin, 1938); Zenith Jones Brown, *Road to Folly* (New York: Scribner's, 1940).

110. Pinckney, *Three O'Clock Dinner.*

111. Katherine Ball Ripley, *Crowded House* (New York: Doubleday, Doran, 1936), 43.

112. Ibid., 200.

113. For a similar discussion of changing family patterns and the role of African Americans in maintaining elite white customs, see DuBose Heyward's novel *Mamba's Daughters* (1929; Columbia: University of South Carolina Press, 1995). This book was a widely read Literary Guild selection and was also performed across the country in play form, cowritten by Dorothy Heyward.

114. A few representative examples of writings from the period that took as their subject black culture include Howard Odum and Guy B. Johnson, *The Negro and His Song: A Study of the Typical Negro Songs in the South* (Chapel Hill: University of North Carolina Press, 1925) and *Negro Workaday Songs* (Chapel Hill: University of North Carolina Press, 1926); Guy B. Johnson, *Folk Culture on St. Helena Island, South Carolina* (Chapel Hill: University of North Carolina Press, 1930); Zora Neale Hurston, *Their Eyes Were Watching God* (Philadelphia: J. B. Lippincott Company, 1937) and *Men and Mules* (Philadelphia: J. B. Lippincott Company, 1935); and Langston Hughes, *Fine Clothes to the Jew* (New York: Knopf, 1927) and *The Weary Blues* (New York: Knopf, 1926).

115. Charlestonians were certainly not the first white Southerners to write stories in so-called negro dialect. Instead, they drew upon a tradition of white-related black folktales popularized in large part by the late-nineteenth-century works of Thomas Nelson Page and Joel Chandler Harris. Likewise, in other parts of South Carolina, white authors detailed the dialect, folklore, superstitions, character, and lifestyles of area blacks. In Columbia, E. C. L. Adams produced a volume of "Congaree Sketches," as well as a book of dialect tales called *Nigger to Nigger* (New York: Charles Scribner's Sons, 1928). See also Reed Smith's pamphlet "Gullah: Dedicated to the Memory of Ambrose E. Gonzales" (Columbia: Bureau of Publications, University of South Carolina, 1926). PSSC member Julia Peterkin was not a Charlestonian, but she detailed the life of the Gullah African Americans on her family's South Carolina plantation, Lang Syne. The contours of her fictional works, such as her 1929 Pulitzer Prize–winning novel, *Scarlet Sister Mary* (Indianapolis: Bobbs-Merrill, 1928), and her nonfictional studies, such as *Roll, Jordan, Roll* (New York: R. O. Ballou, 1933), which was illustrated by Northern photographer Doris Ulmann's soft-focused images of daily plantation life, echo the Charleston Group's themes of black primitivism, romanticism, and simplicity. See Sterling A. Brown's critique of Peterkin's romantic

view of blacks in his "Arcadia: South Carolina," *Opportunity: Journal of Negro Life*, February 1934, 59–60.

116. For more on the historical formation of Gullah language and culture, see Margaret Washington Creel, *"A Peculiar People": Slave Religion and Community-Culture among the Gullahs* (New York: New York University Press, 1988); Charles W. Joyner, *Down by the Riverside: A South Carolina Slave Community* (Urbana: University of Illinois Press, 1984); and Hutchisson, *DuBose Heyward*, 7. Early published examples of these Gullah works are John Bennett's buried-treasure romance, *The Treasure of Peyre Gaillard* (New York: Century Company, 1906), and his two-part article, "Gullah: A Negro Patois," *South Atlantic Quarterly* 7 (October 1908): 332–47; and 8 (January 1909): 39–52; Samuel Gaillard Stoney and Gertrude Mathews Shelby, *Black Genesis: A Chronicle* (New York: MacMillan Company, 1930); and Harriet Kershaw Leiding, "Street Cries of an Old Southern City, with Music," pamphlet, 1927, COC.

117. DuBose Heyward, foreword to Stoney and Shelby, *Black Genesis*, n.p. Heyward went on to note that Stoney "adds a knowledge of the dialect so perfect that he thinks in it, and so authoritative that he was recently selected by Columbia University to contribute a phonograph record of Gullah for their permanent collection of American dialects."

118. A sort of quiet competition concerning what constituted "real" Gullah persisted between Bennett and Gonzales, president of the State Publishing Company, which printed, among other things, the Columbia, S.C., newspaper *The State* and the PSSC yearbooks. Bennett once complained to Josephine Pinckney, "What has Mr. Gonzales to do with the endless variants of verbiage in negro spirituals: did he invent the dialect?" (John Bennett to Josephine Pinckney, 2 July 1923, John Bennett Papers, SCHS). See also Yates Snowden to John Bennett, 5 April 1920, John Bennett Papers, SHCS. In an attempt to present the final word on Gullah, its origins, usages, and vocabulary, Gonzales, in his collection of stories, provided a historical sketch of the language, in which he quotes Bennett's conclusions, as well as a glossary. See Ambrose E. Gonzales, *The Black Border: Gullah Stories of the Carolina Coast* (Columbia, S.C.: The State Company, 1922). For more on Bennett's longtime fascination with Gullah culture, see Greene, *Mr. Skylark*.

119. James M. Hutchisson, "Professional Authorship in Charleston," in Hutchisson and Greene, eds., *Renaissance in Charleston*, 113–14.

120. For extensive biographical information on Heyward, see Hutchisson, *DuBose Heyward*, esp. 4–15; and Durham, *DuBose Heyward*, esp. 3–20.

121. Izard is an old aristocratic family name in Charleston, and the saying is a Low Country commonplace. Quoted from Slavick, *DuBose Heyward*, 19.

122. DuBose Heyward, "Your Gifts," in *Skylines and Horizons*, vii–viii.

123. Janie Screven Heyward, "Charleston," "The Shrimp Seller," and "The Land of Bumbye," in the pamphlet "Songs of the Charleston Darkey" ([Charleston]: 1912). Heyward published two other volumes of verse devoted in part to similar themes—*Daffodils and Other Lyrics* (Charleston, S.C.: The Southern Printing and Publishing Company, 1921) and *Brown Jackets* (Columbia, S.C.: The State Company, 1923).

124. Promotional brochure, Janie Screven Heyward Papers, SCHS.

125. Janie Screven Heyward, "Fore-Word," Gullah notebook no. 6, [n.d.], Janie Screven Heyward Papers, SCHS.

126. Janie Screven Heyward, program introduction, Gullah notebook no. 2, [n.d.], Janie Screven Heyward Papers, SCHS.

127. Janie Screven Heyward, "Fore-Word."

128. Janie Screven Heyward, "Silhouette," Gullah notebook no. 2, [n.d.], Janie Screven Heyward Papers, SCHS.

129. Janie Screven Heyward, "What Mauma Thinks of Freedom," Gullah notebook no. 2, [n.d.], Janie Screven Heyward Papers, SCHS.

130. According to Harlan Greene, the original title of DuBose's first novel, *Porgy*, was actually *Porgo*, a term drawn from his mother's recollections. In her professional recitations, Janie Heyward told the story of "Porgo, a little wooden doll brought over from African long ago" that belonged to a little slave girl on Janie's grandfather's plantation. This girl, renamed Chloe, became one of Janie's beloved childhood "Maumas." She recounted to her paying audiences that "Porgo was with us until the burning of our plantation home [in 1865], when with all of our other treasures she went up in flame[s], but there is no child of the family who does not know the story of Mauma and her doll Porgo" (Janie Screven Heyward, "Porgo," quoted in Harlan Greene, "'The Little Shining Word': From Porgo to Porgy," *South Carolina Historical Magazine* 87 [January 1986]: 79, 81).

131. Hutchisson, *DuBose Heyward*, 9.

132. Durham, *DuBose Heyward*, 9; Hutchisson, *DuBose Heyward*, 10.

133. "The Literary Lantern," *Courier Journal* (Louisville, Ky.), 10 October 1925, quoted in Frank M. Durham, *DuBose Heyward's Use of Folklore in His Negro Fiction*, The Citadel Monograph Series, no. 2 (Charleston, S.C.: The Citadel, The Military College of South Carolina, 1961), 2.

134. "Colored People Increase Total," newspaper clipping, DuBose Heyward Scrapbook, DuBose Heyward Papers, SCHS; see also Hutchisson, *DuBose Heyward*, 15. Heyward's future literary mentor, John Bennett, also raised war funds among city blacks.

135. "Literary Lantern," quoted in Durham, *DuBose Heyward's Use of Folklore*, 2.

136. John Bennett, *Madame Margot: A Grotesque Legend of Old Charleston* (New York: Century Company, 1921). See also Greene, *Master Skylark*, 169–78. John Bennett's papers at the SCHS are full of reams of handwritten notes on Gullah culture, language, and lore. See also John Bennett, *Doctor to the Dead: Grotesque Legends and Folk Tales of Old Charleston* (New York: Rinehart, 1946).

137. DuBose Heyward, introduction to *Porgy: A Play*, x, as quoted in Hutchisson, *DuBose Heyward*, 9.

138. DuBose Heyward to Hervey Allen, 15 July 1924, DuBose Heyward Papers, SCHS.

139. "Alfred Kreymborg on DuBose Heyward," *The State*, 26 June 1931, DuBose Heyward Papers, SCHS.

140. DuBose Heyward, "The Negro in the Low-Country," in Augustine Smythe, Herbert Ravenel Sass, Alfred Huger et al., eds., *The Carolina Low-Country* (New York: MacMillan Company, 1931), 186.

141. DuBose Heyward, *Porgy*, 5.

142. *Charleston City Directory* (1924). Heyward later moved to 98 Church Street, which today is considered his official residence. Heyward also modeled his main character, Porgy, after real-life Charleston fixture Samuel Smalls, who begged on the city streets in a goat cart (Durham, *DuBose Heyward*, 47). Another character, Peter the honey man, was also allegedly based on Ralph Bennett, a Charleston street huckster. See "'Honey Man' Is Traffic Victim," *Charleston Evening Post*, 27 December 1927, newspaper clipping, DuBose Heyward Papers, SCHS.

143. DuBose Heyward, *Porgy*, 17.

144. Ibid., 42–43.

145. Ibid., 52.

146. Ibid., 54.

147. Slavick, *DuBose Heyward*, 61.

148. DuBose Heyward, *Porgy*, 190.

149. DuBose Heyward to John Bennett, 28 July 1924, John Bennett Papers, SCHS.

150. Herschell Brickell, "The Creator of Catfish Row," *Baltimore Sun*, 10 March 1929, newspaper clipping, DuBose Heyward Papers, SCHS.

151. "E. S. W., Charlevoix, Mich., Asks Me to Settle a Dispute as to Color of Author of 'Porgy,'" *Saturday Review of Literature*, 30 October 1926, newspaper clipping, DuBose Heyward Papers, SCHS; Hervey Allen, *DuBose Heyward: A Critical and Biographical Sketch* (New York: G. H. Doran, 192[?]).

152. DuBose Heyward, *Porgy*, 108.

153. Ibid., 110.

154. Ibid., 7.

155. Ibid., 8. See also Durham, *DuBose Heyward*, 69.

156. DuBose Heyward, *Porgy*, 115.

157. Ibid., 14. In *DuBose Heyward* (61), William Slavick presents a similar reading of this scene as a victory of the jungle. For more on episodes of primitivism in *Porgy*, see Slavick, *DuBose Heyward*, 64–69.

158. Harry Saltpeter, "DuBose Heyward," *New York World*, 19 February 1928, newspaper clipping, DuBose Heyward Papers, SCHS.

159. Brickell, "Creator of Catfish Row."

160. DuBose Heyward, "And Once Again—the Negro," *Reviewer* 4 (October 1923): 39–42.

161. DuBose Heyward, *Porgy*, 50.

162. Ibid., 51.

163. DuBose Heyward to Yates Snowden, 2 November [post-1924], DuBose Heyward Papers, SCHS.

164. *New York Times Book Review* article reprinted in "Mr. Heyward's Book Porgy Praise in New York Times Book Review," *News & Courier*, 30 September 1925, newspaper clipping, DuBose Heyward Papers, SCHS.

165. James Southall Wilson, "The Perennial Rooster," *Virginia Quarterly Review* 2 (January 1926): 153.

166. Heywood Broun, "It Seems to Me," *New York World*, 14 October 1925, newspaper clipping, DuBose Heyward Papers, SCHS.

167. Eleanor Roosevelt to DuBose Heyward, 26 February 1928, DuBose Heyward Papers, SCHS.

168. W. E. B. DuBois in *Crisis* 32 (October 1926), quoted in Williams, *Devil and a Good Woman Too*, 118.

169. The Heywards invested their earnings in the 1920s bull market and suffered dramatically from the 1929 crash. In 1930, they reported zero combined professional income, but the following year they bounced back with a reported income from literary royalties of over $33,750 (or $362,903.23 in 2002 dollars; see Columbia Journalism Review, Inflation Calculator, ⟨http://www.cjr.org/tools/inflation⟩, accessed 13 August 2004). See income tax returns, DuBose Heyward Papers, SCHS.

170. For a history of the Orphanage Band, see John Chilton, *A Jazz Nursery: The Story of the Jenkin's Orphanage Bands* (London: Bloomsbury Book Shop, 1980).

171. *Porgy* playbill, 1927, DuBose Heyward Papers, SCHS.

172. Dorothy Heyward, "'Porgy's' Native Tongue," *New York Times*, 4 December 1927, newspaper clipping, DuBose Heyward Papers, SCHS.

173. At least one native Charlestonian living in New York, struggling writer Robert Marks, found the production lacking. After seeing the Theatre Guild performance, he wrote Laura Bragg that he "was terribly disappointed. The Harlem colored people were alien to the gullah spirit, over-theatrical and neurotic. And the white portion of the cast—policemen, detectives, etc., seemed to have been recruited from the Bowery" (Robert Marks to Laura Bragg, 26 March 1928, Laura Bragg Papers, SCHS).

174. See *Porgy* reviews, DuBose Heyward Papers, SCHS.

175. Quoted in Hollis Alpert, *The Life and Times of Porgy and Bess: The Story of an American Classic* (New York: Knopf, 1990), 67.

176. Quoted in ibid., 68.

177. Alexander Woolcott, *Porgy* review, *New York World*, [October 1927], reprinted in unidentified Charleston newspaper, newspaper clipping, DuBose Heyward Papers, SCHS.

178. Alpert, *Life and Times of Porgy and Bess*, 70. Jolson also wanted to mount a blackface musical version of *Porgy*, but it never materialized (ibid., 186).

179. George Gershwin, *Porgy and Bess: An Opera in Three Acts*, libretto by DuBose Heyward, lyrics by DuBose Heyward and Ira Gershwin (New York: Random House, 1935).

180. Alpert, *Life and Times of Porgy and Bess*, 188.

181. Slavick, *DuBose Heyward*, 84.

182. White Southerners were not the only group of Americans cultivating and consuming art, literature, and music rife with "romantic" myths about the region. Patrick Gerster and Nicholas Cords argue forcefully for the significant contributions of white Northerners in this process in "The Northern Origins of Southern Mythology," *Journal of Southern History* 43 (November 1977): 567–82. See also Francis Pendleton Gaines classic literary study, *The Southern Plantation: A Study in the Development and the Accuracy of a Tradition* (New York: Columbia University Press, 1924). For

the South's image in film, see Edward D. C. Campbell Jr., *The Celluloid South: Hollywood and the Southern Myth* (Knoxville: University of Tennessee Press, 1981).

Chapter Four

1. This scenery and costuming were standard for Spirituals Society productions by the 1929 Boston concert. For representative descriptions, see Katherine Hutson to Mr. Graham, [Winthrop College, Rock Hill, S.C.], 21 January 1937, SPS Papers, SCHS; and R. L. C., "Spirituals Singing by Society of Charleston is Highly Complimented," *Augusta Chronicle*, 3 March 1930, newspaper clipping, May Martin Scrapbook II, 1930 February–March, SPS Papers, SCHS.

2. "Southern Voices Sing Spirituals," *Boston Post*, 17 June 1929, newspaper clipping, May Martin Scrapbook I, June 1929, SPS Papers, SCHS.

3. Augustine T. Smythe, Herbert Ravenel Sass, Alfred Huger et al., eds., *The Carolina Low-Country* (New York: MacMillan Company, 1931), 230. The spelling of song titles in dialect varies at times; in the case of this spiritual, for example, the word "Cum" appears in the concert program, while the spelling "Come" is deployed in the Smythe volume.

4. "Society Sings Spirituals," *New York Times*, 30 June 1929.

5. Paul Connerton, *How Societies Remember* (New York: Cambridge University Press, 1989), 35–36.

6. Nathan Irvin Huggins, *The Harlem Renaissance* (New York: Oxford University Press, 1971), 248–49; James H. Dorman, "The Strange Career of Jim Crow Rice," *Journal of Social History* 3 (2): 109–22.

7. See M. M. Manring, *Slave in a Box: The Strange Career of Aunt Jemima* (Charlottesville: University Press of Virginia, 1998); and Patricia A. Turner, *Ceramic Uncles and Celluloid Mammies: Black Images and their Influence on Culture* (Charlottesville: University Press of Virginia, 2002). For more on black stereotypes and American consumer culture, see Kenneth W. Goings, *Mammy and Uncle Mose: Black Collectibles and American Stereotyping* (Bloomington: Indiana University Press, 1994); Eric Lott, "Love and Theft: The Racial Unconscious of Blackface Minstrelsy," *Representations* 39 (Summer 1992): 23–50; and Henry Louis Gates Jr., "The Face and Voice of Blackness," in *Facing History: The Black Image in American Art, 1710–1940*, ed. Guy C. McElroy (Washington, D.C.: Bedford Arts, Publishers, 1990), xxix–xliv.

8. Turner, *Ceramic Uncles*, 53. See also Cheryl Thurber, "The Development of the Mammy Image and Mythology," in *Southern Women: Histories and Identities*, ed. Virginia Bernhard (Columbia: University of Missouri Press, 1992), 99; "The Black Mammy Monument," *New York Age*, 6 January 1923, 4; and Cynthia Mills, "Commemorating the Color Line: The National Mammy Monument Controversy of the 1920s," in *Monuments to the Lost Cause: Women, Art, and the Landscapes of Southern Memory*, eds. Cynthia Mills and Pamela H. Simpson (Knoxville: University of Tennessee Press, 2003).

9. Henry Louis Gates Jr. ("Face and Voice of Blackness," xxix) calls this the "white fiction of blackness." For discussions of various aspects of the history of blackface, see Nathan I. Huggins's germinal chapter, "White/Black Faces—Black Masks," in

Huggins, *Harlem Renaissance*. See also Eric Lott, *Love and Theft: Blackface Minstrelsy and the American Working Class* (New York: Oxford University Press, 1993); Michael Rogin, *Blackface, White Noise: Jewish Immigrants in the Hollywood Melting Pot* (Berkeley: University of California Press, 1996); Dale Cockrell, *Demons of Desire: Early Blackface Minstrels and Their World* (New York: Cambridge University Press, 1997); and Susan Gubar, *Racechanges: White Skin, Black Face in American Culture* (New York: Oxford University Press, 1997).

10. Rogin, *Blackface, White Noise*, 12.

11. Lott, *Love and Theft*, 6, 37. See also Eric Lott, "'The Seeming Counterfeit': Racial Politics and Early Blackface Minstrelsy," *American Quarterly* 43 (2):223–54.

12. Rogin, *Blackface, White Noise*, 12–18.

13. Ibid., 12. Likewise, Lott argues, "the minstrel show worked for over a hundred years to facilitate safely an exchange of energies between two otherwise rigidly bounded and policed cultures, a shape-shifting middle term in racial conflict" (*Love and Theft*, 6).

Similarly, Norman Mailer recognized a sort of identity fluidity, white to black, in the philosophy and lifestyle of the white "hipster" of 1950s America. According to Mailer, in the hipster's desire to experience life on the margins of society, and his consequent dabbling in African American culture and its so-called primitivism, he "had absorbed the existential synapses of the Negro, and for practical purposes could be considered a white Negro." See Mailer, "The White Negro: Superficial Reflections on the Hipster," in Norman Mailer, *Advertisements for Myself* (New York: G. P. Putnam's Sons, 1959), 337–58.

14. Rogin, *Blackface, White Noise*, 12.

15. See William J. Mahar, "Ethiopian Skits and Sketches: Contents and Contexts of Blackface Minstrelsy, 1840–1890," *Prospects* 16 (1991): 241–79.

16. For more on constructions of whiteness in American culture, see Grace Elizabeth Hale, *Making Whiteness: The Culture of Segregation in the South, 1890–1940* (New York: Pantheon Books, 1998); and David R. Roediger, *The Wages of Whiteness: Race and the Making of the American Working Class* (New York: Verso, 1991).

17. David Levering Lewis, *When Harlem Was in Vogue* (New York: Oxford University Press, 1981), 209–11.

18. For a fascinating discussion of the "authenticity" of the Fisk Singers spirituals, see Paul Gilroy, *The Black Atlantic: Modernity and Double Consciousness* (Cambridge: Harvard University Press, 1993), 87–93. For general information on Fisk and other black choirs of the late nineteenth and early twentieth centuries, see Andrew Ward, *Dark Midnight When I Rise: The Story of the Jubilee Singers, Who Introduced the World to the Music of Black America* (New York: Farrar, Straus, and Giroux, 2000); and C. Robert Tipton, "The Fisk Jubilee Singers," *Tennessee Historical Quarterly* 29 (1): 42–48. See also C. Robert Tipton, "'A Feeling of Prejudice': Orpheus M. McAdoo and the Virginia Jubilee Singers in South Africa, 1890–1898," *Journal of South African Studies* 14 (3): 331–50; and Ray Allen, "African-American Sacred Quartet Singing in New York City," *New York Folklore* 14 (3–4): 7–22.

19. For more on the American interest in historical re-creations in the first part of the twentieth century, see David Glassberg, *American Historical Pageantry: The Uses*

of Tradition in the Early Twentieth Century (Chapel Hill: University of North Carolina Press, 1990).

20. Alfred Huger to H. S. Latham, editor, MacMillan Company, New York, 10 January 1930, SPS Papers, SCHS.

21. "Many Features for Festival," *News & Courier*, 2 May 1923, newspaper clipping, Katherine Hutson Scrapbook III, 1923–31, SPS Papers, SCHS. In 1929, Solomon Guggenheim purchased 9 East Battery.

22. Mrs. William Grimball, quoted in Elizabeth O'Neill Verner, "Spirituals of the Low Country," Charleston newspaper clipping, [1926], Burkette Scrapbook IV, SPS Papers, SCHS.

23. Ibid. Panchita's sister, Marie Heyward, was a dear friend of Alice Ravenel Huger Smith, who visited the Heyward plantation, Wappaoolah, and based many of her landscape and plantation paintings on what she saw there. See Alice Smith discussion in Chapter 2.

24. Panchita Heyward Grimball (Mrs. William Grimball), interview by Cal Ball, audio cassette, SCHS.

25. "Constitution of the Society for the Preservation of Negro Spirituals," [1924], SPS Papers, SCHS.

26. Minutes, 4 May 1927, SPS Papers, SCHS. While the Society had occasionally given money to individual African Americans in need of assistance, they expanded this work through the formation of an active, formal relief committee beginning in 1927.

27. In describing the SPS, a reporter commented, "You must go to Charleston for a genuinely exclusive club" (M. A. DeWolfe Howe, "The Song of Charleston," *Atlantic Monthly*, July 1930, 109).

28. Alfred Huger to Dr. Cornelia Brant, 22 August 1931, SPS Papers, SCHS.

29. See membership lists and "Constitution of the Society for the Preservation of Negro Spirituals," SPS Papers, SCHS.

30. Membership lists, SPS Papers, SCHS. Several of these individuals also steered other aspects of the city's cultural revival; Josephine Pinckney and DuBose Heyward were cofounders of the Poetry Society, and Albert Simons was the leading architect of the preservation movement.

31. Alfred Huger to Dr. T. E. Oertel, 7 March 1930, SPS Papers, SCHS.

32. Mr. William Elliott Hutson, telephone interview with author, 14 July 1994, Charleston, S.C.

33. Katherine Hutson described the SPS's personal attachment to and the almost therapeutic qualities of the spirituals in this way: "Loving the old songs not only because of their beauty but also because of their association and the memories they evoked, the members of the group found a deep pleasure in singing them" (Katherine Hutson to Mrs. Edwina Kellenberger, 30 July 1930, SPS Papers, SCHS).

34. Publicity information card, 1938, SPS Papers, SCHS.

35. SPS members and journalists describing SPS activities often deployed the terms "darkey," "old-time darkey," "old-time negro," and "primitive" in their private and public writings to characterize rural African Americans who supposedly adhered to pre–Civil War racial traditions in the Low Country.

36. Many Southern white interviewers for the WPA slave narratives project of the late 1930s similarly described Low Country blacks. About an interview with "Uncle Dave White, An Old Time Negro," Laura Middleton noted that White's "quiet unadulterated mode of living and his never changing grateful disposition typifies the true Southern Negro of pre–Civil War days; a race that was commonplace and plentiful at one time, but is now almost extinct, having dwindled in the face of more adequate educational facilities" (George P. Rawick, ed., *The American Slave: A Composite Autobiography*, vol. 3, South Carolina Narrative, pts. 3 and 4 [Westport, Conn.: Greenwood Publishing Company, 1972]).

37. Charles W. Joyner, *Down by the Riverside: A South Carolina Slave Community* (Urbana: University of Illinois Press, 1984), 197. For more about the historical origins and linguistic traditions of the Gullah-speaking people, see ibid., 196–224; and Margaret Washington Creel, *"A Peculiar People": Slave Religion and Community-Culture among the Gullahs* (New York: New York University Press, 1988).

38. Carole Marks, *Farewell We're Good and Gone: The Great Black Migration* (Bloomington: Indiana University Press, 1989).

39. "Many Features for Festival," *News & Courier*, 2 May 1923. See also "Spirituals Concert Tonight," ibid., 20 December 1923.

40. Walter Fraser, *Charleston! Charleston! The History of a Southern City* (Columbia: University of South Carolina Press, 1989), 360, 364. See also National Association for the Advancement of Colored People, Charleston Branch Papers, LC.

41. Eugene Hunt, interview transcript, interview by Lee Drago, 28 August 1980, Avery Research Center for African American History and Culture, College of Charleston, Charleston, S.C. See also Edmund L. Drago, *Initiative, Paternalism, and Race Relations: Charleston's Avery Normal Institute* (Athens: University of Georgia Press, 1990).

For contemporary comments on the importance of black education in Depression-era Charleston, see Jeanette Keeble Cox to William Watts Ball, 2 March 1936, William Watts Ball Papers, Duke.

42. African American tenor George Johnson, who visited Charleston in 1936, is quoted by a local paper as saying, "The spiritual is now familiarly known as one of the Negro's gifts to music. What is not generally known is that this type of music was threatened with extinction at the hands of Negro leaders themselves. A group tried to discourage the singing of spirituals because they smacked of slavery. If this effort had succeeded, the Negro would have been robbed of one of his most sacred heritage" (Johnson quoted in Isabella Leland, "Chant of Old Tribal Drums," *News & Courier Sunday Magazine*, article clipping, 20 March 1960, SPS File, SCHS). See also Pamela Teresa Burns, "The Negro Spiritual: From the Southern Plantations to the Concert Stages of America" (Ph.D. diss., University of Alabama, Tuscaloosa, 1993).

43. Concert notice, unnamed Charleston newspaper, 12 March 1927, Scrapbook I, SPS Papers, SCHS.

44. DuBose Heyward, *Mamba's Daughters: A Novel of Charleston* (1929. Columbia: University of South Carolina Press, 1995), 217.

45. Thomas Wentworth Higginson, "Negro Spirituals," *Atlantic Monthly*, June 1867, 694.

46. William Francis Allen, Charles Pickard Ware, and Lucy McKim Garrison, *Slave Songs of the United States* (1867; New York: Peter Smith, 1929), xx.

47. Thomas P. Fenner, *Cabin and Plantation Songs* (New York: G. P. Putnam's Sons, 1892); Henry Edward Krehbiel, *Afro-American Folk Songs: A Study in Racial and National Music* (New York: Frederick Ungar Publishing Company, 1914).

48. See, for example, *Religious Folk Songs of the Negro as Sung on the Plantations*, arranged by the musical directors of the Hampton Normal and Agricultural Institute (Hampton, Va.: The Institute Press, 1918); R. Nathaniel Dett, *Religious Folk-Songs of the Negro as Sung at Hampton Institute* (Hampton, Va.: The Institute Press, 1927); and Frederick J. Work, *New Jubilee Songs as Sung by the Fisk Jubilee Singer* (Nashville, Tenn.: Fisk University, 1902).

49. James Weldon Johnson and J. Rosamond Johnson, *The Book of American Negro Spirituals* (1925; New York: The Viking Press, 1947), 49.

50. Ibid., 48.

51. Ibid., 49.

52. Executive Committee Minutes, 1 February 1924, SPS Papers, SCHS. In May 1927, the SPS formed a Committee on Permanent Records with an eye toward publishing the spirituals materials gathered by these early committees in the previous years (Minutebook, 1926–27, 4 May 1927, SPS Papers, SCHS).

53. Katherine C. Hutson, "Save Spirituals in Native Form," *News & Courier*, 15 February 1929, newspaper clipping, Burkette Scrapbook IV, 1923–61, SPS Papers, SCHS. See also Murray duQ. Bonnoitt, "Ghost Music of Coastal Carolina Echoes through the White House," *Washington Post*, 1935, article reprinted in *The State* (Columbia, S.C.), 20 January 1935.

54. "Spirituals Are Again a Delight," [unnamed Savannah newspaper], 7 February 1926, newspaper clipping, May Martin Scrapbook I, 1924–29, SPS Papers, SCHS.

55. See "Spirituals Not Printed," *News & Courier*, 14 April 1928, newspaper clipping, May Martin Scrapbook I, 1924–29, SPS Papers, SCHS.

56. See Minutes, 14 May 1923, SPS Papers, SCHS.

57. Hazel Beamer to [Augustine T.] Smythe, 4 March 1931, SPS Papers, SCHS.

58. Harold E. Marshall, Sask[atchewan], Canada, to SPS, [1931], SPS Papers, SCHS.

59. Janet Tobitt, Program Division, Girl Scouts, New York City, to Secretary of Spirituals Society, 31 January 1936, SPS Papers, SCHS.

60. Katherine Hutson to Charles E. Griffith, 24 May 1937, SPS Papers, SCHS. In this instance, the SPS allowed the Silver Burdett Company of Newark, New Jersey, to print, without charge, "Seddown en Res' a Leetle Wile" in a textbook for children. Before it was printed, Hutson made the company aware that she had "made two corrections in the music and [had] written the words in Gullah," pointing out to the Northern music editors that "no negro here would use the correct English as written and as these are the Spirituals of the Gullah Negro you can understand that this is the only authentic version" (Hutson to Winnfred [*sic*] A. Harrison, 29 May 1937, SPS Papers, SCHS).

61. "Spirituals Not Printed."

62. See, for example, Dorothy Scarborough, *On the Trail of Negro Folk-Songs* (Cam-

bridge: Harvard University Press, 1925); Newman I. White, *American Negro Folk-Songs* (Cambridge: Harvard University Press, 1928); Howard Odum and Guy B. Johnson, *The Negro and His Songs: A Study of the Typical Negro Songs in the South* (Chapel Hill: University of North Carolina Press, 1925) and *Negro Workaday Songs* (Chapel Hill: University of North Carolina Press, 1926); Mary Allen Grissom, *The Negro Sings a New Heaven* (Chapel Hill: University of North Carolina Press, 1930); and Johnson and Johnson, *Book of American Negro Spirituals.* What SPS member Josephine Pinckney called "the present vogue for Negro music" also prompted the reprinting in 1929 of *Slave Songs of the United States*, a compilation of songs originally published in 1867 (see William Francis Allen, Charles Pickard Ware, and Lucy McKim Garrison, *Slave Songs of the South* [New York: Peter Smith, 1929]). Above Pinckney quotation comes from Pinckney's typed review of the Allen et al. reissue in Josephine Pinckney Papers, SCHS.

63. "Spirituals Not Printed."

64. Walter C. Garwick to Josephine Pinckney, 2 February 1936; and George W. Hibbitt to Mrs. William Elliott Hutson, 22 May 1937, SPS Papers, SCHS.

65. Garwick's Southern recording tour ultimately generated "sixty first-hand phonograph recordings of negro legends and folk songs" for Columbia University's collection. See "Charleston Aids Negro Research," *Charleston Evening Post*, 4 April 1937, newspaper clipping, Scrapbook II, January 1936–1937, SPS Papers, SCHS.

66. See Walter Garwick, Sound Recording Instruments, Rye, New York, to Mrs. William Elliott Hutson, 3 April 1937; and Katherine Hutson to Walter Garwick, 1 May 1937, SPS Papers, SCHS. See also "Machine Records Lowcountry Lore," *News & Courier*, 4 July 1937, newspaper clipping, Scrapbook II, January 1936–1937, SPS Papers, SCHS.

67. Walter Garwick to Mrs. William Elliott Hutson, 8 May 1937, SPS Papers, SCHS.

68. Katherine Hutson to Harold Spivacke, Library of Congress, 23 November 1937, SPS Papers, SCHS.

69. "Machine Records Lowcountry Lore."

70. "Crumble Alley—Jan 24" and "Capers—Camanbell Alley—priests in Cambell Alley," Park Dougherty Collection, SPS, Recorded Sound Division, LC. In the latter recording, the pastor of Cromwell Alley Church implores his listeners to save his church from the wrecking ball: "The only way to keep Cromwell Alley that is to help prepare Cromwell Alley and then prepare white people caring and then the government will pass by." For more on the development of the Robert Mills Manor, see Chapter 1.

71. The disc was titled "The Street Cries of Charleston, S.C. The Fish, Flower and Vegetable Vendors as they go about the streets and call out their wares in quaint, original chants" (Executive Committee Minutes, 15 November 1942, SPS Papers, SCHS).

Street cries can also be found on an SPS recording titled "Charleston Street Cries—unidentified," which comprises part of the Park Dougherty Collection, SPS, Recorded Sound Division, LC.

72. See SPS Minutes, 29 October 1937; Katherine Hutson to Walter Garwick, 7

January 1938; Garwick to Hutson, 21 March 1941; and Garwick to Hutson, 16 March 1938, SPS Papers, SCHS.

73. Harold Spivacke to Charles Webb, 22 July 1937; and Katherine Hutson to Harold Spivacke, 23 November 1937, SPS Papers, SCHS. The Library of Congress had to wait almost fifty years for the Society to donate its forty-five 78 rpm aluminum disc recordings, which now make up the Park Dougherty Collection. See Jack Leland, untitled newspaper clipping, 3 May 1982, SPS File, SCHS; and the Park Dougherty Collection, LC.

74. "Spirituals Sung for Folk Record," *News & Courier,* 21 May 1936, newspaper clipping, Scrapbook II, January 1936–1937, SPS Papers, SCHS.

75. "Teachers Jam Theater for Spirituals Society Concert," *News & Courier,* 9 November 1929, newspaper clipping, Scrapbook I, July–December 1929, SPS Papers, SCHS.

76. Another incidence of SPS members instructing blacks on the delicate points of singing spirituals occurred during the rehearsals of *Porgy & Bess* (1935). In this case, SPS members DuBose Heyward and Sam Stoney tutored the Northern black actors in the fine art of Gullah pronunciation and inflection. See discussion in Chapter 3.

77. Minutes, 4 May 1927, SPS Papers, SCHS.

78. Alfred Huger to Mrs. Humbert Barton Powell, 10 October 1929, SPS Papers, SCHS.

79. Minutes, 29 November 1932, SPS Papers, SCHS. A favorite charity was Pinehaven, the African American tuberculosis sanitorium outside the city. In 1929, for example, the Society gave money to the Charleston County Tuberculosis Association to purchase a cart to transport food from the kitchens in the downtown white TB ward to Pinehaven (Alfred Huger to Mrs. Humbert Barton Powell, 10 October 1929, SPS Papers, SCHS).

80. Minutes, 4 May 1927, SPS Papers, SCHS. For historical antecedents, see Barbara L. Bellows, *Benevolence among Slaveholders: The Poor in Charleston, 1670–1850* (Baton Rouge: Louisiana State University Press, 1993).

81. Relief Committee Report, 3 April [1935], SPS Papers, SCHS.

82. See Relief Committee Charity Case Files, 1929–39, SPS Papers, SCHS.

83. In 1932 alone, the year in which the bankrupt city government paid its employees in scrip, the SPS dedicated $800 to charitable works among African Americans. For SPS financial information, see minutebooks and financial statements, SPS Papers, SCHS.

84. See examples in Relief Committee Charity Case Files, 1935, SPS Papers, SCHS.

85. "Backwoods Sufferers Given Help by Spirituals Singers," *News & Courier,* 23 March 1936, newspaper clipping, Scrapbook II, January 1936–37, SPS Papers, SCHS.

86. Concert program, 1928, SPS Papers, SCHS.

87. Matthew Page Andrews to SPS president Dick Reeves, [November 1927], quoted in "Historian Lauds Spirituals Here," *News & Courier,* 26 November 1927, newspaper clipping, May Martin Scrapbook I, 1924–29, SPS Papers, SCHS.

88. Concert program, Charleston High School, 31 March 1924, SPS Papers, SCHS;

Alfred Huger to Mrs. W. C. Moore, 10 October 1929, SPS Papers, SCHS. For more on Janie Screven Heyward's performances, see Chapter 3.

89. "The Negro Spirituals," *News & Courier*, 22 December 1924, newspaper clipping, May Martin Scrapbook I, 1924–29, SPS Papers, SCHS.

90. "Norah (Minor)," in Smythe et al., eds., *Carolina Low-Country*, 240–41.

91. "Somebody Een Yuh, It Mus' Be Jedus," in ibid., 272–73.

92. Douglass quoted in Leslie H. Fishel Jr. and Benjamin Quarles, eds. *The Negro American: A Documentary History* (Chicago: Scott, Foresman and Co., 1967), 116.

93. W. E. B. DuBois, quoted in James H. Cone, *The Spirituals and the Blues: An Interpretation* (New York: Seabury Press, 1971), 62.

94. Johnson and Johnson, *Book of American Negro Spirituals*, 20.

95. "Gwine T' Res' from All My Labuh," in Smythe et al., eds., *Carolina Low-Country*, 244–45.

96. "Ole Egyp'," in ibid., 234–45.

97. "Gottuh Tek Duh Chillun Outuh Pharaoh Han'," in ibid., 290–91.

98. Katherine Hutson, performance notes, correspondence file, 1938–39, SPS Papers, SCHS.

99. Ibid.

100. Robert W. Gordon, "The Negro Spiritual," in Smythe et al., eds., *Carolina Low-Country*, 191–222. See also, "'Real' Spirituals Saved," *New York Times*, 24 March 1935, newspaper clipping, Scrapbook II, January 1933–1935, SPS Papers, SCHS.

101. For discussions of the multivalent layers of African American folk culture during slavery, see Lawrence Levine, *Black Culture and Black Consciousness: Afro-American Folk Thought from Slavery to Freedom* (New York: Oxford University Press, 1977); and Charles Joyner, *Down by the Riverside: A South Carolina Slave Community* (Urbana: University of Illinois Press, 1984).

102. "Sinnuh W'ah Yuh Doin' Down Dere," in Smythe et al., eds., *Carolina Low-Country*, 238–39.

103. Magnetic tape recording, 1936 Azalea Festival, SPS Collection, Archive of Folk Culture, LC.

104. "Siporatin' Line," in Smythe et al., eds., *Carolina Low-Country*, 310–11.

105. Magnetic tape recording, 1936 Azalea Festival, SPS Collection, Archive of Folk Culture, LC.

106. Minutes, 14 May 1923, SPS Papers, SCHS.

107. Concert notice, 12 March 1927, Scrapbook I, SPS Papers, SCHS. SPS concerts were not intended as minstrelsy, but in December 1932, a group of white Charlestonians, calling themselves "The Edisto Island Black Strap Minstrels," performed in blackface for an audience of 400 at the local high school. Tap dances, jokes, burlesque skits, and songs comprised the evening's entertainment, in which several SPS members figured prominently. Other members applauded in the audience. See "Edisto Island Minstrel Mocks Hard Times While 400 Applaud," *News & Courier*, 4 December 1932, newspaper clipping, EONVP, SCHS.

108. "Benefit Concert for Idle Relief," *News & Courier*, 20 March 1923, newspaper clipping, Scrapbook II, January–December 1932, SPS Papers, SCHS.

109. The SPS reinforced this idea of the natural musicality of blacks to white

concert audiences. "One thing the society has tried to do," Huger explained to a group in Boston, "is to tell the colored man that he has a music and can sing it as no other race in the world" ("Southern Voices Sing Spirituals," *Boston Post*, 17 June 1929, newspaper clipping, May Martin Scrapbook I, June 1929, SPS Papers, SCHS). In private correspondence, Huger blamed whites' shortcomings in reproducing the "Negro shout" on a "physiological hindrance" (Huger to Walter Damrosch, 11 March 1930, SPS Papers, SCHS).

110. "Savannah Likes Spirituals," *Savannah Morning News*, [16 February 1924], Scrapbook I, SPS Papers, SCHS.

111. H. B. [Henry Bellamann], "From South Carolina," [November 1931], unnamed newspaper clipping [likely the Columbia *State*], May Martin Scrapbook II, January–December 1931, SPS Papers, SCHS. After hearing the SPS in New York, composer and music critic Walter Damrosch suggested "the guidance of a professional musician" to "enable the white people to carry on the best traditions of the colored people more correctly." He concluded, "Not only does their singing need much more of that sensuous beauty of tone which the negroes have naturally, but in many harmonies, the essential inner voices were often missing" (Damrosch to Marjorie Morawetz, 14 January 1930, SPS Papers, SCHS).

112. Alfred Huger to Walter J. Damrosch, 11 March 1930, SPS Papers, SCHS.

113. T. E. Oertel, "An Appreciation," *Augusta Chronicle*, 3 March 1930, newspaper clipping, May Martin Scrapbook II, February–March 1930, SPS Papers, SCHS.

114. Mrs. Lucile Francis to [SPS], 24 February 1931, SPS Papers, SCHS.

115. [Charles Drayton?] to [A. Jermain] Slocum, 7 November 1929, SPS Papers, SCHS.

116. "The Negro Spirituals," *News & Courier*, 22 December 1924.

117. "Concert Patrons Aid Relief Funds," *Charleston Evening Post*, 20 March 1932, newspaper clipping, Scrapbook II, January–December 1932, SPS Papers, SCHS.

118. [Charles Drayton?] to [A. Jermain] Slocum, 7 November 1929, SPS Papers, SCHS.

119. "Society for Preservation of Spirituals Will Hold Spring Concert Saturday," *News & Courier*, 8 April 1928, newspaper clipping, May Martin Scrapbook I, 1924–29, SPS Papers, SCHS.

120. Howe, "Song of Charleston," 110.

121. Matthew Page Andrews to SPS president Dick Reeves, [November 1927].

122. "Walter Damrosch Thrilled by Concert of Spirituals," *News & Courier*, 22 April 1935, newspaper clipping, Scrapbook II, January 1933–35, SPS Papers, SCHS.

123. "Spiritual Society to Go to Boston," *News & Courier*, [March 1929], newspaper clipping, May Martin Scrapbook I, 1924–29, SPS Papers, SCHS.

124. Ibid.

125. Alfred Huger, "Preserving the Spirituals," *News & Courier*, 14 March 1929, newspaper clipping, May Martin Scrapbook I, 1924–29, SPS Papers, SCHS.

126. Photograph notation, May Martin Scrapbook I, 1924–29, SPS Papers, SCHS.

127. Concert program, 23 March 1929, May Martin Scrapbook I, 1924–29, SPS Papers, SCHS.

128. This happy plantation scene, created by local Charleston artist Edward I. R. Jennings, became a staple illustration for future SPS concerts (concert poster, 23 March 1929, Hutson Scrapbook II, SPS Papers, SCHS).

129. According to Society records (Minutes, 10 and 26 June 1929, SPS Papers, SCHS), this bank loan, cosigned by eighteen SPS members, was repaid two days after the singers returned from Boston.

130. "Spirituals Score in Salem Concert," *News and Courier*, 16 June 1929.

131. Photograph notations, 15 June 1929, May Martin Scrapbook I, June 1929, SPS Papers, SCHS.

132. "Give Concert of Spirituals, Charleston Society Wins Ovation from Music Federation," *Boston Herald*, 17 June 1929, newspaper clipping, May Martin Scrapbook I, June 1929, SPS Papers, SCHS.

133. A. H. M., "Spirituals with a Different Flavor," *Boston Transcript*, 18 June 1929, newspaper clipping, May Martin Scrapbook I, June 1929, SPS Papers, SCHS.

134. Ibid.

135. "Lionized in Boston," *News & Courier*, 18 June 1929, newspaper clipping, May Martin Scrapbook I, June 1929, SPS Papers, SCHS.

136. "Spirituals Score in Salem Concert"; "Give Concert of Spirituals."

137. Untitled newspaper clipping, *Wilmington Morning News*, 19 June 1929, May Martin Scrapbook I, June 1929, SPS Papers, SCHS.

138. "Spiritual Group to Leave Today," *News & Courier*, 8 January 1930, Scrapbook I, July–December 1929, SPS Papers, SCHS.

139. The Spirituals Society elected the Morawetzes as "honorary members" in 1935 in recognition of their support (Katherine Hutson to Marjorie Morawetz, [1935], SPS Papers, SCHS).

140. Alfred Huger to Marjorie Morawetz, 19 September 1929, SPS Papers, SCHS.

141. Ibid.

142. Marjorie Morawetz to Alfred Huger, 6 August 1929, SPS Papers, SCHS.

143. "Spirituals Applause Is Led by Damrosch in New York," *News & Courier*, 11 January 1930; "Gullah Spirituals Sung," *New York Times*, 10 January 1930.

144. "Spiritual Society to Leave Tomorrow on New York Trip," *News & Courier*, 7 January 1930, newspaper clipping, Scrapbook I, SPS Papers, SCHS. As part of its educational program, the SPS established the Junior SPS to maintain the "'word of mouth' method of learning spirituals." In doing so, they guaranteed that future generations of SPS members would learn spirituals not from black singers themselves but from other elite white SPS members. See also Minutes, 16 October 1929, SPS Papers, SCHS.

145. Walter Damrosch to Marjorie Morawetz, 14 January 1930, SPS Papers, SCHS.

146. Morawetz passed Proctor's letter on to the SPS with a handwritten note saying, "Her [Proctor's] opinion really counts." See Mrs. William Proctor to Marjorie Morawetz, January 1930, Scrapbook I, SPS Papers, SCHS.

147. "A High Quality of Publicity," *News & Courier*, 13 January 1930.

148. See, for example, Howe, "Song of Charleston," 108–11; and Maude Barrigan,

"Putting the Spirit into Spirituals," *Etude*, February 1931, article clipping, Scrapbook II, SPS Papers, SCHS.

149. See Correspondence Files, 1930s, SPS Papers, SCHS.

150. Editorial, 1 April 1929, *News & Courier*.

151. "SPS Sings Complimentary Concert," *News & Courier*, 5 April 1930, newspaper clipping, May Martin Scrapbook II, April–December 1930, SPS Papers, SCHS.

152. This concert was broadcast from Charleston's Academy of Music for the 1936 Azalea Festival. It was the Society's debut over national radio (NBC) and was intended to reach, in the words of Mayor Burnet Rhett Maybank, "some of you [who] cannot be with us at the festival this year" (magnetic tape recording, 1936 Azalea Festival, SPS Collection, Archive of Folk Culture, LC).

153. Minutes, 8 December 1931, SPS Papers, SCHS. Given the unpublicized inter-racial character of this concert, it is not surprising that no record exists noting the response of the black audience to the SPS singing. Only one alleged black reaction to a Society concert exists in SPS records. In a letter to the *Spartanburg Herald*, a white member of the audience recounts the pleasure of a "good brother who was lifted to great heights of joy by the lilt and rhythm of song." The writer quotes the African American spectator: "'It seems dat a tousan mockin' burds am turn loose in de troats ob dem singers.'" See "Negroes Appreciate Rendering of Spirituals," *Spartanburg Herald*, [April 1928], reprinted in unnamed Charleston newspaper, newspaper clipping, Hutson Scrapbook III, 1923–31, SPS Papers, SCHS.

154. Concert poster, Stoney Family Papers, SCHS.

155. Alfred Huger to Mrs. A. J. Geer, 15 March 1930, SPS Papers, SCHS.

156. "Restoring the Virginia Birthplace of Robert E. Lee," pamphlet, The Robert E. Lee Memorial Foundation, Inc., 1930, SPS Papers, SCHS.

157. "Of the Old South," *News & Courier*, 6 March 1930, newspaper clipping, May Martin Scrapbook II, February–March 1930, SPS Papers, SCHS.

158. "Spirituals Group Scores Success," *News & Courier*, 8 March 1930, newspaper clipping, May Martin Scrapbook II, February–March 1930, SPS Papers, SCHS.

159. See correspondence files and concert schedules, SPS Papers, SCHS.

160. Mayor Thomas Stoney to Mrs. William Elliott Hutson, 19 December 1929; and Daisy Lee Stuckey to Alfred Huger, 30 December 1929, SPS Papers, SCHS.

161. Minutes, 17 January 1933, SPS Papers, SCHS.

162. A. J. Tamsberg to Mrs. William Elliott Hutson, 29 January 1936, SPS Papers, SCHS.

163. Katherine Hutson to H. M. Pace, 15 January 1936, SPS Papers, SCHS.

164. Sarah Gertrude Knott to Mrs. William Elliott Hutson, 27 April 1935, SPS Papers, SCHS.

165. "Singers to Give Three Concerts," *News & Courier*, 18 January 1935, newspaper clipping, Scrapbook II, January 1933–1935, SPS Papers, SCHS.

166. Bonnoitt, "Ghost Music of Coastal Carolina."

167. "Spirituals Group Enjoys White House Experience," *Charleston Evening Post*, 21 January 1935, newspaper clipping, Scrapbook II, January 1933–1935, SPS Papers, SCHS.

168. Ibid.

169. "High Praise for Singing," *Charleston Evening Post*, 24 January 1935, newspaper clipping, Scrapbook II, January 1933–1935; and Roosevelt photographs, SPS Papers, SCHS. During the War of 1812, British soldiers set fire to the White House, which was reconstructed in 1815–17.

170. Minutes, 31 January 1935, SPS Papers, SCHS.

171. Herbert Ravenel Sass to Yates Snowden, 24 October 1931, Herbert Ravenel Sass Papers, SCHS.

172. Hebert Ravenel Sass, "The Low-Country," in Smythe et al., eds., *Carolina Low-Country*, 15.

173. Alfred Huger to H. S. Latham, 10 October 1930, SPS Papers, SCHS.

174. DuBose Heyward, "The Negro in the Low-Country," in Smythe et al., eds., *Carolina Low-Country*, 185–86.

175. Augustine T. Smythe, "Preface," in ibid., vii.

176. Publicity materials for *The Carolina Low-Country*, [1931], Scrapbook II, SPS Papers, SCHS.

177. DuBose Heyward, "Negro in the Low-Country," 185.

178. Sass, "Low-Country," 5.

179. Alfred Huger, "The Story of the Low-Country," in Smythe et al., eds., *Carolina Low-Country*, 116.

180. Sass, "Low-Country," 3.

181. Huger, "Story of the Low-Country," 121.

182. Thomas R. Waring, "Charleston: The Capital of the Plantations," in Smythe et al., eds., *Carolina Low-Country*, 142.

183. The SPS continues today in a very limited capacity, with members performing an annual concert in the city during the high tourist season, much as their forebears did.

Chapter Five

1. DuBose Heyward, "Charleston: Where Mellow Past and Present Meet," *National Geographic Magazine* 75 (March 1939): 273.

2. All quotations taken from ibid., 273–97.

3. Ibid., 277, 304.

4. Thomas P. Stoney to Susan P. Frost, 17 April 1929; and Alston Deas, SPOD president, to Thomas P. Stoney, 22 April 1929, SPOD Papers, SCHS.

5. On 1 January 1932, Charleston's People's National Bank, which carried the city's payroll, collapsed. With an $11,000,000 debt, the new mayor Maybank was forced to pay his employees with scrip. In two years time, Maybank brought the city out of this financial hole through stringent fiscal policies (Walter Fraser, *Charleston! Charleston! The History of a Southern City* [Columbia, SC: University of South Carolina Press, 1989], 379).

6. DuBose Heyward, "Charleston," 304.

7. John F. Sears, *Sacred Places: American Tourist Attractions in the Nineteenth Century* (New York: Oxford University Press, 1989), 4. For more on tourism, consumer culture, and identity formation, see Dona Brown, *Inventing New England: Regional Tourism*

in the Nineteenth Century (Washington, D.C.: Smithsonian Institution Press, 1995); Leah Dilworth, *Imagining Indians in the Southwest: Persistent Visions of a Primitive Past* (Washington, D.C.: Smithsonian Institution Press, 1996); Richard Wightman Fox and T. J. Jackson Lears, eds., *The Culture of Consumption: Critical Essays in American History, 1880–1980* (New York: Pantheon Books, 1983); Dean MacCannell, *The Tourist: A New Theory of the Leisure Class* (New York: Schocken Books, 1976); Richard D. Starnes, ed., *Southern Journeys: Tourism, History, and Culture in the Modern South* (Tuscaloosa: University of Alabama Press, 2003); and David Lowenthal, *The Heritage Crusade and the Spoils of History* (New York: Cambridge University Press, 1998).

8. W. D. Howells, "In Charleston," *Harper's Magazine*, October 1915, 747.

9. See, for example, the chapter extolling the beauty of Charleston and its suburbs in William Cullen Bryant, ed., *Picturesque America*, vol. 1 (New York: D. Appleton and Company, 1872); and Owen Wister, *Lady Baltimore* (New York: Macmillan Company, 1906).

10. "A New Guide to Modern Charleston," pamphlet (Charleston, S.C.: Walker, Evans & Cogswell, 1911), tourism pamphlets, CM.

11. Newspaper clipping, "Hotel History Missing Pieces," 2 September 1979, Atlantic Beach Hotel File, SCHS.

12. "Aiken South Carolina as a Health and Pleasure Resort," pamphlet (Charleston, S.C.: Walker, Evans & Cogswell, 1889), SCHS.

13. Kay Lawrence, *Heroes, Horses, and High Society: Aiken from 1850* (Columbia, S.C.: R. L. Bryan Company, 1971), 98–100. See also pamphlet titled "Aiken, South Carolina: Queen of Winter Resorts" (Aiken Civic League, ca. 1925), SCHS.

14. Don Doyle, *New South, New Cities, New Men: Atlanta, Nashville, Charleston, and Mobile, 1860–1910* (Chapel Hill: University of North Carolina Press, 1990), 178–80, 182–85. For descriptions of the Exposition and its various behind-the-scenes battles, see T. Cuyler Smith, "The Ivory City," *Frank Leslie's Popular Monthly* 53 (March 1902): 491–517; J. C. Hemphill, "A Short Story of the South Carolina Inter-State and West Indian Exposition," *Yearbook, City of Charleston, South Carolina* (1902), 107–71; and William D. Smith, "Blacks and the South Carolina Interstate and West Indian Exposition," *South Carolina Historical Magazine* 88 (October 1987): 211–19.

15. Charleston Chamber of Commerce, "Historic and Picturesque Charleston, South Carolina" (Charleston, S.C.: Walker, Evans & Cogswell, 1906), 3, tourism pamphlets, CM.

16. Wister, *Lady Baltimore*, 9.

17. Henry James, *The American Scene* (New York: Harper & Brothers, 1907), 414.

18. Mildred Cram, *Old Seaport Towns of the South* (New York: Dodd, Mead & Company, 1917), 125.

19. Quoted in Louis D. Rubin Jr., *Seaports of the South: A Journey* (Atlanta: Longstreet Press Inc., 1998), 4.

20. See Jim McNeil, *Charleston's Navy Yard* (Charleston, S.C.: CokerCraft Press, 1985).

21. Some of these visitors influenced Charleston's burgeoning cultural scene. Several Northern women artists, for example, spent winters in Charleston during the First World War and shared their etching skills with Alice Ravenel Huger Smith;

Smith, in turn, nurtured the career of Elizabeth O'Neill Verner and helped establish the Charleston Etchers' Club in 1923. See discussion in Chapter 2.

22. Edward Hungerford, *The Personality of American Cities* (New York: McBride, Nast & Company, 1913), 138. A large portion of Hungerford's chapter on Charleston was reprinted in Edward Hungerford, "Charleston of the Real South," *Travel*, October 1913, 32–35, 57.

23. "Much Impressed with Charleston John D. Rockefeller, Jr.," *News & Courier*, 11 April 1919; "Rhode Islanders Here," ibid., 1 April 1921; "Tourist Season Sure to Be Heavy," ibid., 15 December 1919.

24. See, for example, Charleston Chamber of Commerce, "Annual Report 1918," CCA; and Chamber of Commerce, "Charleston: Where the Visitor is Welcome," promotional pamphlet [1920], Chamber of Commerce File, DCRA.

25. See *Journal of the City Council, Charleston, S.C.* (1919) and Albert Simons Papers, SCHS. Simons was the chairman of the subcommittee in 1919.

26. Fraser, *Charleston! Charleston!* 341, 352–58. For an overview of Grace's political career, see also Doyle W. Boggs, "John Patrick Grace and the Politics of Reform in South Carolina, 1900–1931" (Ph.D. diss., University of South Carolina, 1977); and John Joseph Duffy, "Charleston Politics in the Progressive Era" (Ph.D. diss., University of South Carolina, 1963). For an example of Grace's views on improvements as conduits primarily for industrial commerce, see his inaugural address for his second term in office, 15 December 1919, in *Journal of the City Council* (1919), 2–7.

27. Fraser, *Charleston! Charleston!* 368.

28. *Journal of the City Council* (1923), 1254.

29. Fraser, *Charleston! Charleston!* 370.

30. Thomas P. Stoney, "Mayor Stoney's Annual Review," *Year Book, City of Charleston, South Carolina* (1924), liv–lx.

31. Ibid., lx. Both Fredericksburg and Williamsburg, Virginia, questioned the legitimacy of Charleston's self-applied slogan, holding themselves alone worthy of the honor of "America's Most Historic City." In a country bent on national self-examination in the 1920s, such a moniker held weight with the public, and neither city was willing to allow Charleston to usurp the title without challenge. The Tourist and Convention Bureau of the Charleston Chamber of Commerce proposed a debate between the cities for September 1928, but no evidence has been found suggesting it occurred. See "City Challenged on Its History," *News & Courier*, 1 March 1927; "Upholds City's Historic Claim," *News & Courier*, 3 March 1927; "Williamsburg Cites Its History," *News & Courier*, 7 April 1927; and "History Debate Next September," *News & Courier*, 30 March 1927.

32. "A Palmetto Boulevard," *News & Courier*, 4 March 1924; "Charleston a State Playground," ibid., 24 April 1924; "Tourists and Conventions," ibid., 17 July 1924.

33. "Tourist Business History Traced," ibid., 6 April 1939.

34. "Helpful Publicity," editorial, quoted in J. Gilmore Smith, Charleston Board of Trade, to *Charleston Evening Post*, 9 November 1925.

35. "Will Stimulate Tourist Trade," *News & Courier*, 14 July 1924.

36. Meigs B. Russell, "Report of the Manager of the Charleston Chamber of Commerce," printed in *News & Courier*, 18 February 1924.

37. Ibid.

38. "Proceedings of the Council, February 24, 1925," *Journal of the City Council* (1925).

39. "Articles on City in the Motorist," *News & Courier*, 21 October 1924; see also "Tourists Urged to Come This Way," ibid., 24 September 1924.

40. "Tourist Folders Distributed," ibid., 9 December 1924.

41. "Mayor Stoney's Annual Review," *Year Book, City of Charleston* (1930), xix–xxi.

42. Ibid. (1925), xxii.

43. "The Story of the Bridge," pamphlet published by the Francis Marion Hotel, 8 August 1929, COC. See also "Francis Marion to Open Today," *News & Courier*, 7 February 1924.

44. "Francis Marion to Open Today." DuBose Heyward's mother, Janie Screven Heyward, was among the winners of the contest held to name the new hotel ("Francis Marion Hotel Name," *News & Courier*, 18 March 1920).

45. Fort Sumter Hotel brochure, tourism pamphlets, CM.

46. "Fort Sumter Hotel 'On the Battery' Formally Opens Today," *News & Courier*, 6 May 1924.

47. Tourist figures in Robert Lee Frank, "The Economic Impact of Tourism in Charleston, South Carolina, 1970" (M.A. thesis, University of South Carolina, 1972), 35.

48. "Apartments for Tourists Needed," *News & Courier*, 18 October 1926; "Tourist Demand Here for Apartments Growing Daily," ibid., 4 January 1927.

49. J. Gilmore Smith, president, Charleston Board of Trade, to *Charleston Evening Post*, 14 April 1932, Thomas Waring Papers, SCHS.

50. Loutrel W. Briggs, "City's Big Charm in Old Buildings," *News & Courier*, 26 November 1933. For more tourist figures, see Frank, "Economic Impact of Tourism in Charleston," 6, 35.

51. "Charleston Opens $6,000,000 Bridge," *New York Times*, 9 August 1929. For background on bridge financing and structural specifics, see also "Mayor Stoney's Annual Review," *Year Book, City of Charleston* (1929), xxiv–xxix; "Story of the Bridge"; and Jason Annan and Pamela Gabriel, *The Great Cooper River Bridge* (Columbia: University of South Carolina Press, 2002).

52. See "Mayor Stoney's Annual Review," *Year Book, City of Charleston* (1929), xxiv–xxix.

53. "An Achievement and an Augury," *News & Courier*, 8 August 1929.

54. Louise Polk Hugee, "Aloof Charleston Calls Outer World," *New York Times Magazine*, 10 November 1929, 21.

55. Katherine Ball Ripley, quoted in Fraser, *Charleston! Charleston!* 374.

56. "Mayor Stoney's Annual Review," *Year Book, City of Charleston* (1930), xxi. See also *Year Book, City of Charleston* (1929), 320–21.

57. See Thomas P. Stoney to J. C. Barbot, 21 August 1929, quoted in "Proceedings of Council, September 10, 1929," *Journal of the City Council* (1929), 294.

58. William G. Sheppard to *News & Courier*, 7 December 1933, newspaper clipping, Scrapbook, SPOD Papers, SCHS.

59. Alfred Hutty to *News & Courier*, 8 December 1933, newspaper clipping, Scrapbook, SPOD Papers, SCHS. Similarly, Howard S. Hadden, of Spring Bank Plantation, Kingstree, S.C., wrote to the *News & Courier*, "These old historic landmarks are the real interest of your many thousands of visitors and they are in fact the chief reason for making Charleston one of the four unique cities of America" (Hadden to *News & Courier*, 5 December 1933, newspaper clipping, Scrapbook, SPOD Papers, SCHS).

60. Charles Hosmer, *Preservation Comes of Age: From Williamsburg to the National Trust, 1926–1949* (Charlottesville: University Press of Virginia for the National Trust for Historic Preservation, 1981), 1:240; Robert P. Stockton, "Historic Preservation in Charleston," undated essay, Historic Preservation File, SCHS.

61. In 1925, longtime Preservation Society president Susan P. Frost argued in a letter to the editor of a local newspaper, "It is entirely compatible with commercial progress that we, at the same time, be careful to preserve our old buildings and the names of our streets that are connected with the early days of our city. These things are not without their meaning and their great value, they give tone and stability to our city, they bring people of culture and artistic taste, as well as people of large means to our city and we mutually benefit from each other" (Susan Pringle Frost to "The Editor," 28 January 1925, unnamed local newspaper clipping, Scrapbook, SPOD Papers, SCHS).

62. "Proceedings of Council, August 13, 1929," *Journal of the City Council* (1929), 285.

63. Letterhead from the St. John Hotel, March 1937, William Watts Ball Papers, Duke.

64. "Proceedings of Council, August 13, 1929," *Journal of the City Council* (1929), 285. To achieve the hoped-for aesthetic balance, Simons made use of original materials salvaged from the 1929 demolition of the early-Republican-era home of architect and rice planter Gabriel Manigault (Jonathan Poston, *The Buildings of Charleston: A Guide to the City's Architecture* [Columbia: University of South Carolina Press, 1997], 188).

65. "Romantic Charleston" (Charleston, S.C.: Elliman, Huyler & Mullally, Inc., [193?]).

66. "Proceedings of Council, November 12, 1929," *Journal of the City Council* (1929), 327.

67. "Proceeding of Council, November 25, 1930," *Journal of the City Council* (1930), 531.

68. City directories reveal the new infrastructural orientation toward tourism. Listings for restaurants, tearooms, tour guides, and small hotels increase in the period. While the *Charleston City Directory* of 1919 contains no listing for "gift shops," for example, by 1928 sixteen are listed; three years later that total had grown to twenty-six. Similarly, listings for establishments providing automotive services, including mechanics and gasoline stations, which served both locals and tourists, grew from covering one page in 1919, to covering four and a half in 1928, to comprising seven full pages in the 1931–32 directory. See *Charleston City Directories*. For numbers concerning transportation services, accommodations, and entertainment venues by the end of the 1930s, see *South Carolina: The WPA Guide to the Palmetto State* (1941; Columbia, S.C.: University of South Carolina Press, 1992), 184.

69. "Zoning Ordinance," quoted in Albert Simons to Susan Pringle Frost, 23 December 1933, Albert Simons Papers, SCHS.

70. *South Carolina: The WPA Guide*, 186. For address and ownership information, see *Charleston City Directory* (1934).

71. William Watts Ball to Sara [Ball Copeland], 6 January 1938, William Watts Ball Papers, Duke.

72. See Clara E. Laughlin, *So You're Going South!* (Boston: Little, Brown and Company, 1941), 403; George W. Seaton, *What to See and Do in the South* (New York: Prentice-Hall, Inc., 1941), 136; and *South Carolina: The WPA Guide*, 192.

73. Elizabeth Verner Hamilton, interview by author, 30 November 1993, Charleston, S.C.

74. "Romantic Charleston."

75. Ibid.

76. See Church Street listings in *Charleston City Directory* (1934).

77. "Writers 'Shocked' at Commercialism," *News & Courier*, 25 December 1933, newspaper clipping, Scrapbook 1932–45, SPOD Papers, SCHS; see also Dorothy Ducas, "Success of 'Porgy' Abolished the 'Catfish Row' That it Made Famous," *New York Evening Post*, [1930s], newspaper clipping, DuBose Heyward Papers, SCHS.

78. "Ancient Beauty of Once Neglected Buildings in Lower City Regained," *News & Courier*, 17 December 1928.

79. Petition to the Honorable City Council, 23 May 1922, Alston Deas Papers, SCHS.

80. In addition to Heyward's novel, the 1935 Gershwin opera *Porgy & Bess* solidified Cabbage Row as a "must-see" feature in Charleston. See "Charleston Expects Boom Possibilities via Gershwin's 'Porgy,'" *Variety*, 7 August 1935, EONVP, SCHS.

81. Loutrel W. Briggs to editor, *News & Courier*, 27 December 1933, newspaper clipping, Scrapbook 1932–45, SPOD Papers, SCHS.

82. Susan Pringle Frost to Albert Simons, 21 December 1933, Albert Simons Papers, SCHS. See also Susan Pringle Frost to James O'Hear [BAR], 26 September 1934, Susan P. Frost File, CCRMD.

83. Susan Pringle Frost to Albert Simons, 21 December 1933, Albert Simons Papers, SCHS.

84. John Patrick Grace to William Watts Ball, 9 May 1929, William Watts Ball Papers, Duke. Grace echoed a long-standing sentiment among early-twentieth-century boosters of local industrial development that the city's commercial past had been neglected. See, for example, "Souvenir Album of Charleston" (Charleston, S.C.: Walker, Evans & Cogswell, 1907), tourism pamphlet, CM. The 1941 WPA guide to South Carolina also comments on this selective orientation to the past; see *South Carolina: The WPA Guide*, 5.

85. "Proceedings of Council, September 10, 1929," *Journal of the City Council* (1929), 296.

86. Dick Reeves to editor of *Charleston Evening Post*, 23 September 1929, in Thomas R. Waring Sr. Papers, SCHS.

87. "R. A. Y." to *News & Courier*, [1937–38], William Watts Ball Papers, Duke.

88. Alice Ravenel Huger Smith to *News & Courier*, 21 October 1938, ARHSP, SCHS.

89. Nell Pringle's daughter explained the shift in how white Charlestonians perceived Northerners from the Civil War to the 1920s and 1930s: "They used to pray, 'Please God, save us from the Yankees, and then they prayed, 'Please God, send us the Yankees'" (Childs interview).

90. C. W. Johnston, *The Sunny South and Its People* (Chicago: Press of Rand McNally & Co., 1918), 201.

91. Hungerford, "Charleston of the Real South," 32. See also Howells, "In Charleston," and Johnston, *Sunny South and Its People*.

92. Margaret Lathrop Law, "Charleston—Queen of Colonial America," *Travel*, November 1929, 22–26, 46.

93. "To Reproduce Battle of Fort Moultrie," *News & Courier*, 28 June 1926.

94. "An Old City Speaks," videocassette, CM.

95. See "List of Persons who Assisted Lorenzo del Riccio," Albert Simons Papers, SCHS.

96. "Notable Film of Charleston," *News & Courier*, [1932], newspaper clipping, Heyward-Washington House File, SCHS.

97. "The Charm of Charleston," *McNaught's Monthly*, reprinted in unnamed Charleston newspaper, [early 1930s], Tourism File, SCHS.

98. Rev. C. F. Wimberley, "Charleston—Sui Generis," *St. Louis Christian Advocate*, [1930s], Tourism File, SCHS.

99. "Chicago Tribune Writer Devotes Column to Charms of Charleston," reprinted in unnamed Charleston newspaper, [1930s], Tourism File, SCHS. After the Second World War, Charleston attempted to distance itself slightly from this self-created characterization. In *Charleston Grows*, a volume published by the city's Civic Services Committee in 1949, Herbert Ravenel Sass argued for Charleston's industrial and economic potential. He noted, "A beguiling legend has grown up here and, beguiled by it ourselves, we have unwisely spread it—the legend of a beautiful but languid and indolent lotus-eater in the bustling sisterhood of American cities. No conception could be more false" (Civic Services Committee, *Charleston Grows: An Economic, Social and Cultural Portrait of an Old Community in the New South* [Charleston, S.C.: Carolina Art Association, 1949], 1).

100. Fraser, *Charleston! Charleston!* 368; John Chilton, *A Jazz Nursery: The Story of the Jenkin's Orphanage Bands* (London: Bloomsbury Book Shop, 1980), 25; "Gives Charleston's Origins," *New York Times*, 19 January 1926.

101. James De Rain to *Charleston Evening Post*, 15 January 1926, Thomas R. Waring Sr. Papers, SCHS. See also "Publicity and the 'Charleston,'" *News & Courier*, 1 February 1926; "Visit Prompted by 'Charleston,'" *News & Courier*, 16 February 1926; and Archie P. Owens to editor, *Charleston Evening Post*, 4 March 1926, Thomas R. Waring Sr. Papers, SCHS.

102. "'Charleston' Is Exploited," *News & Courier*, 1 February 1926.

103. For an excellent discussion of the colonial revival in America, see Sarah L. Giffen and Kevin D. Murphy, eds., *"A Noble and Dignified Stream": The Piscataqua Region*

in the Colonial Revival, 1860–1930 (York, Maine: Old York Historical Society, 1992); and Alan Axelrod, ed., *The Colonial Revival in America* (New York: W. W. Norton for the Henry Francis du Pont Winterthur Museum, 1985).

104. Richardson Wright, "Charles-Town," *House & Garden*, March 1939, 27.

105. See *House & Garden*, November 1939.

106. Secretary to the Trustees of the Museum to Board of Trustees, Charleston Museum, 15 May 1940, Albert Simons Papers, SCHS.

107. Law, "Charleston—Queen of Colonial America," 22.

108. Advertisement, *News & Courier*, 29 March 1926.

109. Advertisement, "What to See, Where to Go in Historic Charleston," tourist pamphlet (winter 1929–30), published by the Charleston Board of Trade, SPOD Papers, SCHS.

110. Robert Goodwyn Rhett, *Charleston: An Epic of Carolina* (Richmond, Va.: Garrett & Massie, Inc., 1940), 341. For more on Cypress Gardens, see "The Cypress Gardens, in Berkeley," *News & Courier*, 19 June 1931, newspaper clipping; and "Cypress Gardens," promotional material, [1930s], Cypress Gardens File, SCHS.

111. "The Garden Club of Charleston" (1972), pamphlet, Garden Club of Charleston File, SCHS.

112. Jean F. Chisholm, untitled article from *Resort Life*, April 1931, reprinted in *News & Courier*, 6 April 1931.

113. See Dale Rosengarten, *Row upon Row: Sea Grass Baskets of the South Carolina Lowcountry* (Columbia, S.C.: McKissick Museum, University of South Carolina, 1987), 31–33. See also Dale Rosengarten, "Lowcountry Basketry: Folk Arts in the Marketplace," *Southern Folklore* 49 (3): 240–55.

114. Laura Bragg, typed essay, [1930–31], Laura Bragg Papers, SCHS.

115. *South Carolina: The WPA Guide*, 187.

116. For historical and architectural details of the Miles Brewton/Pringle House, see "27 King Street" and "Information for Guides of Historic Charleston," Tourism Commission, City of Charleston (1985), 285–87; and Susan Pringle Frost, "Highlights of the Miles Brewton House" (Charleston, S.C.: Privately published, 1944).

117. Photograph, "Streets/27 King Street/Miles Brewton House," MK 3200, CM.

118. In March and April 1929 alone, over thirteen hundred tourists crossed under the double-porticoed threshold of the Brewton/Pringle House. Tens years later, in April 1939, nearly twenty people visited the home each day. See Miles Brewton House guest books, 29 December 1919–March 1931 and 29 March 1930–March 1953, Peter Manigault private collection, 27 King Street, Charleston, S.C.

119. Harvey B. Gaul, "Southern City Combines Attractions of Others," *Pittsburgh Sunday Post*, 24 April 1921, Miles Brewton House Scrapbook, Alston/Pringle/Frost Papers, SCHS.

120. Elisabeth E. Thorne to "My dear Miss Mary," [late 1920s–early 1930s], Miles Brewton House Scrapbook, Alston-Pringle-Frost Papers, SCHS.

121. Caroline H. Gaffields to "My dear Hostesses," 10 January 1931, Miles Brewton House Scrapbook, Alston-Pringle-Frost Papers, SCHS.

122. Elizabeth Covell, essay, 11 April 1937, reprinted in Frost, "Highlights of the Miles Brewton House."

123. For an example of hotel occupancy rates and the geographic origins of Charleston's visitors, see "Tourists Crowd Hotels of City," *News & Courier*, 10 February 1929.

124. William Watts Ball to Dr. Yates Snowden, 22 March 1929, William Watts Ball Papers, Duke.

125. Albert Simons to Thomas R. Waring Sr., 27 July 1933, Albert Simons Papers, SCHS.

126. See "Black Border Plantations Lure Wealthy Northerners," *News & Courier*, 21 April 1929; "Attracted by Climate Northerners Become Landowners," ibid., 15 December 1929; and "Charleston, South Carolina," *Fortune*, March 1933, 81; see also Samuel Gaillard Stoney, Albert Simons, and Samuel Lapham Jr., *Plantations of the Carolina Low Country* (1938; Charleston, S.C.: Carolina Art Association, 1964); and Louisa Cheves Stoney, ed., *A Day on the Cooper River* (Charleston, S.C.: A. E. Miller, 1932).

127. For details, see Chlotilde R. Martin, "Wappaoolah, Berkeley County Estate," *News & Courier*, 22 March 1931, newspaper clipping; and "Cleveland Man Buys Wappaoolah," *News & Courier*, 3 July 193[?], newspaper clipping, Wappaoolah Plantation File, SCHS; and Stoney et al., *Plantations of the Carolina Low Country*, 47–48.

128. Stoney Simons, quoted in Virginia Christian Beach, *Medway* (Charleston, S.C.: Wyrick & Company, 1999), 32.

129. Stoney et al., *Plantations of the Carolina Low Country*, 47–48; Richard N. Cote, "Preserving the Legacy of Medway Plantation on Back River," pamphlet, SCHS; Chlotilde Martin, "Medway," *News & Courier*, 26 April 1931; "A New Map Showing the Principal Plantations of the South Carolina Coast," 1932, CM.

130. Gertrude Sanford Legendre, *The Time of My Life* (Charleston, S.C.: Wyrick & Company, 1987), 70.

131. For details, see Martin, "Wappaoolah"; and "Cleveland Man Buys Wappaoolah," *News & Courier*, 3 July 193[?], newspaper clippings, Wappaoolah Plantation File, SCHS.

132. The 900 acres of land on which the Yeamans Hall Club was built in 1924 had originally belonged to the second Landgrave Thomas Smith and was held by his descendants for over two centuries. See "Yeamans Hall, Built in 1865 by Landgrave Thomas Smith," *News & Courier*, 22 January 1933; "Ancestral Lands of Carolina Planters Appeal to Wealthy for a Playground," *News & Courier*, 23 November 1931; and "Yeamans Hall Winter Season Begins," *News & Courier*, undated newspaper clipping, Yeamans Hall File, SCHS.

133. "Charleston, South Carolina," 78.

134. Herbert Ravenel Sass to Susan Pringle Frost, 18 September 1939, Herbert Ravenel Sass Papers, SCHS.

135. Yeamans Hall Proprietors (1 November 1931), Yeamans Hall File, SCHS.

136. James Derieux, "The Renaissance of the Plantation," *Country Life*, January 1932, as quoted in Beach, *Medway*, 41.

137. Roy S. MacElwee, commissioner of port development, "Why Big Business Chooses Charleston," pamphlet (Charleston, S.C.: Tourist and Convention Bureau, Chamber of Commerce, June 1926), 11, COC.

138. Solomon Guggenheim, quoted in Rhett, *Charleston*, 354.

139. Edward Twigg, "Charleston: The Great Myth," *Forum*, January 1940, 2.

140. For an excellent discussion of the value of a plantation home as a form of "cultural capital" for newcomers, see James Henry Tuten, "Time and Tide: Cultural Changes and Continuities among the Rice Plantations of the Lowcountry, 1860–1930" (Ph.D. diss., Emory University, 2003), 9–10.

141. Josephine Pinckney, notes, [1940s], Josephine Pinckney Papers, SCHS.

142. Tuten, "Time and Tide," 394–97. See also Bernard Baruch, *Bernard Baruch: The Public Years* (New York: Holt, Rhinehart and Winston, 1960).

143. Edith Wilson quoted in Baruch, *Bernard Baruch*, 146, in Tuten, "Time and Tide," 397.

144. Stoney et al., *Plantations of the Carolina Low Country*, 68.

145. Diary of Sidney Legendre, quoted in Beach, *Medway*, 52.

146. Language choices, for example, sometimes served as a cultural divide for Charlestonians and their new "planter" neighbors. In 1933, for example, Albert Simons took offense at a Northerner's use of the term "slave quarters," which Simons considered inappropriate and ahistorical to the Low Country. In discussing an architectural alteration request placed before the Board of Architectural Review, Simons told the city engineer, "Lieutenant Porter might be interested to know that servants' quarters were never referred to as 'slave quarters' even in slavery times. The term 'slave quarters' is a recent invention of our winter colonists, the general use of which should be discouraged" (Albert Simons to J. H. Dingle, City Engineer, 6 May 1933, Albert Simons Papers, SCHS).

147. Sylvia Jukes Morris, *Rage for Fame: The Ascent of Clare Boothe Luce* (New York: Random House, 1997), 299.

148. "Negro Wedding Collection Brings Dusky Couple $40," *News & Courier*, 4 February 1929.

149. Chalmers S. Murray to Herbert Ravenel Sass, [February–March 1934], Hebert Ravenel Sass Papers, SCHS.

150. Ball quoted in Walter Edgar, *South Carolina: A History* (Columbia: University of South Carolina Press, 1998), 493.

151. "Ancestral Lands of Carolina Planters Appeal to Wealthy for a Playground," *News & Courier*, 23 November 1931.

152. "Mayor Stoney's Annual Review," *Year Book, City of Charleston* (1930), xxi.

153. "Ancestral Lands of Carolina Planters."

154. Albert Simons to Samuel G. Stoney, 6 May 1929, Albert Simons Papers, SCHS.

155. Margaretta Pringle Childs described winter colonists as "very discriminating, sophisticated people" (Childs interview).

156. Eola Willis to Benjamin R. Kittredge, Dean Hall, 17 December 1932, Eola Willis Papers, SCHS.

157. Chalmers S. Murray to Herbert Ravenel Sass, [February–March 1934], Herbert Ravenel Sass Papers, SCHS.

158. Legendre, *Time of My Life*, 76.

159. "Charleston, South Carolina," 78.

160. See "Historical Commission Reports," *Year Book, City of Charleston* (1932–38), and Minutes of the Historical Commission, 1933–45, Historical Commission Papers, CCRMD.

161. The Azalea Festival appears to have been the brainchild of Robert Bradham of the *News & Courier* and Lucy Lee Wilbur, who became the festival committee's program chair for 1934. The two saw the idea "as a wonderful opportunity to advertise Charleston and to make even better known [its] charms and attractions." The Maybank administration fully backed the festival from its inception. See "Story If Told of Beginning of City's Big Spring Event," *News & Courier*, 11 March 1934.

162. See report concerning tourist camps in "Proceedings of Council, December 22, 1936," *Journal of the City Council* (1936), 245.

163. "Elaborate Nine-Day Azalea Festival Is Planned for City," *News & Courier*, 11 February 1934. For details of events, see also "Azalea Festival Program Shaping," *News & Courier*, 20 February 1934; and "Parade to Open Azalea Festival This Afternoon," *News & Courier*, 16 March 1934.

164. "Azalea Festival Edition," *News & Courier* and *Charleston Evening Post*, 16–24 March 1934.

165. A. J. Tamsberg to Mrs. William Hutson, 29 January 1936, SPS Papers, SCHS.

166. Photo caption in DuBose Heyward, "Charleston," iv.

167. "Scenes from Pirate Pageant and Street Carnival," *News & Courier*, 15 April 1937.

168. "Negro Programs Will Be Offered," *News & Courier*, 5 March 1934.

169. Rosa Warren Wilson, "'My Privilege': A Romance of America's Most Historic City, Charleston, South Carolina" (Charleston, S.C.: Walker, Evans & Cogswell, 1934), 35–36. See also "Negro Programs Will Be Offered" and "Azalea Festival Program Shaping."

170. "Azalea Festival Program Shaping."

171. "Azalea Festival Huxters, No. 1, 1938," Aluminum disc recording, Park Dougherty Collection, SPS, Recorded Sound Division, LC; see also Josephine Pinckney, "Huckster's Progress," *Town & Country*, March/April 1936, 48–49, 86.

172. "Rice Show Draw Many to Museum . . . Negroes Sing at Work," *News & Courier*, 21 March 1937; "Negroes to Husk Rice at Museum," ibid., 15 March 1937.

173. Edgar, *South Carolina*, 479.

174. Minutes, Board of Trustees, Charleston Museum, 12 March 1937, Albert Simons Papers, SCHS.

175. "Rice Hucksters Recall Congo to Woman Explorer of Wilds," *News & Courier*, 26 March 1937.

176. "Society Clear $700," *News & Courier*, 13 April 1934, newspaper clipping, Notebook, SPOD Papers, SCHS; "Tours of Houses to Be Conducted," ibid., 1 April 1935.

177. "Charleston Art Show Is Planned," *News & Courier*, 4 March 1934.

178. Katherine Hutson to Walter Garwick, 1 May 1937, SPS Papers, SCHS.

179. A magnetic tape recording of the Society's 1936 Azalea Festival Concert is held at the Archive of Folk Culture, LC.

180. Correspondence and telegrams, 15 April 1936, SPS Papers, SCHS.

181. Twigg, "Charleston," 1.

182. Henry W. Lockwood, "Mayor's Message to Charleston of the Future," *Charleston Evening Post*, 30 January 1939.

183. Center for Business Research, Charleston Metro Chamber of Commerce, "Charleston Metro Area Visitor Industry Impact Overview," 2003, ⟨http://pressomatic. com/charlestonchamber/upload/visindustryfacts.pdf⟩, accessed 13 August 2004.

184. Lockwood, "Mayor's Message."

185. Indeed, today the website of the Charleston Convention and Visitors Bureau declares: "Charleston, Where history lives." See Charleston Convention and Visitors Bureau website, ⟨http://www.charlestoncvb.com⟩, accessed 15 August 2004. See also "1996 Charleston Area Visitor Profile Study," 9, CCA.

Afterword

1. Walter Fraser, *Charleston! Charleston! The History of a Southern City* (Columbia: University of South Carolina Press, 1989), 383.

2. Albert Simons, "Dock St. Theatre, Planters Hotel, Add to City's Architectural Wealth," *News & Courier*, 21 November 1937, newspaper clipping, Green Scrapbook, May 1937–February 1938, Gibbes.

3. DuBose Heyward, "The Dock Street Theatre," *Magazine of Art*, January 1938, 11–15.

4. Harry Hopkins, quoted in "City's Culture Made Theatre Gift Possible, Hopkins Says," *News & Courier*, 27 November 1937, newspaper clipping, Green Scrapbook, May 1937–February 1938, Gibbes.

5. Alicia Rhett, a cast member of "The Recruiting Officer," later played India Wilkes in the 1939 film *Gone with the Wind*. See "India Wilkes of 'Gone With The Wind' Finds Radio Broadcasting as Exciting as Hollywood," *News & Courier*, 12 May 1940. For information on the Footlight Players and Charleston's "little theater" movement, see Footlight Players Papers, COC.

6. DuBose Heyward, "Dock Street Theatre," 15.

7. "Dock Street Theatre Opens Tomorrow Night," *News & Courier*, 25 November 1937; "The Restoration and Dedication of the Dock Street Theatre," *Year Book, City of Charleston, South Carolina* (1937), 187–95.

8. David Lowenthal, *The Heritage Crusade and the Spoils of History* (New York: Cambridge University Press, 1998), 6.

9. Record album liner notes, c. 1952–54, SPS Papers, SCHS.

10. James G. Harrison, "South Carolina's Poetry Society: After Thirty Years," *Georgia Review* 7 (Summer 1953): 204–9; James G. Harrison, "The Poetry Society of South Carolina, 1934–1950," pamphlet (Charleston: Poetry Society of South Carolina, 1972).

11. For more on the Historic Charleston Foundation, see Robert Weyeneth, *Historic Preservation for a Living City: Historic Charleston Foundation, 1947–1997* (Columbia: University of South Carolina Press, 2000).

12. Jonathan Poston, *The Buildings of Charleston: A Guide to the City's Architecture* (Columbia: University of South Carolina Press, 1997), 188.

13. Ibid., 30.

14. Center for Business Research, Charleston Metro Chamber of Commerce, "Charleston Metro Area Visitor Industry Impact Overview," 2003, ‹http://pressomatic.com/charlestonchamber/upload/visindustryfacts.pdf›, accessed 13 August 2004.

15. Margaret Mitchell, *Gone with the Wind* (New York: MacMillan Company, 1936), 1034.

SELECTED BIBLIOGRAPHY

Manuscript Collections

Avery Research Center for African American History and Culture, College of
Charleston, Charleston, South Carolina
Eugene Hunt interview transcript, interview by Lee Drago, 28 August 1980
Phyllis Wheatley Club Papers
Charleston Chamber of Commerce Archives, Charleston, South Carolina
Chamber of Commerce Annual Reports, 1915–40
"Charleston Area Visitor Industry Impact Study," 1996
"1996 Charleston Area Visitor Profile Study"
"Charleston Metro Area Visitor Impact Overview," 2003, ‹http://pressomatic.
com/charlestonchamber/upload/visindustryfacts.pdf›
Charleston County Public Library, King Street Branch, Charleston, South Carolina
Coastal Topics, 1931–38
Elizabeth Verner Hamilton, "Four Artists on One Block and How They Got
Along," unpublished manuscript
Charleston Museum, Charleston, South Carolina
Laura Bragg Papers
Edwin Harleston File
"A New Map Showing the Principal Plantations of the South Carolina Coast,"
1932
"An Old City Speaks," 1932, videocassette
Tourism Pamphlets
City of Charleston Records Management Division
Chamber of Commerce File
Susan Pringle Frost File
Historical Commission Papers
Housing Authority File
Robert Mills Manor File
Gibbes Museum of Art, Charleston, South Carolina
Associated Artists of Charleston, Minutebook, 1927–41
Charleston Pamphlets and Brochures
Gibbes Exhibition Files
Scrapbooks
Alice Ravenel Huger Smith Papers, Sales Recordbooks, and Scrapbooks
Thomas R. Waring Sr., Correspondence File

Historic Charleston Foundation, Charleston, South Carolina
    Director's Correspondence
Library of Congress, Washington, D.C.
    Archive of Folk Culture
    Frances Benjamin Johnston Collection, Division of Photographs
    Harmon Foundation Papers
    National Association for the Advancement of Colored People, Charleston
        Branch Papers
    Park Dougherty Collection, Society for the Preservation of Spirituals, Recorded
        Sound Division
    Society for the Preservation of Spirituals Collection, Archive of Folk Culture
Peter Manigault Private Collection, 27 King Street, Charleston, South Carolina
    Miles Brewton House Guest Books
Preservation Society of Charleston, Charleston, South Carolina
    Society for the Preservation of Old Dwellings Papers
Rare Books, Manuscripts, and Special Collections Library, Duke University,
        Durham, North Carolina
      William Watts Ball Papers
      Michael Francis Blake Papers
      Postcards (United States) Collection
Robert Scott Small Library, Special Collections Department, College of Charles-
        ton, Charleston, South Carolina
    Charleston Pamphlet Collection
    Footlight Players Papers
    Francis Marion Hotel, "The Story of a Bridge," pamphlet, 8 August 1929
    Harriet Kershaw Leiding, "Street Cries of an Old Southern City, with Music,"
        pamphlet, 1927
    Roy S. MacElwee, "Why Big Business Chooses Charleston," pamphlet, 1926
South Carolina Historical Society, Charleston, South Carolina
    Aiken (S.C.) File
    Hervey Allen File
    Alston/Pringle/Frost Papers
    Atlantic Beach Hotel File
    John Bennett Papers
    Laura Bragg Papers
    Miles Brewton House Guest Books
    Civic Club of Charleston Records
    Richard N. Cote, "Guide to the Alston/Pringle/Frost Manuscript Collection"
    Robert Cuthbert Papers
    Cypress Gardens File
    Alston Deas Papers
    Susan Pringle Frost File
    Garden Club of Charleston File
    Panchita Heyward Grimball (Mrs. William Grimball), interview by Cal Ball,
        audio cassette

Edwin Harleston Papers
DuBose Heyward Papers
Janie Screven Heyward Papers
Heyward-Washington House File
Historic Preservation File
Alfred Hutty File
Joseph Manigault House Papers
Josephine Pinckney File
Josephine Pinckney Papers
Anita Pollitzer Papers
Herbert Ravenel Sass Papers
Albert Simons Papers
Harriet Simons Papers
Alice Ravenel Huger Smith Papers and File
Society for the Preservation of Spirituals File
Society for the Preservation of Spirituals Papers
Society for the Preservation of Old Dwellings Papers
Samuel Gaillard Stoney File
Stoney Family Papers
Tourism File
Tourism Pamphlets
Elizabeth O'Neill Verner File and Papers
Wappaoolah Plantation File
Thomas R. Waring Sr. Papers
Eola Willis Papers
Yeamans Hall File
South Caroliniana Library, University of South Carolina, Columbia, South
    Carolina
    DuBose Heyward Papers
Southern Historical Collection, University of North Carolina, Chapel Hill, North
    Carolina
    Mabel Pollitzer interview transcript, 19 September 1973, Southern Oral History
    Project
The Tradd Street Press, Inc., Warrenton, Virginia
    Elizabeth O'Neill Verner, Artist's Sketchbook, [pre–1 August 1935], property
    of David Verner Hamilton

Interviews Conducted by Author

Margaretta Pringle Childs, 22 November 1993, Charleston, South Carolina
Ruby P. Cornwell, 16 November 1993, Charleston, South Carolina
William Halsey, 26 November 1993, Charleston, South Carolina
Elizabeth Verner Hamilton, 30 November 1993, Charleston, South Carolina
Eugene Hunt, 26 October 1993, Charleston, South Carolina

William Elliott Hutson, telephone interview, 14 July 1994, Charleston, South
    Carolina
Anna Dewees Kelley, 18 November 1993, Charleston, South Carolina
Mary Julia and Jervey Royall, 17 November 1993, Mount Pleasant, South Carolina
Anna Wells Rutledge, 29 June and 9 November 1993, Charleston, South Carolina
Martha Severens, 18 October 1993, Gibbes Museum of Art, Charleston, South
    Carolina
Patricia Whitelaw, 16 November 1993, Charleston, South Carolina
Harriet Simons Williams, 25 March 1993, Durham, North Carolina
John A. Ziegler Jr., 15 November 1993, Charleston, South Carolina

Newspapers

Charleston Evening Post
Charleston News & Courier
The New York Times
The State (Columbia, S.C.)

Published Primary Sources

Adams, E. C. L. *Nigger to Nigger.* New York: Charles Scribner's Sons, 1928.
Allen, Hervey. "Amy Lowell as a Poet." *The Saturday Review of Literature,* 5 February
    1927, 557–58, 568.
———. *DuBose Heyward: A Critical and Biographical Sketch.* New York: G. H. Doran,
    192[?].
———. *New Legends.* New York: Farrar & Rhinehart, 1929.
———. *Wampum and Old Gold.* New Haven: Yale University Press, 1921.
Allen, William Francis, Charles Ware Pickard, and Lucy McKim Garrison. *Slave
    Songs of the United States.* 1867. New York: Peter Smith, 1929.
*Alice Ravenel Huger Smith of Charleston, South Carolina: An Appreciation on the Occasion
    of Her Eightieth Birthday from Her Friends.* Charleston, S.C.: Privately published,
    1956.
Ball, William Watts. *The State That Forgot: South Carolina Surrenders to Democracy.* In-
    dianapolis: Bobbs-Merrill Company, 1932.
Bennett, John. *Doctor to the Dead: Grotesque Legends and Old Tales of Old Charleston.*
    New York: Rhinehart, 1946.
———. "Gullah: A Negro Patois." *South Atlantic Quarterly* 7 (October 1908):
    332–47; 8 (January 1909): 39–52.
———. *Madame Margot: A Grotesque Legend of Old Charleston.* New York: Century
    Company, 1921.
———. *The Treasure of Peyre Gaillard.* New York: The Century Company, 1906.
Brown, Sterling. "Aracadia: South Carolina." *Opportunity: Journal of Negro Life,* Feb-
    ruary 1934, 59–60.
"Charleston, South Carolina." *Fortune* (March 1933): 78–83.
Civic Services Committee. *Charleston Grows: An Economic, Social and Cultural Portrait*

of an Old Community in the New South. Charleston, S.C.: Carolina Art Association, 1949.

Couch, W. T., ed. *Culture in the South.* Chapel Hill: University of North Carolina Press, 1934.

Curtis, Elizabeth Gibbon. *Gateways and Doorways of Charleston, South Carolina in the Eighteenth and Nineteenth Centuries.* New York: Bonanza Books, 1926.

Fields, Mamie Garvin. *Lemon Swamp and Other Places: A Carolina Memoir.* New York: Free Press, 1983.

Frost, Susan Pringle. "Highlights of the Miles Brewton House." Charleston, S.C.: Privately published, 1944.

Gaines, Francis Pendleton. *The Southern Plantation: A Study in the Development and the Accuracy of a Tradition.* New York: Columbia University Press, 1924.

Gershwin, George. *Porgy & Bess: An Opera in Three Acts.* Libretto by DuBose Heyward, lyrics by DuBose Heyward and Ira Gershwin. New York: Random House, 1935.

Gonzales, Ambrose E. *The Black Border: Gullah Stories of the Carolina Coast.* Columbia, S.C.: The State Company, 1922.

Grissom, Mary Allen. *The Negro Sings a New Heaven.* Chapel Hill: University of North Carolina Press, 1930.

Harrison, Birge. "Old Charleston as Pictured by Alfred Hutty." *The Magazine of American Art* 12 (November 1922): 479–83.

Hemphill, J. C. "A Short Story of the South Carolina Inter-State and West Indian Exposition." *Yearbook, City of Charleston.* 1902, 107–71.

Heyward, DuBose. "And Once Again—the Negro." *Reviewer* 4 (October 1923): 39–42.

———. "Charleston: Where Mellow Past and Present Meet." *National Geographic Magazine* 75 (March 1939): 273–304.

———. "Contemporary Southern Poetry: The Audience." *The Bookman* 62 (January 1926): 561–64.

———. "Contemporary Southern Poetry: The Poets." *The Bookman* 63 (1) (March 1926): 52–55.

———. "The Dock Street Theatre." *Magazine of Art,* January 1938, 11–15.

———. *Mamba's Daughters.* 1929. Columbia: University of South Carolina Press, 1995.

———. *Peter Ashley.* New York: Farrar & Rhinehart, 1932.

———. *Porgy: A Novel.* Charleston, S.C.: Tradd Street Press, 1985.

———. *Skylines and Horizons.* New York: MacMillan Company, 1924.

Heyward, DuBose, and Hervey Allen. *Carolina Chansons: Legends of the Low Country.* New York: MacMillan Company, 1922.

Heyward, DuBose, and Herbert Ravenel Sass. *Fort Sumter.* New York: Farrar & Rhinehart, 1938.

Heyward, DuBose, et al., eds. *Poetry: A Magazine of Verse,* April 1922.

Heyward, Janie Screven. *Brown Jackets.* Columbia, S.C.: The State Company, 1923.

———. *Daffodils and Other Lyrics.* Charleston, S.C.: The Southern Printing and Publishing Company, 1921.

———. "Songs of the Charleston Darkey." Pamphlet. [Charleston]: 1912.

Higginson, Thomas Wentworth. "Negro Spirituals." *Atlantic Monthly*, June 1867, 685–94.

Howe, M. A. DeWolfe. "The Song of Charleston." *Atlantic Monthly*, July 1930, 108–11.

Howells, W. D. "In Charleston." *Harper's Magazine*, October 1915: 747–57.

Hugee, Louise Polk. "Aloof Charleston Calls Outer World." *New York Times Magazine*, 10 November 1929).

Hughes, Langston. *Fine Clothes to the Jew.* New York: Knopf, 1927.

———. *The Weary Blues.* New York: Knopf, 1926.

Hungerford, Edward. "Charleston of the Real South." *Travel*, October 1913, 32–35, 57–58.

Hurston, Zora Neale. *Their Eyes Were Watching God.* Philadelphia: J. B. Lippincott Company, 1937.

———. *Mules and Men.* Philadelphia: J. B. Lippincott Company, 1935.

James, Henry. *The American Scene.* New York: Harper & Brothers, 1907.

Johnson, Guy B. *Folk Culture on St. Helena Island, South Carolina.* Chapel Hill: University of North Carolina Press, 1930.

Johnson, James Weldon. *The Book of American Negro Spirituals.* 1925. New York: Viking Press, 1947.

Johnston, C. W. *The Sunny South and Its People.* Chicago: Press of Rand McNally & Co., 1918.

Law, Margaret Lathrop. "Charleston—Queen of Colonial America." *Travel*, November 1929, 22–26, 46.

Legendre, Gertrude Sanford. *The Time of My Life.* Charleston, S.C.: Wyrick & Company, 1987.

Leiding, Harriet Kershaw. *Charleston: Historic and Romantic.* Philadelphia: J. B. Lippincott Company, 1931.

Ludwig Lewisohn. "South Carolina: A Lingering Fragrance." *The Nation*, 12 July 1922, 36–38.

Mitchell, Margaret. *Gone with the Wind.* New York: MacMillan Company, 1936.

Monroe, Harriet. "Southern Shrines." *Poetry: A Magazine of Verse* 18 (May 1921): 91–96.

Odum, Howard, and Guy B. Johnson. *The Negro and His Songs: A Study of the Typical Negro Songs in the South.* Chapel Hill: University of North Carolina Press, 1925.

———. *Negro Workaday Songs.* Chapel Hill: University of North Carolina Press, 1926.

Peterkin, Julia. *Roll, Jordan, Roll.* New York: R. O. Ballou, 1933.

———. *Scarlet Sister Mary.* Indianapolis: Bobbs-Merrill, 1928.

Philips, Duncan. *American Etchers, Alfred Hutty.* Vol. 2. New York: T. Spencer Hutson, 1929.

Pinckney, Josephine. "Charleston's Poetry Society." *Sewanee Review* 38 (January–March 1930): 50–56.

———. *Hilton Head.* New York: Farrar & Rhinehart, 1941.

———. "Huckster's Progress." *Town & Country* (March/April 1936): 48–49, 86.

————. *Sea-Drinking Cities*. New York: Harper & Brothers, 1927.

————. *Three O'Clock Dinner*. 1945. Columbia: University of South Carolina Press, 2001.

Ravenel, Mrs. St. Julien [Harriott Horry]. *Charleston, the Place and the People*. New York: MacMillan Company, 1906.

————. *The Life and Letters of Eliza Lucas Pinckney*. New York: Charles Scribner's Sons, 1896.

————. *The Life and Times of William Lowndes, 1782–1822*. Boston: Houghton Mifflin, 1901.

Rhett, Robert Goodwyn. *Charleston: An Epic of Carolina*. Richmond, Va.: Garrett & Massie, Inc., 1940.

Ripley, Katherine Ball. *Crowded House*. New York: Doubleday, Doran, 1936.

"Romantic Charleston." Charleston, S.C.: Elliman, Huyler & Mullally, Inc., [193?].

Rubin, Louis D., Jr., ed. *The Yemassee Lands: Poems of Beatrice Ravenel*. Chapel Hill: University of North Carolina, 1969.

Sass, Herbert Ravenel. *Look Back to Glory*. Indianapolis: Bobbs-Merrill Company, 1933.

Scarborough, Dorothy. *On the Trail of Negro Folk-Songs*. Cambridge: Harvard University Press, 1925.

Simons, Albert, and Samuel Lapham Jr. *The Early Architecture of Charleston*. New York: Press of the American Institute of Architects, Inc., 1927.

Smith, Alice R. Huger. *A Carolina Rice Plantation of the Fifties*. New York: William Morrow and Company, 1936.

————. "Doorways, Gateways and Stairways of Quaint Old Charleston." *Art in America* 4 (August 1916): 292–302.

————. "Reminiscences." In *Alice Ravenel Huger Smith, an Artist, a Place and a Time*, by Martha R. Severens. Charleston, S.C.: Carolina Art Association, 1993.

————. *Twenty Drawings of the Pringle House on King Street*. Charleston, S.C.: Lanneau's Art Store, 1914.

Smith, Alice R. Huger, and D. E. Huger Smith. *The Dwelling Houses of Charleston*. Philadelphia: J. B. Lippincott Company, 1917.

Smith, Reed. "Gullah: Dedicated to the Memory of Ambrose E. Gonzales." Columbia: Bureau of Publications, University of South Carolina, 1926.

Smith, T. Cuyler. "The Ivory City." *Frank Leslie's Popular Monthly* 53 (March 1902): 491–517.

Smythe, Augustine T., Herbert Ravenel Sass, Alfred Huger et al., eds. *The Carolina Low-Country*. New York: MacMillan Company, 1931.

South Carolina: The WPA Guide to the Palmetto State. 1941. Columbia, S.C.: University of South Carolina Press, 1992.

Stoney, Louisa Cheves, ed. *A Day on the Cooper River*. Charleston, S.C.: A. E. Miller, 1932.

Stoney, Samuel Gaillard. *This Is Charleston: A Survey of the Architectural Heritage of a Unique American City*. 3d ed. Charleston, S.C.: Carolina Art Association, 1964.

Stoney, Samuel Gaillard, and Gertrude Mathews Shelby. *Black Genesis: A Chronicle*. New York: MacMillan Company, 1930.

Stoney, Samuel Gaillard, Albert Simons, and Samuel Lapham Jr. *Plantations of the Carolina Low Country.* 1938. Charleston, S.C.: Carolina Art Association, 1964.

"The Black Mammy Monument." *New York Age,* 6 January 1923.

Twelve Southerners. *I'll Take My Stand: The South and the Agrarian Tradition.* New York: Harper, 1930.

Untermeyer, Louis. *The New Era in American Poetry.* New York: Henry Holt & Company, 1919.

Verner, Elizabeth O'Neill. *Mellowed by Time: A Charleston Notebook.* 3d ed. Charleston, S.C.: Tradd Street Press, 1978.

———. *Prints and Impressions of Charleston.* Columbia, S.C.: Bostick & Thornley, Inc., 1939.

White, Newman I. *American Negro Folk-Songs.* Cambridge: Harvard University Press, 1928.

Willis, Eola. *The Charleston Stage in the Eighteenth Century, with Social Settings of the Times.* Columbia, S.C.: The State, 1924.

Wilson, Rosa Warren. "'My Privilege': A Romance of America's Most Historic City, Charleston, South Carolina." Charleston, S.C.: Walker, Evans & Cogswell, 1934.

Wister, Owen. *Lady Baltimore.* New York: MacMillan Company, 1906.

Wootten, Bayard, and Samuel Gaillard Stoney. *Charleston: Azaleas and Old Bricks.* Boston: Houghton Mifflin, 1937.

Wright, Richardson. "Charles-Town." *House & Garden,* March 1939, 27.

Year Book of the Poetry Society of South Carolina. Charleston, S.C.: The Society, 1921–33.

Government Documents

Charleston City Directory. Charleston, S.C.: various publishers, 1920–45.

Journal of the City Council, Charleston, S.C. Charleston, S.C.: various publishers, 1919–45.

Year Book, City of Charleston, South Carolina. Charleston, S.C.: various publishers, 1920–45.

Museum Catalogs

Myers, Lynn Robertson, ed. *Mirror of Time: Elizabeth O'Neill Verner's Charleston.* Columbia, S.C.: McKissick Museum, University of South Carolina, 1983.

Books

Allen, Louis Anderson. *A Bluestocking in Charleston: The Life and Career of Laura Bragg.* Columbia: University of South Carolina Press, 2001.

Alpert, Hollis. *The Life and Times of Porgy and Bess: The Story of an American Classic.* New York: Knopf, 1990.

Anderson, Benedict. *Imagined Communities: Reflections on the Origin and Spread of Nationalism.* London: Verso, 1983.

Anderson, Mary Crow. *Two Scholarly Friends: Yates Snowden—John Bennett, Correspondence, 1902–1932.* Columbia: University of South Carolina Press, 1993.

Annan, Jason, and Pamela Gabriel, *The Great Cooper River Bridge.* Columbia: University of South Carolina Press, 2002.

Axelrod, Alan, ed. *The Colonial Revival in America.* New York: W. W. Norton for the Henry Francis du Pont Winterthur Museum, 1985.

Ayers, Edward L. *The Promise of the New South: Life after Reconstruction.* New York: Oxford University Press, 1992.

Baigell, Matthew. *The American Scene: American Painting of the 1930s.* New York: Praeger Publishers, 1974.

Bellows, Barbara L. *Benevolence among Slaveholders: The Poor in Charleston, 1670–1850.* Baton Rouge: Louisiana State University Press, 1993.

Bhabha, Homi K., ed. *Nation and Narration.* New York: Routledge, 1990.

Bland, Sidney R. *Preserving Charleston's Past, Shaping Its Future: The Life and Times of Susan Pringle Frost.* Westport, Conn.: Greenwood Press, 1994.

Blight, David W. *Beyond the Battlefield: Race, Memory, and the American Civil War.* Amherst: University of Massachusetts Press, 2002.

Bloom, Clive, and Brian Docherty, eds. *American Poetry: The Modernist Ideal.* New York: St. Martin's Press, 1995.

Bodnar, John. *Remaking America: Public Memory, Commemoration, and Patriotism in the Twentieth Century.* Princeton: Princeton University Press, 1992.

Brear, Holly Beachley. *Inherit the Alamo: Myth and Ritual at an American Shrine.* Austin: University of Texas Press, 1995.

Brown, Dona. *Inventing New England: Regional Tourism in the Nineteenth Century.* Washington, D.C.: Smithsonian Institution Press, 1995.

Brownwell, Blaine A. *The Urban Ethos in the South, 1920–1930.* Baton Rouge: Louisiana State University Press, 1975.

Brundage, W. Fitzhugh, ed. *Where These Memories Grow: History, Memory, and Southern Identity.* Chapel Hill: University of North Carolina Press, 2000.

Bussman, Marlo Pease. *Born Charlestonian: The Story of Elizabeth O'Neill Verner.* Columbia, S.C.: The State Printing Company, 1969.

Campbell, Edward D. C., Jr. *The Celluloid South: Hollywood and the Southern Myth.* Knoxville: University of Tennessee Press, 1981.

Campbell, Gavin James. *Music and the Making of the New South.* Chapel Hill: University of North Carolina Press, 2004.

Chabot, C. Barry. *Writers for the Nation: American Literary Modernism.* Tuscaloosa: University of Alabama Press, 1997.

Chatterje, Partha. *The Nation and Its Fragments: Colonial and Postcolonial Histories.* Princeton: Princeton University Press, 1993.

Chibbaro, Anthony. *The Charleston Exposition.* Charleston: Arcadia, 2001.

Cockrell, Dale. *Demons of Disorder: Early Blackface Minstrels and Their World.* New York: Cambridge University Press, 1997.

Coclanis, Peter A. *Shadow of a Dream: Economic Life and Death in the South Carolina Low Country, 1670–1920.* New York: Oxford University Press, 1989.

Cone, James H. *The Spirituals and the Blues: An Interpretation.* New York: Seabury Press, 1971.

Connerton, Paul. *How Societies Remember.* New York: Cambridge University Press, 1989.

Corn, Wanda. *Grant Wood: The Regionalist Vision.* New Haven: Yale University Press, 1983.

Creel, Margaret Washington. *"A Peculiar People": Slave Religion and Community-Culture among the Gullahs.* New York: New York University Press, 1988.

Davis, Jack E. *Race against Time: Culture and Separation in Natchez Since 1930.* Baton Rouge: Louisiana State University Press, 2001.

Degler, Carl N. *Place over Time: The Continuity of Southern Distinctiveness.* Baton Rouge: Louisiana State University Press, 1977.

Denning, Michael. *The Cultural Front: The Laboring of American Culture in the Twentieth Century.* New York: Verso, 1996.

Dilworth, Leah. *Imagining Indians in the Southwest: Persistent Visions of a Primitive Past.* Washington, D.C.: Smithsonian Institution Press, 1996.

Donnachie, Ian, and Christopher Whatley, eds. *The Manufacture of Scottish History.* Edinburgh: Polygon, 1992.

Dorman, Robert L. *Revolt of the Provinces: The Regionalist Movement in America, 1920–1940.* Chapel Hill: University of North Carolina Press, 1993.

Doss, Erica. *Benton, Pollock, and the Politics of Modernism: From Regionalism to Abstract Expressionism.* Chicago: University of Chicago Press, 1991.

Douglas, Ann. *Terrible Honesty: Mongrel Manhattan in the 1920s.* New York: Farrar, Straus, and Giroux, 1995.

Doyle, Don, *New South, New Cities, New Men: Atlanta, Nashville, Charleston, and Mobile, 1860–1910.* Chapel Hill: University of North Carolina Press, 1990.

Drago, Edmund L. *Initiative, Paternalism, and Race Relations: Charleston's Avery Normal Institute.* Athens: University of Georgia Press, 1990.

Dubin, Steven C. *Displays of Power: Memory and Amnesia in the American Museum.* New York: New York University Press, 1999.

Durham, Frank. *DuBose Heyward: The Man Who Wrote Porgy.* Columbia: University of South Carolina Press, 1954.

———. *DuBose Heyward's Use of Folklore in His Negro Fiction.* The Citadel Monograph Series, no. 2. Charleston, S.C.: The Citadel, The Military College of South Carolina, 1961.

Edgar, Walter. *South Carolina: A History.* Columbia: University of South Carolina Press, 1998.

Fishel, Leslie H., Jr., and Benjamin Quarles, eds. *The Negro American: A Documentary History.* Chicago: Scott, Foresman and Company, 1967.

Flores, Richard R. *Remembering the Alamo: Memory, Modernity, and the Master Symbol.* Austin: University of Texas Press, 2002.

Foster, Gaines M. *Ghosts of the Confederacy: Defeat, the Lost Cause, and the Emergence of the New South, 1865–1913.* New York: Oxford University Press, 1987.

Fox, Richard Wightman, and T. J. Jackson Lears, eds. *The Culture of Consumption: Critical Essays in American History, 1880–1980.* New York: Pantheon Books, 1983.

Fraser, Walter J. *Charleston! Charleston! The History of a Southern City.* Columbia: University of South Carolina Press, 1989.

Gaston, Paul M. *The New South Creed: A Study in Southern Mythmaking.* Baton Rouge: Louisiana State University Press, 1970.

Gerdts, William H. *Art Across America: Two Centuries of Regionalist Painting, 1710–1920.* Vol. 2. New York: Abbeville Press Publishers, 1990.

Giffen, Sarah L., and Kevin D. Murphy, eds. *"A Noble and Dignified Stream": The Piscataqua Region in the Colonial Revival, 1860–1930.* York, Maine: Old York Historical Society, 1992.

Gillis, John R., ed. *Commemorations: The Politics of National Identity.* Princeton: Princeton University Press, 1994.

Gilroy, Paul. *The Black Atlantic: Modernity and Double Consciousness.* Cambridge: Harvard University Press, 1993.

Glassberg, David. *American Historical Pageantry: The Uses of Tradition in the Early Twentieth Century.* Chapel Hill: University of North Carolina Press, 1990.

———. *Sense of History: The Place of the Past in American Life.* Amherst: University of Massachusetts Press, 2001.

Glover, Lorri. *All Our Relations: Blood Ties and Emotional Bonds among the Early South Carolina Gentry.* Baltimore: Johns Hopkins University Press, 2000.

Goings, Kenneth W. *Mammy and Uncle Mose: Black Collectibles and American Stereotyping.* Bloomington: Indiana University Press, 1994.

Gray, Richard. *The Literature of Memory: Modern Writers of the American South.* Baltimore: Johns Hopkins University Press, 1977.

Greene, Harlan. *Mr. Skylark: John Bennett and the Charleston Renaissance.* Athens: University of Georgia Press, 2001.

Gubar, Susan. *Racechanges: White Skin, Black Face in American Culture.* New York: Oxford University Press, 1997.

Hale, Grace Elizabeth. *Making Whiteness: The Culture of Segregation in the South, 1890–1940.* New York: Pantheon Books, 1998.

Handler, Richard, and Eric Gable, *The New History in an Old Museum: Creating the Past at Colonial Williamsburg.* Durham, N.C.: Duke University Press, 1997.

Hobsbawn, Eric, and Terence Ranger, eds. *The Invention of Tradition.* New York: Cambridge University Press, 1983.

Hosmer, Charles B. *Presence of the Past: A History of the Preservation Movement in the United States before Williamsburg.* New York: Putnam, 1965.

———. *Preservation Comes of Age: From Williamsburg to the National Trust, 1926–1949.* Vols. 1 and 2. Charlottesville: University Press of Virginia for the National Trust for Historic Preservation, 1981.

Huggins, Nathan Irvin. *The Harlem Renaissance.* New York: Oxford University Press, 1971.

Hutchisson, James M. *DuBose Heyward: A Charleston Gentleman and the World of Porgy and Bess.* Jackson: University of Mississippi Press, 2000.

Hutchisson, James M., and Harlan Greene, eds. *Renaissance in Charleston: Art and*

Life in the Carolina Low Country, 1900–1940. Athens: University of Georgia Press, 2003.

Jaher, Frederick Cople. *The Urban Establishment: Upper Strata in Boston, New York, Charleston, Chicago and Los Angeles.* Chicago: University of Illinois Press, 1982.

Joyner, Charles. *Down by the Riverside: A South Carolina Slave Community.* Urbana: University of Illinois Press, 1984.

Kammen, Michael. *Mystic Chords of Memory: The Transformation of Tradition in American Culture.* New York: Knopf, 1991.

Kantrowitz, Stephen. *Ben Tillman and the Reconstruction of White Supremacy.* Chapel Hill: University of North Carolina Press, 2000.

King, Richard H. *A Southern Renaissance: The Cultural Awakening of the American South, 1930–1955.* New York: Oxford University Press, 1980.

Lawrence, Kay. *Heroes, Horses, and High Society: Aiken from 1850.* Columbia, S.C.: R. L. Bryan Company, 1971.

Lears, T. J. Jackson. *No Place of Grace: Antimodernism and the Transformation of American Culture, 1880–1920.* 2d ed. New York: Pantheon Books, 1981.

Levine, Lawrence. *Black Culture and Black Consciousness: Afro-American Folk Thought from Slavery to Freedom.* New York: Oxford University Press, 1977.

Levinson, Sanford. *Written in Stone: Public Monuments in Changing Societies.* Durham, N.C.: Duke University Press, 1998.

Lewis, David Levering. *When Harlem Was in Vogue.* New York: Oxford University Press, 1981.

Lindgren, James M. *Preserving Historic New England: Preservation, Progressivism and the Remaking of Memory.* New York: Oxford University Press, 1995.

————. *Preserving the Old Dominion: Historic Preservation and Virginia Traditionalism.* Charlottesville: University Press of Virginia, 1993.

Linenthal, Edward T., and Tom Englehardt, eds. *History Wars: The Enola Gay and Other Battles for the American Past.* New York: Metropolitan Books, 1996.

Lott, Eric. *Love and Theft: Blackface Minstrelsy and the American Working Class.* New York: Oxford University Press, 1993.

Lowenthal, David. *The Heritage Crusade and the Spoils of History.* New York: Cambridge University Press, 1998.

————. *The Past Is a Foreign Country.* New York: Cambridge University Press, 1985.

MacCannell, Dean. *The Tourist: A New Theory of the Leisure Class.* New York: Schocken Books, 1976.

Mailer, Norman. *Advertisements for Myself.* New York: G. P. Putnam's Sons, 1959.

Manring, M. M. *Slave in a Box: The Strange Career of Aunt Jemima.* Charlottesville: University Press of Virginia, 1998.

Marks, Carole. *Farewell We're Good and Gone: The Great Black Migration.* Bloomington: Indiana University Press, 1989.

McBride, Ian, ed. *History and Memory in Modern Ireland.* Cambridge: Cambridge University Press, 2001.

McDowell, Dorothy Kelly. *DuBose Genealogy.* Columbia, S.C.: R. L. Bryan Company, 1972.

McKay, Ian. *The Quest of the Folk: Antimodernism and Cultural Selection in Twentieth-Century Nova Scotia*. Montreal: McGill-Queen's University Press, 1994.

McNeil, Jim. *Charleston's Navy Yard*. Charleston, S.C.: CokerCraft Press, 1985.

Michaels, Walter Benn. *Our America: Nativism, Modernism, and Pluralism*. Durham, N.C.: Duke University Press, 1995.

Mills, Cynthia, and Pamela H. Simpson, eds. *Monuments to the Lost Cause: Women, Art, and the Landscapes of Southern Memory*. Knoxville: University of Tennessee Press, 2003.

Mires, Charlene. *Independence Hall in American Memory*. Philadelphia: University of Pennsylvania Press, 2002.

Morris, Sylvia Jukes. *Rage for Fame: The Ascent of Clare Boothe Luce*. New York: Random House, 1997.

Moutoussamy-Ashe, Jeanne. *Viewfinder: Black Women Photographers*. New York: Dodd, Mead & Company, 1986.

Muir, Edward. *Civic Ritual in Renaissance Venice*. Princeton: Princeton University Press, 1981.

Nash, Gary B. *First City: Philadelphia and the Forging of Historical Memory*. Philadelphia: University of Pennsylvania Press, 2002.

Newell, George Willson, and Charles Cromartie Compton. *Natchez and the Pilgrimage*. Kingsport, Tenn.: Southern Publishers, 1935.

O'Brien, Michael. *The Idea of the American South, 1920–1941*. Baltimore: Johns Hopkins University Press, 1979.

———. *Rethinking the South: Essays in Intellectual History*. Baltimore: Johns Hopkins University Press, 1988.

O'Brien, Michael, and David Moltke-Hansen, eds. *Intellectual Life in Antebellum Charleston*. Knoxville: University of Tennessee Press, 1986.

Pearson, Edward A., ed. *Designs against Charleston: The Trial Record of the Denmark Vesey Slave Conspiracy of 1822*. Chapel Hill: University of North Carolina Press, 1999.

Pease, William H., and Jane H. Pease. *The Web of Social Progress: Private Values and Public Styles in Boston and Charleston, 1828–1843*. New York: Oxford University Press, 1985.

Pennington, Estill Curtis. *Look Away: Reality and Sentiment in Southern Art*. Spartanburg, S.C.: Saraland Press, 1989.

Poston, Jonathan. *The Buildings of Charleston: A Guide to the City's Architecture*. Columbia: University of South Carolina Press, 1997.

Powers, Bernard E. *Black Charlestonians: A Social History, 1822–1885*. Fayetteville: University of Arkansas Press, 1994.

Radway, Janice A. *A Feeling for Books: The Book-of-the-Month Club, Literary Taste, and Middle-Class Desire*. Chapel Hill: University of North Carolina Press, 1997.

Rawick, George P., ed. *The American Slave: A Composite Autobiography*. Vol. 3, South Carolina Narratives, Parts 3 and 4. Westport, Conn.: Greenwood Publishing Company, 1972.

Reed, John Shelton. *The Enduring South: Subcultural Persistence in Mass Society*. Lexington, Mass.: Lexington Books, 1972.

Roberts, Randy. *A Line in the Sand: The Alamo in Blood and Memory.* New York: Free Press, 2001.

Roediger, David R. *The Wages of Whiteness: Race and the Making of the American Working Class.* New York: Verso, 1991.

Rogers, George C., Jr. *Charleston in the Age of the Pinckneys.* Norman: University of Oklahoma Press, 1969.

Rogin, Michael. *Blackface, White Noise: Jewish Immigrants in the Hollywood Melting Pot.* Berkeley: University of California Press, 1996.

Rosengarten, Dale. *Row upon Row: Sea Grass Baskets of the South Carolina Lowcountry.* Columbia, S.C.: McKissick Museum, University of South Carolina, 1987.

Rubin, Louis D., Jr. *Seaports of the South: A Journey.* Atlanta: Longstreet Press Inc., 1998.

———. *The Writer in the South: Studies in a Literary Community.* Athens: University of Georgia Press, 1972.

Said, Edward. *Orientalism.* New York: Pantheon Books, 1978.

Saunders, Boyd, and Ann McAden. *Alfred Hutty and the Charleston Renaissance.* Orangeburg, S.C.: Sandlapper Publishing Company, Inc., 1990.

Savage, Kirk. *Standing Soldiers, Kneeling Slaves: Race, War, and Monument in Nineteenth-Century America.* Princeton: Princeton University Press, 1997.

Schwartz, Barry. *Abraham Lincoln and the Forge of National Memory.* Chicago: University of Chicago Press, 2000.

Scott, James C. *Weapons of the Weak: Everyday Forms of Peasant Existence.* New Haven: Yale University Press, 1985.

Sears, John F. *Sacred Places: American Tourist Attractions in the Nineteenth Century.* New York: Oxford University Press, 1989.

Severens, Kenneth. *Charleston: Antebellum Architecture and Civic Destiny.* Knoxville: University of Tennessee Press, 1988.

Severens, Martha R. *Alice Ravenel Huger Smith, an Artist, a Place and a Time.* Charleston, S.C.: Carolina Art Association, 1993.

Shackel, Paul A. *Memory in Black and White: Race, Commemoration, and the Post-Bellum Landscape* (Walnut Creek, Calif.: Altamira Press, 2003.

Silber, Nina. *The Romance of Reunion: Northerners and the South, 1865–1900.* Chapel Hill: University of North Carolina Press, 1993.

Singal, Daniel Joseph. *The War Within: From Victorian to Modernist Thought in the South, 1919–1945.* Chapel Hill: University of North Carolina Press, 1982.

Slavick, William H. *DuBose Heyward.* Boston: Twayne Publishers, 1981.

Starnes, Richard D., ed. *Southern Journeys: Tourism, History, and Culture in the Modern South.* Tuscaloosa: University of Alabama Press, 2003.

Taylor, William R. *Cavalier and Yankee: The Old South and American National Character.* Cambridge: Harvard University Press, 1979.

Thane, Elswyth. *Mount Vernon Is Ours: The Story of Its Preservation.* New York: Duell, Sloan and Pearce, 1966.

Tindall, George B. *The Emergence of the New South, 1913–1945.* Baton Rouge: Louisiana State University Press, 1967.

Turner, Patricia A. *Ceramic Uncles and Celluloid Mammies: Black Images and their Influence on Culture.* Charlottesville: University Press of Virginia, 2002.

Wallace, Mike. *Mickey Mouse History and Other Essays on American Memory.* Philadelphia: Temple University Press, 1996.

Ward, Andrew. *Dark Midnight When I Rise: The Story of the Jubilee Singers, Who Introduced the World to the Music of Black America.* New York: Farrar, Straus, and Giroux, 2000.

Whisnant, David. *All That Is Native and Fine: The Politics of Culture in an American Region.* Chapel Hill: University of North Carolina Press, 1983.

Williams, Susan Millar. *A Devil and a Good Woman Too: The Lives of Julia Peterkin.* Athens: University of Georgia Press, 1997.

Wood, Peter H. *Black Majority: Negroes in Colonial South Carolina, 1670 through the Stono Rebellion.* New York: Knopf, 1974.

Wright, Patrick. *On Living in an Old Country: The National Past in Contemporary Britain.* London: Verso, 1985.

Articles and Essays

Allen, Ray. "African-American Sacred Quartet Singing in New York City." *New York Folklore* 14 (3–4): 7–22.

Benjamin, Walter. "Theses on the Philosophy of History." In *Illuminations.* New York: Harcourt, Brace & World, 1968.

Brundage, W. Fitzhugh. "White Women and Historical Memory." In *Jumpin' Jim Crow: Southern Politics from Civil War to Civil Rights,* edited by Jane Dailey, Glenda Elizabeth Gilmore, and Bryant Simon, 115–39. Princeton: Princeton University Press, 2000.

Datel, Robin Elisabeth. "Southern Regionalism and Historic Preservation in Charleston, South Carolina, 1920–1940." *Journal of Historical Geography* 16 (2): 197–215.

Deas, Alston. "Charleston First Zoning Ordinance." *Preservation Progress* 27 (January 1983): 3.

———. "They Shall See Your Good Works." *Preservation Progress* 7 (May 1962): 1–5.

Donaldson, Susan V. "Songs with a Difference: Beatrice Ravenel and the Detritus of Southern History." In *The Female Tradition in Southern Literature,* edited by Carol S. Manning, 175–92. Urbana: University of Illinois Press, 1993.

Dorman, James H. "The Strange Career of Jim Crow Rice." *Journal of Social History* 3 (2): 109–22.

Durham, Frank. "The Poetry Society's Turbulent Year: Self-Interest, Atheism, and Jean Toomer." *Southern Humanities Review* 5 (Winter 1971): 76–80.

———. "South Carolina's Poetry Society." *South Atlantic Quarterly* 52 (April 1953): 277–85.

Fant, J. Holton. "Tea and Talk: A Preservation Memoir." *Preservation Progress* (Fall 1990): 1–4, 17.

Fenhagen, Mary Pringle. "Descendants of Judge Robert Pringle." *South Carolina Historical Magazine* 62 (July 1961): 151–64; (October 1961): 221–36.

Gates, Henry Louis, Jr. "The Face and Voice of Blackness." In *Facing History: The Black Image in American Art, 1710–1940*, edited by Guy C. McElroy, xxix–xliv. Washington, D.C.: Bedford Arts, Publishers, 1990.

Gerster, Patrick, and Nicholas Cords. "The Northern Origins of Southern Mythology." *Journal of Southern History* 43 (November 1977): 567–82.

Glassberg, David. "Public History and the Study of Memory." *The Public Historian* 18 (2): 7–24.

Greene, Harlan. "'The Little Shining Word': From Porgo to Porgy." *South Carolina Historical Magazine* 87 (January 1986): 75–81.

Harrison, James G. "The Poetry Society of South Carolina, 1934–1950." Pamphlet. Charleston: Poetry Society of South Carolina, 1972.

———. "South Carolina's Poetry Society: After Thirty Years." *Georgia Review* 7 (Summer 1953): 204–9.

Harvey, Bruce. "Architecture for the Future at the Charleston Exposition, 1901–1902." In *Exploring Everyday Landscapes*, edited by Annmarie Adams and Sally McMurray, 115–30. Perspectives in Vernacular Architecture, no. 7. Knoxville: University of Tennessee Press, 1997.

Heisser, David C. "'The Warrior Queen of Ocean': The Story of Charleston and Its Seal." *South Carolina Historical Magazine* 93 (July/October 1992): 167–95.

Herman, Bernard L. "The Embedded Landscapes of the Charleston Single House, 1780–1820." In *Exploring Everyday Landscapes*, edited by Annmarie Adams and Sally McMurray, 41–57. Perspectives in Vernacular Architecture, no. 7. Knoxville: University of Tennessee Press, 1997.

Heyward, James B. "The Heyward Family of South Carolina." *South Carolina Historical Magazine* 39 (January 1938): 15–35.

Johnson, Thomas L. "Charleston was Charleston." *State Magazine*, 17 February 1985, 12–13.

Kelleher, Margaret. "Hunger and History: Monuments to the Great Irish Famine." *Textual Practice* 16 (2): 249–76.

Kelley, Robin D. "'We Are Not What We Seem': Rethinking Black Working-Class Opposition in the Jim Crow South." *Journal of American History* 80 (June 1993): 75–112.

Kirschke, Amy. "The Southern States Art League: A List of Members." *Southern Quarterly* 26 (Winter 1988): 51–63.

———. "The Southern States Art League: A Regionalist Artists' Organization, 1922–1950." *Southern Quarterly* 25 (Winter 1987): 1–23.

Klein, Kerwin Lee. "On the Emergence of *Memory* in Historical Discourse." *Representations* 69 (Winter 2000): 127–50.

Lockhart, Matthew A. "'Under the Wings of Columbia': John Lewis Gervais as Architect of South Carolina's 1786 Capital Relocation Legislation." *South Carolina Historical Magazine* 104 (3) (July 2003): 176–97.

Lott, Eric. "Love and Theft: The Racial Unconscious of Blackface Minstrelsy." *Representations* 39 (Summer 1992): 23–50.

———. "'The Seeming Counterfeit': Racial Politics and Early Blackface Minstrelsy." *American Quarterly* 43 (2): 223–54.

Lounsbury, Carl. "The Dynamics of Architectural Design in Eighteenth-Century Charleston and the Lowcountry." *Exploring Everyday Landscapes*, edited by Annmarie Adams and Sally McMurray, 58–71. Perspectives in Vernacular Architecture, no. 7. Knoxville: University of Tennessee Press, 1997.

Mahar, William J. "Ethiopian Skits and Sketches: Contents and Contexts of Blackface Minstrelsy, 1840–1890." *Prospects* 16 (1991): 241–79.

Mayrant, Drayton [Katherine Drayton Mayrant Simons]. "'If Any Man Can Play the Pipes': A Sketch of the Poetry Society of South Carolina." *South Carolina Magazine* 14 (September 1951): 9, 21–22.

"Memory and American History." Special edition of *Journal of American History* 75 (March 1989).

Nora, Pierre. "Between Memory and History: Les Lieuxs de Memoire." *Representations* 26 (Spring 1989): 7–25.

O'Brien, Michael. "'The South Considers Her Most Peculiar': Charleston and Modern Southern Thought." *South Carolina Historical Magazine* 94 (April 1993): 119–33.

O'Neill, Frank Q. "Light on the Water: The Golden Age of Charleston's Art." *Kiawah Islands Legends* 2 (Spring/Summer 1991): 28–36.

Parker, Ellen. "Historical Sketch and Catalogue of the Old Powder Magazine, 79 Cumberland Street, Charleston, South Carolina." 3d ed. Charleston, S.C.: The South Carolina Society of Colonial Dames, 1946.

Radford, John. "Identity and Tradition in the Post–Civil War South." *Journal of Historical Geography* 18 (1) (1992): 91–103.

Richardson, Emma B. "Dr. Anthony Cordes and Some of His Descendants." *South Carolina Historical Magazine* 42 (1942): 133–55, 219–42; and 44 (1943): 17–42, 115–23, 184–95.

Rosengarten, Dale. "Lowcountry Basketry: Folk Art in the Marketplace." *Southern Folklore* 49 (3): 240–55.

Severens, Martha R. "Charleston in the Age of *Porgy and Bess*." *Southern Quarterly* 28 (Fall 1989): 5–23.

Singal, Daniel Joseph. "Towards a Definition of American Modernism." *American Quarterly* 39 (1): 7–26.

Smith, William D. "Blacks and the South Carolina Interstate and West Indian Exposition." *South Carolina Historical Magazine* 88 (October 1987): 211–19.

Stockton, Robert P. "Charleston's Preservation Ethic." *Preservation Progress*, special ed. (Spring 1993): 11–12.

Thelen, David. "Memory and American History." *Journal of American History* 75 (4) (March 1989): 1117–29.

Thurber, Cheryl. "The Development of the Mammy Image and Mythology." in *Southern Women: Histories and Identities*, edited by Virginia Bernhard, 87–108. Columbia: University of Missouri Press, 1992.

Tipton, C. Robert. "The Fisk Jubilee Singers." *Tennessee Historical Quarterly* 29 (1): 42–48.

Webber, Mabel L. "The Thomas Pinckney Family of South Carolina." *South Carolina Historical and Genealogical Magazine* 39 (January 1938): 15–35.

Wilson, James Southall. "The Perennial Rooster." *Virginia Quarterly Review* 2 (January 1926): 152–55.

Woodward, C. Vann. "The Search for Southern Identity." In *The Burden of Southern History*, by C. Vann Woodward, rev. ed. Baton Rouge: Louisiana State University Press, 1968.

Young, Dwight. "How the Perseverance of Miss Ann Pamela Cunningham Helped Give Birth to a Movement." *Preservation* (July/August 1996): 116.

Dissertations and Theses

Boggs, Doyle W. "John Patrick Grace and the Politics of Reform in South Carolina, 1900–1931," Ph.D. diss., University of South Carolina, 1977.

Burns, Pamela Teresa. "The Negro Spiritual: From the Southern Plantations to the Concert Stages of America." Ph.D. diss., University of Alabama, Tuscaloosa, 1993.

Cann, Marvin Leigh. "Burnet Rhett Maybank and the New Deal in South Carolina, 1931–1941." Ph.D. diss., University of North Carolina at Chapel Hill, 1967.

Cox, Headley M., Jr. "The Charleston Poetic Renascence, 1920–1930." Ph.D. diss., University of Pennsylvania, 1958.

Davis, Gwen Shepherd. "The Charleston Etchers' Club and Early South Carolina Printmaking." M.A. thesis, University of South Carolina, 1982.

Duffy, John Joseph. "Charleston Politics in the Progressive Era." Ph.D. diss., University of South Carolina, 1963.

Fenton, Michael Kevin. "'Why Not Leave Our Canvas Unmarred?': A History of the Preservation Society of Charleston, 1920–1990." M.A. thesis, University of South Carolina, 1990.

Frank, Robert Lee. "The Economic Impact of Tourism in Charleston, South Carolina, 1970." M.A. thesis, University of South Carolina, 1972.

Hanckel, William Henry. "The Preservation Movement in Charleston, 1920–1962." M.A. thesis, University of South Carolina, 1962.

Moltke-Hansen, David. "Southern Genesis: Regional Identity and the Rise of the 'Capital of Southern Civilization,' 1760–1860." Ph.D. diss., University of South Carolina, 2000.

Peale, Marjorie Elizabeth. "Charleston as a Literary Center." M.A. thesis, Duke University, 1941.

Press, Nancy. "Cultural Myth and Class Structuration: The Downtown Group of Charleston, South Carolina." Ph.D. diss., Duke University, 1986.

Radford, John P. "Culture, Economy and Urban Structure in Charleston, South Carolina, 1860–1880." Ph.D. diss., Clark University, 1975.

Tuten, James Henry. "Time and Tide: Cultural Changes and Continuities among the Rice Plantations of the Lowcountry, 1860–1930." Ph.D. diss., Emory University, 2003.

Francis Marion Hotel, 164–65, 167
Fraser, Charles, 54, 64
Frost, Mary: and Miles Brewton/
Pringle House, 175–77
Frost, Robert, 93
Frost, Susan Pringle, 8, 40, 169, 172, 189,
209 (n. 33); founding of Society for
the Preservation of Old Dwellings,
24–25; suffrage work, 26; employ-
ment, 26–27; Tradd Street restora-
tion, 30–31; and the Miles Brewton/
Pringle House, 31, 65, 175–77
Fugitive poets. *See* Nashville Agrarians

Garden Club of Charleston: and flower
vendors, 86; and Gateway Walk,
173–74
Georgetown, S.C., 75, 177
Gibbes Art Gallery, 42, 73, 75, 174; and
Guggenheim paintings, 12, 183; and
local artist shows, 55–56, 187. *See also*
Carolina Art Association; Gibbes
Museum of Art
Gibbes Museum of Art, 193. *See also*
Carolina Art Association; Gibbes
Art Gallery
Gone with the Wind, 71, 113, 126, 129, 173,
193
Gonzales, Ambrose, 115
Grace, John P., 4, 162, 164; as opponent
of historic preservation, 42, 169
Greenfield Village (Mich.), 12, 21, 35
Griffiths, D. W., 62, 128
Grimball, Panchita Heyward, 132–33,
172
Guggenheim, Solomon, 179; art collec-
tion of, 12, 56, 67, 183; as Low Coun-
try property owner, 37, 177, 179, 238
(n. 21)
Gullah, 9, 69, 86, 115, 117, 118, 125, 132,
138, 184, 231–32 (n. 115); origins of,
134; and sea grass baskets, 174. *See
also* Spirituals Society: spirituals
collecting

Hampton, Wade, 4, 133
Harlem Renaissance, 15, 115, 131
Harleston, Edwin: NAACP activities
of, 5; artistic training and career of,
58; *The Nurse*, 58
Harleston, Elise, 58
Harrison, Birge, 63–64
Heyward, Dorothy Kuhns, 118, 124,
226 (n. 43)
Heyward, DuBose, 16, 38, 40, 80, 82,
115, 190, 192; *Porgy*, 38, 92, 115, 118–
26, 137, 168–69; and founding of
Poetry Society, 89, 93–96; poetic vision of, 92, 103, 104–5; family background of, 94–96; and Southern literature, 101–2; *Carolina Chansons*,
104–9; *Skylines and Horizons*, 109–
10; and decline of Poetry Society,
111–12; as novelist, 115–26; mother's influence upon, 116–17; and
contact with African Americans,
117–18; *Porgy and Bess*, 126–27, 158;
and Spirituals Society, 135, 154, 15;
and tourism, 157–59, 172, 187, 188
Heyward, Janie Screven, 99; and depictions of African Americans, 116–17,
142
Heyward, Thomas, 40, 95
Heyward-Washington House, 29, 38,
43, 45, 60, 119, 167, 186, 193; preservation of, 39–42; historical lineage
of, 40, 95, 174
Historical memory: workings of, 9–11,
190, 192; national controversies over,
11; and historic preservation, 30–31,
34, 42, 45, 51–52; and gentrification,
50; and fine arts, 62–63, 66, 70, 79–
83; in literature, 89–90, 106–8, 115–
16; and spirituals, 132, 146, 150; and
tourism, 159, 166, 169–70, 187–88
Historic Charleston Foundation, 192–
93
Historic preservation, 64, 151; male pro-
fessionalization of, 24, 40, 42; as complement to commercial progress, 26–

Southern States Art League, 76, 193
Spartanburg, S.C., 3
Spirituals: declining use of, 134–35, 140; history of, 136; interpretations of, 143–44. *See also* Society for the Preservation of Negro Spirituals
Spirituals Society. *See* Society for the Preservation of Negro Spirituals
Spoleto Festival, 193
Standard Oil Company, 34, 35
Stein, Gertrude, 12, 93, 112
Stoney, A. T. S., 75, 151, 172
Stoney, Samuel Gaillard, 9, 172, 183; *Charleston: Azaleas and Old Bricks*, 35, 36; and Regional Planning Committee, 50–51; and Gullah, 116, 125
Stoney, Thomas Porcher, 8, 153; and "Most Historic City" declaration, 14, 162; and historic preservation, 42–43, 166; and tourism, 162, 164–67
Street vendors, 14, 83–86, 107, 116, 139–40, 172, 174, 184, 186

Tate, Allen, 16, 101, 229 (n. 88)
Taylor, Anna Heyward, 55
Tillman, Ben, 4
Timrod, Henry, 89, 92
Toomer, Jean, 16, 224–25 (n. 28)
Tourism, 7, 173–75, 188; and historical memory, 11; city government and business leaders' support for, 14, 161–65; and World War I, 36, 161; and historic preservation, 31, 37, 50, 166; and fine arts, 65–67, 77–80; and poetry, 108; and spirituals, 145–46, 149–51, 153; and Azalea Festival, 153, 183–87; and modernization, 157–59, 164–65, 167–68; early history of, 160–61; Church Street development, 167–69; tensions about, 167–71, 182–83; and nationalism, 171–72, 175–77, 179; and winter colonists, 177–83; contemporary, 193

Vanderbilt Agrarians. *See* Nashville Agrarians

Verner, Elizabeth O'Neill, 7, 31, 54, 99, 118, 133, 155, 172, 174, 183, 193; artistic vision of, 57–58; art studio of, 60, 168, 174; family background of, 73–75; artistic training of, 75; cultural activism of, 75–78; as business professional, 77; clientele of, 78–80; *Prints and Impressions of Charleston*, 80; artistic vision of, 80–87; *Mellowed by Time: A Charleston Notebook*, 81; and depictions of African Americans, 82–87. *See also* Southern States Art League; Street vendors
Villa Margherita, 41, 164, 174

Waring, Leila, 55
Waring, Thomas, 43, 96, 98, 99, 155; and tourism, 162–63, 172, 184
Washington, George, 40, 42, 108, 174
Whitelaw, Robert N. S., 75, 172; and historic preservation, 42; and Regional Planning Committee, 50; and promotion of local artists, 56. *See also* Carolina Art Association; Gibbes Art Gallery
Whites: artistic depictions of, 57, 71; as slaveowners, 68–69; literary depictions of, 91, 105–6, 115, 120
Willis, Eola, 55
Winter colonists, 18, 35, 161, 173, 177–83, 238 (n. 21); and historic preservation, 37–38, 256 (n. 146)
Wister, Owen, 92, 161
Works Progress Administration, 15, 55, 138, 168, 175, 189
Word War I, 5, 16, 46, 101, 118; and navy yard expansion, 4, 161; as catalyst to domestic tourism, 36
World War II, 46, 51, 68

Yeamans Hall, 178, 182–83
Yemassee, 103

Zoning ordinance, 43, 166, 167, 170